Employment, Technology and Development

Employment, Technology and Development

A study prepared for the
International Labour Office
within the framework of the
World Employment Programme

AMARTYA SEN

WITH A FOREWORD BY
LOUIS EMMERIJ, I.L.O.

CLARENDON PRESS · OXFORD
1975

Oxford University Press, Ely House, London W. 1

GLASGOW NEW YORK TORONTO MELBOURNE WELLINGTON
CAPE TOWN IBADAN NAIROBI DAR ES SALAAM LUSAKA ADDIS ABABA
DELHI BOMBAY CALCUTTA MADRAS KARACHI LAHORE DACCA
KUALA LUMPUR SINGAPORE HONG KONG TOKYO

CASEBOUND ISBN 019 877052 9
PAPERBACK ISBN 019 877053 7

Copyright © 1975 International Labour Office

Printed in Great Britain

by Fletcher & Son Ltd., Norwich

Foreword

The choice of technology is one of the key instruments of a development strategy, but the whole field of 'appropriate technology' is still largely virgin territory for economists and engineers alike, since the hard facts about the possibilities of substituting labour for capital are hard to come by.

The employment implications of technological choice in a development strategy can usefully be examined in terms either of those which call for the spread of new knowledge (innovations such as new seed varieties, the development of new 'intermediate' technologies), or of those which involve putting to use existing knowledge through an adequate institutional and incentives structure and pricing policies regarding factor inputs and products.

The present study[1] by Professor Amartya Sen falls into this second category. It is an analytical piece of work intended to provide a conceptual framework and guidelines for further work in the field. One of the main features of the study is the importance it attaches to institutional factors and to economic and political feasibility considerations connected with appropriate technological choices. Even if appropriate technological alternatives are known to exist and are economically efficient, they are unlikely to be easily disseminated and applied unless adequate decision-making criteria, institutions and policies are intro-

1. The study is the first of a series of monographs resulting from research in the technology and employment field being done under the ILO's World Employment Programme (WEP), which was launched in 1969 and represents the contribution of the International Labour Organization to the International Development Strategy for the Second United Nations Development Decade. This and other research under the WEP has been made possible through a generous grant from the Swedish government to the ILO for this purpose

duced to change the factor- and product-mix in favour of greater labour intensity and employment creation. The appendices to Professor Sen's study, which illustrate the application of his conceptual and analytical framework to concrete situations, confirm how important it is for appropriate institutions and policies to accompany identification of feasible technological alternatives.

Two important sets of general guidelines emerging from Professor Sen's study are worth mentioning. First, the household production modes which are prevalent in agriculture and services in less-developed countries have important implications for the utilization of technologies with domestic non-wage labour which may not be available for factory work. This is an area which is being explored further by the ILO in empirical case studies relating to questions of technology choice in agriculture and services.

Secondly, the study shows that too much emphasis should not be placed on the development of *new* intermediate technologies through research and development. At any point in time there is already a set of evolved techniques (the so-called 'technology shelf') which is a relevant frame for making *current* policy choices and decisions. To quote Professor Sen: 'The view that the past menu is basically "inappropriate" and we must rely on "making" our own technology by looking for it, while full of healthy vigour is not always a very useful approach. To recognize that a whole lot of techniques already exist no matter what we do would seem to be not entirely a negligible thought.'

There are also specific guidelines emerging from Professor Sen's study. Thus, as regards the particular field of road construction, it provides the basis for answering such questions as (i) is the adoption of labour-intensive techniques for this area of activity *socially* desirable? And, if so, (ii) what is the 'ideal' system of fiscal devices to ensure that private contractors use the socially optimal technique? Part V of the study, on employment, technology and evaluation, sets out principles and criteria for estimating 'shadow' prices required to determine socially optimal techniques and to evaluate the gains from specific projects to migrants, peasant families and society in terms of increases in income, savings, employment, etc. The study also emphasizes that the framework for social cost-benefit analysis should not be considered simply as a mechanical exercise, noting that social valuation of labour and the exercise of project evaluation depend very significantly on such institutional factors as modes of employment (wage-based or family-based) and ownership and control of projects (public or private). These considerations are being built into ILO case studies now being undertaken in the field of road construction.

There are other policy implications emanating from Professor Sen's study which go beyond the range of guidelines for ILO research and action in the field of technology and employment. Since these implications have an important bearing on the World Employment Programme as a whole, a few words on each of the major ones may be in order.

In the first place the distinction which Professor Sen makes between the various aspects of the employment problem is illuminating not only for the purposes of pure analysis but also for identifying the magnitude of the problem and formulating policies tailored specifically to its different aspects and dimensions. In most less-developed countries one-dimensional measurements of unemployment are likely to be a misleading and inadequate basis for employment policy.

Secondly, the policy implications of employment expansion through the instrument of appropriate technical choices can be examined most realistically only with reference to the relevant modes of production. For instance, non-wage or self-employment can be an important means of employment generation which offers some advantages over wage modes of employment for the utilization of labour-intensive techniques. If schemes can be designed in such a way that work can be done outside the wage system, the institutional wage rigidities need not conflict with the expansion of employment. The co-operative work projects in which the reward for additional work is not immediate, and is in the form of greater output for the co-operative rather than of wage payments, are a useful method of overcoming the disadvantages of small-scale operations in a non-wage family system.

Thirdly, poor project planning and design, administrative rigidities, inadequate analysis of the nature of the employment problem and lack of criteria for the selection of projects have often resulted in public employment schemes failing to meet their objective of helping the 'working poor' below the poverty line Some knowledge of the size and distribution of different income groups below the poverty line is necessary if the public employment schemes' purpose of catching the really poor is not to be thwarted.

The functioning of the programmes of the Small Farmer Development Agency (SFDA) in India, reviewed by Professor Sen in Appendix B to his study, shows that, because of the lack of a clear definition of 'potentially viable' small and marginal farmers as target beneficiaries, it is not necessarily the poorest who have always benefited. There is evidence to suggest that SFDA assistance has frequently gone to farmers who operate holdings much larger than those stipulated by the agency in terms of ownership, or who have other sources of income.

Fourthly, another issue of employment policy brought out by Sen is that of prices as signals for decision-taking. In market-oriented economies the prices of factors and products are often out of line with their real scarcity and abundance, with the result that managerial decisions are not conducive to the achievement of socio-economic goals of employment. This provides justification for the use of shadow prices as tools for decision-taking. These pricing signals, if communicated to the decentralized manager or project evaluator, will induce him to take right decisions regarding technological choices. Thus, an appropriate incentives structure is an essential prerequisite of an adequate employment policy.

To sum up, Professor Sen's study takes the reader beyond the narrow confines of a purely economic approach to employment and technological choice. One of the most significant conclusions of the study is that economic policies, if formulated in isolation from the specific political, social, and institutional context, are almost bound to flounder. These non-economic aspects and constraints are of fundamental importance for employment policy.

LOUIS EMMERIJ

Chief of the Employment
Planning and Promotion Department,
International Labour Office

Preface

This monograph is concerned with presenting an approach to technological choice as a part of employment policy in developing countries. Since some of the confusing issues of employment policy arise from ambiguities about the concept of employment, the book begins with an attempt to distinguish clearly between different aspects of employment. There are several distinct – though related – concepts of employment (and, of course, unemployment), all of which have some relevance for employment policy, but which have to be distinguished precisely for an understanding of the different issues involved.

Aside from these conceptual questions, the book is much concerned with institutional issues. Technological choice involves a variety of institutional considerations and the rationale of employment policy depends significantly on the institutional framework. The focus of this work lies in the exploration of the interrelationships between institutions, technology and employment. In particular, differences between alternative modes of production and systems of employment have been studied in some detail to bring out their implications for policy making.

The increasing use of benefit-cost analysis in general and of 'accounting prices' in particular has also made it particularly relevant to relate employment policy to the literature on optimal allocation of resources. Parts IV and V of this monograph are concerned with this question in the light of the relationships between institutions, technology, and employment explored in the earlier sections.

While the book is largely analytical, the focus of attention is India. Aside from references to India in the text, there are four appendices dealing with empirical problems of unemployment measurement and employment policy in India. The conceptual contrasts are illustrated in this context, as are the interrelationships between institutional features and technological choice. The emphasis is on agriculture, and the current debate on tractorization is analysed in the light of the available empirical data.

I have received considerable help from discussions with Ajit Bhalla, Louis Emmerij and Mark Leiserson of the ILO. For comments and criticisms I am also very grateful to Pranab Bardhan, Robert Cassen, D. P. Chaudhri, S. C. Chaudhuri, Partha Dasgupta, Heather Joshi, Vijay Joshi, J. Krishamurty, Richard Layard, Shakuntla Mehra, Ashok Mitra, Dharm Narain, Hanumantha Rao, S. K. Rao, Ashok Rudra, S. R. Saini, R. K. Sharma, Frances Stewart, and R. Thamarajakshi. For skilful typing, I am much indebted to Celia Turner.

AMARTYA SEN

London School of Economics
March 1973

Contents

I | Basic Concepts

1 | The Concept of Employment

1.1 Introduction

PEACHUM: *Turning his back to the second beggar.* Between 'giving people a shock' and 'getting on their nerves' there's obviously a difference, my friend. I need artists. To-day, only artists can give people the right sort of shock. If you'd work properly, your public would be forced to appreciate you.[1]

True enough, of course. But is this 'artist' *employed*? Surely yes, since he is hired by Jonathan Jeremiah Peachum and he works for him diligently with his rubber arm and his artificial scabs. But clearly no, since a beggar is not 'producing' anything, except perhaps sympathy, and that is not thought to be a 'product'. On the other hand, he works hard, makes money for his boss and gets a wage. But no, his services will not be taken as saleable output in the national income accounts, and his chances of getting registered as 'employed' in the national statistics are not very bright. And if, for some reason, the statistical authorities let him get by, it is clear that Polly Peachum's sweetheart Macheath will never make it. And yet Macheath is 'a first class burglar, a far-sighted and experienced street-robber', and as Polly sees it, 'a few more successful enterprises and we can retire to a little house in the country, just like that Mr Shakespeare father admires so much'.[2] But then, was Shakespeare 'employed', or did he live on patronage and 'transfer payments'?

To say that employment is a complex concept does not get us very far. We have to ask: *why* is it complex? Essentially, the concept of

1. Bertolt Brecht, *The Threepenny Opera,* Act One, Scene Three. In *Bertolt Brecht Plays,* Vol. I, Methuen, London, 1961, pp. 126–7.
2. Ibid., p. 127

employment has to be related to some notion of the 'value' of the work. And the 'value' would vary depending on the persons from whose point of view the work is evaluated. The beggars are producing income for Jonathan Jeremiah Peachum and getting a part of it themselves. But they are not selling any output to the public (though on this there can also be some doubt in view of the 'artistic' element stressed by Peachum). Macheath, of course, is not offering commodities to the public — in fact, he is taking them away — but he is giving himself an income. Whether such people are to be regarded as employed or not depends on the person whose valuation of the work is to be used.

This question of valuation is inescapable since employment cannot be defined in terms of physical activity as such. To live is to indulge in some activity or other, even if it involves just lying in a bed, which — incidentally — for an artist's model can be quite remunerative as well. And when the question of valuation is raised much depends on from whose point of view the calculations are made.

It is interesting that, despite this inherent complication, the question of measurement of employment has received remarkably little attention in economic theory (it has come in mainly in development economics and that only indirectly), and the limelight has been on the question of measurement of capital. In his *General Theory* Keynes treated the measurement of employment as essentially a trivial problem,[3] and the tradition is a well-established one. It may be thought that this makes sense for an advanced capitalist economy since in such an economy it is fairly straightforward to decide whether people are employed or not, thanks to the developed system of wage employment. But the concept of 'disguised unemployment' was developed not in the context of Mexican peasants or Indian hawkers, but in relation to members of the British working class.[4] People selling matches in the Strand in London during the thirties were certainly employed from their own point of view but not so — it was alleged — from that of making a productive contribution to the national output. Macheath or Peachum's brigade flourished in a glorified Soho and perhaps, in some number, can be found there to-day. The measurement problem is not exclusively that of developing countries.

But, of course, it is a more serious problem for the developing countries than for countries like Britain or America. The concept of

3. Keynes (1936), p. 41.
4. 'The cause of this diversion a decline in effective demand, is exactly the same as the cause of unemployment in the ordinary sense, and it is natural to describe the adoption of inferior occupations by dismissed workers as *disguised unemployment*.' (Robinson (1937), p. 62.)

employment is notoriously vague in any economy in which the wage system is weak and in which 'self-employment' and 'unpaid family labour' are common.[5] Indeed for an economy of peasants and artisans the concept of employment loses its straightforward meaning and economic activity merges into a wider complex of family-based activities. The criterion of being paid a wage does not apply, and that of productivity is difficult to use since it is not easy to separate out the productive contribution of any particular member of the family in the total family enterprise.

1.2 The Three Aspects of Employment

At the risk of over-simplification we can distinguish between three different aspects of employment:

    (i) *the income aspect*, employment gives an income to the employed;

    (ii) *the production aspect*, employment yields an output;

    (iii) *the recognition aspect*, employment gives a person the recognition of being engaged in something worth his while.

It may look as if we have listed them in order of increasing complexity and this probably is the case. But the fact is that each of these aspects is quite complex and all of them require careful treatment.

Consider the recognition aspect first. Employment can be a factor in self-esteem and indeed in esteem by others. Much, of course, depends on the class one comes from. To a member of the 'leisured class' the fact that one does not work for one's living may be, in fact, a source of pride, but for those who have to work for a living, lack of 'employment' is not only a denial of income, it can also be a source of shame. In the same way, if a person is forced by unemployment to take a job that he thinks is not adequate for his purpose, or not commensurate with his training, he may continue to feel unfulfilled and indeed may not even regard himself as 'employed'. The phenomenon of people having a job but nevertheless regarding themselves as 'unemployed' is a common one and has been observed in various countries. In assessing whether a person is 'employed' or not, clearly his own views on the subject have to be given some weight, and the question of employment is one of having not only a gainful occupation but one which also satisfies some of the minimal expectations of the job-seekers.

The question is of a certain amount of practical interest. The ILO mission to Ceylon (now Sri Lanka) discussed cases 'where people said they were "unemployed" when they meant that they did not have a regular job offering security and some sort of steady income'. The

5. See Reddaway (1962), pp. 24–5.

mission went on, legitimately, to conclude: 'To the extent that respondents thought in these terms and interviewers did not probe very deeply, the data on the number shown as openly unemployed may be somewhat overstated.'[6] On the other hand, the question remains whether joblessness is the best way of viewing unemployment, and because of its emphasis on 'matching employment opportunities and expectations', the mission was, in fact, forced to view employment in a wider perspective.

The question of recognition can influence one's choice of jobs, if such a choice should arise. For example, a marked preference for working for oneself rather than for others may partly relate to this problem of recognition in terms both of status and of one's reaction to being ordered around. M. I. Finley has argued that the absence of wage employment in ancient Greece was related to this question: 'What we rarely find is the free wage labourer, for such a man was "under the restraint of another", in Aristotle's phrase, and even the poorest Greek avoided that position if he possibly could.'[7] Marxian discussions of 'alienation' relate closely to this question.[8] So do the recent discussions on the 'dualism' of the labour market in the developing countries – in particular the reluctance of peasants to accept wage employment elsewhere unless the wages are relatively high.[9]

A specific aspect of this question is the position of women. While women have not always followed Benjamin Franklin's advice to Catherine Ray: 'Go constantly to Meeting – or church – till you get a good Husband, – then stay at home, nurse the Children, and live like a Christian',[10] women's ability – and indeed their inclination – to accept outside employment has usually been severely constrained. On the other hand, the jobs done by women within the home have typically not been regarded as 'employment' at all, and the story of the man marrying his cook, thereby reducing both the national income as well as the employed work force, has rarely been viewed as an economic scandal.[11]

6. ILO (1971), p. 26.
7. Finley (1959).
8. Cf. Gintis (1972).
9. See, for example, P. Visaria, 'The Farmers' Preference for Work on Family Farms', in *Report of the Committee of Experts on Unemployment Estimates,* Government of India, New Delhi, 1970.
10. Dated 16 October 1755, reproduced in *The Autobiography of Benjamin Franklin,* selected and arranged by C. van Doren, Pocket Books, New York, 1940, p. 254.
11. After discussing the valuation of the services of domestic servants, Alfred Marshall did, however, devote precisely one sentence to those families which did not, it seems, keep servants: 'There is however some inconsistency in omitting the heavy domestic work which is done by women and other members of the household, where no servants are kept.' (Marshall (1890), p. 67.)

1.3 The Production Aspect

Consider the advice, which has cropped up in so many forms throughout history:

'And do not think of the fruit of action.'
'Fare forward.'[12]

It would not do, I fear, for the hired worker; he would be forward but fired. Employment is commonly judged precisely by 'the fruit of action'.

But what about the economist? Would he view employment thus? Frequently enough the answer is yes. Not only for the hired labour force but also for those who are self-employed. Nowhere is this seen more clearly than in the theory of 'disguised unemployment'. The discussion seems to have concentrated on the number of people who can be removed from the traditional sector (usually peasant agriculture) without affecting the output level there.[13]

Consider the following example, involving a peasant family of four working members with a small plot of land – providing enough fruitful work for two full-time workers but no more. Each of the four working members worked half time (or with half the 'intensity' of effort), and when one person left for the town the others worked that much harder, leaving the total labour effort and total output unchanged.[14] before this man left, had he been 'unemployed'? He was certainly working and earning something, and conceivably he also valued being in the family enterprise. Clearly he was *not* 'unemployed' in some sense, but this is thought to be a case of 'disguised unemployment' in the sense of the family output being unaffected by his departure. The latter is a production-oriented point of view and furthermore judges changes specifically from the point of view of family production.

The question of the valuation of the output can be quite complex and much would depend on from whose point of view the valuation is made. In the case just described, from the *individual* as opposed to the *family* point of view the departing man was producing something and was, therefore, not unemployed even in terms of the production-based definition. The contrast is here between the individual and the family (and of course the society). In other fields, there could be a relevant contrast

12. T. S. Eliot, 'The Dry Salvages', in *Four Quartets,* Faber, London, 1944, p. 31. Eliot interprets thus Krishna's admonition of Arjuna in *Bhagavadgeeta.*
13. See among others, Rosenstein-Rodan (1943), (1957), Nurkse (1953), Lewis (1954), Eckaus (1955), Mellor and Stevens (1956), Leibenstein (1957), Raj (1957), Viner (1957), Oshima (1958), Kao, Anschel and Eicher (1964), Schultz (1964), Sen (1966), (1967), Mehra (1966).
14. For the assumptions necessary and sufficient for this to happen see Sen (1966). See also Chapter 4 below.

between a firm and the society. Peachum's beggars do produce an 'output' from the point of view of his firm, 'The Beggar's Friend', and Macheath gets the value of his acquisitions, but the National Income Office may see in this no contribution to the gross national product. The point of view that the evaluator adopts is crucial for all this.

1.4 The Income Aspect

When a labourer sells his labour for a wage, he is accepting employment in exchange for some earnings, and these earnings may frequently be the primary consideration in taking up employment. What presumably interests the employer in the case of a profit-oriented firm is the cost of hiring this worker vis-à-vis what the employer expects to get by hiring him, but from the point of view of the worker the primary concern would typically be what wages he is paid.

This income aspect of employment may sometimes be altogether divorced from the production aspect. If, for example, the government wants to increase the income of a certain group of people, or of a certain region, one of the most effective means of achieving this end would be to expand employment in it. Keynes thought of paying wages for digging holes and filling them up for expanding effective demand in a situation of unemployment, and similar policies may also be relevant for redistributing income between regions or communities, even when the total output is unresponsive to an expansion of effective demand.[15] Employment has often been thought of as an effective means of income distributional policy. While the same function can be served simply by paying doles or subsidies, the political difficulties of the latter may well be considerable.

The income aspect of employment is concerned with that part of one's income which is received on condition that one works. If one enjoys a share of the joint family income whether one works or not, then that share is, obviously, not covered by the income aspect of employment. The focus of the income aspect of employment as used in this work is, therefore, on this question of conditionality, and not just on whether the income level is high or low.[16]

In the case of self-employment, the income aspect is not easy to separate from the production aspect. A family farm's income comes from

15. See Chopra (1972).
16. Contrast the Report of the ILO Mission to Kenya, which 'puts the greatest emphasis on . . . the poverty level of returns from work' (ILO, 1972, p. 1). Needless to say, poverty and low productivity will be among the major considerations in our discussion of technological choice, but not as a reflection of 'unemployment' as such.

its production and contributing to the latter expands the former as well. But what about the individual? Or the nuclear family as it breaks away from a joint family in the process of migrating to the town? The identification no longer holds. Even though the nuclear family might not have been contributing anything in the net to the joint family output (as in the example discussed in §.1.3), it was receiving a share of the joint family income and was in fact living on it. While the contribution to net output might have been zero or low, the amount of income enjoyed was more than that.

It could, however, be asked whether the income enjoyed was related in any way to the work done, rather than being a 'social' requirement for a joint family. There seems to be a clear relation. One would, in fact, have precious little chance of enjoying a share of the joint family income if one refused to be an economic part of the family and to share some part of the family work.[17] Thus, even though the departure of this man (or this nuclear family) might leave the total joint family output unchanged, so that from the production point of view he (or it) would have been a part of 'disguised unemployment', nevertheless from the income point of view the man (or the working members in the nuclear family) might have been 'employed'. This might, for example, explain the discrepancy between the low estimates of unemployment in rural India according to the National Sample Surveys[18] and the high estimates obtained by using the production approach.[19] There will be occasion to examine this question later on in this work. The contrast between the different *aspects* of employment suggests contrasting *estimates* of employment and unemployment.

1.5 Aggregation of Employment

There are two distinct problems in the evaluation of employment:

(i) identification of who is 'employed' and who is not;

(ii) weighting of different types of employment to arrive at a total figure.

I have been commenting so far only on (i). Coming now to (ii), it is worth noting that Keynes measured the quantum of employment in terms of 'the wage unit', i.e., total employment was measured in units of common, unskilled labour, weighting skilled labour in terms of relative wages:

17. Cf. Dumont (1957) and Chayanov (1966).
18. See Table A.3 in Appendix A below.
19. See, for example, Mehra (1966), and Table A.2 in Appendix A below.

For, in so far as different grades and kinds of labour and salaried assist-ance enjoy a more or less fixed relative remuneration, the quantity of employment can be sufficiently defined for our purpose by taking an hour's employment of ordinary labour as our unit and weighting an hour's employment of special labour in proportion to its remuneration, i.e., an hour of special labour remunerated at double ordinary rates will count as two units.[20]

The rationale of this weighting is not altogether straightforward. From the point of view of the worker it can, of course, be argued that he would earn just the same amount of income by working for ten hours at $1 per hour as by working for five hours at $2 per hour. But the worker is not merely concerned with his income and he could easily prefer making the same money in five hours' work rather than in ten hours' toil. It is reasonably clear that Keynes was, in fact, viewing the problem from the point of view of productive contributions and this weighting is crucial to his 'employment function'.[21] The 'elasticity of employment' measures 'the response of the number of labour units employed in the industry to changes in the number of wage-units which are expected to be spent on purchasing its output'.[22] Evidently there is some underlying notion that a unit of labour which is paid twice the wage rate of another would be needed in half the amount for the same productive contribu-tion, and this, of course, ties up neatly with the marginal productivity theory of distribution, i.e., with the idea that the productive factor is paid at a rate equalling its marginal product. The rationale of the weighting would depend on the credibility of that theory.

For our purpose in this work we shall not need to aggregate hetero-geneous labour into one homogeneous measure through some sophisti-cated technique. We can think of employment not as a number but as a vector, i.e., as a set of numbers giving employment of each kind of labour. When it comes to calculating the volume of total 'unemployment' we shall need to aggregate the different categories of employment in some way, in order to compare that total with the available work force and to estimate the unemployed work force. But for that purpose an *unweighted* sum of all categories of employment will prove the most relevant. For some problems the simplest procedure is also the most convenient.

20. Keynes (1936), p. 41.
21. See Keynes (1936), Chapter 20.
22. Keynes (1936), p. 282.

2 | Technology and Efficiency

2.1 Introduction

'A technique is', wrote J. D. Bernal in *Science in History*, 'an individually acquired and socially secured way of doing something; a science is a way of understanding how to do it in order to do it better.'[1] The gap between understanding how something would work and making it actually work can be quite a substantial one, and some of the major problems of technological advance in developing countries seem to arise from difficulties in the translation of science into technology.[2]

In the context of employment policy this contrast between science and technology is relevant. Between the development of 'intermediate technology' (or whatever the technological panacea for poor countries might currently be) in well-endowed laboratories, and its actual use in production, lies a whole host of problems — partly economic, partly social, partly ones of pure organization. Technology involves a great deal more than the mechanical processes of turning iron ore into steel, and in this study one must take a wider view of the technological problem. For example, if the social and economic structure of a country permits the use of multiple-shift working in a factory but not in a household operation, this is a relevant aspect of the technological contrast.[3] Similarly, if household production permits the use of domestic labour not available for factory work,[4] the two kinds of labour have to be treated as different kinds of inputs, making the technological contrast more complicated than it would otherwise have been.

Another aspect of the practical nature of technology concerns its

1. Bernal (1969) Vol. 1, p. 47.
2. See Hirschman (1967).
3. See Sen (1964).
4. See the Report of the ILO mission to Kenya, ILO (1972).

11

evolution. New techniques are invented only when there is an active search for such methods. This is true of even the purely mechanical processes of production, which seem to emerge in response to economic needs and active pursuit. Habakkuk's study of the impact of labour scarcity in the United States on the type of technology that evolved provides an important illustration of this phenomenon.[5] Technological progress cannot be viewed independently of actual production.[6]

This approach to the problem is particularly relevant to the vigorous debate which has been going on for some time on 'appropriate technology' or 'intermediate technology' for developing countries. The approach warns us, on the one hand, against taking technological possibilities as 'given', and against making development planning a choice out of a given 'menu' of alternative technologies. It also warns us, on the other hand, against the frequently held belief that 'intermediate techniques' would emerge if some research institutions began to work in that direction, even if the institutions were relatively remote from actual production. But most importantly it induces us to face the following questions: If certain types of intermediate technology would be economically most appropriate for a class of developing countries, are the industries there not actively looking for these techniques? If they are, why have they not got them? If they are not, why not? These questions relate to the logic of the operation of particular economic systems, which we shall take up later.[7]

There is, however, a danger in taking too 'dynamic' a view of the problem of technology. Technology is certainly created by looking for it, but there also exists at any point of time a vast collection of already evolved techniques. In some ways our direct choice must be related to the existing stock, even though the choices made will alter the stock and add to it, and indeed this will be an important consideration in the optimal choice of techniques. The view that the past menu is basically 'inappropriate' and we must rely on 'making' our own technology by looking for it, while full of healthy vigour, is not always a very useful approach. To recognize that a whole lot of techniques already exist no matter what we do would seem to be not entirely a negligible thought. Tolstoy recalls in his *Childhood, Boyhood and Youth* that he had such a total fixation about matter being created by the human mind that he would drive himself insane looking rapidly round to one side hoping to

5. See Habakkuk (1962), (1963); also Temin (1966), Rosenberg (1969), and Nordhaus (1969).
6. See Kaldor (1957), Kaldor and Mirrlees (1962), Arrow (1962), Atkinson and Stiglitz (1969).
7. See Part III below.

catch a glimpse of the emptiness *before* his mind had time to create matter on that side. There is perhaps a moral in this story for the technology-maker.

2.2 Technical Efficiency

We shall here explore a few of the 'basic' concepts of technological economics. Technical efficiency has been widely discussed in the literature of resource allocation. A situation can be described as technically efficient if it is impossible to move to an alternative such that the change yields something for nothing. Suppose we are producing a certain bundle of goods x, using a certain bundle of inputs y, through a combination of techniques that I shall call A. Imagine now that someone points out that by using another combination of techniques B we can get more of some output and no less of any other output and use up no more of any input. This means that by shifting from A to B we get something for nothing, and if B is available when we choose A, we are being 'technically inefficient'. We are technically inefficient also if some available combination C can produce no less of any output while using less of some input and no more of any other input. If there are no such 'superior' technological possibilities compared with A, then A can be described as technically efficient.[8]

In the resource allocation literature it is common to begin by weeding out technically inefficient combinations and then to go on to choose the best of the efficient combinations. Efficiency is taken as the first step, on the ground that if something could be got for nothing it should be grabbed straightaway without further ado.

This picture is rather misleading, for a number of reasons. First, given the dynamic view of technology discussed in the last section, it is not easy to decide whether B or C was 'available' when A was chosen. Availability does not imply existence in some book of blueprints and technology can be invented when it is searched for. This does not, of course, prevent us from criticizing the choice of a technology combination such that a superior combination to it is *already known* to exist, but the fact that no known combination is superior need not be taken to be a proof of technical efficiency from the operational point of view.

Secondly, the great appeal of technical efficiency lies in the fact that no matter what the prices are — as long as they are not negative — a combination A that is superior to another B would yield no lower profits than B, so that the choice is independent of the actual prices used for the

8. For an illuminating analysis of the concept and its relevance, see Scitovsky (1952).

evaluation. This is indeed so *as long as* the same prices are applied to all technical combinations. There may, however, be cases in which a particular input may be available at a cheaper price if technique A is used than if technique B is chosen.[9] For example, for reasons discussed in the last chapter, a farmer could use a higher supply price of his labour for working elsewhere than the compensation he would accept for working on his own farm. Under these circumstances, even if the technique that involved working outside the farm required less labour and no more of the other inputs in order to produce the same volume of output, it might not necessarily be more economic to use that technique. In a formal sense one can avoid this problem by considering 'family labour' and 'wage labour' as two *different* inputs, but the more one brings in such differentiation, the more one reduces the usefulness and cutting power of the concept of technical efficiency.

Thirdly, the general question as to what is to count as a separate output and what as a separate input nevertheless remains. The difficulty can be illustrated in terms of the regional aspect of production and efficiency. Suppose technique A produces more output compared with B, but all at location x rather than at location y where B is situated. Is it more efficient? This is not clear at all, since the regional distribution desired might involve a lot of movements from x to y in the case of A, which could be relatively expensive. One way of viewing the problem of efficiency is to compare A and B inclusive of transportation costs to the ultimate destination. But then the efficiency comparison is specific to the particular assumption about destination, and the optimum destination may itself be a subject of locational planning.[10] And if an attempt is made to do this comparison for all possible destination assumptions, the cutting power of the efficiency criterion can be substantially reduced. Furthermore, technical efficiency requires calculation not of 'costs' but of uses of specific resources, and if more of any one resource (e.g., diesel for transportation) is needed for A than for B for the same output distribution, A will not be technically superior. The problem becomes even more complicated if political constraints on commodity movements are also included in the picture, e.g., Indian restrictions on movements of foodgrains between states and sometimes between different zones within a state.

Fourthly, the distinction between 'input' and 'output' may not be the relevant one in some cases. Industrial waste is an 'output' but is not much loved, whereas one's latent talent may be an 'input' but its use may

9. See Sen (1960), Chapter IV and Appendix C.
10. See Lefeber (1958), Rahman (1963), Datta-Chaudhuri (1967), Manne (1967), and Lefeber and Datta-Chaudhuri (1971).

not be thought to be a bad thing. Further, some outputs may be desirable from a private point of view but not necessarily from the social viewpoint, e.g., daggers. Use of some inputs, e.g., employment of labour, may be a private cost but involve a benefit from the social point of view. Also, a good may be desirable at a certain level of availability but not beyond that, e.g., certain types of industrial by-products with a limited demand.

All these considerations make the concept of technical efficiency deeply problematic in its relevance. When all the qualifications have been added, technical efficiency may come out victorious, but only by becoming an empty box for practical purposes. This is a question of some importance, since controversies on employment policy and technological choice have frequently been geared to the notion of technical efficiency.

2.3 Economic Efficiency

Aside from all the problems discussed in the last section about the conception and use of technical efficiency, there is also the fact that it is a very weak criterion of economic performance. Consider a peasant trying to decide how much time to spend in weeding his field. The more time he spends the more weeds he can remove and the more will be the net output. In this case, the alternative decisions on time are all technically efficient, since compared with any decision there is no alternative which would yield more output with no more input (or yield no less output with less input). All that technical efficiency would require in this case is that the person should not spend more effort if that would yield no additional output. That is fair enough, but it need not take one very far.

The concept of *economic efficiency* (as opposed to technical efficiency) is a bit closer to policy prescriptions. This is the notion of Pareto optimality familiar in welfare economics. A situation x is Pareto–superior to another y if someone is better off at x than at y and everyone is at least as well off at x as at y. So Pareto superiority means superiority for one person and inferiority for none. A situation is economically efficient if no Pareto-superior position is available, i.e., if there is no way of making someone better off without making somebody else worse off.

In a Robinson-Crusoe economy consisting of one man, economic efficiency would be a complete criterion for policy-making. Taking the peasant—effort example discussed above, Robinson would have to decide how much weeding to do and whatever he thinks is best for him is best for the society too, for he *is* the society. But as soon as we shift our attention from the strange world of Robinson Crusoe, economic efficiency ceases to be a complete criterion for action. Situation x may make person A better off and person B worse off compared with situation y, but both x and y would be economically efficient in this two-alternative choice. The concept of economic efficiency gears itself to individual welfare and makes pronouncements only on those choices in which no inter-personal conflicts arise. Problems of income distribution are completely left out of the discussion of economic efficiency and as a criterion of policy-making it is of very limited help. In real policy debates inter-personal and inter-class conflicts of interest have to be faced and in this study we must go much beyond the criterion of economic efficiency.

3 | Employment Modes and the Non-wage Sectors

3.1 Introduction

Wage labour, as a dominant form of employment, is of comparatively recent origin. Even to-day the vast majority of the labour force of the world works outside the wage system. Before going into the analytical issues involved in this problem, some factual questions are worth investigating. In particular, it is important to know something about the orders of magnitude of the prevalence of different modes of employment, and to note any inter-country or inter-sectoral regularities that might be present.

In Table 3.1 a breakdown of the economically active population in terms of modes of employment in the aggregate as well as for the different sectors, is presented for twenty-eight countries.[1] The data are taken from the *Demographic Yearbook 1964* of the United Nations and while the reference year varies from country to country, the information relates to some year in the late 1950s or early 1960s. An alternative source of data is the ILO's *Yearbook of Labour Statistics 1971*. Despite its later date of publication, much of the data relate to a common period; later issues of the UN *Demographic Yearbook* do not provide this breakdown. Some countries are missing from the ILO *Yearbook* and others from the UN *Demographic Yearbook*, and important qualifications are specified for data of some other countries covered in the list. For our purpose, however, an overall general impression is all that is required. The arbitrariness of some of the information has to be borne in mind in interpreting the findings.

---

1. See Sen (1973*a*).

Table 3.1
Breakdown of the Economically Active Population according to
Employment Status: Total and Sectoral
(percentages)

Country and sector	Employees	Unpaid family workers	Workers on own account	Employers	Not classifiable
Thailand					
Total	12	58	30	0	1
Agriculture	3	66	30	0	0
Manufacturing	50	17	31	2	0
Commerce	12	40	46	1	0
Turkey					
Total	19	48	28	1	4
Agriculture	7	63	30	1	0
Manufacturing	52	8	33	5	1
Commerce	27	5	61	6	1
Ghana					
Total	20	13	62		6
Agriculture	10	20	70		0
Manufacturing	22	2	76		0
Commerce	12	4	84		0
South Korea					
Total	21	29	44		6
Agriculture	6	44	50		0
Manufacturing	64	8	28		0
Commerce	13	9	78		0
Philippines					
Total	27	23	42	1	7
Agriculture	11	34	54	0	0
Manufacturing	41	14	44	1	0
Commerce	31	13	53	2	0
Morocco					
Total	34	16	37	2	11
Agriculture	19	27	50	2	1
Manufacturing	50	3	39	2	5
Commerce	26	3	63	3	5
Greece					
Total	34	29	32	3	3
Agriculture	8	51	39	2	0
Manufacturing	64	3	26	6	0
Commerce	35	6	49	10	0

Table 3.1 (continued)

Country and sector	Employees	Unpaid family workers	Workers on own account	Employers	Not classifiable
Honduras					
Total	37	20	35	2	6
Agriculture	25	29	44	2	0
Manufacturing	55	6	37	1	0
Commerce	41	4	53	1	0
Iran					
Total	44	10	40	1	4
Agriculture	29	16	54	1	0
Manufacturing	64	3	30	2	0
Commerce	21	3	73	2	0
Ecuador					
Total	46	8	41	2	3
Agriculture	39	11	47	3	0
Manufacturing	39	6	52	3	0
Commerce	21	4	72	3	0
UAR					
Total	49	19	22	7	2
Agriculture	35	30	25	10	0
Manufacturing	79	4	13	4	0
Commerce	26	8	56	10	0
Japan					
Total	54	24	19	3	0
Agriculture	6	58	35	1	0
Manufacturing	86	5	6	3	0
Commerce	57	16	21	5	0
Malaysia					
Total	56	8	34		1
Agriculture	45	13	42		0
Manufacturing	66	3	31		0
Commerce	41	4	55		0
Jamaica					
Total	59	6	31	3	1
Agriculture	41	7	48	3	0
Manufacturing	47	10	40	3	0
Commerce	43	4	47	6	0
Venezuela					
Total	60	5	30	3	2
Agriculture	33	14	51	3	0
Manufacturing	68	1	27	4	0
Commerce	50	1	41	7	0

Table 3.1 (continued)

Country and sector	Employees	Unpaid family workers	Workers on own account	Employers	Not classifiable
Tanzania					
Total	61	0	22	11	7
Agriculture	61	0	14	22	4
Manufacturing	62	0	18	15	5
Commerce	40	0	40	14	7
Mexico					
Total	64	1	33	1	1
Agriculture	54	2	43	0	1
Manufacturing	82	0	17	1	0
Commerce	38	1	59	2	0
El Salvador					
Total	67	8	22	2	2
Agriculture	63	12	23	2	0
Manufacturing	60	3	28	4	5
Commerce	38	3	55	3	0
Uraguay					
Total	69	2	15	8	6
Agriculture	54	7	23	15	1
Manufacturing	74	0	18	7	1
Commerce	64	1	18	17	1
France					
Total	70	9	15	4	3
Agriculture	22	34	37	7	0
Manufacturing	91	1	5	3	0
Commerce	69	6	19	6	0
Austria					
Total	71	13	16		0
Agriculture	16	48	36		0
Manufacturing	88	3	9		0
Commerce	80	5	15		0
Chile					
Total	73	2	19	1	5
Agriculture	67	5	23	2	3
Manufacturing	76	0	21	2	1
Commerce	45	1	50	3	1
Denmark					
Total	77	2	20		0
Agriculture	40	6	54		0
Manufacturing	90	1	9		0
Commerce	70	4	26		·0

Table 3.1 (continued)

Country and sector	Employees	Unpaid family workers	Workers on own account	Employers	Not classifiable
Netherlands					
Total	80	5	7	8	0
Agriculture	29	20	24	27	0
Manufacturing	92	1	3	4	0
Commerce	66	9	13	12	0
New Zealand					
Total	80	0	10	9	1
Agriculture	41	1	33	24	1
Manufacturing	91	0	3	4	1
Commerce	84	0	7	8	1
Switzerland					
Total	81	5	15		0
Agriculture	23	27	50		0
Manufacturing	90	2	8		0
Commerce	81	3	16		0
USA					
Total	83	1	11		5
Agriculture	33	6	57		4
Manufacturing	92	0	2		6
Commerce	80	2	14		4
Sweden					
Total	83	3	11	3	0
Agriculture	35	14	47	4	0
Manufacturing	94	1	3	2	0
Commerce	81	3	11	5	0

Aside from the total labour force, breakdowns for three sectors are presented, viz, 'agriculture', 'manufacturing', and 'commerce'. Employment categories covered are 'employees', 'unpaid family workers', 'workers on own account', 'employers', and 'not classifiable'. Apart from the three sectors covered in the table, the total figures incorporate data for 'construction', 'mining and quarrying', 'electricity, gas, water and sanitary services', 'transport, storage and communication', 'services', and 'activities not adequately described'. This explains the fact that occasionally percentages for the 'total' lie outside the range defined by the percentages of the three sectors included in the table. There is a persistent tendency for this to happen for the column of 'not classifiable' people, largely because the 'sector' labelled 'activities not adequately described', which is not included in our table, frequently covers people described as 'not classifiable'.

There are some interesting general patterns in the classification. First, it would appear that unpaid family work as a category of employment is an important one for many countries, and indeed for some countries it is the dominant form of employment.[2] As a category this has to be distinguished from that of 'workers on own account', because the motivational problems involved are rather different − a fact that is frequently overlooked in the analytical literature. The unity of interest that can be assumed in the case of labourers working for themselves would be an inappropriate assumption for unpaid family workers, especially since the size of the 'extended family' in some of the pre-capitalist economies is very large.

Secondly, the relative importance of wage employment seems to increase quite noticeably as we move from poorer to richer countries. The countries in Table 3.1 have been arranged in increasing order of the percentage of 'employees' in the total economically active labour force and even a cursory examination of the sequence brings out the general relation between income per head and the dominance of 'employees' as a category. Indeed, the growing importance of wage-labour is recognized to be a significant aspect of the process of economic development.

Thirdly, for most countries the importance of 'employees' seems to be much greater in manufacturing than in other sectors. Even the less developed countries rely to a large extent on the wage sector in manufacturing, and for the more advanced countries the manufacturing sector is almost wholly dominated by wage-labour.[3] In contrast, in agriculture the importance of the non-wage sector is very much greater and remains relatively so even for the richer countries. Commerce seems to come somewhere in between, and while for the less developed countries the non-wage sector is dominant, precisely the opposite seems to be the case for the more advanced economies.

In discussing problems of technological choice and employment we have to bear in mind this empirical framework. The policy implications of employment expansion can be studied only with reference to the relevant modes of production.

2. For the European countries covered in the table, except for France and Greece, family workers receiving pay are included in the category of 'unpaid family workers' in these UN data, and the same happens for Japan among the non-European countries. The importance of unpaid family workers remains even after making allowance for this.

3. Although our data give the number of 'employees', we are making statements about 'wage-labour'; this is justified only because the wage is the standard form of payment to 'employees'. In fact that is how 'employees' are usually defined.

3.2 Employment and the Utilization of Labour

Consider first an extremely simple model. Let x be the amount of labour time supplied by a typical labourer; if there are n labourers, the total amount of labour time (L) is:

$$L = nx. \tag{3.1}$$

Output Q is assumed to be simply a function of L, increasing at a diminishing rate as more and more labour is applied:

$$Q = f(L), \text{ with } f' > 0 \text{ and } f'' < 0. \tag{3.2}$$

The effort involved in working is a function of the amount of labour. To simplify the picture it is assumed that the required compensation for an additional unit of work z is constant, measured in units of output.[4] $S(x)$ expresses the total compensation required for x amount of labour.

$$S(x) = zx. \tag{3.3}$$

The work equilibrium will, therefore, be characterized by the condition of equating z with the gain from an additional unit of work. It is assumed that of the additional output produced by such work the labourer gets a proportionate share of α, with $0 \leqslant \alpha \leqslant 1$. The labourer values a unit of output going to others at h per unit (in terms of units of output enjoyed by himself),[5] with $0 \leqslant h \leqslant 1$. If he is completely 'alienated' from others $h = 0$.

In a situation of 'work equilibrium' the cost of an additional unit of labour would equal the reward from it:[6]

$$z = f'(nx) [\alpha + (1 - \alpha)h]. \tag{3.4}$$

Since output Q increases at a diminishing rate with L, Q can also be seen to be a function of f', such that the lower the value of f' the higher is the total output produced:

$$Q = G(f'), \text{ with } G \text{ diminishing.} \tag{3.5}$$

4. This is an over-simplification; see § 3.3. below.
5. The value of h will depend not only on one's 'concern' for others but also on their respective income levels; if one is richer than others it is even possible that $h > 1$. For a more general analysis, see Sen (1966), (1966a). See also Hymer and Resnick (1969), Wellisz (1968), W. C. Robinson (1969), (1971), Jorgenson and Lau (1969), and Zarembka (1972).
6. There must be some 'boundary conditions' on the total amount of labour that can be supplied by a typical person, i.e., $x \leqslant x^*$, and there is no guarantee that equation (3.4) would hold for $x \leqslant x^*$. I postpone discussion of this problem to § 3.3.

Putting equations (3.4) and (3.5) together, we obtain:

$$Q = G(z/[\alpha + (1 - \alpha)h]), \text{ with } G \text{ diminishing.} \qquad (3.6)$$

We conclude that output and employment will be larger if:
 (i) α is larger
 (ii) h is larger
 (iii) z is smaller.

This shockingly simple framework is, nevertheless, broad enough to permit a preliminary sorting out of issues for the different modes of employment on a comparative basis. However, there are also variations in technological parameters, particularly where the possibility arises of using technologies that require a larger scale of operation. The production function that is open to a large wage-based factory enterprise might not be available to a small household production unit. This is not very easy to integrate into the framework outlined here and we shall do it — shamefully näively — through a 'technology parameter' β. The object of the exercise is to be able to catch the relative advantages of the different modes in terms of output and when a mode is open to larger scale operation we shall express this advantage by a higher value of the multiplicative parameter β applied to f.

$$Q = \beta f(L), \text{ with } \beta > 0 \qquad (3.7)$$

$$Q = G(z/\beta [\alpha + (1 - \alpha)h]), \text{ with } G \text{ diminishing.} \qquad (3.8)$$

In Table 3.2 a rough schematic structure of the four influences (α, h, z and β) is considered for four modes of labour use, viz., 'family system', 'extended family system', 'wage employment' and 'co-operative system'; these are, of course, only very rough stereotypes.[7]

Table 3.2

Variations of Parameters among Employment Modes

Category	Parameter	Family	Extended family	Wage employment	Co-operative
Share	α	High	Medium	High?	Low
Concern	h	High	Medium	Low	Medium?
Cost advantage	$1/z$	High	High	Low	High?
Technology	β	Low	Medium	High	High

7. In the table we take the inverse of z rather than z itself, so that 'high' means a positive influence rather than a negative one.

As far as α is concerned, it is obviously high for the family system since a family is a small unit and each worker will receive a high proportion of his contribution to output.[8] This share will be less for an extended family since α may correspond roughly to $1/n$, where n is the number of people involved, which will be larger for the extended family. For a co-operative run on a larger scale, α will tend to be smaller still, if the distribution system in the co-operative is geared towards some family-type criterion. A co-operative that is run on the basis of payments according to work rather than on some criterion of needs may approximate 'wage employment' in essential respects and should be put under that category.[9]

As far as wage employment itself is concerned, if the marginal productivity theory of wages held, α should equal 1, but the weaknesses of that theory are well-known. In any case, if there are monopolistic elements in the product market or monopsonistic elements in the labour market, the wage earner will get less than his marginal product even according to neo-classical theory.

Coming now to h, members of the same family are likely to have a high degree of concern for each other, so that h should be high. This may be less so for the extended family and still less for a large co-operative, even though it will depend very much on the values and social consciousness of the society in question. With the capitalist wage system, the wage earner's interest in the welfare of the capitalist, who takes away a part of his product, may be expected to be rather little.

As far as z is concerned, one of the common features of models of the 'dual' economy is the relatively low level of the supply price of labour in the family system (and this should apply to the extended family, as well as to a co-operative organized in a community-centred way), as opposed to capitalist wage employment. We discussed this question in Chapter 1. The capitalist is deterred from choosing relatively labour-intensive techniques by the level of the wage he has to pay. But the height of the wage rate may reflect institutional constraints (see Chapter 6 below) and the labour cost calculations of the family enterprise may be completely different. To what extent this cost advantage will apply to a co-operative enterprise as well will depend on how alienated the members of the co-operative feel from the management and from each other. At one extreme is the case of the co-operative being one big family and at the other is the case in which members treat their work simply as jobs to be

8. For share-cropping and other feudal systems in agriculture, α will be smaller.
9. There are, however, also some special problems associated with co-operative payment according to work, on which see Ward (1958), (1971), Domar (1966) and Sen (1966a).

done to earn some income. The value of z will depend on the appropriate assumption.

Each system, therefore, seems to have some advantage over others and some disadvantages. As far as Table 3.1 is concerned, it is easy to guess why wage employment tends to dominate in manufacturing but not in agriculture; the technological possibilities opened up by larger scale production are incomparably greater for manufacturing than for agriculture.[10] As far as commerce is concerned, in a largely rural economy the scale advantages may not be very great, but in the highly urbanized societies of the advanced economies commerce can make substantial use of the benefits of large scale. In general, economic development opens up technological possibilities of exploitation of large scale production and this factor tends to outweigh the advantages of higher values of α, h and $1/z$ in the non-wage family systems. The differential advantages would have different net balances at different stages of economic development.

The balance of advantages discussed above, however, reflects an essentially static picture. There is also the question of dynamic forces of change, such as capital accumulation and technological progress. This is precisely where modern wage-based systems have a distinct advantage, because they tend to show much greater dynamism than the more traditional economic systems. Opportunities for expansion of output and employment depend to a great extent on these forces.[11]

3.3 Some Further Observations

The model outlined in the last section is extremely over-simplified, but it permits us to bring certain important points into focus. A few critical observations on the assumptions of the last section may now be considered. First, the required compensation for work, viz., z, should be expected to rise rather than to remain constant as the amount of work x increases. Instead of equation (3.3), we can take: $S'(x) > 0$ and $S''(x) > 0$, i.e., the imputed 'cost' of labour increases at an increasing rate. The other relations remain unaffected as long as we replace z everywhere by $S'(x)$. Furthermore, by assuming that $S'(x)$ rises without bound as x approaches some x^*, we can also ensure an equilibrium of the kind given by equation (3.4) for $x \leqslant x^*$.

Secondly, output Q may not be a function of labour alone, so that other factors have to be brought in. Our intention was, however, to catch the advantages and disadvantages on the labour side and bringing in other

10. Plantation agriculture is an exception and this largely explains the high ratio of 'employees' in the agriculture of such countries as Malaysia.
11. See Part IV below.

factors would not affect this, even though the functional relations and the equilibrium conditions would have to be redefined.

Thirdly, labour may have outside employment opportunities. A 'dual' market equilibrium may take place with z_1, the supply price of labour for peasant cultivation, falling short of z_2, the supply price for capitalist production. We shall have occasion to examine such 'dual' equilibria later on in this work.

Fourthly, as argued in the last chapter, production possibilities depend on actual experience and the practical search for new technology. The value of β and the function f must be seen to depend on the actual history of the different modes.

Fifthly, the employment modes have been compared an terms of output production, but it may be argued that what is needed is some concept of welfare which should take into account the cost of labour. Consider the group welfare function W as a maximand:

$$W = \beta f(L) - zxn, \tag{3.9}$$

which is simply the output level *minus* the sum of the supply prices of labour. It is obvious that all the directional relations in the light of which Table 3.1 was presented remain unaffected. Clearly a higher β increases W, given other things. However, greater effort involves a larger cost (z per unit) in addition to greater benefit. Is there a net gain from higher effort? Note that:

$$\frac{dW}{dx} = [\beta f'(L) - z]n. \tag{3.10}$$

Given $1 > \alpha$ and $1 > h$, the work equilibrium would imply:

$$\beta f'(L) > z. \tag{3.11}$$

Therefore, a larger x involves a greater W. The analysis of the preceding section dealt with more or less output Q in terms of more or less labour x and precisely the same directional relation holds for welfare W as well. A higher α and a higher h (for $\alpha < 1$) involve a larger welfare level, given other things.

So does a lower z, for two reasons: viz., (i) it would induce a larger *value of x*, and (ii) the negative part of the welfare function (3.9) would simply be lower. The former is much like having a higher value of α or h, whereas the latter reflects a direct advantage of the preferred (and possibly less alienated) forms of employment.

Note that equation (3.9) values the benefit from output simply in natural units, whereas the worker's own valuation of it depends on his concern for others and the share going to them. From his personal point of view, the net gain in his welfare V from more effort is given by:

$$\frac{dV}{dx} = \beta f'(L)\,[\alpha + (1 - \alpha)h] - z. \qquad (3.12)$$

However, the others gain too, viz, to the extent given by $\beta f'(L)(1 - \alpha)$. Assuming symmetrically that they value income coming to them at one per unit while valuing at h per unit the income going to the people whose efforts yield these outputs (and similarly their efforts), and adding the whole thing up, the total social gain when everyone increases his effort x would be found to be:

$$\frac{dW}{dx} = [\beta f'(L) - z]\,(1 + h)n. \qquad (3.13)$$

All the directional relations are preserved as in equation (3.10), and furthermore there is a direct gain from a higher h, through getting more from a given volume of output due to greater concern for each other. Equation (3.13) is simply a blown-up version of (3.10), making allowance for social concern to the extent of $(1 + h)$.

Various alternative assumptions about social welfare are possible.[12] It may be objected that a different value of h simply means different individual preferences and that the definition of social welfare W may be problematic under these circumstances. There is something in this, but there is nothing wrong in principle in making social welfare W vary with individual preferences. In any case, it is clear that all the directional relations discussed with respect to output levels, and in terms of which Table 3.1 was drawn up, remain true for all the different welfare cases considered. So the directional analysis does not seem to be affected by the particular variant of the welfare function chosen.

Finally, variations of preferences based on people's interdependence with others do, in fact, reflect an essential aspect of work choice, especially under non-wage systems. A conception of social welfare which ignores this aspect of the question misses an important dimension of employment decisions. An individual is a social being and his work is a social act. These are significant facts which can scarcely be overlooked in evaluating the conflicting considerations favouring different modes of employment. When we discuss employment policy this aspect of the question will assume some prominence.

---

12. I have tried to discuss these questions in Sen (1970), (1973).

II | Some Measurement Problems

4 | Surplus Labour and Disguised Unemployment

4.1 Introduction

It was said of the burghers of Ghent that they had 'two great sources of strength', viz., 'their towers' and 'their kinsfolk'.[1] In contrast the unemployed in the poor countries have only their kinsfolk, and their survival depends on their ability to bank on this source of strength. In a country without a system of dole for the unemployed or social security arranged by public bodies, a person can live with no source of income only if he has kin to fall back on.

But could he get away without doing any work for the family on which he lives? The answer is, by and large, no.[2] He would be expected to help with the family chores. But what are these chores? In a system of wage employment, he may not be able to help the employed members of the family directly in their formal work, but he can help in various activities like marketing, cooking, looking after the children and other such things. So far so good; the statistician is not confused — this man is unemployed and he is not undertaking any 'gainful activity', as that peculiar concept is defined. But suppose he lives in a peasant family. What are the chores that he will now be expected to share? Perhaps the cultivation itself. Certainly ancillary activities, like carrying things from place to place. But then he *is* 'gainfully employed' and the statistician is in a dilemma. How can we tell this man from others who are 'genuinely' employed?

1. Bloch (1965), p. 124.
2. There is a primitive sense of justice in this which crops up in different forms in different contexts. It is caught best by St Paul's rather stark injunction: 'If any one will not work, let him not eat.'

This is roughly the background to the concept of 'disguised unemployment'. Following the distinction between the three aspects of employment analysed in Chapter 1, we can use one of three possible tests.

(i) *The production approach:*   If this man leaves the family would the output of the family enterprise go down?

(ii) *The income approach:*   Is this man's income (including direct consumption and any other income that he is given) a reward for his work, and will he cease to get it if he stops work?

(iii) *The recognition approach:*   Does he think of himself as 'employed'? Do others?

The literature on 'disguised unemployment' has concentrated on the first approach only, but there are problems for which the two latter approaches are relevant. I shall discuss them in turn.

4.2 Disguised Unemployment under the Production Approach

Much blood has been shed on crusades about disguised unemployment viewed from the production point of view. There are two fronts in the battle, viz., the analytical and the empirical. The former will be discussed first.

In the production sense, disguised unemployment means that a withdrawal of a part of the labour force from the traditional field of production (usually peasant agriculture) would leave total output unchanged. Is this consistent with rational behaviour by the peasants? It is not immediately obvious why it should not be, but it depends on what the precise explanation of the phenomenon is meant to be. Ragnar Nurkse argued that 'in technical terms, the marginal productivity of labour, over a wide range, is zero'.[3] This could explain why a reduction in the use of labour would not affect output,[4] but it is open to the question: since it is fruitless, why is labour being applied over this 'wide range'? There would seem to be something unnatural in such behaviour.

The answer lies in the distinction between labour time and the number of labourers and in arguing that the phenomenon is essentially

3. Nurkse (1953), p. 33.
4. 'A number of people are working on farms or small peasant plots, contributing virtually nothing to output, but subsisting on a share of their family's real income.' (Nurkse (1953), p. 33.) 'All this work is not necessary, all the same it does occupy a great deal of a person's time.' (Telang (1954), p. 150.)

connected with variations in labour time per person (or 'effort' per person).[5] Consider a simple example. Four persons may be doing the work of two if there is no more fruitful work to be done, i.e., the marginal product of labour touches zero. There will be no work done that is 'not necessary' – the marginal product would not be zero 'over a wide range' – but the necessary work will be spread over more people than are needed to get that work done.

There are, however, two further problems. First, it has been argued that the marginal product of labour can hardly fall to zero. Viner put this point of view most eloquently:

As far as agriculture is concerned, I find it impossible to conceive of a farm of any kind on which, other factors of production being held constant in quantity, and even in form as well, it would not be possible by known methods, to obtain some addition to the crop by using additional labor in more careful selection and planting of the seed, more intensive weeding, cultivation, thinning, and mulcting, more painstaking harvesting, gleaning and clearing of the crop. [6]

Secondly, even if the marginal product of labour could fall to zero for some total amount of labour, that would not be a point of work equilibrium unless the peasants had no disutility from work whatsoever. With a positive marginal disutility of effort, the work equilibrium would be at a positive marginal product of labour.[7]

There is clearly something in these criticisms, but where they go wrong is in the simple fact that a work equilibrium at zero marginal product of labour is not necessary (nor, incidentally, is it sufficient) for the thesis of disguised unemployment. In terms of the model of Chapter 3, z need not be zero and indeed all we need for disguised unemployment is the *constancy* of z in the relevant region. That is, eqn (3.3) will do nicely irrespective of the value of z. This is obvious from eqn (3.6) or (3.8). As long as z, α and h are constant, so will be output Q, despite the withdrawal of some working members of the family, and all that will change is x, i.e., the amount of work done per person.[8]

The main limitation of such a model of disguised unemployment lies in the problem discussed in § 3.3, viz, that the supply price of labour

5. See Sen (1960), pp. 3–5. See also Myint (1964) and W. C. Robinson (1971).
6. Viner (1957), p. 18. See also Schultz (1964).
7. 'Why should the workers continue to work though they are not producing anything? More particularly, why don't they stop working at a level above zero marginal productivity? Is it assumed that work does not represent any disutility?' (Myrdal (1968), p. 2053.)
8. If α rises when members of the joint family leave (thereby making the remaining unit smaller), constancy of z is unnecessarily strong, and surplus labour can exist even if z rises somewhat.

effort $S'(x)$ can be an increasing function of work time, and then a withdrawal of a part of the work force will reduce output.[9] Further, there will clearly be a maximum amount of work time x^* per person over a given period of time. If we assume that $S'(x)$ is constant at a value z subject to x being no more than x^*, the model of disguised unemployment can work perfectly well, provided the withdrawal of part of the labour force does not push the amount of work effort per person beyond x^*. The model is spelt out explicitly below.

$$L = nx \tag{3.1}$$

$$Q = f(L), \text{ with } f' > 0 \text{ and } f'' < 0 \tag{3.2}$$

$$S(x) = zx, \text{ subject to } x \leqslant x^* \tag{3.3*}$$

$$z = f'(nx)\,[\alpha + (1-\alpha)h], \text{ subject to } x \leqslant x^* \tag{3.4*}$$

$$Q = G(z/[\alpha + (1-\alpha)h]), \text{ with } G \text{ diminishing, and}$$

$$f^{-1}(Q) \leqslant nx^*. \tag{3.6*}$$

Eqn (3.1) gives the equal work-sharing rule among the n working members of the peasant family. Eqn (3.2) gives the total output as a function of labour, given the amounts of other factors of production. Eqn (3.3*) states that the compensation that a cultivator requires is constant at z per unit, subject to a maximum amount of work of x^* per person. Eqn (3.4*) reflects the work equilibrium of the typical peasant. For a cohesive and non-alienated family, full concern for others may imply, given an equal distribution of income and work, $h = 1$, thereby substantially simplifying (3.4*) and (3.6*), but that is a special case and the existence of disguised unemployment does not depend on it. Eqn (3.6*) expresses output as a function of z, α and h, subject to the work of each person being no more than x^*. The work done per person is given by:

$$x = f^{-1}(G(z/[\alpha + (1-\alpha)h]))/n. \tag{4.1}$$

A reduction in the labour force leaves the *total* work time and the level of total output completely unchanged (the reduction in numbers being completely balanced by the increase in work per person) as long as x given by eqn (4.1) is no more than x^*. Once that limit is reached, everyone's work level gets fixed at this maximum value x^* and a reduction of the work force will reduce output. So the necessary and sufficient condition for the existence of disguised unemployment in this model is:

$$x^* \geqslant f^{-1}(G(z/[\alpha + (1-\alpha)h]))/n \tag{4.2}$$

9. A rise in z will reduce Q since G in eqn (3.8) is a diminishing function.

in which n is the number of working people left in the family *after* the withdrawal of part of the work force.[10]

It is clear that the analytical framework for disguised unemployment can be made quite rigorous to fit easily into the usual conception of reasoned economic behaviour. Whether Viner (1957) was right in arguing that marginal productivity of labour *cannot* fall to zero also turns out to be irrelevant, since the conditions for the existence of surplus labour do not depend on this.[11] This is worth recognizing, especially since some development economists seem to have found the criticisms of Viner and others to be 'incontrovertible'.[12]

There has also been a vigorous debate on the detailed empirical evidence in favour of or against the thesis of disguised unemployment. Some, e.g., Mellor and Stevens (1956), Sarkar (1957), ILO (1961), Mehra (1966), Sanghvi (1969), seem to have found evidence of its existence. Others, e.g., Oshima (1958), Schultz (1964), Jorgenson (1967), Hansen (1966), have, on the other hand, presented evidence to the contrary.

The empirical part of the debate is particularly difficult to settle, for two separate reasons. First, it is not easy to find an actual case of a withdrawal of part of the labour force with other things remaining the same. Typically such a withdrawal would take place side by side with other changes.[13] Furthermore, the type of withdrawal one is concerned with takes place in response to economic incentives and other types of withdrawal may be quite different. For example, sudden deaths through epidemics would not give relevant information on this question, since in an epidemic working members would be killed off indiscriminately (in

10. This model is a variant of the one presented in Sen (1966), which also examined the underlying utility function. See also Hymer and Resnick (1969), Wellisz (1968), Myrdal (1968) Appendix 6, Uppal (1969), W. C. Robinson (1969), (1971), and Lal (1972).

11. Nor is it easy to get excited about Elkan's (1973) worry: 'But clearly those who remain behind will not work longer or harder if they can continue to obtain the same amount of food as hitherto by working only five hours' (p. 72). The return per unit of extra effort would rise if the smaller population left behind were to keep their effort per person unchanged, and this would give them an incentive to increase efforts (unless they had already attained 'bliss'!).

12. Myrdal (1968), p. 2055.

13. Cf. Marx's analysis of the creation of a 'reserve army of labour' in England: 'In spite of the smaller number of its cultivators, the soil brought forth as much or more produce, after as before, because the revolution in the conditions of landed property was accompanied by improved methods of culture, greater co-operation, concentration of the means of production etc., and because not only were the agricultural wage-labourers put on the strain more intensely, but the field of production on which they worked for themselves, become more and more contracted.' (Marx (1887), pp. 769–70.)

fact, wiping out some families altogether while not affecting others much), and not selectively from families with relatively more labour compared with land and other assets. Schultz's (1964) observation that in the year following the influenza epidemic in India in 1918–19 the Indian agricultural output did decline, while perfectly accurate, does not establish whether output would have declined had a comparable proportion of the agricultural population left for other occupations in response to economic incentives.[14]

Secondly, while economists seem to have a preference for proving the existence of *or* the absence of disguised unemployment in the developing countries *in general*, it is of course perfectly possible that the thesis of disguised unemployment is reasonably correct for some countries or regions and not for others. Furthermore, the relevant issue is not of the yes–no type, and there are questions both of (i) the *volume* of surplus labour if present, and (ii) the *quantitative impact* of labour withdrawal on output, which could be high or low; whether or not it is exactly zero is not the only interesting question.[15]

4.3 Disguised Unemployment and the Income Approach

Suppose the output produced by a peasant family of five working members would remain unaffected if one of them should leave. That is, one person is in disguised unemployment in the production sense. We may not be able to say which *particular* person is in this state, since any one person could go and the output would still be the same. But assume now that some person A does go, and we find that from the production point of view he was unemployed in 'disguise'. How would it look from the income point of view?

He was working and earning something in return. Clearly, from the income point of view he need not have been considered unemployed. Is there a distinction to be drawn in this case as well and is there a criterion for deciding whether he was unemployed or not? The crucial question concerns the relation of his earnings (including direct consumption, such as food and shelter, as well as any other emoluments) to his work.

A contrast between two cases may be helpful in bringing out the distinction. Consider first a case of joint ownership of land and other productive assets, and let the system be that each member of this joint family is entitled to some income from the joint property. If person A stays in the village he helps in the productive activities, but if he takes up employment elsewhere, he cannot do this; but in either situation let us

14. See Sen (1967) and Schultz (1967). See also Appendix A below.
15. A quantitative formulation of the decline of output resulting from the withdrawal of part of the population is given in Sen (1966), with surplus labour as a special case.

assume that he receives his share of the farm income. This being the case, if he is 'unemployed' in the production sense, he will be so according to the income approach as well. What he earns from the farm is independent of his own work, and his work, therefore, has no income consequence. Contrast this case with that of the man who is supported only on condition that he helps in the family work and who would not receive any income if he should leave. In this second case clearly the man is employed in the income sense.

In many traditional economies, to be entitled to the implicit rent from land and other agricultural property, one has to be on the farm and work in it. By going away one forfeits one's right to a part of the family's joint income.[16] This means that the income approach yields different results from the production approach.

Is the distinction significant for employment? I would argue that it is. First of all, it focuses on employment as a vehicle of income distribution, which is indeed an important aspect of public policy (see Chapter 9). The dichotomy between the income aspect and the production aspect of disguised unemployment is relevant in that context. Finding an outside job for a person who was employed in terms of the income approach has an impact not only on his own well-being but also on those left behind in the farm, since they now get what he was earning while on the farm. The results would be quite different if the person were unemployed in the income sense as well.

Secondly, the determination of the supply price of labour to outside enterprises would depend on whether disguised unemployment existed only from the production point of view, or also in terms of the income approach. If the former, then a labourer (or a nuclear family) migrating elsewhere for a job would want compensation for the loss of his share of income from the joint family enterprise and his wage rate would have to cover at least that. Despite his being unemployed from one point of view, the opportunity cost of his taking up a job elsewhere may be quite high. If, on the other hand, he were unemployed from both the production and the income points of view, there would not be such an opportunity cost. If a joint family stays joint and completely merged together in terms of income, even after part of the family migrates elsewhere in search of employment, and the migrating members do not have to seek compensation for an income loss, the supply price of labour will be lower to that extent.

This type of question seems to have a bearing on the survival and

16. See Appendix A.

success of the so-called 'informal' sector,[17] since its effective labour cost will remain low vis-à-vis that of the organized sector operating outside the family orbit. It also has some relevance for the pattern of migration of industrial labour in some countries,[18] since short-period wage employment might permit one to continue to enjoy part of the joint family income and assets. The distinction between disguised unemployment in the production sense and in the income sense is relevant to a number of issues of employment policy.

4.4 The Income Approach to Unemployment

To avoid possible confusion I should comment on the distinction between the income approach to unemployment as developed here and the view that 'an adequate level of employment must be defined in terms of its capacity to provide minimum living to the population'.[19] The ILO mission to Kenya took an approach to unemployment similar to the latter, and indeed put 'the greatest emphasis on ... the poverty level of returns from work'.[20] This criterion of unemployment – essentially as one of inadequate income – has appeared in other works as well.[21]

As a criterion for the existence of a social problem, inadequate income is of obvious relevance. The question is whether this is best viewed as a criterion of *unemployment* as such. It seems to me that perhaps there is a good case for keeping 'poverty' as a concept distinct from 'unemployment', without of course assuming them to be independent of each other. Employment is an important means of generating and distributing income (see Chapter 9), but a person can be rich yet unemployed, if he has other sources of income, and also a person can work very hard and still be very poor. Poverty is a function of technology and productivity, of ownership of the means of production, and of exploitation and social arrangements for production and distribution. To identify unemployment with poverty seems to impoverish both notions since they relate to two somewhat different categories of thought.

17. On the importance of this sector for Kenya, see ILO (1972), Chapter 13; for India, see Appendix B below.
18. See § 8.4 below.
19. Dandekar and Rath (1971). Dandekar and Rath are primarily concerned with poverty and consider employment through work programmes as a means of redistribution. The value of their work is not diminished by their somewhat limited definition of unemployment, since nothing crucial in their analysis depends on it.
20. ILO (1972), p. 1.
21. See Raj Krishna's (1973) illuminating study of the alternative approaches to the estimation of unemployment in India. See also Rao (1973).

In contrast, the income approach used in this work is not concerned with checking whether a person's income is high or low, but whether the emoluments he receives are conditional on the work he performs.[22] From this point of view, a member of a joint family working in the family farm is to be regarded as unemployed if he would continue to receive economic support even if he did not work in that farm, but is to be taken as employed if his emoluments would cease if he stopped working in that farm. The criterion is not whether his income is high or low, but whether his income is conditional on his work.

4.5 Unemployment and the Recognition Aspect

Consider a person who is in disguised unemployment in both the production sense and the income sense, but who works, survives economically and does not view himself as 'unemployed'. In terms of the recognition approach the question could be raised as to whether he is best viewed as unemployed or not. The distinction between objective categories and subjective ones is not easy to draw in this case. Precisely because the person in question regards himself as employed, certain actual behaviour patterns may be expected to follow.

One of them relates to the question of seeking work elsewhere. For example, it has been observed in many traditional agrarian economies that even people who have a very low intensity of work in their own farms and suffer from acute poverty frequently do not look for work elsewhere and could not be persuaded to take up wage employment elsewhere even if it were offered to them.[23] The fact that a member of the peasant family might be a case of 'disguised unemployment' is certainly relevant for some purposes, but it may not induce him to offer himself as a wage labourer in the market; indeed he may not even regard himself as 'unemployed'.

Each economic system seems to produce its own values, its own illusions, its own ideology. The conviction of a peasant that he is 'employed' relates to a certain structure of thought to which the concept of 'disguised unemployment' does not really belong. While that is no reason

22. If his emoluments are conditional on only a part of the work that he actually does, then the remainder represents the proportion of unemployment in the income sense. The income approach to unemployment does not require an 'all-or-nothing' approach.
23. The Indian National Sample Survey reports that in 1961–2 among the group of rural workers with only 15–28 hours of work per week, only 27 per cent said that they were available for additional work if offered. Among workers who had only 1–14 hours of work per week, the proportion willing to accept additional work was even lower, viz. 23 per cent. See National Sample Survey, 17th Round (1961–2), Table 3.9. See Appendix A for a detailed discussion of this problem.

for dismissing the notion of 'disguised unemployment' as a 'Western category'[24] — the contrast is certainly not between the East and the West but (i) between different economic and social modes that may exist side by side in the same country and (ii) between different ways of viewing unemployment related to different economic questions — it is necessary to view the behaviour patterns of human beings also in terms of their own assessments of their position. The question of women's employment is, of course, a typical example of this problem. The type of household work that might convince a woman in one society that she was fully employed might make her feel in another society that she was totally wasting her time, and her behaviour pattern would depend on what she herself would see her own state to be.

Unemployment is a state of being without fruitful work and the perception of the fruitfulness of work is, to a large extent, a result of social conditioning. In studying economic behaviour and the problems of economic policy, the concept of unemployment has to be viewed not only in the light of production and income but also in terms of the perception of the people caught by the statistician's slide rule. The problem is not quite comparable to counting the number of surplus cattle in India or Thailand.

24. Myrdal (1968), p. 2221.

5 | Capital Intensity and Technology

5.1 Introduction
A million X million matrix is not a delight to handle. But there are certainly at least a million goods in the world[1] and the construction of an input—output table involving all of them would require massive amounts of paper and patience. It is, therefore, fair to assume that, leaving aside a handful of hardened masochists, nobody would be totally opposed to aggregation. Economists do frequently do their sums in terms of rice (and not always in terms of rice of specific varieties), of the total supply of food grains (and not only of rice, wheat, etc.), and even of the total supply of consumer goods (and not only of food grains, clothing, etc.). Virtually any economic analysis seems to involve some aggregation.

Why then do some economists rise indignantly in protest when it comes to the aggregation of capital goods? The question is of more than academic interest since discussions on employment policy tend to be much concerned with concepts like 'capital intensity', and problems of aggregation of capital are of obvious relevance for defining capital-intensity. The questions we must ask are the following:
   (i) What are the special problems of valuation of capital?
   (ii) How do they affect statements on the capital intensity of invest-
        ment in connection with employment policy?

5.2 Capital as a Factor of Production
The recent controversies in capital theory have engaged a large number of economists and have produced — in less than two decades — a monu-

---

1. Remember that different books are different products, which is a good start even without taking account of different editions.

mental literature.[2] This is not the occasion to launch a full-scale review of the debate and I shall confine my discussion of the problem to a few remarks only.[3]

First, quite a bit of the controversy is not concerned with the measurement of capital at all, but with the use of capital as a factor of production in an aggregate production function and with the concept of marginal productivity of capital and its identification with the rate of profit. Even if there is only one homogeneous capital good along with a homogeneous consumer good, there is a problem of the *value* of capital in terms of output. In neo-classical models with an aggregate production function, the value of output per labourer is taken to be a non-decreasing function of the value of capital per labourer (evaluated at the competitively determined prices) and the rate of profit equals the marginal impact of the latter on the former.[4] It is easy to check that even with one homogeneous capital good such a functional relation between the two sets of *values* may not exist. The relation between the value of capital goods and that of consumer goods depends on the rate of profit. The value of capital in equilibrium equals past costs accumulated at the appropriate rate of profit and also equals future rentals discounted at the appropriate rate of profit. Therefore, a variation of the rate of profit implies a variation of the value of capital. Viewing the value of output per head as a non-decreasing function of the value of capital and equating the rate of profit to the marginal response of the former to a change in the latter raise important problems of internal consistency. These neo-classical relationships can be restored only with very special assumptions,

2. The contributions include, among many others, Robinson (1954), (1956), (1970), (1971), Champernowne (1954), Solow (1956a), (1957), (1960), (1962), (1963), Swan (1956), (1960), Kaldor (1957), Johansen (1959), (1961), (1972), Salter (1960), Sraffa (1960), Hicks (1960), (1965), (1973), Arrow, Chenery, Minhas and Solow (1961), Arrow (1962), Kaldor and Mirrlees (1962), Samuelson (1962), Pyatt (1963), Hahn and Matthews (1964), Morishima (1964), (1969), Fisher (1965), (1969), (1971), Levhari (1965), Pasinetti (1965), (1966), (1969), Bhaduri (1966), (1969), Bruno, Burmeister and Sheshinski (1966), (1968), Garegnani (1966), (1970), (1970a), Hahn (1966), (1970), Jorgenson (1966), Levhari and Samuelson (1966), Jorgenson and Griliches (1967), Shell and Stiglitz (1967), Robinson and Naqvi (1967), Bliss (1968), (1970), Spaventa (1968), (1970), Asimakopulos (1969), P. Bardhan (1969), Bruno (1969), Ferguson (1969), Harcourt (1969), (1972), Nuti (1970), (1970a), Burmeister and Dobell (1970), von Weizsäcker (1971), Rymes (1971), McIntosh (1972), Burmeister (1974), and Wright (1974).
3. See also Sen (1974).
4. The rate of profit is a pure number independent of units. The marginal product of a capital good viewed in physical terms would be so many units of output per additional unit of the capital good. To get from the latter to the former we have to bring in the relative prices of the capital good and the consumer goods.

in particular that the different sectors have the same factor intensity, i.e., the same ratio of physical capital to labour.[5] The fact that in this case there is only one homogeneous capital good is not sufficient to establish the neo-classical relations between the value of capital and that of output.[6]

Secondly, it is of course possible to compare alternative positions of equilibrium (stationary or moving), each having a given rate of profit and a given wage rate, and the technique used in any particular equilibrium position can be associated with a given value of capital per head and a given value of output. Linking up these values of capital and output per man we get a 'pseudo-production function',[7] choosing the most profitable technique for each set of prices. But this is a case of pure *comparison* of alternative positions in respective equilibrium at different rates of profit; a movement from one position to another is not covered by this relationship and therefore the question of using this pseudo-production function as a basis of defining the marginal product of capital and getting a rate of profit out of that does not really arise.[8]

Thirdly, there has been a riotous debate on whether the phenomenon of 'multiple switching' can or cannot occur under certain specified circumstances. Multiple switching refers to the possibility that a technique that might be more profitable than another at a high interest rate and less profitable at a lower one, could be again more profitable at a still lower interest rate. Multiple switching makes the conception of a neo-classical production function more problematic.[9] However, it is

---

5. See Samuelson (1962) and Garegnani (1970). McIntosh (1972) establishes an alternative condition in terms of savings behaviour that would permit the formulation of such a 'surrogate production function', but as he himself points out, the condition is very restrictive and 'the results presented do nothing to redeem the surrogate production'.
6. The surrogate production function holds for heterogeneous capital goods as well (indeed the main purpose of Samuelson (1962) was to show this) *if* the highly restrictive assumption of equal factor intensity holds. Under less restrictive conditions one can construct a 'chain index' measure of capital such that there will be a neo-classical-looking, production function and such that in any situation the equilibrium rate of profit will equal the partial derivative of output with respect to capital at the appropriate chain index value of Capital (Champernowne (1954)). The trick lies in the revaluation of capital and the neo-classical model is not restored despite the superficial resemblance.
7. See Robinson (1956), (1970).
8. Whether the results may hold approximately for 'slow' shifts is a question worth discussing analytically as well as empirically. There is, however, not much evidence that the shifts are typically slow.
9. For example, Champernowne's chain index does not work in this case, as he noted in his paper (Champernowne (1954)).

important to note that even if multiple switching were never to occur, it would still not be possible to construct a Samuelsonian surrogate production function unless the more restrictive assumptions discussed earlier held.[10] Nor would it be possible to consider *shifts* along a pseudo-production function which gives alternative positions of long-run equilibrium. In the debate that took place on multiple switching, the issue undoubtedly received undue prominence, possibly for purely strategic reasons.

Fourthly, it is very important to bear in mind the motivation of the capital theory debate. Those attacking the neo-classical parable (such as Sraffa or Joan Robinson) were not asking whether the neo-classical model would give *approximately* good predictions, but whether the model was logically sound and perfectly consistent with reality within its own frame of reference, once the rigid assumption of a one-commodity world was dropped. Sraffa put the distinction thus:

one should emphasize the distinction between two types of measurement. First, there was the one in which the statisticians were mainly interested. Second there was measurement in theory. The statisticians' measures were only approximate and provided a suitable field for work in solving index number problems. The theoretical measures required absolute precision ... The work of J. B. Clark, Böhm-Bawerk and others was intended to produce pure definitions of capital, as required by their theories, not as a guide to actual measurement. If we found contradictions, then these pointed to defects in the theory, and an inability to define measures of capital accurately.[11]

Sraffa's motivation can be contrasted with that of, say, Fisher (1969), (1971), who has examined the question of the relative accuracy of econometric analysis and empirical predictions based on the assumption of a neo-classical aggregate production function.[12] Fisher also comes to a negative conclusion about the advisability of using the neo-classical aggregate model, especially 'when widely diverse industries are included' (Fisher (1969), p. 576), but his question is very different from that of Sraffa.

Fifthly, one particular difficulty with a version of the neo-classical aggregate model that has been widely used lies in its use of the assumption of 'malleability'. This takes the form of assuming that capital goods already in existence are 'versatile' in the sense that they can be recast — costlessly — to be transformed into capital goods of different specifica-

10. The Samuelsonian assumption of equal factor intensities implies the absence of multiple switching, but the converse is not true.
11. Sraffa, quoted in Lutz and Hague (1961), pp. 305–6.
12. See also Robinson (1970).

tions.[13] For example, if labour becomes relatively expensive, the existing machinery can be reshaped into less labour-intensive forms. Also the fruits of the technical progress that has taken place since the old machinery were built can be incorporated into them — again costlessly. The implausibility of this position is glaring.[14] (With the recent developments in the technology of making chemical fertilizers, many managers of old factories would have dreamt longingly of *ex post* malleability.) A more reasonable assumption is what is sometimes called 'putty-clay', where there is subsitutability *ex ante*, i.e., before the capital goods are built, but not *ex post*, when they become rigid like clay.[15] The problem of *ex post* fixity makes the evaluation of the capital stock much more difficult than that of the investment flow.

5.3 Capital-intensity and Employment Policy
The debate about capital theory is of obvious relevance to employment policy, but too much should not be read into this. The motivation of the debate — the debunking and the defence of the neo-classical aggregative school — does not have a great deal to do with the more mundane pursuits of the practical policy-maker. What Sraffa calls the 'statistician's measures' may be of more relevance for him than 'the measurement in theory' requiring 'absolute precision'. Furthermore, while the neo-classical aggregative model permits statements on capital intensity, it is not a prerequisite for such statements. To say that in a cheap labour 'economy'[16] there is a case for using less capital-intensive techniques does not require one to become a card-carrying member of the neo-classical club. In the same book in which Joan Robinson presents her definitive attack on the neo-classical treatment of aggregate capital as a factor of production, she is also found observing — in my judgment sensibly — that 'when there is persistent unemployment in a stagnant economy the redundant workers may take to employing themselves with tiny quantities of capital (say as shoe-blacks and pedlars)'. (Robinson (1956), pp. 157–8).

It is important to distinguish between different elements in the recent critique of neo-classical capital theory.

First, when one recommends choosing less capital-intensive techniques

13. Used, for example, in Solow (1956), Swan (1956), and Meade (1961).
14. See Solow (1960), (1962).
15. See Bliss (1968) for a penetrating study of the problem. Among the early contributions in this field are Robinson (1956), Johansen (1959), Salter (1960) and Solow (1960), (1962).
16. Whether labour, is in fact, cheap or not in a given economy is, however, a fairly complex question; see Part V below.

in a cheap labour economy, one is usually making a statement about investment and not about the existing capital stock. In this context problems arising from *ex post* fixity are not relevant.

Secondly, at a given rate of profit ruling in an economy, the capital costs of a particular investment project can be assessed without running into problems of inconsistency, and the fact that the rate of profit may not be determined by 'the marginal productivity of capital' need not be in the least disturbing.

Thirdly, there are, of course, problems of aggregation even for investment, and if the projects are large one has to consider the problem of interdependence between the quantities of inputs absorbed and their appropriate prices. The relative capital intensities of two projects could depend on these price variations, but frequently they will not be affected by small changes in valuation. Let $(q_1^1, \ldots, q_n^1)$ be the amounts of n types of capital goods inputs needed per unit of output under technique 1 and $(q_1^2, \ldots, q_n^2)$ those required under technique 2. We refer to them as vectors $\mathbf{q}^1$ and $\mathbf{q}^2$ respectively. The appropriate shadow prices[17] might depend on the choice of technique and might not even be known with very great precision. Suppose the planner only knows that the price vectors $\mathbf{p}^1$ and $\mathbf{p}^2$ in the two cases would belong to some set π. Then we would be able to say that $\mathbf{q}^1$ is more capital-intensive than $\mathbf{q}^2$ if for *every* pair of price vectors $\mathbf{p}^1$ and $\mathbf{p}^2$ (not necessarily distinct) taken from π we have:

$$\mathbf{p}^1 \mathbf{q}^1 > \mathbf{p}^2 \mathbf{q}^2. \tag{5.1}$$

When it comes to assessing the capital-intensity of the technique of shoe-blacking done by hand and brush, as opposed to that done by the automatic machines found in American airports, it is unlikely that the exact choice of the price vectors within the easily specifiable limits will cause any particular problem. In general, of course, the ranking relation defined by eqn (5.1) would be a partial ordering, i.e., it could be incomplete for some pair-wise comparisons involving closely competing cases. But that fact does not rule out the possibility of making firm statements on many other comparisons in terms of a precisely defined criterion.[18] Sraffa's difficulty with 'the measurement in theory' remains, but it does not deliver a fatal blow to the policy-maker.

17. See Chapters 11–3 below, especially pp. 112–4.
18. I have tried to argue elsewhere that by insisting on a complete ordering, the economist often rules himself out of court when he could have said a lot in terms of a quasi-ordering, which seems to be a more natural concept in many of these problems. See Sen (1970), (1973).

5.4 Mechanization

I turn now to a rather more mundane question compared with the debate on capital theory. The case for a lower 'capital intensity' is sometimes confused with that for a lower degree of 'mechanization', but the two concepts are really rather different. The degree of mechanization is concerned with the ratio of the value of the stock of machinery to the number of labourers who can be employed *at a point of time when the machinery is in operation*. Or else it can be seen as the ratio of the former to the output flow *at a point of time when in operation*. In contrast, capital-intensity is concerned with the ratio of capital stock to the total amount of labour time *over a given period* (say a day, a week, a month, or a year), taking into account the points of time when the machinery is in operation as well as those when it is not. Alternatively capital intensity can be seen as the ratio of the former to the output produced *over a given period*.

Whether we take the capital–labour ratio or the capital–output ratio, it is clear that mechanization differs from capital intensity in the treatment of time. For example, a more mechanized technique requiring a lot of machinery per person (or per unit of output per unit of time when in operation) may nevertheless have a lower degree of capital intensity, defined as the capital stock per labour hour over a week (or that per unit of output over a week), if it is *utilized* more intensively through working round the clock.[19] A handloom may have a lower degree of mechanization, but if it is used only in one shift for a small number of days in the year, its capital-intensity may be quite high.[20] At the risk of oversimplification one can say that mechanization concentrates mainly on technical facts, whereas capital intensity takes full account of social factors, such as the number of shifts worked per day and the number of days worked per year.

A second distinction arises from the items that are included in the value of the capital stock. Mechanization is concerned with machinery and possibly other types of fixed capital, like buildings, but working capital would not be included under this heading. For capital intensity, however, it is necessary to include working capital. The ratio of working capital to physical capital in different forms of investment may vary quite widely and will frequently tend to be higher for relatively less mechanized techniques. The inclusion of working capital could make the

---

19. Cf. Winston (1971).
20. This may explain the widely observed phenomenon that despite the existence of slack seasons in agriculture, handloom weaving is very rarely a seasonal operation supplementing the agricultural work pattern.

ordering of capital-intensity of different techniques quite different from that of mechanization.[21] The two are very different concepts and involve different measurement problems. For employment policy the distinction is of significance, especially since less mechanized techniques are frequently associated with a lower degree of utilization and a high ratio of working capital to fixed capital.

A third difference arises from investment in education. Skill formation involves capital investment and contributes to capital intensity. It is frequently the case that the more costly the machinery, the more expensive the types of skill that are needed to go with it (e.g., pilots are expensive, as are aeroplanes), and it may be thought that adding in the value of 'human capital' will simply reinforce the high capital intensity of the more mechanized techniques. But this correspondence does not always hold, and sometimes a high degree of skill may go with relatively little use of machinery (e.g., in music and dance). The ranking of investment projects in terms of capital intensity may change substantially if human capital is introduced into the sums.

5.5 Valuations of Specific Resources and Capital-intensity

It is, however, worth remarking that aggregate values of capital intensity may be objectionable even from a practical point of view, and not merely from the sophisticated viewpoint of capital theory surveyed in § § 5.1–5.3. There are, of course, general problems of evaluation of the sacrifice of present consumption vis-à-vis that in the future involved in all types of capital investment (see Chapter 10). But in addition at any point of time there are specific shortages and a need to economise on specific resources.

Shortage of skilled manpower of one type may exist side by side with a surplus of other types of skill and indeed even with abundance of savings and investment funds. The current valuation of the particular skilled labour in short supply can be quite substantially higher than that in the long run, when educational institutions can be expanded and a new supply created, and this type of changing valuation over time makes it particularly difficult to rank technologies in terms of their aggregate capital intensity. Of course, for some comparisons this change in valuation will not alter the ranking of capital intensities and a partial ordering of the type discussed in § 5.3 can be quite extensive, but in general one has to be concerned with specific values of specific resources.[22]

21. That this makes a substantial difference for alternative techniques in small-scale Indian industries is demonstrated in Sen (1960), Appendices C and D, Dhar and Lydall (1961), and Bhalla (1964), (1965). See also Hewavitharana (1971), Appavadhanulu (1971), and the reports of the ILO missions to Ceylon and Kenya, ILO (1971), (1972).
22. See Chapter 11.

III | Institutions, Technology, and Labour

6 | Dual Labour Markets

6.1 Introduction

In the controversial field of economic development one of the few areas of agreement is over the existence of multiple labour markets in many developing countries. People who cross swords on the subject of the existence of surplus labour and disguised unemployment, nevertheless seem to agree on the prevalence of a gap in wages (and labour costs) in different sectors of the underdeveloped economy. The existence of wage gaps is a common feature of such different models of growth as those of Lewis (1954) and Fei and Ranis (1964), on the one hand, and those of Jorgenson (1961) and Zarembka (1972), on the other; and there are also the models of Marglin (1966), Dixit (1968), Hornby (1968), and Stern (1972), to mention just a few.

In the case of the wage system the gaps are readily noticeable in terms of differences in the wage rates for the same kind of labour in different labour markets. However, when one contrasts a wage-based labour market with labour use under a non-wage system, one has to be careful about defining real labour costs appropriately. For the case of 'self-employed labour' or 'unpaid family labour', the appropriate cost of labour is given by the rate of substitution between output and non-work that is acceptable to the labourer.[1] If a self-employed person accepts two units of output as making it just worth his while to put in an additional unit of work, then 2 is the relevant 'real labour cost' expressed in terms of output.

One has to be careful in interpreting the real labour cost, since the substitution in question is not that between the person's labour and his *own share* of output, but that between the former and the *entire* output

---

1. If the non-wage labourer simply obeys the commands of the head of the family enterprise, then the valuation has to be that of the head in question.

51

produced by that unit of his labour. For example, if he gets one half of the output contribution he makes, and regards two units of output, of which he gets one unit, to be just adequate compensation for his work, then the real labour cost is 2 and not 1. In terms of the model of Chapter 3, the real labour cost j is not given by z but by:

$$j = z/[\alpha + (1 - \alpha)h]. \qquad (6.1)$$

Only with a homogeneous family unit — typically a nuclear family rather than a joint family — when one's 'own share' is the whole (i.e., $\alpha = 1$), or when concern is total (i.e., $h = 1$), can we have the special result:[2]

$$j = z. \qquad (6.1.1)$$

In general it is j and not z that has to be compared with the ruling market wage w, since j and w play identical roles in decisions on labour allocation.

While the formula given by eqn (6.1) involves psychological factors, estimating j on the basis of observed choices need not bring in these factors explicitly. In such an exercise of estimation one would have to check the precise point at which the labourer in question would stop and to observe the value of j implied in terms of production possibilities. The value of eqn 6.1 lies not in this estimation, but in understanding the underlying process and in interpreting the estimates.

The problem of estimation is relatively simpler for wage-based labour markets, in which the operating wage rates can be simply observed. However, there is a need for caution in interpreting the wage rate as the real labour cost in any market in which imperfections exist. For example, if labour is available at a given wage rate w but the output thus produced is sold in an imperfect product market, then the profit-maximizing capitalist would apply labour to the point such that:

$$w = pf'(L)\left[1 - \frac{1}{e}\right], \qquad (6.2)$$

where e is the elasticity of demand for the product of this firm and p the price of it. In units of output, the 'real labour cost' j would then be not w, but:

$$j = w/\left[1 - \frac{1}{e}\right]. \qquad (6.3)$$

Similar corrections would have to be made if there were monopsonistic elements in the labour market.[3]

2. Cf. Sen (1966).
3. Robinson (1933).

Needless to say, if the output of the non-wage unit is sold in an imperfect product market, then a correction similar to eqn (6.2) would have to be made in the formula given by (6.1) as well. Frequently this would not be needed, since family-based producers typically tend to sell their product in a market with innumerable sellers, e.g., in peasant agriculture, but there can be exceptions, e.g., in the case of family-based production units making specialized handicrafts, in which each producer may enjoy a substantial share of the market.

Finally, it may sometimes be the case that essentially identical labour may be sold at different prices because of artificial distinctions. A typical example of this is the Indian phenomenon of using highly educated labour in jobs that do not require that type of education.[4] For the purpose of the work at hand the two kinds of labour may be identical; nevertheless the selection process, for various administrative and political reasons, may give preference to those who have acquired the additional bit of irrelevant education. Through this process the educated labourer may end up getting the relatively better paid job, but may do no more specialized work than those without this education employed in lower paid positions.[5] Thus dual markets may exist even when they are not visible, since apparently heterogeneous labour may in fact be essentially homogeneous in such cases. The problems of diagnosis are by no means negligible for a study of dual labour markets.

6.2 Causes of Dualism

Dualism of labour markets can arise from a number of different causes, and since their implications are quite different, it is necessary to distinguish clearly between the different types of causation. The following are some of the alternative causes that can be relevant.

(1) *Labourers' job preferences.* The labourer in question could actually prefer to be in one sector rather than in another, e.g., working in peasant agriculture rather than in wage employment in the town. It would be foolish to attribute all such preferences to 'irrationality' of some kind or other; there may be nothing remotely irrational in having a preference for being one's own master in one's farm even at a lower income, rather than working as a 'wage slave' in some factory, or indeed

4. On this see Blaug, Layard and Woodhall (1969), and Sen (1971).
5. This is certainly one reason for the rush for university education in countries like India or Ceylon. The Indian situation is discussed in the *Report of the Education Commission* 1964–66, Government of India, Delhi, 1966; Blaug, Layard and Woodhall (1969); and Sen (1971). For the situation in Ceylon, see the report of the ILO mission, ILO (1971).

in some other farm. What is, however, more easy to argue is the case for
avoiding the assumption of stationary tastes. Preferences about one's way
of life and location are typically the result of one's past experience and
an initial reluctance to move does not imply a perpetual dislike. The
distinction has some bearing on the welfare aspects of employment
policy, since the importance that one wishes to attach to the wage gap as
a reflection of the labourer's preferences would tend to depend on the
extent to which tastes are expected to vary as a consequence of the
movement itself.

(2) *Indivisibilities in labour supply*. A labourer could prefer to work
half time in his farm and half time in a factory, but he may not be able
to do this, given the physical problems of location and organizational
problems of the factory system. To take up a job in the factory he may
have to leave his farm altogether or at least for long stretches of time,
and the same may be true of accepting a job in, say, an irrigation project.
The high level of transportation costs, including the monetary and
psychological costs of settling in, may persuade the labourer to stick to
his farm unless the reward elsewhere is very high. But settled in his own
farm the supply price of labour z and the real cost of labour j for hours
(or days) of extra effort may be comparatively low.

(3) *Loss of share of family income*. A movement away from one's
farm may involve the loss of one's share of the family income. In terms
of orthodox economic theory it is possible to split the earnings of the
peasant into two parts — one being the reward for labour and the other
that for being a joint owner of family resources, in particular the plot of
land. But — as argued in Chapters 1 and 4 — there is a kind of labour
theory of value which tends to determine the distributional principles in
a peasant society, and the possibility of the ex-peasant working in the
town but nevertheless cashing in on the 'implicit rent' on his share of the
land is frequently rather remote. This 'income aspect' of employment we
distinguished from its 'production aspect' in earlier chapters, and it is
clear that the peasant in question may have an economic incentive not to
move, even when his marginal contribution to the family output is negligible or low.[6] What wage he will accept as minimal compensation
depends partly on the exact distribution system in the peasant set-up and
partly on his concern for the welfare of the joint family as compared

6. See Appendices A and B. Incidentally, the classical argument, of which a modern
version is presented by Lewis (1954), that industrial wages must be determined by
subsistence requirements, arises from this notion that when someone moves to the
town he will have to support himself entirely on his wage income.

with his own welfare (or the welfare of the nuclear family).[7] The greater his concern, the more willing he will be to move, since his loss of implicit rent is a gain for the others in the joint family.

(4) *Labour legislation and union pressure.* In many countries there is labour legislation specifying a minimum wage for employment in the organized sector and even if the number of people seeking such jobs far exceeds the number of jobs available, the wage rate will still not decline. The same result is sometimes achieved by unionized labour through wage bargaining. This provides a straightforward institutional explanation of the wage gap between organized and unorganized sectors.[8]

(5) *Employers' incentives for paying high wages.* The employer is, under certain circumstances, better off by paying wages higher than the minimum at which he can recruit labour. First, the costs of rapid labour turnover can be very high for the firm in terms of work disruption and frequent rearrangements, and the industrialist may have an incentive to offer higher wages to discourage the employee's inclination to move. Secondly, fear of discontent and potential labour strife is another reason for offering higher wages and for aiming at a loyal labour force. Since many industrial firms use rather heavily mechanized techniques, the share of labour cost even at a comparatively high wage may be quite low, while the loss from strife and discontent in reducing the effectiveness of the machines may be relatively much higher.[9] Thirdly, higher wages may also have a direct impact on labour productivity through better nutrition and greater ability to work hard.[10] While the first two considerations apply especially to wage labour in the modern industrial sector, this third consideration is thought to be particularly relevant for hired labour within the agricultural sector itself.

7. For contrasting assumptions on the welfare functions, see Sen (1966) and Guha (1969).
8. Bhalla (1970) argues that it may not be in the interest of self-employed labour to bid down the wages of their relatives working in the high-wage sector, since they benefit from income transfers from their wage earning relatives. This implies some kind of implicit collusion between different families placed in similar situations. By bidding down the wages slightly a family can get more of its working members employed in the high wage sector and its gain will be greater than its own loss, even though other families will suffer. The Bhalla case would seem to depend, therefore, on the actual existence of such implicit collusion, which is rather like the phenomenon of 'tacit collusion' in the theory of oligopoly (see Stigler (1952), Chapter 13).
9. For discussions of these issues and some related ones, see Sen (1966), Frank (1968), Todaro (1969), Stiglitz (1969), (1972), and Pack and Bhalla (1970).
10. On this see Leibenstein (1957), Mazumdar (1959), and Galenson and Pyatt (1964).

6.3 Migration, Employment, and Expected Income

The consequences of a dual labour market depend on the cause of the phenomenon. For example, if the wage gap arises from labour legislation or union pressure (cause 4), or from the employers' incentives for paying high wages (cause 5), then not only would we have different wages in different markets, but labourers from the low labour-cost sector would be available in substantial numbers to move to the high-wage sector. The high wages would be restrained from falling by legislation, or union action, or the employers' expected profit calculations, but many people would be looking for jobs and be ready to work even at somewhat *lower* wages. If, however, the causation is labourers' job preferences (cause 1), indivisibilities in labour supply (cause 2), or loss of share of family income (cause 3), the wage gap would be a reflection of labour supply constraints, and there would not be a mass of people hanging around in readiness to work at *lower* wages.[11]

The wage gap under causes 4 and 5 leads to rather complicated decision problems for the potential wage labourer. If he gets a job at the ruling wage he will clearly prefer it to working in the family-based production unit. On the other hand, he prefers his current work to unemployment. Given such a ranking it can be argued that he would be indifferent between the certainty of his job in the family system and a certain probability mixture of getting a high wage job in the organized sector and being unemployed.[12] This crucial probability ρ^* of getting a high wage job is given by eqn (6.4), in which $U(w)$ stands for his utility from employment in the high-wage sector, $U(y)$ for that from his current family-enterprise employment, and $U(0)$ for that from unemployment, with $U(w) > U(y) > U(0)$:[13]

$$U(y) = \rho^* U(w) + (1 - \rho^*) U(0). \tag{6.4}$$

Obviously, $1 > \rho^* > 0$. A rather simpler version of this has been presented by Harris and Todaro (1970), in which the calculation is done not in terms of utility but directly in terms of incomes. If y is the income

11. There may, however, be a large 'reserve army of labour' available for work *at* the ruling wage rate given by the subsistence level in one version of cause 3; see Marx (1887). Also Lewis (1954).

12. This is not an analytic requirement and there is obviously no mathematical reason why such a probability must exist. However, it can be regarded as a reasonable behaviouristic postulate and it implies essentially a continuity assumption. On this see von Neumann and Morgenstern (1947).

13. See von Neumann and Morgenstern (1947), or Marschak (1950). A very lucid presentation of utility theory under uncertainty can be found in Luce and Raiffa (1957), Chapter 2. On the interpretation of utility in this framework and the possible pitfalls, see Luce and Raiffa (1957), pp. 31–2.

of the person in the unorganized sector and w that in the high-wage sector, with $w > y$, then the person is assumed to be indifferent between the certainty of getting y and the probability ρ^* of getting w and $(1 - \rho^*)$ of getting nothing when:[14]

$$\rho^* = \frac{y}{w}. \tag{6.5}$$

If the actual probability ρ of getting high-wage employment in the town is greater than ρ^* then this person moves to town and if it is less he does not. If $\rho > \rho^*$, more and more people crowd to the towns, thereby raising the incidence of unemployment and reducing the proportion of the work force that is employed there, until their subjective probability of employment ρ comes down to ρ^*. The opposite happens if we start from $\rho < \rho^*$, and the equilibrium given by $\rho = \rho^*$ is stable according to this adjustment process.

This is a theory of the determination of the subjective probability ρ of finding a job. More has, however, been read into it, and a model of the determination of urban unemployment ratio has been based on it.[15] By assuming that the subjective probability of employment in this hign-wage sector is equal to the ratio of the employed to the total work force in that location, the condition of subjective equilibrium[16] given by eqn (6.5) has been converted into a theory of the determination of the *actual* ratio of the employed to the work force.

One consequence of making this translation and of thus interpreting eqn (6.5) is to make the market wage rate equal the opportunity cost of labour. For every employed person in the urban sector there must be $(1/\rho^*)$ people in the urban work force, and to get one man to work in the town, $(1/\rho^*)$ men will have to be drawn there from the rural sector involving a sacrifice of income of y per person in that sector. Thus the alternative earnings foregone per person employed in the urban area

---

14. This corresponds exactly to (6.4) if utility is a linear function of income. Choosing the origin arbitrarily as $U(0) = 0$, we get $U(w) = w$ and $U(y) = y$ through appropriate choice of units.

15. See Todaro (1969) and Harris and Todaro (1970).

16. Strictly speaking, the equilibrium condition is:

$$\rho = \frac{y}{w} \tag{6.5.1}$$

Clearly, (6.5) is an equilibrium condition only when ρ^* is reinterpreted as the *actual* expectation of probability of getting a high-wage job.

turns out to be (y/ρ^*), which by virtue of (6.5) exactly equals w.[17] What the market pays the labourer equals, on this interpretation, the corrected opportunity cost of his employment. The Invisible Hand strikes again!

There are, however, several difficulties with this analysis. First the workers in question need not have the behavioural characteristics implied by eqn (6.4), i.e., may not be expected utility maximizers. On matters of 'life and death' (what happens if the worker draws blank?) and on questions of one's entire economic existence, the Neumann–Morgenstern axioms are indeed very restrictive. Second, even if they do follow eqn (6.4) they may not follow (6.5), requiring them to maximize expected *income* and not expected utility, which corresponds to the von Neumann–Morgenstern theory only under very special assumptions, ruling out diminishing marginal utility.

Third – and perhaps more important – the people in question may not think of the possibility of employment in terms of a given probability of getting a job *independent of time*, but in terms of a period of *waiting* after which they can expect to get employed. Studies of unemployment in several developing countries have indicated that the way the labour market adjusts to variations of excess supply is mainly through a variation of the length of time for which a person has to wait before he gets his first job.[18] On this interpretation, the way to bring the excess labour supply situation into the individual's rational calculations is through a discounting of future higher incomes and not through a probability weight independent of time. Various intermediate possibilities can also be considered.[19] Eqn (6.5) holds only for the time-independent extreme case.

Finally, even if people do think exclusively in terms of expected probability of employment, i.e., in the terms given by (6.5), they may

17. See also Harberger (1971), pp. 568–72. Stiglitz (1972) provides an alternative set of assumptions that also lead to induced unemployment just offsetting the gap between the wage rate and the opportunity cost of labour, in a model in which the government directly controls the urban employment level and the ratio of urban unemployment, or equivalently directly controls the urban employment level and the urban wage rate.
18. See Blaug, Layard and Woodhall (1969), and the report of the ILO missions to Ceylon and Kenya, ILO (1971), (1972). See also Appendix A on the average lag between registration in Indian employment exchanges and the first call.
19. See Anand (1971).

not identify their subjective probability of employment with the actual ratio of the employed to the work force, and it is only under this very special interpretation that the Invisible Hand could grab the prize.[20]

20. Note also that even if this theory of urban unemployment were accepted, it would equate the wage rate w only to the private income interpretation of the opportunity cost of labour from the traditional sector. The latter can diverge from the 'production aspect' of the opportunity cost when the 'implicit rent' from his share of the joint ownership of land is lost to the migrant as he moves. Indeed there can be surplus labour (and therefore no opportunity cost in terms of production) but a positive y reflecting the opportunity cost of private income per migrant. Bringing in the subjective costs of effort would not eliminate this problem, as can be readily checked by resetting the discussion in terms of the model of Chapters 3 and 4.

7 | Ownership, Classes, and Allocation

7.1 Introduction

The economic decision processes that determine the technology and the level of employment in a given economy depend on the pattern of ownership of the means of production and the relations between the different economic classes. In the last chapter, the focus was on the contrast between the use of family-based labour and that of hired labour. That distinction is only one among many that are relevant for a study of the production structure.

The use of own labour may go with the use of owned land (e.g., peasant ownership farms) or with rented land (e.g., tenant farms). Owned land can be of different types, e.g., co-operative farms involving many families working together, and peasant farms involving one family. The latter can still involve quite a few working members, since the family may be a 'joint' one, involving relations in addition to the nuclear family, but nevertheless its size is severely limited compared with co-operative farms.

Rented land can also be of several types and the distinction between fixed-rent arrangements and the share-cropping system may be of some importance. Rental contracts vary in many different ways and some of these variations can be significant for resource allocation and income distribution.

As far as hired labour is concerned, the main form in use to-day is the free wage system. In contrast bonded labour systems were common until quite recently and still survive in some areas to-day. The wage system permits recontracting within short periods. On the other hand, contracts over many years were quite common for indentured labour in early plantations. Slavery is the extreme form of bonded labour, in which the bondage can apply to the progeny as well.

The wage system has been used in publicly owned enterprises as well as in capitalist concerns. The differences between these depend on their respective economic motivations, and the motivation of a public enterprise firm would vary with the nature of the economy as well as the general political situation. Variations in the motivation of private enterprises have also attracted a lot of attention recently.

The categorization outlined above is shown in Fig. 7.1. The examples all come from agriculture, to enable us to focus on the contrasts in question rather than incidental differences arising from other variations, such as that between industry and agriculture. Further, Fig. 7.1 represents only the 'pure' types. A Soviet 'kolkhoz' (collective farm) involves a complex mixture of 'co-operative farms' (it is, in principle, a co-operative organization), 'state owned farms' (the operational procedures involve some important features of public enterprises) and 'peasant farms' (collective farm households have their own small plots of land as well).[1] Similarly, in many so-called peasant economies, farms do hire some outside labour in the peak agricultural seasons, so that the labouring operations are not purely of the own labour type, nor is there complete reliance on hired labour. These mixtures have to be borne in mind in any policy-making exercise. The purpose of Fig. 7.1 is to catch the contrasts between the pure systems, but the insights gained from studying the pure systems will need modification before they can be used.

There are other significant contrasts which have not been brought into the classification given in Fig. 7.1. The financial arrangements are important, and the contrast between dependence on monopolistic money lenders and the availability of cheap institutional credit may be very significant for decisions affecting technology and employment.[2]

7.2 Labour Use and Dualism

While in Chapter 6 the wage gap was defined in fairly general terms, the focus of our attention was on rural—urban differences. There are, however, important problems that arise from dual labour markets *within* the agricultural sector itself. Consider the model of labour use outlined in Chapters 3 and 4. The total amount of labour L applied in a family farm and the output Q produced in the farm are given respectively by the

1. See Bergson (1964), pp. 17–19, and Dobb (1948).
2. In some economies there are important links between landlordism and money-lending, which have to be viewed together. See Bhaduri (1973).

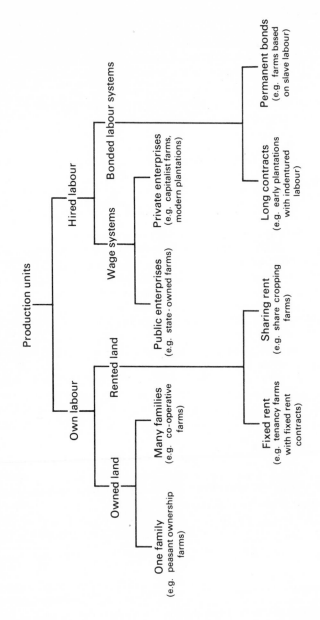

Fig. 7.1. *Categorization of Farms: Pure Types*

following relations, in which j stands for the 'real labour cost' equalling $z/[\alpha + (1 - \alpha)h]$.

$$L = f^{-1}(G(j)) = E(j) \tag{7.1}$$

$$Q = G(j). \tag{7.2}$$

Both E and G are strictly diminishing functions of the real labour cost. For wage-based farms with the same production possibilities, eqns (7.1) and (7.2) give the relevant relationships if j is replaced by the wage rate w.

The essence of dualism lies in the simple fact that:

$$w > j. \tag{7.3}$$

It follows from the fact that E and G are strictly diminishing functions of j that:

$$E(w) < E(j) \tag{7.4}$$

$$G(w) < G(j). \tag{7.5}$$

That is, the family farmers could yield a higher value of labour and output per acre than the wage-based farms.[3] It has been argued[4] that eqns (7.4) and (7.5) explain why the relatively smaller farms in India tend to have higher productivity per acre than relatively larger ones, since the dependence on hired labour tends to go up as farms of larger size groups are considered.[5]

A special case of (7.5) has been much discussed in the context of 'the relative efficiency' of peasant agriculture and capitalist farming. Taking the real labour cost of 'overpopulated' peasant economies to be zero ($j = 0$), we get:

$$G(w) < G(0). \tag{7.5.1}$$

Bauer (1948) had observed as early as 1948 that rubber cultivation in Malaya and Indonesia reflected this inequality relation:

In the choice of planting density the rational course is not the same for estates and small holders. The majority of small holders incur no cash wage costs and attempt to maximize the gross yield per surface unit. On

---

3. Sen (1962), (1966).
4. Sen (1962), (1964), in which some alternative explanations were also presented.
5. The analytical and empirical issues involved in this thesis have been thoroughly examined in a vigorous controversy on the subject. See Appendix C.

their densely planted holdings the trees are of smaller girth and yield per tree lower than on estates, but the yields per surface area are higher.[6]

Georgescu-Roegen (1960) has shown the relation of this result to the historical 'Agrarian Doctrine'.[7]

In view of the seasonal nature of agriculture, this argument needs to be somewhat extended, as spelt out in Sen (1966). But I shall postpone a discussion of this aspect of the problem until Chapter 8.

The assumption that the same production function f, and therefore the same E and G functions, hold for farms with different modes of production and employment is, however, a restrictive one. In so far as the wage-based production units can use techniques involving larger scale that are not available to smaller family-based units, the relationship will not be a simple one. It is usually assumed that in farming the possibilities of technological economies of scale are not very great. This could well be the case, though evidence on the subject is not conclusive, but it is quite clear that there are scale economies in several operations ancillary to agriculture, such as irrigation projects. To what extent the advantages of the low real labour cost of the family farm and of the scale flexibility of wage-based farms can be combined through co-operative farming remains an interesting policy issue.

Turning now to the rural—urban wage-gap as opposed to dual labour markets *within* agriculture, it is difficult to apply the inequalities (7.4) and (7.5) to this contrast. This is largely because the composition of the products varies between different sectors and any comparison of 'productivity' must bring in relative prices. Also the two-factor land—labour analysis breaks down completely for industrial production in view of the predominance of capital goods and it is not easy to find the industrial analogue of 'productivity per acre'. Nevertheless, the differences in the real labour cost are of relevance in the calculation of the shadow prices of labour, which will be discussed in Part V of this book.

Finally, it is worth mentioning that eqns (7.4) and (7.5) apply to wage gaps caused by 'labourers' job preference', 'loss of share of family income', or 'labour legislation and union pressure', but not necessarily to 'employers' incentives for paying high wages'. In the last case, the relevance of (7.4) and (7.5) will depend on the precise reasons behind the employers' higher wage offers. If the reasons are based on higher productivity (say, due to the influence of nutrition on productivity), the

---

6. Bauer (1948), p. 363. See also Bauer and Yamey (1957), pp. 94−5.
7. See also Nicholls (1960), Dandekar (1962), Myint (1964) and Kumar (1970). For discussions of the advantages of self-employment, see also Sen (1960), Meade (1961) and Bhalla (1970).

effective labour cost may not be higher even when wages are greater. The relationships discussed in this section hold only for differences in effective real labour cost after correction for productivity differences.

7.3 Dualism, Used Machinery and Capital Value

One aspect of technological variation related to dualism concerns the choice of the appropriate age of machinery. Consider two sectors A and B of an economy, of which sector A has a higher wage and a lower interest rate. (We can think of A as 'advanced' and B as 'backward'.) The relative prices of old and new machines that would be equilibrating from the point of view of profits in sector A would not offer the same rates of profit in sector B, and this provides a case for trade in second-hand machinery.

Begin with the simplest case first. Let the gross profits (quasi-rents) of a machine with a fixed life be P per year in both sectors A and B. But the interest rate is lower in sector A, i.e., $r_a < r_b$. The equilibrium price of a machine one year before the end of its life in sectors A and B will be respectively $P/(1 + r_a)$ and $P/(1 + r_b)$, and the corresponding prices two years before its end will be $[P/(1 + r_a)] + [P/(1 + r_a)^2]$ and $[P/(1 + r_b)] + [P/(1 + r_b)^2]$ respectively. The price ratios of the 'one-years-left' machine to the 'two-year-left' machine in sectors A and B are respectively:

$$\rho_a = (1 + r_a)/(2 + r_a) \tag{7.6}$$

$$\rho_b = (1 + r_b)/(2 + r_b). \tag{7.7}$$

Since $r_b > r_a > 0$, it is clear that:

$$\rho_b > \rho_a. \tag{7.8}$$

Thus an older machine is a relatively better investment for the high-interest backward sector B. The argument can be easily generalized for all periods of time. If the new and old machines all sell in the advanced sector A at relative prices such that they are equally profitable investments in sector A, then in the absence of transport costs an investor in sector B will always find it more profitable to buy an older machine rather than anything of newer vintage.[8]

Of course, it is likely that sector B will have not merely a higher interest rate but also a higher gross profit P, since the wage rate there is lower. Will the above argument be affected if we take P_a and P_b as the

8. Sen (1962a)

respective quasi-rents and assume that $P_a < P_b$? The answer is: not at all. In fact, the ρ_a and ρ_b given by eqns (7.6) and (7.7) are completely independent of P_a and P_b. The relative advantage in favour of older machinery, i.e., eqn (7.8), holds even though the lower wage sector may have a higher gross profit per machine and not merely a higher interest rate.[9]

Export of second-hand machinery from countries with high wages and low interest to those with lower wages and higher interest does, of course, take place on a substantial scale. A factor that acts against this is transportation cost, which is larger if machinery has to be frequently replaced and imported. Also, in countries with import control and licensing, the industrialist may feel more inclined to import a new machine that will last for a long time rather than one which will have to be replaced very soon, thereby requiring a new licence. The latter issue is, however, inoperative for transfers between sectors *within* a country, and the transport costs will also be typically lower in comparison with inter-country transfers. Such inter-sectoral transfers have been observed on a very large scale in Japan as well as in India.[10] The dualism characterized by differential capital and labour costs not only affects the extent of mechanization in different sectors, but also influences systematically the optimal age structure of capital goods in use.

7.4 Tenancy and Share-Cropping

When the cultivator rents land from a landlord his production decisions are guided by the rental arrangements. In this context the distinction between fixed rent contracts and share-cropping arrangements (where the landlord gets a percentage, say 50 per cent, of the product) is thought to be significant. A fixed rent can be seen to be simply a subtraction of a constant value from the value of output Q and it does not therefore affect the *marginal* relationships like eqns (3.4), (3.5), (3.6), (3.8) or (4.1). On the other hand, share-cropping can be seen as a system in which a part of the marginal product goes to the landlord, and which does, therefore, affect the marginal conditions. One way of viewing this case is to regard share-cropping as a mode of production which makes the value of α (the relative share coming to the cultivator) smaller, due to the landlord's take, and also the value of h lower, since the cultivator is likely to have less concern for the landlord's income than for the income going to other members of his own family. Both these will tend to push up the

9. See Sen (1962a). The model can be extended to take account of labour input variation with age and of technical progress related to vintage; see Smith (1972).
10. See Shinohara (1962), and Mehta (1954). Regarding the interpretation of the Indian experience, see also Bagchi (1972), pp. 252–3.

real labour cost j, which equals $z/[\alpha + (1 - \alpha)h]$. Hence by eqns (7.4) and (7.5), the share-cropping farmer will apply less labour and produce less output than the peasant cultivator.[11]

This conclusion has recently been challenged by a number of authors, notably Cheung (1968), (1969). Cheung proposes a model of the share-cropping system such that the 'inefficiency' result will not hold. This is easily done by assuming that the landlord himself takes the decision as to how much labour will be put in by the share-cropping cultivator.[12] The cultivator's subjective work equilibrium, therefore, drops out of the picture, and Cheung constructs a simple general equilibrium model incorporating this feature.[13]

Without specifying the amount of work to be done by the cultivator explicitly or by implication, the inefficiency result for share-cropping cannot be eliminated. Johnson (1950) had noted this and discussed alternative ways of forcing the cultivator to do the right amount of work:

Three techniques are available to the landlord for enforcing the desired intensity of cultivation. The first is to enter into a lease contract that specifies in detail what the tenant is required to do. A second is to share in the payment of expenses to the same extent as in the sharing of the output. The third is to grant only a short term lease, which makes possible a periodic review of the performance of the tenant.[14]

The first is the line that Cheung explores and he gives some examples of contracts in which the sharing agreement includes specification of the number of men, the type of crop and the use of fertilizer, animal power and other non-labour inputs. The difficulty with this procedure lies in the fact that it is very difficult to formulate and execute an agreement on the exact intensity of effort. It is one thing to specify the number of men, but it is quite another to specify the amount of labour hours to be spent, and it is still more complex to have a contract on the intensity of work per unit of labour time. The great advantage of the peasant system lies in the fact that the cultivator is guided to the appropriate efforts by his own calculations. If a formal contract for intensive effort is needed,

11. See Johnson (1950).
12. See Cheung (1968), pp. 1113–14, and Cheung (1969), p. 20.
13. Bardhan and Srinivasan (1971) criticise Cheung's assumptions about labour allocation, and construct an alternative model in which — as in Cheung's model — the labour market is perfect, but — unlike in Cheung's model — the work decisions in the share-cropping farms are taken by the cultivators themselves. Newbery (1973), (1973a) has raised questions about the internal consistency of the Bardhan–Srinivasan model, especially about whether a competitive equilibrium can exist in the Bardhan–Srinivasan case, and has proposed a more complex model of share-tenancy equilibrium.
14. Johnson (1950), p. 118.

the game is already partly lost, since the specification of work intensities as well as the verification of the actual work done are both very difficult.[15]

Newbery (1973), (1973a) shows that there may not exist a competitively determined rental share that would equate the demand for and supply of land if the landlords do not take the production decisions. The argument is simplest in the case in which the marginal product of more land for a given share-cropper stays positive—however small—no matter how much land he hires. Since the share-cropper gets a proportion of the total output, he does better and better by leasing in more and more land; he gets a given fraction of the always positive marginal product of land. And this is true for every rental share. So demand for land to be leased in is indefinitely large and always exceeds supply at *all* rental shares and the landlord has to ration his land between the share-croppers.

Even if the marginal product of land to the share-cropper falls to zero, so that demand may not exceed supply at every rental share, a similar problem may arise. If the equilibrium rental share maximizes the landlord's income per acre, it is fine for him. But if not, he still has the option of cutting down the rental share and creating an excess demand, and then rationing out his land. It would appear that the landlord can try to maximize his income by using the rationing procedure, and this quite independently of the actions of other landlords. In contrast Cheung's assumption, by which the landlord also determines the work intensity, offers a simpler picture and one in which the share-cropping system is efficient.[16]

The main difficulty with Cheung's line of reasoning lies in the problem of specifying a work intensity contract and in executing it. It is certainly the case that this lacuna leaves the competitive mechanism with a problem in the determination of rental shares, but it is not by any means clear that the competitive mechanism is the right framework of analysis for this problem anyway. Indeed the fact that rental shares are typically very sticky — regions with widely different labour and land supply conditions seem to have ½:½ sharing or 2/3:1/3 sharing — indicates that the competitive determination of rental shares may not be

15. Not surprisingly, none of the contracts that Cheung mentions does in fact specify the intensity of work.
16. However, Cheung does not demonstrate any advantage of the share-cropping system over the fixed-rent-and-fixed-wage system, and Newbery (1973) establishes that under these assumptions, even after introducing uncertainty, share tenancy is at best equivalent to a combination of fixed rent and fixed wage contracts, and argues that one has to find *additional* reasons to account for the widespread existence of share-cropping, some of which he suggests. See also Rao (1971) and Bardhan and Srinivasan (1971).

even superficially plausible. Certainly, the institutional and even historical factors in the determination of rental shares would seem to be very
important.

The second method suggested by Johnson, viz. the sharing of costs in
the same proportion as output, may reduce the misallocation of non-
labour factors, but it does not cure the labour use distortion since labour
cost is not a part of the sharing arrangement.[17] Johnson himself concentrated on the third technique, viz., granting only short-term leases and
periodically reviewing the performance of the tenant. This is a phenomenon that is fairly frequently observed in share-cropped agriculture,
and in fact it is this aspect of share tenancy that has increasingly come
under special attack in proposals for land reform. It might be tempting to
conclude from this that this kind of land reform, though beneficial from
the point of view of the tenant's security, would be pernicious in its
impact on efficiency, since the threat of eviction of the tenant (in the
absence of security of tenure) would be a way of making the share-
cropper do the right amount of work. Is land reform then a move in the
direction of inefficiency — humane but counter-productive?

Even if this argument were correct, it would not be a crushing blow
against land reform, since efficiency is a very limited goal anyway and
the single-minded pursuit of it would not get us very far (see Chapter 2).
It is, however, also the case that the long-run efficiency requirements
would conflict with insecurity of tenure. Those improvements of land
that bear fruit over a long period of time, e.g., digging feeder channels
from irrigation sources, are typically neglected by tenants without
security of tenure and for good reason. Thus the very process of forcing
the share-cropper to expend more labour on current production, by
keeping him on tenterhooks, would also reduce his incentive to put in
effort for long-run improvements of the land he tills.

It would, thus, appear that the distortion of labour use caused by
share-cropping arrangements may not indeed be very easy to cure *within*
that system.

7.5 Financial Heterogeneity and Investment Cost

Imperfections in the market for credit in developing countries are an
institutional feature of much significance. In some ways they work in the
opposite direction to the dual labour market, in the sense that just as
peasant farmers may have cheaper labour they tend to face much dearer
credit. While the impact of dearer credit on land utilization tends to

---

17. On other aspects of cost-sharing see Bardhan and Srinivasan (1971), Section V,
and Newbery (1973). See also Dumont (1957).

work in the opposite direction to cheaper labour, as far as the relative use of labour and capital goods are concerned they reinforce each other. The peasant farmer with cheap labour and dear credit has strong incentives to economize on the use of capital goods, whereas the capitalist farmer with dearer labour and cheaper credit may choose very different technological combinations of labour and capital goods.[18]

There is, however, one type of capital for which peasant farming does have an advantage over capitalist farming. This concerns the requirement of working capital in the form of work-in-progress. Since agriculture involves a substantial time lag in the production process, work-in-progress can be very substantial. Indeed in the classical model of Ricardian agriculture, it was the work-in-progress in the form of wages advanced that was taken to represent the value of capital investment.[19] For a wage-based farm, such wage advances are an essential part of the production process. But in the case of peasant agriculture based on own labour, no advance payment need be involved. Of course, the peasant would have to eat to live, but his consumption need not be related to the amount of his labour, except in so far as his calorific requirements go up with greater effort. The contrast can be clarified by considering the case of applying more fertilizers and more labour in a peasant farm and in a capitalist farm. In the latter, aside from the price of the fertilizer, the capitalist farmer has to advance wages to hired labour to apply the extra fertilizer. If, however, the fertilizer is used in peasant agriculture without the use of hired labour, this may lead to some higher food intake caused by greater activity, but there is no need for the payment of wages to anyone. When the output comes, *then* the peasant family will be richer, but there is no time lag between payment for labour and the arrival of the output, as under the wage system.[20]

Thus peasant farming has two advantages vis-à-vis capitalist farming as far as the labour-cost component of the work-in-progress is concerned. First, the real labour cost may be less for peasant farming, i.e., $j < w$. Second, the compensation for the cost is postponed and there is thus no labour-content in the work-in-progress, except in so far as more work involves greater immediate food consumption. It may be argued that if the capital market were perfect and savings optimal, the latter consideration would make no difference whatever. Everyone's rate of discount would have been the same and would have equalled the market rate of interest r per period, and the peasant would have expected a marginal reward per unit of effort of $j (1 + r)$ one period later when the output

18. Cf. Appendix D.
19. See Ricardo (1815).
20. Sen (1964*a*).

arrived, whereas the wage labourer could have been paid either w now or $w (1 + r)$ then. And with optimal savings the planners would not care whether j, or w, were to be paid now, *or* $j (1 + r)$, or $w (1 + r)$, respectively one period later. But with an imperfect capital market and especially with sub-optimal savings (see Chapter 10), a postponement of consumption may be regarded as an important advantage. And the advantage relates entirely to institutional and social differences. Two identical techniques with the same streams of physical inputs and outputs would represent two quite different capital requirements and therefore two contrasting economic alternatives precisely because of differences in the mode of employment.

8 | Seasonal Variations and Employment

8.1 Introduction

What happens to agricultural employment when the busy season comes? It goes up, of course, which is not surprising, but so, it seems, does the size of the labour force itself, according to the usual definitions. For example, the Indian rural labour force as a percentage of the rural population as given by the National Sample Survey (14th round) varies from 39.9 per cent in May-June to 43.4 per cent in July-August.[1] More workers simply materialize. While this reflects, partly, a definitional problem — the labour force should not perhaps be defined in such short-run terms[2] — the phenomenon does catch one aspect of the economic reality of traditional agriculture, viz., the dependence of rural economic life on the seasonal rhythm.

It is necessary to relate our discussion of surplus labour (Chapter 4) and dual labour markets (Chapter 6) to a framework that takes full note of this important feature of seasonality in the agricultural production process. It is also worth enquiring how this technological feature of seasonality affects the capital requirements of agricultural production. The latter is a relatively simpler issue, and I shall try to comment on this question first.

Lewis (1955) has argued that 'the capital requirements of agriculture are usually underestimated', pointing out that 'the working capital is

---

1. National Sample Survey, 14th Round, 1958–9. Students in rural schools tend to have a high rate of absenteeism during the agricultural peak periods. See Agricultural Economic Research Centre, Delhi (1971).
2. See Appendix A.

large because the crop is seasonal'.[3] Much depends, however, on the appropriate definition of working capital. If all inventories are included, then clearly food stocks are part of working capital. But why should all inventories be part of working capital? The crucial test is whether the stock in question has to be increased as a part of the process of increasing production, or whether it is simply a *result* of the increased production?

In the last chapter the dependence of working capital on institutional arrangements was discussed. The same type of reasoning would seem to apply here. In wage-based cultivation an expansion of employment will involve an immediate expansion of the wage bill and will thus lead to an expansion of the demand for foodgrains.[4] This will require an additional supply of foodgrains *before* this season's harvest comes, and this means that some stock has to be put aside for this purpose from last season's harvest. This stock is clearly a type of working capital. Consider, now, the same process of expanding employment in a family-labour farm. In this case there is no need for a larger inventory of foodgrains out of last season's harvest (except in so far as harder work may require more food). When the output comes in the next harvest, the stock becomes larger, but it is then a *result* of increased production rather than a *requirement* of the expansion of the production process. Thus whether the food grains stock related to the seasonality of agriculture is a part of the working capital requirement of production depends on the institutional structure, and in particular on the mode of employment.

8.2 Seasonality and Surplus Labour

The surplus labour model developed in Chapter 4 was based on a non-seasonal interpretation of the production relations. This is clearly a limitation, since seasonality is a major factor in agricultural production and it cannot be assumed that labour applied in the slack season is a perfect substitute for that applied in the busy season. In fact, the simplest interpretation of the model of Chapters 2 and 4 would be to assume *perfect complementarity* between labour applied at different times of the year, so that they can be applied only in fixed proportions. Then z, x and w can be taken to be the weighted averages respectively of

3. Lewis (1955), p. 270. See also Kindleberger (1958), chapter on 'Capital'.
'... since agricultural output is produced at one time of the year and consumed evenly over the year as a whole, half of output on the average is in inventories at a given time. This is a higher ratio than industry or services. In consequence, since the proportion of agricultural output in total output declines as income grows, the ratio of inventories to output declines.' (Kindleberger (1958), p. 38.)
4. Cf. Ricardo (1815).

the supply prices, the real costs of labour and the wage rates, in the different seasons.[5]

In some models of labour allocation it has been argued that if the seasonality of the production process is taken into account, then surplus labour cannot exist. Perhaps the most interesting of these models is that of Stiglitz (1969). As he puts it, 'we have proved that, provided leisure is a superior good and labour supplied at harvest and planting times and at other times of the year are complementary, output must fall as labour migrates to the urban sector: labourers cannot be in surplus'.[6] Explaining the difference between his results and those of a model similar to the one outlined in Chapter 4, Stiglitz says:

This result can be contrasted with that of Sen (1966). He argues that agricultural output will remain unchanged as labour leaves the agricultural sector if and only if there is constant marginal utility of leisure and income (so the indifference curves are straight lines). The reason for the divergence between our results and his is his strong assumption that L^1 and L^2 (labour supplied at different periods of the year) are perfect substitutes. Even if we allow L^1 and L^2 to be substitutes, but not perfect substitutes, his results will not obtain.[7]

This is, if correct, a very serious criticism of the model of surplus labour presented in Chapter 4, since we do know with certainty that labour applied in different seasons is not perfectly substitutable. We cannot replace a day's work at harvest time by a day's effort at sowing time, or by a day's work when the crop is quietly growing in the fields while the cultivator is resting his limbs without having much to do. But is the criticism correct?

It would be surprising if it were. As argued earlier, we can easily interpret the model of Chapter 4 (and of Sen (1966)) as one of perfect *complementarity* between labour of different seasons, and as long as the weighted average of the supply prices of labour z in different seasons remains constant as labour is withdrawn, so will the total amount (including the seasonal distribution) of labour used, and the output must remain the same. In each season there may be a separate supply function $S(x)$ for labour, but as long as it is flat in the relevant region and $x \leqslant x^*$ in each season, total output Q cannot be affected by the withdrawal of some labourers. Clearly, therefore, the difference in question cannot lie in the assumption about substitutability of labour. But then what does it lie in?

5. See Sen (1966), eqn (50).
6. Stiglitz (1969), p. 11.
7. Stiglitz (1969), p. 11.

The crucial difference rests in Stiglitz's assumption that in at least one of the seasons of the year, each person is already doing the maximum amount of work that he *possibly* can, and this combined with the fact that labour applications in different seasons are not perfect substitutes immediately produces the no-surplus-labour consequence. Stiglitz explains his assumption thus:

> For simplicity, we shall divide the year into two periods, planting and harvesting, during which labourers are assumed to be fully utilized (i.e., *work the maximum that is possible at those times*), and the other times of the year, during which the supply of labour (hours worked per week) by each labourer is determined so as to maximize utility.[8]

No wonder that this model produces the result that 'labourers cannot be in surplus', since it begins by assuming that there is no slack whatsoever in one season, which, combined with the perfectly reasonable assumption that labour in other seasons cannot fully substitute for busy season labour, must yield the no-surplus-labour result. The difference *does not* lie only in the assumption about substitutability.

8.3 Dual Labour Markets and Seasonal Variations

How would the dual labour market (Chapter 6) and its allocational consequences (Chapter 7) be affected by the pattern of seasonality? Consider two seasons, in one of which there is a wage gap, viz., $j_1 < w_1$, while there is none in the other, viz., $j_2 = w_2$. If complete complementarity is assumed, so that labour is used in fixed proportions (say, in the ratio $b:1$), the effective cost of a composite unit of labour in the family farm would be $(bj_1 + j_2)$ and that in the wage-based farm $(bw_1 + w_2)$. It follows immediately from the strictly diminishing nature of the E-function and the G-function that:

$$E(bj_1 + j_2) > E(bw_1 + w_2) \tag{8.1}$$

$$G(bj_1 + j_2) > G(bw_1 + w_2). \tag{8.2}$$

That is, the employment level and output volume per acre would be higher in the family farm than in the wage-employment farm.

It is obvious that this result can be easily extended to a model allowing for many seasons, and the directional results will hold as long as there is a wage gap in *at least* one season. Furthermore, it is not necessary that labour in different seasons be perfectly complementary. If we assume that a greater use of labour in one season increases the productivity of

8. Stiglitz (1969), p. 3; italics added.

labour in other seasons,[9] the result will hold. Greater use of labour in the slack season would stimulate employment in the other seasons as well. Thus, a lower real labour cost of slack season labour in the family farm would stimulate greater labour use in that farm in the busy season also. And the output per unit of land would, of course, be higher under those circumstances.

8.4 Non-seasonal Unemployment and the Income Aspect

While neither the possibility of the existence of surplus labour nor the consequences of dual labour markets are essentially altered by the technological fact of the seasonality of agriculture, it is certainly the case that the incidence of worklessness tends to vary quite substantially between different seasons in an agricultural economy. Seasonal unemployment can be very large in agrarian societies.

However, the appropriate measure of seasonal employment depends on precisely which concept of unemployment is invoked.[10] There is, in particular, a contrast between the production aspect and the income aspect of employment related to the seasonal pattern of work. Consider the case of a member of a peasant family who works elsewhere during much of the year but joins in the family cultivation during some peak period of activity, e.g. harvesting. In so far as his co-operation increases the output level, he is productively employed in his family farm in addition to whatever else he might be doing. However, even if the family output were to be completely unaffected by his labour contribution, he might still decide to give a helping hand to the family to cut down the efforts of others. In this case he is certainly making a contribution, but not to the output level, and from the production point of view he is still surplus. But nevertheless he may not be unemployed in terms of the income aspect. His right to a part of the family income may depend crucially on his doing this bit of work in the peak season. If his income is conditional on such seasonal activity, he cannot be regarded as unemployed from the income point of view, even if his joining in leaves the total output of the farm completely unchanged.

This distinction is of some importance in assessing the extent of surplus labour at the height of the peak seasons. It is quite common for labourers engaged in other activities, e.g., services and industries, to migrate to their family farms during the agricultural busy weeks. This may often reflect the fact that but for their joining in, the agricultural output will be lower, but it need not necessarily indicate this at all.

9. That is, the 'cross partials' are positive.
10. See Chapters 1 and 4.

Working is not merely a method of producing output, it is also a way of establishing one's rights to a share of the family income from a joint farm. It is, therefore, possible to over-estimate the work force requirement during the peak seasons if we go only by the actual numbers sharing in the activities in those periods, some of whom may be leaving other work to do so. One has to take into account the institutional set up and the principles of income-sharing that are in use in peasant communities.[11]

8.5 Technological Choice and Seasonality

While the extent of unemployment from the production point of view may not be negligible even in the peak seasons, unemployment in the slack season tends to be very large from every point of view in many agricultural economies. Two sets of policy questions are immediately raised by such seasonal unemployment.

First, is it possible to find seasonal work, preferably involving little capital investment, to supplement the agricultural operations, so that a cultivator can do such work in the slack seasons? Obviously, a lower real labour cost (or a greater excess supply of labour at the same real labour cost) in the slack seasons would justify such a pursuit. It is, in fact, not at all difficult to think of technological possibilities that involve a low degree of mechanization, but part-time seasonal use would tend to make the capital intensity relatively high by reducing the rate of utilization of the capital goods over the year.[12] Thus in a capital-scarce economy finding seasonal supplementary work does involve some problems. Furthermore, those operations which require next to no machinery, e.g., primitive road building, may, however have a considerable working capital requirement if slack season labour is used under the wage system.[13] The ideal solution is, of course to find some type of fruitful work that requires little machinery and can be done outside the wage system.

Secondly, is it possible to change the pattern of seasonality in the demand for labour? The seasons as climatic factors may not, of course, be amenable to easy manipulation, but seasonality in the economic sense is as much a reflection of prevailing technical knowledge as of basic climatic factors. For example, irrigation cuts down the dependence on

11. The fact that sometimes male labourers moving to the towns to work as domestic servants or industrial workers leave their nuclear family behind with the rest of the joint family frequently puts them under a straightforward obligation to come and help in the peak farming activities. The relation between economic support and work obligation is a particularly complex one in traditional agrarian societies.
12. See Chapter 5.
13. See Chapter 7.

rain during planting, and even though this does not, in itself, seem to alter substantially the time scheduling of the usual crops (largely because of dependence on other climatic factors, e.g., temperatures, atmospheric humidity and the sun), it does make the peak season of planting and transplanting somewhat more flexible. Similarly, some of the new varieties of crop have a shorter maturing period, e.g., *taichung* rice as opposed to the traditional varieties grown in India, and this alters the harvesting time (and sometimes the planting time). In so far as seasonal variations in the employment situation are significant, technological research geared towards changing the seasonal pattern must be recognized to be important. Luckily, the seasonality of employment depends on a great deal more than the four seasons.

IV | Policy Objectives and Employment

9 | The Employment Objective

9.1 Introduction

Is employment a benefit or a cost? This question is not quite as jejune as it sounds, and in analysing the objective of employment creation we can do worse than face it head on. There may seem to be some inconsistency in our attitude to employment. On the one hand we seem to be taking for granted that employment creation is a good thing and a cause for rejoicing, while on the other whenever we come to discussing the prospect of increased employment we rush into doing little sums involving 'the real cost of labour'. Are we being schizophrenic, or at least involved in some kind of a Freudian 'erroneous performance of action' to fulfil some latent wish?[1]

In fact, the scope for schizophrenia in pursuing the employment objective is quite considerable. A cheap way out of this dilemma would be to say: people prefer to be employed because they earn an income that way, but employment is not valuable in itself, and no one would want to work if he were not compensated for it. This line of reasoning concentrates on what we have been calling 'the income approach'[2] and it is a no-nonsense justification of employment as a means to the end of earning an income. But it is not by any means clear that people prefer to have a job *only because* it brings them some money. A job can be a source of satisfaction in itself and the thrust of what we called 'the recognition approach' lies in this direction. But if so, why should people

---

1. Cf. 'Or, as happened to one of my patients whom I had forbidden to telephone the lady he was in love with, he "by mistake" and "thoughtlessly" gave the wrong number when he meant to telephone me [Freud], so that he was suddenly connected with her.' (Freud (1924), p. 81.)
2. See Chapter 1.

demand 'compensation' for work in the form of wages rather than offering to pay for the privilege of being employed?

Part of the answer clearly lies in the fact that the person may not have any money to give if he is in fact unemployed. It is not unusual to find a very rich person spending money so as to be involved in some work that he or she thinks is worthwhile. The reason why this type of luxury is not open to others is simply that they have to earn money through employment, because – as Marx put it – they have only their labour power to sell. In fact, Marx did argue that work may ultimately become 'life's prime want' when people are provided for economically, irrespective of their work.[3] The question also relates to the person's perception of who gets the fruits of his labour; he may like to work but may refuse to do it free for a profit-earning capitalist.[4]

There is also an important contrast between the valuation of being employed and that of putting in an extra unit of effort. The recognition aspect of a job tends to be related more to the former – to the feeling of self-esteem and esteem from others which comes from being employed and also to the feeling of fulfilment if the work is satisfying – but the incentive system is also geared to the latter. In fact, the person may prefer having (a) *some* work and a lot of income, both to having (b) *no* work and the same income, and to having (c) *more* work and the same income;[5] but his decision problems do not really involve a choice between (a) and (b).

Employment policy would, therefore, have to be aware not only of the production resulting from employment and of the income earned by the employed, but also of 'the recognition aspect' of the problem. The fact that compensation may be demanded for work does not make employment a cost rather than a benefit in itself (in addition to the production and income consequences of it). Of course, it will frequently be the case that production and income considerations will be the dominant issues in employment policy, but 'the recognition aspect' must also figure.

In fact, from the point of view of the policy maker there are other positive consequences of employment, that might be very important in his calculations even though they might not figure in the decisions of the

3. Marx (1875).
4. The real labour cost j relates inversely to h, viz., the person's concern for the beneficiary of his efforts. Aside from the usual 'welfare' considerations, ideas of fairness and justice are also involved in these decisions.
5. In terms of the model of Chapter 3, $S'(x)$ may not be positive for small values of x, but positive after that. If it is flat in the relevant region after it becomes positive, the possibility of surplus labour (Chapter 4) will remain unaffected.

job seekers. Worklessness induces vagrancy and crime, whose impact on others may be quite considerable. Similarly, expansion of female employment may be a great force for change in a traditional society and may be welcomed by many for that reason. Employment does, indeed, involve more than production and income.

9.2 Feasibility Constraints and Income Distribution

On the production approach employment is not desired for its own sake but for the output that is produced. On the income approach as well, employment is a means to an end. From the point of view of employment policy, the relation of employment to income distribution is frequently an important one. There are very few methods of distributing income that are thought to be as effective as offering employment. It is worth enquiring why this should be so.

For this discussion, the production aspect is best left out altogether. Keynes' example of 'digging holes and filling them up' will do for this. Consider the proposal that the government offers jobs to people in a poverty-stricken area in which unemployment is rampant; the purpose is to give them something with which to buy goods.[6] The question can be asked whether this aim could not be better served by simply paying these people subsidies which would give them their income although they would not be required to work. In order to concentrate on the income approach alone, we leave out of this picture the recognition aspect, just as the production aspect has already been excluded; people may prefer to receive income for work rather than be on the dole, but let us not go into this question here. So we now have a case of employment that has no consequence for production and that has no recognition aspect. Under these circumstances, it could well be asked: why make the poor people work rather than simply handing them subsidies?

Two types of issues seem to be relevant in answering this question, and both involve more than economics. First, a widespread system of pure subsidies in a developing economy may be difficult to run because of the possibilities of corruption involved in it. By relating payment to employment, these possibilities are substantially reduced, since the records are easier to check and fictitious payments by corrupt officials easier to eliminate. Second, if the subsidy mechanism is not broad enough to cover everyone, either due to a lack of funds or due to the

6. In the Keynesian case the purpose would be a general expansion of effective demand to increase total employment through the multiplier effect (Keynes (1936)), whereas here the objective may be one of pure redistribution. On this see Marglin (1967) and Chopra (1972). See also the report of the ILO mission to Kenya, ILO (1972), Chapters 7, 9 and 16.

limitations of the administrative machinery, there is a serious problem of selection of beneficiaries for special favour. By offering people jobs rather than pure subsidies the government may be less likely to be charged with arbitrary discrimination, and indeed the bureaucracy may in fact succeed in discriminating in favour of those who most need support and are ready to work for it. This type of administrative and political consideration may provide the rationale of employment schemes for the purpose of income redistribution, such as the one with the somewhat odd name of the Crash Scheme for Rural Employment, launched in India in 1971.[7]

There is, however, a problem of feasibility even in the case of the employment-method of redistributing income. Suppose n jobs are to be offered at w wage rate. If only n people wish to work at that wage rate, then clearly there is no problem of selection, though in that case the question can be raised as to whether the wage rate is enough of a hidden income subsidy. If, on the other hand, more than n people try to get these jobs, the question of selection and therefore of arbitrary discrimination reappears.[8] So does the possibility of corruption and bribery. Employment may not, therefore, be as fine a method of income redistribution as it is sometimes made out to be. The fact of the matter is that the whole purpose of pure redistribution is to give something free, and given that fact — no matter how the process is administered — it will tend to generate pressures influencing the officials involved in the give-away. Whether the employment mechanism minimizes these problems compared with other vehicles of redistribution is an open question.

9.3 Employment and Consumption

One of the commonest problems of employment policy is to consider the choice between two alternatives, one of which, say, alternative A, produces more output but yields less employment than the other B, given all other resources. Can it be argued that despite the lower productivity of B, it can be chosen if employment is regarded as an important goal? No doubt such an argument can be made, but it is not necessarily an easy one to defend. Alternative B is, of course, technically inefficient, but this need not in itself be a sufficient reason for rejecting it.[9] The important question is: what determines the aggregate level of employment? Does the level of output in one enterprise influence that in others?

7. See Appendix B.
8. In the Indian experiment this seems to have been a problem. See Appendix B.
9. If employment is a desirable goal in itself, B can be 'superior' from the social point of view despite technical inefficiency.

If more employment is sought, we have to ask why is it not possible simply to hire more people in some public sector project, e.g., road building? From what we have already said it would appear that the main difficulty in this way of solving the employment problem lies in the requirement of consumer goods to meet the additional demand arising from the additional wages bill [10] When more people are hired, more wages will be paid out, thereby creating more effective demand. In a situation of Keynesian unemployment, this would, of course, lead to more supply, but not so in the developing economy, given the fact that typically in such an economy output is restricted by resources and organization rather than by effective demand.[11] Thus the extra demand arising from the additional wages bill would simply have to be met by reallocation of the existing output, e.g., through inflationary readjustments, which may have considerable political and economic repercussions, and can also involve reduction of employment elsewhere.

It is this fact which casts serious doubt on the view that aggregate employment can be easily raised at the cost of reducing output of consumer goods. If in the choice posed earlier, alternative B is chosen, yielding more employment and less output, the opportunity of creating employment elsewhere will be less, because of the reduction of output.[12] In fact, at the risk of over-simplification, the total opportunity of wage employment $\hat{E}$ can be viewed as being given by the available supply of wage goods M and the real wage rate w, assuming that all wages are consumed.

$$\hat{E} = \frac{M}{w} \tag{9.1}$$

A reduction in output would tend to reduce M, so that even if direct employment in this project is larger, its overall impact on total employment can be negative.[13]

This type of consideration has an important bearing on the framework in terms of which employment policy may be discussed. For example,

10. See Chapters 7 and 8.
11. See A. K. Das-Gupta (1954), (1956), and V.K.R.V. Rao (1956).
12. The argument is immediate if the output in question is of goods consumed by the wage earners. If the product consists of capital goods, a similar argument exists through the possibility of shifting resources between the production of capital goods and consumer goods. The same holds for the case of consumer goods of other kinds.
13. If alternative B involves a lower real wage rate, that fact will tend to work in the opposite direction, but it need not fully cancel out the greater employment potential of the larger output of A. However, the picture is simplest when there is a uniform wage rate, as is assumed in (9.1).

important contributions have been made in recent years in analysing the generation of 'indirect employment' through input—output relationships. The creation of demand for related goods can be taken to expand employment through their labour content.[14] If this is interpreted as a model of *determination* of total employment (direct plus indirect), there are obvious problems, since what the process really implies is the creation of a market demand for labour.[15] In a completely free enterprise economy, this may be the way employment is determined, but if there is employment planning by the government, the real bottleneck to employment expansion will arise from the wage goods supply, rather than from the demand side, which the government can in any case alter through public sector projects if wage goods are available. The framework of analysis in terms of direct and indirect employment is useful in exploring the creation of market demand for labour, but to interpret it as a process of determination of employment would be a hang-over from the Keynesian model of demand bottleneck. A government seriously pursuing the employment objective should always be able to make up the gap between the employment opportunity as given by eqn (9.1) and the existing demand for labour. The distinction will be important when doing project evaluation in terms of the employment objective, because the question will arise as to whether to take credit for 'the indirect employment' to be generated by the project through the demand for related goods and thus through the derived demand for labour. The answer really depends on the government's own policy. If it merely maintains law and order, and does not pursue any employment policy, then it may make sense to count in 'the indirect employment', since demand may also be a bottleneck. If, however, the government does try to expand employment subject to the constraint given by eqn (9.1), it can always make up for any demand gap, so that (9.1) will be the binding constraint. Employment will then depend simply on the supply of wage goods.

One final point. This analysis is based on the use of the wage system at a given real wage rate. The advantage of a lower real cost of labour for certain modes of production and employment have already been discussed earlier. One way of breaking through the barrier of eqn (9.1) is to use a non-wage system of employment generation, e.g., through co-operative work projects in which the reward for extra work comes only later in the form of greater output for the co-operative and the com-

14. See, for example, Hazari and Krishnamurty (1970), Gaiha (1972), and Parikh (1972).
15. In this sense it is an extension of the older concept of the 'employment multiplier' (Keynes (1936)).

munity. This is essentially a method of extending the advantages of a non-wage family system (see Chapter 7) to operations of larger scale. There have been some attempts to use this strategy in China,[16] and whether eqn (9.1) would be binding in such a system would depend on the possibility of expanding employment outside the wage system. Questions of work motivation are crucial for the possibility of exploring this avenue.[17]

16. See Ishikawa (1973). See also Eckstein, Galenson and Liu (1968), Perkins (1969), and Wong (1971). The use of non-wage labour in water projects in China is discussed eloquently in Huang Chen *et al.* (1972).
17. See Riskin (1973) and Sen (1973), Chapter 4. See also von Weizsäcker (1972).

10 | Employment in the Long Run

10.1 Introduction

It was argued in the last chapter that under the wage system the volume of employment would be closely related to the output of consumer goods consumed by the wage earners. But the future output of consumer goods will depend on the growth of productive capacity, and that in its turn will depend on the level of investment to-day. And the higher the proportion of to-day's output that is invested, the lower – given other things – will be to-day's consumption and employment. And there we have a conflict between employment to-day and employment tomorrow, as well as between consumption to-day and consumption tomorrow.

This is, of course, not surprising. People have been talking about 'jam to-day versus jam tomorrow' ever since jam was invented. But mundane though it is, the conflict adds substantial complexity to the problem of technological choice. Consider a wage-based farm in which labourers are hired at the wage rate w. Consider alternative degrees of labour intensity. As more and more labour is applied, the additional output generated by it falls. Assume that there is surplus labour in the economy and further – to simplify the problem – that the disutility of effort is zero. In terms of the maximization of the value of current output of this farm, it makes sense to go on applying more and more labour as long as the additional output q generated by an additional unit of labour is positive.

However, let us consider the consequence of applying a unit of labour which contributes less to output than the wage that is to be paid to it, i.e., $q < w$. If all wages are consumed, what will be the impact of this additional employment on the surplus available for reinvestment? Output is increased by q, but consumption rises by more, viz., w, and clearly the volume of investible surplus is now *lower*. So the growth of the future productive capacity is less and, given other things, the future output and employment will be lower as well. The conflict between present and future employment has come into the choice of labour intensity. Indeed choice of techniques seems to be an integral part of this conflict.[1] How do we propose to tackle this intertemporal conflict in technological decisions?

10.2 The Social Cost of Labour

When a conflict of the kind discussed in the last section occurs, one has to consider whether to increase output, irrespective of its division between investment and consumption, or to put some additional weight on the share of investment. If we feel that the overall division of the national output between consumption and investment is correct, then we should really put the same weight on investment as on consumption and need not be concerned about how the income from the marginal project is divided between savings and consumption. In choosing technology for the marginal project, we can then concentrate on the maximization of total output irrespective of the wage bill and irrespective of the consumption generated by it. On the other hand, if the overall share of investment in the national output is thought to be below the optimum, then greater weight should be given to the marginal unit of investment than to the corresponding amount of consumption. And then we would no longer be involved in maximizing the market value of total output irrespective of the amount of additional consumption generated by the wages bill in this project. Indeed we would then stop short of the point where the productive contribution of additional employment falls to zero. How short? That would clearly depend on how sub-optimal we think the investment level is and, in particular, on the relative weighting of investment vis-à-vis consumption.

Let s be the proportion of the output Q of this project that is saved and invested (we still stick to the complete homogeneity of all outputs implicitly assumed in the preceding argument) and let p^I be the weight attached to an extra unit of investment vis-à-vis an extra unit of consumption. The weighted value of the output level is then given by:

$$R = Qsp^I + Q(1 - s). \tag{10.1}$$

Consider now the production relation:

$$Q = f(L), \text{ with } f' > 0 \text{ and } f'' < 0. \tag{3.1}$$

1. I have discussed this conflict extensively elsewhere; see Sen (1960). See also Galenson and Leibenstein (1955), Dobb (1956), (1960), Eckstein (1957), Sen (1957), (1968), Marglin (1966), Dixit (1968), Lefeber (1968), Bose and Dixit (1969), S. Chakravarty (1969), Newbery (1972), Stern (1972) and Pattanaik (1972).

What determines the savings ratio s? Let the savings ratio out of wages be s^1 and that out of the project profits be s^2. Further, the project profits π will equal the difference between the output value and the wage bill:

$$\pi = Q - Lw. \tag{10.2}$$

Putting together these bits and pieces, we get the maximand as:

$$R = f(L)\,[1 + s_2(p^I - 1)] - Lw[(s_2 - s_1)(p^I - 1)]. \tag{10.3}$$

The labour intensity that maximizes R can be found by setting the marginal contribution of labour L to the weighted value of output R at zero, i.e., putting $(dR/dL) = 0$. This yields the following relation:

$$0 = \frac{dR}{dL} = f'(L)\,[1 + s_2(p^I - 1)] - w[(s_2 - s_1)(p^I - 1)]. \tag{10.4}$$

What is 'the social cost of labour' w^*, defined as the magnitude to which the nominal marginal product of labour should be equated in order to maximize the weighted valuation of output R?[2] It is obvious from (10.4) that:

$$w^* = \frac{w(s_2 - s_1)(p^I - 1)}{1 + s_2(p^I - 1)}. \tag{10.5}$$

If there is no sub-optimality of savings and we attach the same weight to investment as to consumption, i.e., $p^I = 1$, we have:

$$w^* = 0. \tag{10.6}$$

If, on the other hand, the sub-optimality is so severe that the weight p^I on investment is very large, we get:

$$w^* = \frac{w(s_2 - s_1)}{s_2}. \tag{10.7}$$

This, with the additional assumption that all wages are consumed, yields:

$$w^* = w. \tag{10.8}$$

It would, thus, appear that in this surplus labour economy, the social cost of labour is zero if there is no sub-optimality of savings, and that it is given by the market wage rate if all the weight is on investment as

2. Sen (1968).

opposed to immediate consumption, and if there are no savings out of wages.[3]

10.3 The Premium on Investment
In the foregoing analysis a crucial role is played by the premium on investment $(p^I - 1)$ compared with consumption. What should determine this weight p^I? In the first place, why should p^I exceed unity at all, i.e., why should there be a premium on investment? As we saw, the last question is essentially equivalent to asking why the investment level should be taken to be sub-optimal.

There are various reasons for expecting sub-optimality of market-determined savings as viewed by the planners. First of all, the planners may believe that individual decisions on savings tend to be too low, since people in the present generation do not attach sufficient weight to the welfare of future generations, and they may wish to correct this.[4] Secondly, they may believe that even if the present generation has sufficient concern for the future, there is an 'externality' involved, in that each person prefers that others should save more for the sake of future generations, which would tend to make market savings sub-optimal.[5] It is not my purpose here to evaluate these arguments, which I have tried to do elsewhere,[6] or to present other arguments relevant to this diagnosis.[7] What seems to be fairly widely conceded is that the planners in most developing countries assume that the market-determined savings rates are less than optimal.

But if this is so, why does the government not correct the sub-optimality by taxation and other means? This is where the feasibility constraints on taxation and other means of increasing savings are relevant. Taxation as an instrument is partly political, and fear of political repercussions might prevent the necessary taxes from being imposed and the sub-optimality of savings from being corrected. There is a distinction between the planners' own values and their reading of feasibility, given the political balance of power in the country.

So much for the reasoning behind the existence of a premium on investment, i.e., for $p^I > 1$. But how should p^I be calculated in any actual economic evaluation?

3. The view that $w^* = 0$ has been expressed in Polak (1943), Kahn (1951), Lewis (1955), Bator (1957), among others. That $w^* = w$ is implied by Galenson and Leibenstein (1955) and Dobb (1960), among others.
4. See Dobb (1960).
5. See Sen (1961) and Marglin (1963).
6. See Sen (1967a).
7. See Feldstein (1964) and Phelps (1965), among others.

Let the rate at which the government wishes to discount future consumption benefits be i per year, let g be the yield per year in terms of consumer goods output of an additional unit of investment, and s the proportion of this yield that is saved and reinvested. It is assumed that i, g, s and p^I remain constant over time. In such a model sub-optimality of savings corresponds exactly to: $g > i$.[8] Clearly the return from a unit of investment is a flow of consumption equalling $g(1-s)$ and a flow of investment gs valued, in units of consumption, at gsp^I. Treating this dual flow as a perpetuity, we get the value of a unit of investment as given by the capitalized sum of its future benefits discounted at i. This value must equal p^I itself. Hence:

$$p^I = \frac{g(1-s) + gsp^I}{i}. \tag{10.9}$$

Solving this we get:[9]

$$p^I = \frac{(1-s)g}{i - sg}. \tag{10.10}$$

What if the sub-optimality is to be cured at time $\hat{t}$ and will not last for ever? This case corresponds to $g = i$ from point $\hat{t}$ onwards and of course $p^I = 1$ after $\hat{t}$. It can be shown[10] that in this case, we have a more complex expression for p^I_t, where p^I_t is the weight on investment at point of time t.

$$p^I_t = \frac{(1-s)g}{i-sg}\left[1 - \left(\frac{1+sg}{1+i}\right)^{\hat{t}-t}\right] + \left(\frac{1+sg}{1+i}\right)^{\hat{t}-t} \tag{10.11}$$

If $i > sg$ and $\hat{t}$ is large, it is easily verified that approximately:

$$p^I_t = \frac{(1-s)g}{i-sg}$$

We are back again to (10.10), now true in approximate terms but without the assumption that the sub-optimality of savings lasts for ever.

8. Marglin (1966), Sen (1968), and UNIDO (1972).
9. Note that if $i < sg$, then this formula does not work. This is perhaps an unlikely occurrence and would, in any case, imply that the social discount should be higher, since this is a situation in which the investment yield sg of a unit of investment as a perpetuity exceeds the discount rate i, making the present value of investment unbounded.
10. UNIDO (1972), pp. 194–7.

10.4 Future Consumption and Future Employment

In terms of the reasoning of Chapter 9, the choice between consumption to-day and tomorrow was seen to be very close to that between employment to-day and tomorrow. It was this relationship that permitted us to approximate the problem of evaluation of long-run employment in terms of that of long-run consumption. In deciding on the weight to be put on consumption in the future vis-à vis consumption to-day, we have to consider the respective employment potentials implicit in each and the relative importance of employment at the two points of time. We could, for example, argue: 'Consumption this year is worth much less than that in the future since (a) the community will be richer in the future, and (b) the level of unemployment will by then be lower, so that the employment implications of a unit of extra consumption, given by eqn (9.1), will also be less valuable by comparison with to-day.' In the determination of relative weights for the future consumption stream, its employment implications and their relative significance will have to be woven in. This would come into R, the weighted value of the product, through the value of p^I.

In thinking systematically about this weighting problem a distinction should be made between (i) estimating the employment content of additional consumption, and (ii) estimating the social value of an additional unit of employment. In the first exercise the main consideration would be the magnitude of the wage rates, as is clear from (9.1), and also the importance of the wage system, the relevance of which in this context was discussed in § 9.3. In the latter exercise one would have to be particularly careful about 'the recognition aspect' (Chapter 1), as well as the social consequences of employment which do not affect private decisions but do influence our reading of social welfare (§ 9.1). The distributional consequences related to 'the income aspect' could either be considered under employment, or directly as a distributional judgment. The production aspect goes into the derivation of the consumption stream itself.

Other general sets of considerations have also to be kept in view. First, the fiscal constraints that make the expansion of employment dependent on the availability of wage goods may themselves change over time. If they do change, the implications of this change for the weighting of consumption will have to be worked out, since the tightness of the fiscal constraints will affect the employment implications of consumption and therefore the value of that consumption. Second, the development of non-wage systems of employment, even in the absence of a relaxation of fiscal constraints, can affect the employment aspect of the valuation of consumption substantially. The greater the use of non-wage systems, the less will be the dependence of employment on the availability of wage goods. The valuation of future consumption will depend on these institutional issues as well.

V | Economic Evaluation

11 | Shadow Prices and Resource Allocation

11.1 Introduction

The view that in developing economies labour should be valued not at its market price but at its correct 'shadow price' has been expressed with increasing frequency in recent years and there would now seem to be a remarkable degree of agreement on this proposition. However, it seems, alas, to be the case that this unanimity about 'the need for' using shadow prices is not altogether matched by an agreement on the *meaning* of shadow prices. The solidarity may have been partly caused by a play on words.

Ideas on shadow prices diverge for two different reasons. First, the definition of shadow prices varies remarkably. Second, even within the framework of a given definition, the formulation of the exercise varies substantially. The first problem is taken up in this chapter and the second will come up in Chapter 12, in the specific context of the pricing of labour. In this chapter four different approaches to shadow pricing will be compared and contrasted.

11.2 Programming and the Dual

Consider an exercise of optimization through the use of mathematical programming. In particular, consider the problem of maximizing some concave objective function W subject to a set of concave constraints including one that represents 'the excess supply' of the particular resource, the shadow price of which we are seeking.[1] The objective func-

1. A function $f(\mathbf{x})$ is concave if and only if a weighted average of $f(\mathbf{x})$ and $f(\mathbf{y})$, i.e., $[tf(\mathbf{x}) + (1-t) f(\mathbf{y})]$, for $0 < t < 1$, would be no higher than $f(t\mathbf{x} + (1-t)\mathbf{y})$, i.e., than the value given by that function for the weighted average of $\mathbf{x}$ and $\mathbf{y}$. It is linear if the two are exactly equal, which is a special case. For example, we have for a concave production function diminishing *or* constant marginal productivity, whereas a linear function will imply constant marginal productivity only. Linear programming is a special case of concave programming.

tion W represents a certain view of social welfare, while the constraints represent various conditions that would have to be satisfied for a programme of action to be feasible, e.g., the use of each resource being no larger than its supply (i.e., 'the excess supply' of each resource being non-negative), the amount of each output being non-negative, and so on.

Associated with each constraint is a 'dual' variable, which will have the value zero if the constraint is not binding (e.g., if there is a strictly positive excess supply of the resource in question), but which can take a positive value if the constraint does bind (e.g., if supply just equals the use of that resource). The interpretation of the dual variable of a resource is that it represents the additional amount of W (the social welfare to be maximized) that is generated by having one more unit of that resource, on each occasion solving the programming problem to obtain the maximized value of W. If with a given resource m being available in amount σ we can produce a maximum value W_1 in terms of the objective function subject to the given constraints, and if with one more unit of that resource available and everything else unchanged, the maximum value of the objective that can be produced subject to the constraints is W_2, then $(W_2 - W_1)$ corresponds to the 'dual' variable associated with resource m. In fact, $(W_2 - W_1)$ will lie precisely in between the dual for m in the first programming problem, with the amount of m being σ, and that in the second programming problem, with the amount of m equalling $\sigma + 1$. Therefore the marginal contribution made by the resource to social welfare is one interpretation of the shadow price of that resource

More formally,[2] let there be a set of production processes available which produce outputs from resources, and let $\mathbf{x}$ be the process selection vector specifying the intensity of each activity. The objective function W is some concave function $W(\mathbf{x})$ and the 'slack' (excess supply) of each resource k is a concave function $\mu_k(\mathbf{x})$. With n types of resource, the set $\mu_k(\mathbf{x})$ can be represented as $\mu(\mathbf{x})$. A simple programming problem is given by:

$$\text{Maximize } W = W(\mathbf{x}) \tag{11.1}$$

$$\text{subject to } \mu(\mathbf{x}) \geqslant 0 \tag{11.2}$$

$$\mathbf{x} \geqslant 0. \tag{11.3}$$

2. For a lucid exposition of linear and concave programming, see Dorfman, Samuelson and Solow (1958). For a more advanced treatment, see Karlin (1959). Heal (1973) goes in depth into the programming framework for planning.

With resource m being available in amount σ, we get a particular $\mu_m(\mathbf{x})$ and we can write the general relation as $\xi_m(\mathbf{x},\sigma)$. We replace $\mu(\mathbf{x})$ by $\xi(\mathbf{x},\sigma)$. Let the solution of the problem in this case yield:

$$U(\sigma) \equiv \max_{\mathbf{x}} W(\mathbf{x}), \text{ subject to } \xi(\mathbf{x}, \sigma) \geqslant 0 \text{ and } \mathbf{x} \geqslant 0. \qquad (11.4)$$

With the amount of resource m being raised to $(\sigma + 1)$, we get:

$$U(\sigma + 1) \equiv \max_{\mathbf{x}} W(\mathbf{x}), \text{ subject to } \xi(\mathbf{x}, \sigma + 1) \geqslant 0 \text{ and } \mathbf{x} \geqslant 0. \quad (11.5)$$

The duals associated with the constraint ξ_m in the two cases are given respectively by $p_m{}^*(\sigma)$ and $p_m{}^*(\sigma + 1)$. It can be established that:

$$p_m^*(\sigma) \geqslant U(\sigma + 1) - U(\sigma) \geqslant p_m^*(\sigma + 1). \qquad (11.6)$$

Thus, the shadow price of a resource in the programming sense corresponds to its marginal impact on the objective function W. Roughly, it is the marginal welfare contribution of that resource. Obviously, if the resource is in excess supply, then having one more unit makes no difference, and its shadow price in the sense of the dual would be zero.

11.3 Shadow Price as a Signal for Decision Taking
A second approach to the problem lies in the definition of shadow prices as those pricing signals which, if communicated to the decentralized manager or project evaluator, would induce him to take the right decision in the sense of maximizing the planning objective subject to the constraints. The shadow prices in this sense are those prices which would lead to an optimal programme if the decision takers maximize the shadow profits corresponding to those prices.[3]

By this definition the shadow price would tend to correspond to the dual in the programming sense. Obviously, for the right use of any resource m it is not sufficient that the shadow price of resource m alone should be right; so should all the shadow prices.

Shadow prices are, however not merely calculating devices; they are also instruments for communication. Sometimes the use of appropriate shadow prices might be made difficult by traditional habits of thought, which could misinterpret the meaning of the appropriate shadow prices in the sense of the 'dual'. In some problems any departure from the 'correct' shadow prices anywhere would lead to incorrect decisions, but in others departures can be made in limited areas without affecting the

3. On prices 'associated with an optimum', see Malinvaud (1967), Hurwicz (1971), Koopmans and Montias (1971), and Heal (1973).

results. While $(p_1{}^*, p_2{}^*, p_3{}^*)$ may be the 'correct' shadow prices, the use of $(p_1{}^*, p_2{}^{**}, p_3{}^{**})$ may lead to the same decisions in some particular area of decision-taking. And if $(p_1{}^*, p_2{}^{**}, p_3{}^{**})$ corresponds more closely to the understanding of the people involved, then that price vector, though not correct for the exercise as a whole, may be taken to be the shadow prices in this limited sense for this restricted exercise.

This may look like an elaborate way of messing up a perfectly decent system of shadow prices p^* and it may not be clear what the rationale could be for undertaking this exercise. The main advantage does not lie in doing the sums well but in relating valuation and decisions to ideas and concepts in common use. In the exercise on the social cost of labour in Chapter 10, the value of the shadow price of labour in the programming sense for maximizing R was obviously (dR/dL), which was in fact zero, since the constraint on the excess supply of labour was not binding. One could thus have said that the proper shadow price of labour was zero, which means that labour was in some sense 'costless'. But given the usual meaning of costlessness of labour,[4] this could have been interpreted to mean that one could go on using more and more labour as long as it had a positive marginal product, i.e., as long as $f'(L) > 0$. Clearly, this would have been quite wrong, since it is the marginal impact on social welfare R that is to be reduced to zero, not the marginal product $f'(L)$ in the market sense. An extra unit of employment produces some extra output and also necessitates a shift from investment to consumption. The market value of the marginal product does not take the latter into account, partly because it is not part of the usual definition of marginal product, but also because the shift *is* costless at market prices, since corresponding units of investment and consumption have the same price. But at the right shadow prices there is a premium $(p^I - 1)$ on investment vis-à-vis consumption and (dR/dL) differs from $f'(L)$. The definition of the social cost of labour as that value (w^*) which if equated to $f'(L)$ would yield the optimal labour intensity is thus not an exercise in introspection on optimal allocation but one in communication.[5] That has its value, and the shadow price of labour can sometimes be usefully defined in a sense different from the programming dual.[6] In Section 12.2, this will be discussed further.

4. See, for example, Lewis (1955), p. 386.
5. In this example, with 1 = consumption, 2 = investment and 3 = labour, for the particular exercise of choice of labour intensity, we have: $p_1{}^* = 1$, $p_2{}^* = p^I$, $p_2{}^{**} = 1$, $p_3{}^* = dR/dL$, and $p_3{}^{**} = w^*$.
6. See Sen (1960), (1968), and Marglin (1966). See also UNIDO (1968), Dixit (1968), (1971), Little and Mirrlees (1969), Lal (1972), Newbery (1972), V. Joshi (1972), and Stern (1972).

11.4 Competitive Equilibrium Prices

A third kind of shadow prices is that set of prices which equates demand and supply in a perfectly competitive market. In his pioneering exercise in using 'accounting prices' for development planning, Tinbergen (1958) took this approach:

They [accounting prices] are the prices at which supply is just sufficient to satisfy demand; they represent the value of the marginal product to be obtained with their aid, since projects showing no surplus above the cost, at accounting prices, of the factors used, will be on the margin between acceptance and rejection.[7]

This conception is, obviously, close to the notion of the shadow price to guide decentralized decision-taking, since perfect competition is a method of decentralized resource allocation. But the difference between the two approaches is quite substantial. The existence of competitive equilibrium would guarantee only Pareto optimality (and that under certain specific circumstances[8]), and an arbitrary competitive equilibrium need not at all correspond to the maximization of the objectives of planning, even if those objectives include *inter alia* Pareto optimality.[9]

This concentration on the competitive market led Tinbergen into an unduly narrow framework of accounting prices and also made him come out with a rather limited set of reasons for which accounting prices should differ from the market prices.

In other words, there are two reasons why market prices do not truly reflect 'intrinsic values'. First, the realization of the investment pattern will itself influence these values, but only after some time, since investment processes are essentially time-consuming. Secondly, there do exist, in underdeveloped countries especially, a number of 'fundamental disequilibria'.[10]

This leaves out divergences of accounting prices from market prices arising from the planning objectives being different from whatever the particular competitive mechanism may achieve when in equilibrium.[11] Some of the more important reasons for the divergence between market prices and accounting prices may have nothing whatsoever to do with either of the two reasons suggested by Tinbergen and may relate instead to income distributional judgments, the existence of certain types of non-

7. Tinbergen (1958), p. 40.
8. See Koopmans (1957), Essay 1.
9. Further, certain circumstances may rule out the achievement of Pareto optimality through the competitive mechanism, but not decentralized procedures in general.
10. Tinbergen (1958), p. 39.
11. Cf. Dasgupta and Pearce (1972).

market interdependences between individuals and groups,[12], and so on.

It should be noticed that while the difference between the first and the second approaches to shadow pricing is one of presentation and there is no real conflict between the two, the same does not hold for the differences between the third approach and the earlier two. The prices that would equate demand and supply under the competitive mechanism in a given economic environment may indeed have nothing very much to do with shadow prices in the two earlier senses.

11.5 Directional Corrections

Finally, a fourth approach to shadow pricing attempts only to adjust the results in 'the right direction', and chooses the exact shadow prices quite arbitrarily. For example, Mahbub-ul-Haq's (1963) suggestion that if u is the proportion of the employed labour force to total labour force and w the wage rate, then uw is an appropriate shadow price of labour, is of this type. Since u will be between 0 and 1, it will put the shadow price of labour between 0 and w, and the more severe the unemployment problem the lower will the shadow wage be. These qualitative characteristics would appeal to many, and the direction of correction may well be right under most circumstances, even though the exact formula used may lead to undercorrection *or* overshooting.

Another approach quite often used is to make an accounting cut in the wage rate in an arbitrary ratio for any economy with surplus labour and dual labour markets and to raise the interest rate correspondingly to get the shadow interest. These may induce the choice of more labour-intensive techniques than at market prices and such a change may be thought to be 'better'.

It is difficult to evaluate these exercises, since the motivation of the approach is quite different from those discussed earlier. One should also distinguish between the arbitrariness of having to do a lot of guesswork to estimate shadow prices according to one of the earlier approaches,[13] and the planned arbitrariness of this fourth approach. The motivations of these different approaches would seem to be completely different from each other, and the formulae used in the fourth approach cannot be evaluated in the same way as the formulae under the first three. These rules of thumb are, however, quite widely used, and while the meek may or may not inherit the earth, the humbler shadow prices have certainly conquered one government after another.

12. Some types of 'externalities' would rule out the existence of shadow prices in the sense of the dual, but not all.
13. The gaps in our information make such guesswork inevitable even for full-fledged programming models; see Chakravarty and Lefeber (1965), Srinivasan (1965), Manne and Rudra (1965), Weisskopf (1967), and Eckaus and Parikh (1968).

12 | Valuation of Labour

12.1 Introduction

The social cost of labour, as defined in Chapter 10, concentrated on only two aspects of employment, viz., its impact on present consumption and its impact on investment, i.e., on future consumption. While eqn (9.1) provided a relation between the supply of wage goods and employment, and therefore between future consumption and future employment, the framework was by no means robust enough to bear the weight of the many considerations that influence decisions on employment and labour use.

We may now begin by distinguishing between the different facets of economic life which may be influenced by an additional unit of employment in a particular project. First, there is the impact on the output of the project, say q. If the wage paid to the person thus employed is w, then $(q - w)$ is the change in project profits. Second, the person employed gains because his income rises to w from y, which is what he was earning previously. The value of y represents his income from some other job (e.g., in the unorganized sector), or his share of the family income if he was involved in a family enterprise. His gain is $(w - y)$. In Chapters 6 and 8 the reasons for $(w - y)$ being positive were discussed. Third, if he was in a family enterprise, or was being supported by his relatives, it is possible that he was producing a smaller value m of output than the income he was enjoying. If he came from the pool of the unemployed, then his contribution m to output would have been zero. This would be immediately obvious, if he was *openly* unemployed, while if he was in a state of disguised unemployment the fact of his zero net contribution to output would be hidden.[1] The gain of others who were

1. See Chapter 4.

supporting him, or the gain of the members of this joint family, would be $(y - m)$, since they were giving him y and getting back m from him in terms of his net productive contribution. The reasons for $(y - m)$ being positive were discussed in Chapter 6.

Fourth, we ought to look at the impact on the savings of these three groups, which would be $(q - w) s_1$, $(w - y) s_2$ and $(y - m) s_3$ respectively, when s_1, s_2 and s_3 are the savings ratios for the respective groups.

Fifth, even if the output of the family enterprise remains the same, there is no presumption that the rest of the family members would not have to work harder to make up for the loss of the person who is now employed elsewhere. In the model of Chapter 4, the conditions which would enable them exactly to make up for the loss were analysed.[2] These additional efforts, whether or not they compensate fully for the loss of the labour of the person leaving, do represent some cost for those who will now be working harder.[3]

Sixth, the person taking up this new job in the project may also be typically involved in harder work compared with what he was used to. This too would need evaluation in addition to the loss of output, if any.

Seventh, there is the recognition aspect of employment. This will add directly to the benefit side.[4]

Eighth, there are also other social consequences of additional employment not reflected in the market prices. The need to build up civic facilities and in general the costs of social investment related to additional employment must be brought in where relevant. This would raise the cost side, but the benefit side may be pushed up by the reduction of vagrancy and crime usually associated with open unemployment (and sometimes with disguised unemployment as well).

2. Representing the elasticity of marginal disutility from work with respect to individual hours of work as n, the absolute value of the elasticity of marginal utility of income with respect to individual income as m, the elasticities of output and marginal product of labour with respect to hours of work as G and g respectively, it can be shown that the elasticity η of the total supply of work with respect to the number of working members in the joint enterprise will be given by:

$$\eta = (n + m)/(n + mG + g). \tag{12.1}$$

The corresponding elasticity θ of output with respect to the number of working members will then equal:

$$\theta = \eta G. \tag{12.2}$$

On this see Sen (1966). See also Hymer and Resnick (1969).
3. See Chapter 4 and Sen (1966).
4. See Chapters 1 and 6.

12.2 The Shadow Wage

The considerations discussed in the last section are systematically presented in Table 12.1, leaving out the recognition aspect and the social effects.

Table 12.1

Components of the Shadow Wage

	Increase in income	Increase in savings	Increase in efforts
1. The project	$q - w$	$(q - w)s_1$	—
2. The migrant	$w - y$	$(w - y)s_2$	z_2
3. The peasant family	$y - m$	$(y - m)s_3$	z_3

Denoting the item in the ith row and jth column as r_{ij}, we can sum up these differences caused by additional employment in the wage sector by weighting them with a set of value parameters v_{ij}. The net result of these particular effects in terms of the given value weights is:[5]

$$\gamma = \sum_i \sum_j v_{ij} r_{ij}. \tag{12.3}$$

If the set of v_{ij} were the appropriate value weights in the programming sense and they represented all the relevant avenues of impact of employment on social welfare, then γ could be interpreted as the shadow price of labour (corresponding to the dual).[6] This corresponds to (dR/dL) in Chapter 10, and if there are no other constraints, we should go on using more labour as long as $\gamma > 0$.

We can also bring in the recognition aspect and what we called the social effects. Putting Λ for our assessment of the welfare value of the recognition aspect, and Γ for that of the direct social effects of additional employment,[7] we get the shadow price of labour p_{ϱ}^* as:

$$p_{\varrho}^* = \gamma + \Lambda + \Gamma. \tag{12.4}$$

5. Note that $r_{11} = (q - w)$, $r_{21} = (w - y)$, and so on. Also $r_{13} = 0$. See Sen (1972).
6. The additive form of (12.3) would be approximately correct for small changes, interpreting the value weights v_{ij} as the appropriate incremental rates.
7. The opportunity cost of labour migration *in excess* of the number of jobs created (cf. Harris and Todaro (1969), Harberger (1971), Stiglitz (1972), Mazumdar (1973) and others), can be included under Γ. See Chapter 6.

Note that Λ will not be negative whereas Γ can be positive *or* negative, since some effects (e.g., less crime, or less vagrancy) would be judged to be socially beneficial whereas others (e.g., social effects of overcrowding in urban centres where the project may be located) would be taken to be detrimental to society.

The shadow price in the other sense, viz., the magnitude to which $f(L)$ should be equated for optimal use of labour (discussed in Chapter 11), will be obtained from eqn (12.4) by solving it for q. This yields:

$$
\begin{aligned}
w^* = [w\{(v_{11} - v_{21}) &+ (v_{12}s_1 - v_{22}s_2)\} + y\{(v_{21} - v_{31}) \\
&+ (v_{22}s_2 - v_{32}s_3)\} + m(v_{31} + v_{32}s_3) - (v_{23}z_2 + v_{33}z_3) \\
&+ \Lambda + \Gamma]/(v_{11} + v_{12}s_1).
\end{aligned} \tag{12.5}
$$

12.3 Ownership, Control and the Shadow Prices

The choice of the value weights and of the objective function and the set of constraints from which these weights will be derived pose a number of problems. Some of them have already been discussed. For example, the considerations underlying the weight on investment p^I in terms of consumption were discussed in Chapter 10.[8] One of the important respects in which the conception of the shadow wage developed in the last section differs from that of the social cost of labour in Chapter 10 is the explicit valuation of income distribution considerations.

In eqns (12.3), (12.4) and (12.5) we have three distinct weights on consumption, viz., v_{11}, v_{21}, depending on whose consumption it happens to be.[9] Similarly, instead of using one price of investment p^I, we have here three alternative weights v_{12}, v_{22} and v_{32}, depending on whose saving it is. The intention of these distinctions is to permit the use of income distributional weights.[10] The objective function for planning may not indeed be indifferent between the consumption of the different groups

---

8. See also O. Eckstein (1957), Marglin (1963a), (1966), (1967), Feldstein (1964), (1972), Sen (1968), Dixit (1968), UNIDO (1968), (1972), and Little and Mirrlees (1969). On the inadequacy of dispensing with p^I and doing the exercise in terms of a weighted average of flow interest rates, a point of view that is often advocated (see, for example, Harberger (1972)), see Feldstein (1972).

9. These are described as weights on income Q, but are in fact weights on consumption, since the parts of the incomes that are saved and invested get additional weights through v_{12}, v_{22} and v_{32}.

10. Income distributional considerations may enter the weighting of z_2 and z_3 as well, i.e., may affect v_{23} and v_{33}.

involved, nor between their investments. In practice the operative relevance of the distinction between weights on the savings of different groups, i.e., between v_{12}, v_{22} and v_{32}, may not be very important, partly because it would be difficult to do the calculations relevant for each,[11] but also because the savings activities of workers and peasants may not really be very large, so that the weighting of these operations need not alter the evaluation of the project substantially. The contrast between the consumption of different classes is, however, a very significant aspect of project evaluation. In eqns (12.3)–(12.5), the distinction between v_{11}, v_{21} and v_{31} would reflect our relative priorities on issues of inter-class distributions. The categorization can, of course, be easily extended to cover different types of workers (e.g., white-collar vis-à-vis manual, or high-salaried vis-à-vis low-paid), so that we need not restrict ourselves to these three groups.

Since the formulae presented here may give the impression that the process of evaluation is essentially a mechanical one, it is worth emphasizing that the precise framework chosen and the value weights to be used will depend on institutional assumptions as well as on a reading of the political situation. For example, it matters a lot whether the project is publicly owned and its profits go to the government, or whether it is under private ownership, with profits being entirely private income except for the part that is taxed away. The income distributional considerations may be thought to have some bite when the project is privately owned, since the weights v_{11}, v_{21} and v_{31}, reflecting the valuation of consumption benefits for capitalists, workers and peasants (or labourers in the unorganized sector), will tend to diverge.

Similarly, the existing tax system and the political and administrative scope for taxation will affect both the quantitative magnitudes involved, particularly the savings ratios s_1, s_2 and s_3, and their weights, particularly the weights on savings v_{12}, v_{22} and v_{32}.[12] The exercise of project evaluation will depend crucially on these political and social questions.

It also makes a lot of difference what the mode of employment happens to be.[13] If the system of employment used in the project is not wage-based, the formulae (12 3)–(12.5) will have to be correspondingly modified. Economic evaluation of non-wage operations in terms of

---

11. Since the distribution of power depends significantly on that of wealth, there is in fact a good case for making the distinction in question, even though the differential weights are difficult to derive from the usual policy objectives of planning.
12. See Chapter 10.
13. See Chapters 3 and 7.

concepts relevant to a wage system can be very misleading indeed.[14] The use of a non-wage framework may not, in fact, prove to be particularly difficult. Essentially this would amount to the merging of project profits with the income of labour, which can be formally brought into the calculations through putting $w = y$, which would make the item $(w - y)$ drop out, and the replacement of $(q - w)$ by $(q - y)$. Furthermore, if the labourers work in their own farms rather than coming from their farms to some non-wage enterprise in the unorganized sector, it will frequently be correct to put $y = m$ as well.[15]

While the existing treatises on project evaluation provide a usable basis for economic evaluation of alternative projects, they have not been too deeply concerned with the institutional aspect of the valuation of labour. With that in mind, in this work the emphasis has been precisely on the institutional side of the problem.[16] Social valuation of labour can be seen to depend on the precise structure of ownership and control, and, of course, on the modes of employment.

14. An important example comes from the *Studies in the Economics of Farm Management* done by the Government of India, in which it was not uncommon to use the market wage in valuing the labour of peasants, which frequently resulted in the conclusion that much of Indian agriculture was being run on 'losses'. 'This is an alarming situation, for if 50 per cent or more of the farmers are carrying on the business at a loss, the farming community cannot be considered to be comfortably placed in any sense of the term.' (*Report on Madras*, 1955–6, p. 146.) Comfortably placed they are not, but not for this reason. On this, see Appendix C.

[15] See Chapters 3 and 6.

[16] The evaluator attempting to use the approach towards employment presented in this book is, however, advised to look also at the *Guidelines for Project Evaluation*, UNIDO (1972), authored jointly by Partha Dasgupta, Stephen Marglin and myself. I have tried to avoid duplication here, and have concentrated on issues specifically relevant for employment policy.

13 | Concluding Remarks

13.1 Introduction

'If by a miracle', sighed Gunnar Myrdal, 'the cultivators in South Asia could be induced to work more diligently, production would rise dramatically.'[1] Perhaps so, perhaps not.[2] What is certainly true is that this diagnosis, even if correct, does not point instantly towards some remedial strategy. Any work on employment policy must begin with a sorting out of things that are within the control of the planners and things that are not, and while attitudes to work can certainly be influenced in the long run (and even in the short, when there are social upheavals), it is not excessively likely that an appeal to diligence will by itself be a riotous success.

At the risk of over-simplification we can distinguish between four sets of structural factors that will constrain employment policy: (i) technological possibilities, (ii) institutional features, (iii) political feasibilities, and (iv) behavioural characteristics. These factors are, of course, interlinked with one another, as we have seen in earlier chapters, and in studying them the interdependence must be borne in mind. The valuation of labour will depend on the totality of all these features. And the appropriate employment policies must be based on an assessment of the extent to which these structural relations can be deliberately influenced. Myrdal's question about the attitude to work is just one of the relations that need examination.

1. Myrdal (1968), p. 1294.
2. As we saw in Chapter 4, the existence of surplus labour is not ruled out by a positive marginal product of labour effort. Myrdal's view can be interpreted as an expression of the belief that 'the real cost of labour' j is relatively high in South Asian agriculture.

13.2 Variables and Constants

Technology, institutions and politics are all variable over time. What is less clear is whether they can also be varied in the short run and in certain planned directions. In Chapter 2, I contrasted two views of technical progress, and argued that much would depend on the precise extent to which technology can be expected to respond to our research, experience, and learning by doing. Given the particular problems of utilization of labour in developing countries, the case for aiming technical progress in certain specific directions can be easily argued. The directions involved may vary from the general pursuit of superior labour-intensive techniques (Chapters 2 and 5) to the development of techniques yielding a different seasonal pattern of production, so as to redistribute the demand for labour more evenly over different months (Chapter 8). Since the variation of the quality of output is frequently one barrier to the use of less mechanized techniques,[3] technical progress aimed at improving the output quality in 'the informal sector' is obviously also an important pursuit.

At the general level of economic analysis there is not a great deal we can say on this type of issue, except to indicate certain broad directions for research and experimentation. In those fields where technical research tends to be relatively removed from practical economic operations, the need for deliberate orientation towards important economic issues seems substantial. For example, the fact that institutional research on the technology of producing rice has been conducted largely under conditions of assured water supply in experimental stations may have been a barrier to the evolution of strains that would have greater immediate applicability in the fields.[4]

Economic forces do, of course, always influence the direction of technological adaptation in the actual fields of operation. This applies not merely to the development of new technologies but also to the use of existing ones. The utilization of second-hand machinery in sectors with low wages and high interest rates is a case in point. In effect, the equilibrium prices of old and new machinery in a high-wage sector reflect differential profitability for the low-wage sector and it can be shown that

---

3. See Stewart (1972), (1972a) and (1972b). Also the Report of the ILO mission to Kenya, ILO (1972). Frances Stewart also brings out the importance of shifting the pattern of demand to variants of the same good which can be produced by more labour-intensive techniques.
4. The contrast between the success of the green revolution in wheat and the relatively indifferent results in rice relates partly to this. See Sen (1972a). Also Srinivasan (1971) and Dharm Narain (1972). See also Ishikawa and Ohkawa (1972).

the older machinery will be the more profitable choice for the latter when transportation costs are low.[5]

As far as institutional structures are concerned, I have tried to discuss in some detail their relevance to labour use, technological choice and employment policy (Chapters 3–10). Institutions come into employment policy in two different ways. First, optimal technological choices depend substantially on the precise institutional framework within which the choice has to be made, and the alternatives have to be evaluated with explicit reference to the mode of employment, methods of organization, patterns of ownership, and such features. Second, employment policy may also be geared towards institutional restructuring which would bring about better utilization of the labour force. While the first range of policies would be institution–specific, the second would have to go beyond that into the dynamic of institutional change. Evaluations of labour cost and employment, as presented in Chapters 11 and 12, help primarily in the former exercise, but they also provide the background to the latter task, since the case for institutional change in the context of employment policy can be brought out explicitly only in terms of the relative performance of different modes of employment and other institutional features.[6]

The third set of features, viz. political feasibilities, relates closely to the institutional structure. Different types of political constraints affecting employment policy were discussed in Chapters 7, 9 and 10, and their implications were explored. The extent to which one has to take these constraints as given is a matter of fundamental importance for employment policy. This question takes us well beyond the limits of economics, but, as we have seen, economic policies can be discussed only in a specific political and social context.

The question of behavioural characteristics referred to by Myrdal (1968) is also crucial to labour use. In considering the attitude to work one must look not only at the 'cultural pattern',[7] but also at the institutional structure, since the behaviour of people will be a reflection of both. The point can be easily illustrated in terms of the model of non-wage labour allocation presented in Chapter 3 and used extensively in subsequent chapters. The variable h is essentially a cultural one, while the variable α is largely institutional. The latter represents the sharing arrangements of the output produced and reflects the institutional back-

5. See § 7.3 above. Also Sen (1962a) and Smith (1972).
6. Even for bargaining with foreign suppliers of technical know-how, a systematic analysis of alternative benefits and costs is an important strategic requirement. See Sen (1971a), UNCTAD (1972), and Cooper (1972).
7. Myrdal (1968), p. 1078. See also the critique of Myrdal's position by Lal (1972a).

ground, such as the type of ownership, the relation of ownership to operation, the mode of employment, and so on. Even when the value of h is entirely given and 'the cultural pattern' is unchangeable, the allocation of labour will vary depending on the institutional arrangements reflected in α. The 'real cost of labour' j being given by $z/[\alpha + (1 - \alpha)h]$ brings out the mixture of the two types of considerations in their impact on labour use, with which Myrdal is concerned. The interdependence is also clear in employment policy and in the calculation of the shadow price of labour, as is obvious from eq (5.3)–(5.5).

Even the value of capital intensity and the investment requirement for extending employment and output depend on the institutional structure, as was brought out in Chapter 5. The contrast between the degree of mechanization and the degree of capital intensity was based partly on variations in the rate of utilization of capital, as well as on differences in the absorption of resources in the form of working capital; both these issues were seen to be related to institutional features. It is this interrelationship between institutions, feasibilities and behavioural characteristics that makes the determination of employment and technological policies such a complex exercise, involving a great deal more than a vigorous use of optimization techniques.

13.3 Partial Ignorance and Policy-making

One of the difficulties of using a very broad framework of analysis involving institutional, social and political factors, is the near certainty that its practical application will be extremely difficult. Methodologically, one is faced with the choice between, on the one hand, using an uncomplicated model which will be easy to apply, but which will miss many important dimensions of employment policy and technological choice, and on the other, using a more comprehensive model which would be more appropriate if it could be applied but which would be difficult to apply. In some ways in this work we have tried to achieve a compromise between these two approaches. Nevertheless, the difficulties of estimation and evaluation involved in using the structure of shadow prices discussed in Chapters 11 and 12 may be quite considerable.

It is worth emphasizing, in this context, that the exercise of systematic economic evaluation should not be viewed as an all or nothing game. In some circumstances it may be possible to be certain that the relevant shadow prices would lie within a certain range, without knowing precisely what these shadow prices should be. It is this type of constraint that has led to the increasing use of sensitivity analysis in project evaluation.[8] However, sensitivity analysis only shows which shadow prices have

8. See UNIDO (1972). Also Datta-Chaudhuri and Sen (1970).

to be estimated very accurately and which somewhat more approximately. It is, in fact, possible to go beyond that and to define rigorously the decisions that can be made with confidence in a state of partial ignorance and those that cannot. Formally, it is possible to think of social preference as a partial ordering rather than as a complete ordering. This type of a framework has been used in other problems of policy-making and planning,[9] and it can be applied to employment policy as well.

In terms of eq (12.3) one might find that the value of each v_{ij} and each r_{ij} lies within the sets V_{ij} and R_{ij}, respectively. Considering all possible combinations of these values we can easily define the price range H in which the shadow price of labour γ will lie.[10] In evaluating any project one can then use not one combination of shadow prices but a set of combinations and it can be easily checked that this will mean that the ranking of projects will be a partial ordering, which will be transitive, but not necessarily complete. That is, if project A is judged superior to B, and B to C, then project A will also be judged superior to project C. However, cases can arise, and in fact typically will quite often arise, in which two projects cannot be ranked against each other. Such incompleteness of ranking is, however, not a real deficiency, since it only reflects the extent of partial ignorance characterizing the choice problem. Arbitrary choices between them may have to be made, but the approach outlined here would simply define precisely which choices are arbitrary and which can be made with confidence, even in the given state of partial ignorance.

The alternative to this would be to leave out a whole set of questions which we have been discussing in this book, and which, I would argue, make employment an important goal and employment policy a serious exercise. While the complexity of institutional, behavioural, technological and political features does make many of the choices difficult, there is no way in which one can escape this difficulty without shutting

---

9. On its use for income distributional judgments and policies, see Sen (1973). For a more general analysis see also Sen (1970), Chapters 7, 7*, 9 and 9*.

10. That is, H is given by

$$[\inf_{\substack{v_{ij}\epsilon V_{ij} \\ r_{ij}\epsilon R_{ij}}} \sum_i \sum_j v_{ij}r_{ij}, \quad \sup_{\substack{v_{ij}\epsilon V_{ij} \\ r_{ij}\epsilon R_{ij}}} \sum_i \sum_j v_{ij}r_{ij}].$$

Similarly, a range can be defined for the other interpretations of the shadow price of labour given by (12.4) and (12 5).

one's eyes to significant aspects of technological choice and employment policy. A partial ordering derived in the way described would reflect our ability to say something, though not everything, whereas the requirement of a complete ordering is a compulsion to open our mouth on every choice that can arise. Happily, silence and babbling are not the only possible approaches to employment planning.

One final remark. Employment policy is a matter of interest not only for the government, but also for the citizen. A book on employment policy need not, therefore, aim exclusively at those in power. This one certainly does not. Based on the belief that the cause of employment is best served by public awareness of the nature of the problem, much of this book has been devoted to studying employment and technology in very broad terms. The analysis of conceptual questions (Chapters 1–3), measurement problems (Chapters 4–5), and institutional and structural issues (Chapters 6–8) in employment and technology, while relevant for the making of employment policy and technological choice in general (Chapters 9–10) and for the use of cost–benefit analysis in particular (Chapters 11–12), has been geared to something more than that. Policy-making is, ultimately, a social process and not merely a bureaucratic one, and the precise choice of a cost–benefit system, important as it is, may make less eventual difference than a wider understanding of the nature of the employment problem. This work has been aimed primarily at the latter, and at the former only as one part of that general problem.

Appendix A | On the Measurement of Unemployment in India

A.1 Evaluation of Unemployment in India

More, I suspect, has been written on the unemployment problem of India than on that of any other country in the world.[1] There have been varying estimates of the quantum of unemployment in India and the figures obtained have diverged widely.[2] Faced with this problem, there are two alternative ways of proceeding. One is to trace the divergences systematically to differences in concepts and estimation procedures and then to evaluate them in terms of their economic relevance. The other is to cry the whole thing off. I fear that something akin to the latter is now taking place and it is important to discuss whether such pessimism is justified. I would like to re-examine the picture in the light of the conceptual framework outlined in this book.

In his classic study of Asia, Gunnar Myrdal examined 'several important specimen studies of employment, unemployment, and underemployment that were supported by South Asian governments', the pride of place being taken by the Indian estimates.[3] In his concluding section, entitled 'The Fundamemtal Weakness of Attempts to Quantify "Employment" and "Unemployment" in South Asian Countries', Myrdal argued:

In general, these studies have been led to ask the kind of questions Western economists would wish to investigate in their own countries. At

---

1. For a good introduction to the literature, see Sanghvi (1969) and *The Report of the Committee of Experts on Unemployment Estimates*, Planning Commission of India, Government of India, New Delhi, 1970.
2. Including Professor Theodore Schultz's estimation that there was *no* surplus labour in India at the time of the influenza epidemic of 1918–19 (see Schultz (1964)).
3. Myrdal (1968), Appendix 16.

the same time, however, it is often acknowledged that Western categories cannot be transferred intact to a South Asian environment . . . The orientation of these studies – fully as much as the errors in their execution – lies at the root of the problem. Attempts to measure phenomena that have no existence in reality or, at best, lead a shadow life remote from the image in the minds of investigators, are demanded by the modern approach to the study of South Asian countries. Unfortunately, the persons responsible for statistical enquiries in the region, and behind them the Western and indigenous economists and planners, have been reluctant to scrap received doctrine and to begin afresh by formulating a new conceptual kit appropriate to their economic conditions.[4]

The advice to use a new conceptual kit was not, however, accompanied by any concrete suggestion as to what this kit might include, and Myrdal's own focus seems to have been mainly on the necessity 'to scrap received doctrine'. Myrdal's doubts have been shared by others and his advice seems to have been well received. The meaningfulness of the estimates of employment and unemployment has recently been subjected to thundering criticism, very much in tune with Myrdal's attack.

A result of this process of rethinking can be seen in the *Report of the Committee of Experts on Unemployment Estimates.*[5] I shall refer to it, by a rearrangement of the initials, as EUREC.[6] It argues that 'the concept of unemployment is not meaningful in the conditions prevailing in rural India',[7] and makes similar criticisms of unemployment estimates for urban India as well. EUREC ends up with the following conclusion:

In the light of what is said above, it is our view that estimates of growth in the labour force, of additional employment generated by the Plans and of unemployment at the end of the Plan period, presented in one-dimensional magnitudes are neither meaningful nor useful as indicators of the economic situation. We recommend this practice be given up.[8]

That 'one-dimensional magnitudes' can be misleading is certainly true, as is the view that 'Western categories' often do not apply to countries like

4. Myrdal (1968), p. 2221. Everyone seems to accuse others of applying 'Western' concepts to the problems of developing countries. Myrdal meets his match in P. C. Mahalanobis: 'Steeped as he is in the concepts of the West, Myrdal cannot help evaluating the history and events of South Asia within the framework of those concepts.' (Mahalanobis (1969), p. 1119.)
5. See n. 1 above.
6. Since I am going to be somewhat critical of EUREC's recommendations, I take this opportunity of recording my appreciation of the Report for its technical brilliance and for its definitive exploration of one – and, in my judgment, limited – approach to the question.
7. EUREC, p. 13.
8. EUREC, p. 31.

India. That alternative estimates give widely divergent views of the magnitude of unemployment is also true. The question, however, is whether scrapping is the best way of meeting these problems.[9]

EUREC has recommended 'separate estimation of different segments of the labour force, taking into account such important characteristics as region (state), sex, age, rural—urban residence, status or class of worker and educational attainment'.[10] This is certainly a positive step, but it is worth enquiring whether or not it gets us off the hook. I shall argue that it does not.

First, the differences between estimates of unemployment (and of course of employment) arise to a great extent from conflicting *concepts* of employment. These differences hold not only for the 'one-dimensional' total figures but also for figures split up in terms of region, sex, age and such things. For each of these classes different employment estimates would follow from different concepts of employment. A stubborn refusal to come to grips with the conceptual problems underlying unemployment weakens not only the total figures but also the figures for different sectors, classes, etc.[11]

Second, the so-called 'conflicting estimates' of unemployment using different approaches are interesting *precisely because* they conflict. The different concepts of employment correspond to different *aspects* of the phenomenon (see Chapters 1 and 4), and each has some relevance. An attempt to get one 'consistent' estimate only will be, it seems to me, fundamentally misconceived. One would like to see different estimates based on different aspects of unemployment, since the contrasts between them are important for employment policy, as we have seen in earlier chapters. The answer to one-dimensionality does not lie in splitting it up into *sectors*, but in giving alternative calculations of the employment figures using different *approaches* which reflect different *aspects* of employment.

9. Since this monograph was completed, the *Draft Fifth Five Year Plan 1974—79* has been published by the Government of India. It discontinues the earlier practice of presenting estimates of Indian unemployment, without replacing it by anything comparable, and in justification quotes the recommendations of EUREC.

10. EUREC, p. 31.

11. The main 'change in the present procedure of classifying a person as employed or unemployed' recommended by EUREC is in terms of reorienting the various surveys to take note 'of the activity of the respondents on *each day* in the reference week' (p. 31), and not merely in terms of whether the person worked for *any day* during the week. This is an improvement even though entirely *within* the old framework, as is the suggestion that data be collected in terms of sub-rounds, which will catch the seasonal pattern.

Third, the value of employment figures has to be judged not merely in terms of their use by the government but also in the context of their role in educating the public and in facilitating public discussion of policy issues.[12] As we have seen, major problems of employment policy in relation to technological choice arise from 'feasibility constraints', in which the role of social awareness and public involvement is crucial. The public is interested in figures of employment and unemployment from different points of view, and it *is* concerned also with the overall picture, no matter how hungry it may be for sector-wise, region-wise matrices. The over-all figures do have their usefulness, and by giving alternative estimates using different concepts after properly spelling them out, a contribution can be made to public understanding of the magnitude of the problem.

Doubts about the interpretation and relevance of Indian unemployment statistics are perfectly justified. It is the remedy that is worrying.

A.2. The Census Data

There are three main sources of data on unemployment in the Indian working population:

    (i) the decennial censuses;

    (ii) the National Sample Surveys;

and (iii) the employment exchange registers and the Employment Market Information Programme.

While employment data have been collected in one form or another since 1871 and more systematically in each census since 1941, there is currently only one that gives usable data on unemployment for the entire country, viz., the 1961 census.[13] The unemployment data collected by the 1941 census were not tabulated and in the 1951 census data were collected only for three states, viz., Uttar Pradesh, Bihar, and Bombay (including Saurashtra and Kutch). The 1971 census data on unemployment have not yet been processed, and its coverage is, in any case, going to be narrower in some important respects. So we are left with one vintage year, viz., 1961.

12. The Committee of Experts on Unemployment Estimates was, of course, restrained by its terms of reference to 'go into the estimates of unemployment worked out for the previous Plans and the data and methodology used in arriving at them and advise the Planning Commission on the various issues connected therewith, in particular, the alternative methods of analysis, computation and presentation that may be adopted for the Fourth Five Year Plan (1969–74) in the ten-year perspective of 1969–79' (EUREC, p. 1). Whether feeding the public with relevant information on employment and unemployment falls within these terms of reference, is a matter of interpretation.

13. *Census of India* 1961, p. 35, italics added.

The 1961 census found only 1.4 million people unemployed in the whole of India. Of these 0.6 million were in rural areas, and amounted to less than 1 per cent of the rural labour force. For urban areas the percentages of unemployment were 3.25 and 1.48 respectively for males and females.

While these figures are low enough to put many advanced countries to shame, they mainly reflect the stringent nature of the test by which a person is classified as unemployed by the census authorities. For 'seasonal work like cultivation, livestock, dairying, household industry etc., if the person has had *some regular work of more than one hour a day* throughout the greater part of the working season', he was taken as engaged in work. 'In the case of regular employment in any trade, profession, service, business or commerce the basis of work will be satisfied if the person was employed *during any of the fifteen days preceding* the day on which you [the investigator] visited the household.'[14] The unemployed were those who were not thus engaged in work but were 'seeking work', though the instructions did not explain how the enumerators should interpret the concept of 'seeking work'.[15] To qualify as unemployed one had to fail the test of 'working' and pass the test of 'seeking work', overcoming on the way various obstacles like being put under some other category of 'not working' people, such as HW ('housewife', 'engaged in unpaid home duties'), ST ('student'), or B ('a beggar, a vagrant or an independent woman without indication of source of income and others of unspecified source of existence').[16]

How does this relate to the conceptual framework discussed in this book? Obviously it is not based on the 'production approach', since many people in a family can be putting in one or two hours a day in cultivation, although some of them could move elsewhere without affecting output (see Chapter 4). The philosophy of the approach is based

14. *Census of India* 1961, p. 35, italics added. Further, the instructions went on to explain that 'if on the check or the revision round such a person is found to be unemployed no change in the original entry should be made', and that 'a person who is working but was absent from his work during the fifteen days preceding the day on which enumerated or even exceeding the period of fifteen days due to illness or other causes should be treated as *worker*' (p. 35).
15. Two categories were distinguished: 'a person who has not been employed before but is seeking employment for the first time' and 'a person employed before but now out of employment and seeking employment' (p. 39).
16. *Census of India* 1961, p. 39. Here at last we run into a definitive disposal of the problem of Peachum's beggars and of young Macheath, posed in Chapter 1. They were 'not working', but nor were they 'unemployed'! The explanation about 'an independent woman without indication of source of income' puts even Ginny Jenny in danger of getting into this double-negative box.

essentially on a mixture of the 'income aspect' and the 'recognition aspect'. Having 'worked' is of course, in itself an ambiguous concept and the instructions do not specify what should count as 'work'. While no explicit reference is made to income, still, in normal usage, work in this context would be associated with receiving emoluments, either in the form of wages or salaries, or as profits of one's own enterprises, or as part of the income of a family engaged in some family enterprise, e.g., cultivation of land.[17] Further, one has to pass the test of 'seeking work', which relates to the question of 'recognising' oneself as unemployed and would presumably distinguish a worker from kitchen-happy housewives and other 'satisfied' members of the 'not working' population.

The test, therefore, is based on the *intersection* of two criteria (see Fig. A.1). If one recognizes oneself as unemployed and 'seeks work', but regularly does one or two hours of work in the family farm, one does not qualify as 'not working' and therefore has no chance of being taken as unemployed. Similarly if one is 'not working' but *not* 'seeking work', then again one is not unemployed. The census definition of the unemployed covers precisely those who pass *both* the tests. The census-recognised 'unemployed' has to traverse a narrow path between Scylla and Charybdis.

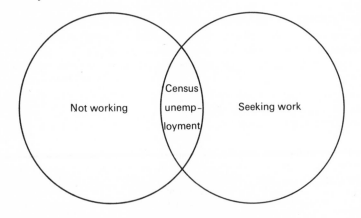

Fig. A.1. *The Census View of the Unemployed*

17. The definition of 'a family worker' is very generous: 'A *Family Worker* is a member who works, without receiving wages in cash or kind, in an industry, business or trade conducted mainly by members of the family and ordinarily does at least one hour of work every day during the working season ... For the purpose of this definition members of a family may be drawn from beyond the limits of the household by ties of blood or marriage.' (*Census of India* 1961, p. 38.)

Not surprisingly the figure is very low. In fact it can be argued that even *within* this framework of the intersection of the two criteria, the census biases the estimation by taking a narrow view of each. 'Seeking work' is not the only possible interpretation of the recognition approach. A person may feel that he or she is unemployed but not seek work if none seems likely to crop up. 'Seeking work' involves a recognition not only of one's own status but also of the state of the labour market as well as one's chances of obtaining something there. The interpretation of the recognition aspect is, therefore, rather narrow.

The same is true of the income aspect. The income approach should, strictly speaking, count as employed only those who would not receive their share of the family income if they stopped working (see Chapter 4). The test is not whether one is working and receiving an income, but whether one is receiving an income *because* one is working. I would not, however, put much weight on this distinction, not only because the contrast is difficult to test empirically (though in principle it is testable), but also because it is commonly presumed – and I think with justification – that sharing the joint family's income from farming and similar activities does involve an obligation to help with the work. An 'unpaid family worker' gets paid through his share of the family income, and if he should go away (or stand around with his hands neatly folded), the chances are that he would not get much economic support. Thus, while the census interpretation of the income approach *is* narrow, it probably does not make a big quantitative difference, given the social system. But precisely for the same reason, the criterion of income – and *a fortiori* its intersection with that of recognition – makes it very difficult for anyone to be enumerated as 'unemployed' in rural India. People must eat to survive and if the economic support the able-bodied male receives is conditional on helping in the family's cultivation and other joint activities, he will tend to be counted in as 'employed', especially since even one or two hours of work a day during the busy season would qualify one for the status of being 'working'. It is, in fact, a bit amazing that people qualifying in the census as 'unemployed' (i.e., 'not working' and 'seeking work') manage to get a living!

The picture is, of course, less demanding for the urban areas, since the wage system makes it difficult for an employed man to get help from his able-bodied dependents. But the amount of remunerative work one has to find to get by is rather little. I have some difficulty with EUREC's argument that 'the definitions used in the 1961 Census cannot be said to have caused an undue bias towards classifying as "employed" those engaged in the *non-agricultural sector*, since employment in this sector is generally more stable than in agriculture and a person reported as working on "at least one day during the fortnight preceding the day of enumeration" may indeed be presumed to have been in some kind of employment'.[18] More stable than in agriculture it certainly is, but is it stable enough to justify the concluding presumption? In fact, we know from the National Sample Survey data for roughly the same period that the number of people who worked for short hours (28 hours or less) just about equalled the number who did not work on a single day during the *week* preceding the survey,[19] and the latter included both those who did not work a single day in the preceding *fortnight* and others who did work in the last but one week but not in the last week.

To conclude, the census figures of unemployment have the following characteristics:

(i) They are based on the *intersection* of the class of the unemployed in terms of the 'income approach' and the class in terms of the 'recognition approach', and are therefore narrower than each.

(ii) The interpretation of the 'income approach' is narrow.

(iii) The interpretation of the 'recognition approach' is also narrow.

(iv) The 'production approach' is not used.

A.3. The National Sample Survey Data

The basic approach of the National Sample Survey is similar to that of the census, but there are some differences. There have been variations from round to round but the basic principle is one of taking the intersection of the class of the unemployed in terms of the 'income approach' and that according to the 'recognition approach'. However, the interpretation of each approach is, on the whole, a little less narrow that in the census, though in one respect it is even more narrow, and in some respects the restrictions are not comparable.

The criteria have varied from round to round. In the 11th, 12th and 13th rounds, surveyed during 1956–8, both one day and one week immediately preceding the day of enquiry were chosen for reference, and a person was treated as 'employed' if he had gainful work on that day. A person not having such work would be classified as 'unemployed' if he were either 'seeking work', or fell into the category of 'not seeking but available for work'. In both respects, therefore, the criterion is less narrow than in the census. However, since the 14th round (1958–9) the criterion of being in work has been to have worked 'at least one day during the reference week', which narrows the concepts towards the census test. Further, beginning with the 16th round (1960–1) persons

18. EUREC, p. 24.
19. National Sample Survey, 17th Round (1961–2). See also EUREC, p. 86.

below the age of 15, or aged 60 or more, have been excluded from the figure of the unemployed even if they are actively seeking work. Moreover, since the 16th round for the urban areas the category of people 'not seeking but available for work' has been excluded from the class of the unemployed. Both these changes make the criterion of unemployment substantially narrower. By virtue of the age restriction, the NSS unemployed now correspond to the intersection of three sets, viz., those 'not employed' (in terms of the reference week of one week), those available for work, and those between 15—60 years of age. By virtue of the second restriction, those counted as available for work in the urban areas includes only people who were 'looking for work', rather than being just 'available for work'.

After the 17th round (1961—2), the rural labour surveys were discontinued, since 'it was felt that the concept of unemployment as the term is generally understood, was not applicable to rural areas'.[20] The data on rural unemployment were obtained only from 'the integrated household schedule'.[21]

The 'unemployed' as defined by the NSS have tended, on the whole, to form a somewhat broader category than the 'unemployed' according to the census of 1961. Not surprisingly, the unemployment count in the 1961 census is less than that in the corresponding National Sample Surveys (the 16th round, 1960—1, and the 17th round, 1961—2), as can be seen from Table A.1.

The percentage of unemployment is much lower according to the census in every category except for urban males. The shortfall of the census figure is large in rural areas and remarkably so for females. This is not surprising in view of what has been said already. The criterion of being 'available' for work, even if not actively 'seeking' work, did give the NSS a wider coverage. This is especially important in rural areas where the channels for seeking work are not always accessible, particularly for women, who frequently cannot seek work actively given the social arrangements. There is also the difference of the reference period being one week for the NSS and a fortnight for the census for non-seasonal activities. However, since the census had a fixed reference period of a fortnight in February, while the NSS had a moving reference week and usually three visits a year to each household, the direction of the difference is not clear. For rural areas the census criterion of merely an hour's work each day during the busy season is, of course, a remarkably easy

20. EUREC, p. 25.
21. EUREC has recommended the resumption of rural labour force surveys (p. 25) and has made a number of other recommendations which would bring in additional data (see EUREC, Chapters IV and V).

Table A.1

'Unemployment' as a Percentage of the Labour Force in Urban and
Rural India according to the 1961 Census and the 16th and the 17th
Rounds of the National Sample Survey

Sector	Sex	Census	NSS 16th round 1960–1	NSS 17th round 1961–2
Rural	Males	0.50	2.59	3.74
	Females	0.10	6.49	8.53
Urban	Males	3.23	2.47	3.02
	Females	1.42	2.21	3.32

Source: EUREC, Appendix II, by P. Visaria, Table 20, p. 86.

test to pass in order to be classed as 'working', thereby yielding a very narrow coverage for the 'not working'. I have discussed this earlier.

The only surprising result, therefore, is that the census count for the unemployed *urban males* turns out to be *larger* than that of the NSS. While the factors that give the NSS a wider coverage would be less important for urban males (e.g., urban males *can* 'seek' work relatively easily), there is no clear reason to expect a *reversal* of the usual ranking. The exclusion of people over 60 or under 15 from the NSS data for these rounds may be a factor, but it is not likely that this would explain much of the difference. Perhaps part of the explanation lies in the organizational structure of the two enquiries, e.g., the selection of households, the training of the investigators, the coverage of the NSS sample frame (the NSS sample was based on the 1951 census, which had a different definition of urban areas), and such differences.[22]

There is also a question of timing, since unemployment figures do fluctuate over time and the timing of the NSS surveys differed from that of the census. The census data were collected during February and March 1961, while the 17th round of the NSS was conducted during September 1961–July 1962, and the 16th round, which was meant to cover July 1960–June 1961, was in fact fielded almost entirely during July–

22. Heather and Vijay Joshi have told me that in their study of the Bombay labour situation they felt that the difference could have arisen from the fact that the pavement dwellers were often missed out by the NSS due to its concentration on 'households'; in comparison, the census enumerators tried to get a more complete coverage.

December 1960. It is often argued that urban unemployment is a reflection of rural unemployment and that 'any seasonal influx into urban areas of the unemployed from rural areas would probably occur during the slack agricultural season, usually after December'.[23] If so, this could explain part of the difference between the 16th round and the census.[24] The difference between the 17th round and the census figures for urban male unemployment is not all that great anyway, the respective percentages being 3.23 and 3.02 — a difference of 0.21 per cent of the urban male labour force.

A.4. Data from the Employment Exchanges

The live registers of the employment exchanges give information on the number of job seekers. These figures have been used in the past by the Indian Planning Commission to construct estimates of urban unemployment in India. There is an obvious problem in this, since a person can be employed and still seek another job, and the employment exchanges do not ask whether one is already employed or not. Not surprisingly, the number of people on the live registers of the employment exchanges tends to exceed the unemployment figures of the NSS.

The difference is, in fact, huge. In December 1966 the number on the live registers of the employment exchanges was 2.6 million; it was 2.7 million in December 1967.[25] On the other hand the proportion of the unemployed in the urban labour force according to the 21st round of the NSS, surveyed during 1966–7, was only 1.6 per cent.[26] Given that the urban labour force was about 33 million, this amounted to a total unemployment figure of 0.53 million, i.e., about one-fifth of the number on the live registers.[27] How do these figures tally with each other?[28]

23. EUREC, p. 85.
24. Note that despite this fact the *rural* unemployment figures are much larger for the 16th round NSS than for the census. There is, however, no contradiction here, since it can be argued that the downward bias of the census coverage of the unemployed is so strong for the rural areas that the NSS figures are larger, despite the fact that the census covered the slack period of February and March which the NSS 16th round did not. It is significant to note that the rural as well as urban unemployment figures in the 17th round are substantially larger than those in the 16th round.
25. See Krishnamurty (1972).
26. National Sample Survey, 21st round (1966–7), Table S.9.
27. The gap seems to have widened since then, with the number of people on the live registers in employment exchanges going up about three times to the 8 million mark, and with a relatively much smaller rise in the NSS unemployment count.
28. Krishnamurty goes into this question in EUREC, Appendix III, and in Krishnamurty (1972). While my conclusions are somewhat different from his, the methodology used here has been much influenced by Krishnamurty's work.

A recent survey conducted by the Directorate General of Employment and Training (DGET) of the Ministry of Labour and Employment, of a sample of about 18,000 job seekers on the live registers on March 1968, indicated that: (i) about 34 per cent of the registered job seekers were 'normally resident in rural areas', and (ii) about 50 per cent of the urban registrants were unemployed, the rest being already in employment (about 43 per cent) or students (about 7 per cent).[29] Taking these ratios, we would guess that around 1.8 million registrants in 1966–7 were urban and that of these about 0.9 million were unemployed. This is still substantially larger than the NSS figure of 0.53 million.

Furthermore, the NSS 21st round found that only 44 per cent of the urban unemployed were in fact registered with the employment exchanges. Hence the 0.9 million registered urban unemployed would correspond to a total of 2.05 million urban unemployed. The difference from the NSS figure of 0.53 million is now stunningly large.

It has been asked whether 'the D(irectorate) G(eneral) of E(mployment) and T(raining) Survey, conducted by virtually the same agency as the Employment Exchanges, prevented some respondents from admitting that they were employed'.[30] There is, alas, no alternative survey conducted by any other agency for the whole of urban India, but the other party in this dispute, viz., the NSS, did survey a sample of the Calcutta registrants in 1965.[31] This survey indicated that about 20 per cent of the registrants were unemployed.[32] Applying this ratio to 1.8 million, it would appear that about 0.36 million registrants were 'unemployed' in the NSS sense. With a 44 per cent registration ratio, this would correspond to a total urban unemployment figure of 0.82 million. The NSS estimate of 0.53 million is less than this, though larger than the figure of registered unemployed of 0.36 million.

I do not think that these differences are worth pursuing in minute detail, since the questions the respondents have to answer look superficially much less ambiguous than they in fact are. Even the question:

29. EUREC, p. 27.
30. EUREC, p. 145.
31. 'Survey of Employment and Attitudes to Registration in Calcutta: 1965', conducted by the NSS Department of the Indian Statistical Institute, under the direction of Mr Sudhir Bhattacharya. I am most grateful to Mr Bhattacharya and Professor Deb Kumar Bose for drawing my attention to this unpublished report and to the Indian Statistical Institute for making the report available to me.
32. 198 persons out of 973. The proportion of 'students' is much smaller than in the DGET Survey, in which it was 7 per cent. The category of 'neither employed nor unemployed' (in the schedule, Block 2, Item 4: 'n.l.f.', not in labour force), which included students among others, amounted to less than 1 per cent of those surveyed.

'Whether on live register of employment exchange for better employment' (Column 19, Block 3, Household Schedule 10: Urban Labour Force, NSS, 21st Round) is not an easy one for a respondent to answer. It is one thing to know that one has registered in the past, but it is quite another to be able to tell whether one is still on 'the live register'. The Calcutta survey of registrants revealed that the time lag between first registration and first calling was more than three months for 85 per cent of the registrants, more than six months for 69 per cent, more than one year for 35 per cent, and more than two years for 9 per cent.[33] Under the circumstances it is a bit difficult for a respondent to be confident that some 'live register' is still carrying his name and that the wheels are turning to help him out. The proportion who say that they *are* registered has fluctuated substantially from year to year,[34] and it is not at all clear that one ought to devote a lot of energy to squaring these figures with each other.

The differences between the unemployment figures from different sources reflect a variety of factors, but the heterogeneity of the concept of unemployment is certainly a major element in this contrast. As explained before, both the NSS approach and the census approach use the intersection of two criteria of unemployment based on 'the income aspect' and 'the recognition aspect' respectively, and both take a relatively narrow view of each. In contrast the live registers of the employment exchanges reflect a variant of the recognition aspect only. This is relatively broad-based in one respect; it is based merely on dissatisfaction with one's current state of activity, whether or not one has a 'job'. But it is narrow in other respects, viz., only those are covered who bother to register, leaving out those who doubt that employment exchanges can help, or those who are too far away from an exchange. The latter is a fairly serious consideration, since most towns in India do not have an employment exchange. And the coverage of the rural areas is, of course, in effect negligible. In trying to construct an overall picture from these figures we have to bear in mind these limitations.

A.5. The Production Approach and Disguised Unemployment
It is remarkable that the Committee of Experts on Unemployment Estimates did not consider a single attempt at estimation of unemployment from the production point of view. In contrast the literature on unemployment in developing countries has concentrated almost entirely

33. 'Survey on employment and Attitude to Registration in Calcutta: 1965', Draft Report, Table 6.
34. EUREC, p. 27.

on 'disguised unemployment' from the production point of view. The question can be asked whether 'disguised unemployment' is at all amenable to actual measurement and in particular whether the model presented in Chapter 4 is usable in any empirical context.

There are two ways of measuring disguised unemployment. The 'direct' approach is to observe a withdrawal of part of the labour force and to see its consequences on production. One serious attempt at applying this approach was that by Schultz (1964), in which he examined the impact of the influenza epidemic of 1918—19 on Indian agricultural output. He found a negative impact on the output level and on the basis of inter-state data he came close to his prior expectation that the elasticity of output with respect to the number of labourers was 0.4. There are methodological problems in Schultz's approach and it has been suggested that he should have taken no change in output as 'the null hypothesis' and seen whether that could be rejected; this is in fact easily done.[35] The real problem lies in the difference between (i) withdrawal of labourers from families with a high ratio of labour to other productive resources, as when labour is attracted elsewhere through the labour market, and (ii) withdrawal of labourers unrelated to resource ratios but following the patterns of the spread of epidemics, as would have been the case with the influenza epidemic in India.[36] The fact of a reduction of output in the latter case leads to no presumption whatsoever about the impact of the former.[37]

The direct approach to the measurement of disguised unemployment is not easy to use, since withdrawal in response to market demand for labour tends to be relatively slow and its impact cannot be easily isolated from the effects of other factors. An alternative is to measure disguised unemployment within the framework of a specific model, assuming that the model holds (or better, after testing that its underlying assumptions are verified). This we can call the 'indirect' approach.

Perhaps the most impressive attempt in this direction is the estimation of surplus labour in Indian agriculture by Shakuntla Mehra (1966). The model on which she based her calculations is similar to the one discussed in Chapter 4.[38] She did not test the model, which would have required checking the supply function of labour effort in peasant families, but assuming the supply curve to be flat she calculated how many could be

35. See Harwitz (1965).
36. See Sen (1967) and Schultz (1967).
37. See also Mehra (1966).
38. For the necessary behaviour assumptions and the implicit utility functions underlying such a model, see Sen (1966). For an important empirical application of a similar approach, but with some significant differences, see Rudra (1973a).

withdrawn from Indian agriculture without affecting total output. Her methodology should be briefly outlined here.

Indian farms classified in terms of size show considerable variation in the amount of work done per person, the intensity of work time being greater for farms with a large amount of land per head. Assuming that the largest farms, which could be expected to have the highest amount of work time per cultivator, have no surplus at all, Shakuntla Mehra calculated the number of people in other farms who would be released if the cultivators there could work for the same amount of time per head as the cultivators in the non-surplus farms.

Mehra's approach is based on the idea that in family farms the shortage of productive work is shared by all and takes the form of a smaller amount of work per head. She treats output as a function of all factors of production including labour time and she considers withdrawal of labour keeping all factors (including labour time) constant. The data relate to 1956–7. Since people are indivisible, and a 0.5 person being surplus does not permit any one to be withdrawn (unless farms are merged together), Mrs Mehra adds the number of the farms to the size of the 'required' work force to obtain the maximal estimate of the necessary labour force and therefore the minimal estimate of surplus labour. The actual surplus will of course, be larger and will lie somewhere between these minimal estimates and the uncorrected (maximal) estimates. In Table A.2 her estimates are given as percentages of the total agricultural work force.

A few observations are in order. First, the volume of disguised unemployment on this measure would seem to be of a totally different order of magnitude than the NSS and census estimates of unemployment: 17 per cent for the country as a whole is indeed a high ratio.

Second, the 'uncorrected' estimates (giving a figure of 29 per cent for India as a whole) are the relevant figures if our focus is on expanding employment opportunities *without* involving migration, e.g., by finding supplementary activities in the local 'informal' sector.

Third, if farms could be merged together, e.g., through a co-operative, the number of people who could shift elsewhere without affecting output would increase substantially. The calculation of the value of unemployment thus depends on social arrangements, e.g., the use of co-operatives.

Fourth, the variation from state to state is quite remarkable. It is interesting that all the states in the east and the north of India have a higher volume of disguised agricultural unemployment than any state in central and southern India. Some viz., Assam, Bihar and Rajasthan, have an 'uncorrected' figure of more than half the rural labour force and a 'mean' figure of more than a third.

Table A.2

Estimates of Disguised Unemployment as a Percentage of the Total Agricultural Work Force in India

State	'Uncorrected' (maximal)	Minimal	Mean
Assam	57.6	21.7	39.6
Bihar	51.5	21.6	36.6
Rajasthan	50.9	20.5	35.7
Uttar Pradesh	47.9	9.8	28.8
West Bengal	46.0	1.9	24.0
Orissa	42.7	6.4	24.5
Punjab	36.6	1.7	19.1
Madhya Pradesh	23.7	–	9.4
Madras (Tamil Nadu)	21.4	–	10.0
Mysore (Karnataka)	12.7	–	1.3
Kerala	8.9	–	–
Gujarat	–	–	–
Andhra Pradesh	–	–	–
Maharashtra	–	–	–
INDIA	29.1	6.4	17.1

Source: Mehra (1966).

Fifth, given Mehra's methodology, the estimate of surplus labour depends on the extent to which larger farms have a higher intensity of effort per person employed. Size is brought in only because data on variations of labour effort are available in terms of size. But in so far as the relation of size to labour effort is not uniform in all areas, the relative orders of magnitude of unemployment in different states in Table A.2 may not be very significant. In fact, it is not the case that the highest work intensity occurs in the largest size group in each region. Among the Indian states, Maharashtra, Andhra Pradesh, Gujarat, Madhya Pradesh, and Kerala involve a violation of this assumption, and for this reason the first three states in fact end up yielding negative volumes of surplus labour in Shakuntla Mehra calculations, which she treats as zero, on the ground that the available labour force is in fact producing the existing output. If, however, one chooses the activity norm not from the largest holding size class, but from whichever size group does in fact happen to have the highest intensity of activity, then the surplus labour figure has to be revised upwards for these five states. It would appear that for India as a whole this adds another 4.6 per cent of the workforce to the total size of surplus labour, taking the uncorrected percentage of 'disguised unemployment' to a staggering 33.7 per cent of the rural labour force.

Sixth, Shakuntla Mehra's calculations are all based on size class averages. It is obvious that averages do soften the blow, and if one could look at the data farm by farm, one would find greater variation of intensity of work and thus a *larger* volume of disguised unemployment.

Seventh, there are, however, some considerations working in the opposite direction. Since the smaller farms have a higher proportion of 'unpaid family labour', it is possible that some people, having other work to do (e.g., household activities), would not be available for full-time work. This will operate in the other direction. Another reason for suspecting over-estimation arises from the fact that some people belonging to the smaller holding size group may in fact be working part of the time as casual labour in the larger farms. If this is ignored, the estimation of surplus labour will be biased in an upward direction for two separate reasons. First, some of the workers in the small holdings, who may appear to be 'surplus', may in fact already be employed as casual labour in the larger holding size groups. Second, intensity of work per head of the workforce of the larger farms will be lower, since the workers classified under the larger size group are supplemented by these part-time labourers in sharing out the total work time calculated from the Farm Management data. This will tend to reduce the work norm.[39]

Finally, much depends on the time pattern of labour inputs. Rather than taking the number of days per year per person, it would be better to take the number of days per person *in each season* and then to choose the maximal work intensity among all size groups for all seasons, as the norm to calculate the work force requirements in each season for each category. The maximal requirements of labour force among the various seasons will yield the binding requirement for each category. It is easily verified that if the application of labour is more even over the seasons for the smaller farms (with lower intensity), then this will have the effect of raising the amount of surplus labour above Mehra's estimates. And this may well be a plausible situation, since the differential of real labour cost tends to be greater during the slack seasons.

A.6. Concluding Remarks

Compared with the low figures of rural unemployment in the census and NSS estimates, based on the intersection of the relatively narrow inter-

39. There may also be state to state variations in the *net* bias, which is a further reason for not attaching very much importance to the relative position of different states in Table A.2. The fact that Punjab apparently had a higher ratio of 'surplus labour' than some other states may have something to do with this, as well as with the question of the relation of holding size to effort intensity discussed earlier. The relative pattern must also have changed a great deal since 1956–7, especially since some areas, like Punjab, have been growing much faster than others.

pretations of the 'income aspect' and the 'recognition aspect', the figures yielded by the 'production aspect' from the point of view of family output seem to be very large. The relevance of the last set of calculations depends on our acceptance of the model presented in Chapter 4.

Much depends also on the purpose for which we wish to use these estimates. For studying the scope for productive employment within the rural structure itself, the very high 'maximal' figures of Mehra are relevant, after the corrections discussed above. For knowing whether people can be moved elsewhere without affecting total output, the lower but still high 'mean' figures of Mehra are important, assuming a symmetric distribution. For calculating the 'availability' of a labour force to work outside their own farms, the production approach in itself is not sufficient, and one has to look into the income aspect and the recognition aspect. The recognition aspect influences a person's decision to seek or accept work elsewhere, and the income aspect is significant in the determination of the wage rate for such employment.

It is mainly in the last two contexts that the NSS and census data become relevant. I have argued in earlier sections that the census and NSS interpretations of the 'income aspect' and the 'recognition aspect' are very narrow. Given the family structure in rural India it is difficult to escape sharing in the economic activities of the family for at least one day in the week (the NSS test) and one can scarcely avoid one hour's work per day in the busy seasons for seasonal activities (the census test). But these criteria do make some rough sense in the context of the 'income approach', even though it is difficult to get a clear answer to the crucial question: Is the person's income dependent on his doing this bit of work? It is arguable that from the income point of view the incidence of unemployment in India is, in fact, rather low.[40]

The census and NSS figures however, take a fairly narrow view of the recognition aspect as well. The test of 'seeking work' is not easy to pass and even that of being 'available for work', where used, is not always easy to interpret.[41] Since both the census and the NSS take the *intersection* of the two aspects, the figures tend to be severely biassed in a

40. However, if one includes those undertaking less than 14 hours of 'gainful' work (who may qualify as near-unemployed by some interpretation of the income criterion), the level of Indian unemployment appears to be much higher. See Raj Krishna (1973), and also the *Report of the Committee on Unemployment*, 1972–3. Raj Krishna takes this as a case of the use of his 'time criterion', which it is, but it corresponds closely to the income criterion, since the 'time' in question is that spent in 'gainful' work (see chapter 1 above).
41. From the 25th round of the NSS, which is currently being tabulated, the questions have been made clearer.

downward direction. Furthermore, there are sharp year to year variations in the NSS figures of unemployment. These are partly due to the definitional changes discussed earlier. Table A.3 gives 'the incidence of unemployment' in the NSS sense from the 14th to the 21st round, the latter being the last for which tabulation has been completed.

Table A.3

NSS 'Unemployed' as a Percentage of the Labour Force

Years	Round	Rural		Urban	
		Male	Female	Male	Female
1958−9	14th	3.6	9.8	3.6	3.7
1959−60	15th	3.2	8.4	5.0	6.7
1960−1	16th	2.6	6.5	2.5	2.2
1961−2	17th	3.7	8.5	3.0	3.3
1964−5	19th	2.7	7.9	2.6	7.3
1966−7	21st	1.8	4.4	1.5	1.8

Source: EUREC, pp. 86, 94−5. The rural unemployment figures for the 19th and the 21st rounds are obtained from the 'Integrated Household Schedule', which has a much smaller sample size.

Finally, the employment exchange data concentrate directly on the offer of labour to the market. Their main limitations are (i) their neglect of rural India, and (ii) their insufficient coverage of urban India, partly because most towns do not have an employment exchange and partly because many job seekers do not register out of scepticism, or due to social barriers which are especially important for unemployed women. Also the act of registration involves some difficulty for the uneducated population, and it is not surprising that a disproportionately high percentage of the registrants turn out to be educated. In December 1970, of 4.07 million registrants 1.82 million were matriculates, graduates and post-graduates.[42] This ratio of 45 per cent is, of course, much higher than the corresponding ratio of educated labour to the total labour force and the contrast cannot be readily explained in terms of differences in the incidence of worklessness. The nature of the search activity involved in the act of registration in the employment exchange introduces a clear bias. This expression of the recognition approach is ideally cut out for the urban educated unemployed and it is particularly suitable for the

42. *Employment Review 1970−71*, Directorate General of Employment and Training, Ministry of Labour, 1972, Appendix 4.4, pp. 90−1.

male. It is not surprising that as many as 38 per cent of the total number of registrants are male matriculates, graduates and post-graduates.[43]

But within these limitations the employment exchange data have their own value if properly interpreted. The fact that a high proportion of the registrants turn out to be 'employed' in the NSS sense does not demolish the relevance of these figures. The NSS test of having some gainful work to do on one day during the preceding week is a very narrow one, and what is remarkable is that not only the sample survey of registrants conducted by the NSS itself, but also that conducted by the Directorate General of Employment and Training, which runs these employment exchanges, should use this narrow NSS concept to classify the employment status of registrants. Furthermore, EUREC has suggested the need to use 'correction factors' based on the NSS estimates in order to 'correct' employment exchange data by eliminating the 'employed' as seen by the NSS.[44] The search for 'consistency' seems irresistible, even when it implies grinding down data based on sharply different concepts into some kind of homogeneous dust.

If the alternative unemployment figures have their value, they have it because of the respective concepts underlying the estimation. While I have tried to analyse the conceptual differences between these various estimates and their respective areas of relevance, some general gaps in information have also clearly emerged. The need for more estimations of unemployment according to the production approach is evident. That for a wider coverage in estimations based on the recognition approach is also clear. The latter is particularly important for the rural labour force and for the urban uneducated job seekers – and, of course, for women in virtually every region and every category.

43. *Employment Review 1970– 71*, Appendix 4.4, pp. 90–1.
44. EUREC, pp. 27–8.

Appendix B | Public Schemes for Employment Expansion in India

B.1 Introduction

A number of schemes for employment expansion have been recently introduced by the Government of India.[1] The main ones are the following:

(1) *Crash Schemes for Rural Employment (CSRE)*. This scheme is aimed at rapidly expanding rural employment and applies to every district in India. One thousand persons are to be hired in each district on an average over a working session of ten months in a year. The wage rate is not to exceed Rs. 100 per month. The scheme, which came into operation in April 1971, is supposed to go on until the end of the Fourth Five Year Plan, i.e., until 31 March 1974. The provision for cost is Rs.50 crores (i.e., Rs. 500 million) per year. While CSRE is geared primarily to employment generation, it aims also at producing works and assets of a durable nature in consonance with local development plans.[2] The projects to be undertaken are to be of the labour-intensive kind, and costs of materials, equipment, etc., should not exceed a quarter of the cost of labour.

(2) *Small Farmer Development Agency (SFDA)*. This programme is aimed at 'small but potentially viable farmers' and the objectives include 'making available to them the inputs, including credit, to enable them to

1. There are also some schemes introduced by the state governments, which are not discussed here. For an analysis of the 'Pilot Employment Guarantee Scheme' introduced by the Government of Maharashtra in July 1969, see Dandekar and Rath (1971), pp. 116–9.
2. Ministry of Food, Agriculture, Community Development and Co-operation, Government of India, *Crash Scheme for Rural Employment*, New Delhi, March 1971, p. 2.

participate in available technology and practise intensive agriculture and diversify their activities'.[3] For the period of the Fourth Five Year Plan a sum of Rs. 67.5 crores has been allotted for 46 projects being set up in selected districts throughout the country. The agency is not to extend credit directly, but is to function as a catalyst and stimulate the flow of credit from various institutional agencies, such as commercial banks and co-operatives. The agency should also assist the institutions concerned with the distribution of inputs, marketing, processing and storage, so that an adequate infrastructure is built up. There is provision for subsidization of the commercial costs of custom services, as well as for meeting part of heavy capital outlays and setting up dairy and poultry units.

(3) *Marginal Farmers and Agricultural Labourers (MFAL)*. This programme is aimed at marginal farmers and agricultural labourers, and 'will help to study in depth' their problems and 'evolve appropriate programmes as well as institutional, financial and administrative arrangements'.[4] Rs. 47.5 crores have been allocated to the programme for the Fourth Five Year Plan and 41 projects are planned. The scheme is aimed at helping the marginal farmers and agricultural labourers very much in the same way as the SFDA scheme is to help small farmers. Credit is to be facilitated though not directly offered, and there are provisions for subsidization of commercial rates for custom services and for meeting one third of the capital investments in agriculture, animal husbandry, poultry farms and other activities.

(4) *Miscellaneous schemes*. While SFDA, MFAL and CSRE are the most talked-of schemes for the expansion of rural employment and production, there are many other programmes as well. The Rural Works Programme for Chronically Drought Affected Areas has been operating for some time, and is now known as the Drought Prone Area Programme. A special programme for schemes to provide employment for the educated unemployed had an outlay provision of Rs. 25 crores during 1971-2. There is a scheme for agro-service centres for training agricultural entrepreneurs in the maintenance and repair of machinery; it provides employment for engineers and technicians.

B.2 Examination of the Crash Scheme for Rural Employment
The Crash Scheme for Rural Employment, the programme with the

3. Ministry of Food, Agriculture, Community Development and Co-operation, Government of India, *Small Farmers Development Agency*, New Delhi, March 1971, p. 2.
4. Ministry of Food, Agriculture, Community Development and Co-operation, Government of India, *Marginal Farmers and Agricultural Labourers*, New Delhi, March 1971, p. 2.

biggest financial implications, focuses on the 'income aspect' of employment. Given the way it is set up., i.e., in terms of providing employment for 1,000 people per district on an average over ten months, the emphasis is clear enough. The formal requirement about production of 'assets of a durable nature' is essentially secondary, especially since no criterion has been proposed for economic valuation of the assets, apart from specifying eight extremely wide fields.[5] CSRE is, therefore, to be judged primarily in terms of its 'income aspect'.

The limits to wage rates have been fixed uniformly for all districts, and even though there is an exhortation to the effect that only the off-season rate for agricultural labourers in the district should be paid, in practice the remuneration rate has been about Rs. 3 per worker per day, or Rs. 100 per month, more or less everywhere. In districts where the market wage rate is much lower, this has been a major draw.[6] Basing my observations on information relating to Bankura and Birbhum, two districts in West Bengal, it would appear that the demand for work at these wages has tended to exceed considerably the stipulated limits, even though these limits of employment have frequently been relaxed substantially. The question of rationing the employment to be offered among the applicants has been an important one.

As discussed in Chapter 10, while employment as a vehicle of income redistribution may be relevant because of feasibility constraints on the fiscal machinery for redistribution, it does have its own feasibility constraints. In Fig. B.1 the demand and supply for labour in the context of a scheme like CSRE are presented; the demand is given by the scheme itself. The case considered is that of a poor region where the scheme wage rate (say, Rs. 3) is high in comparison with the prevailing pattern of remunerations. While W_1 may be the wage rate that equates demand and supply, W_2 is the wage actually offered (Rs. 100 per month, or around

5. These are (a) road building, (b) reclamation and development of land, (c) drainage, embankments, etc. (d) water conservation and ground water recharging, (e) minor irrigation, (f) soil conservation, (g) afforestation, and (h) special repairs.
6. In some areas the wage rate of casual labour is very much lower than Rs.3 per day. For example, in Bankura: 'the most common wage rate for both men and women labourers was between Rs. 2.00–3.00 per day which covered 61 per cent and 80 per cent of the total number of days worked by men and women respectively during the last fortnight in December. The rest of the days in this period, were, however, paid higher wages. As regards the wage rates in April, it was observed that about 70 per cent of the employed days among men and 28 per cent among women were paid between Rs. 2.00–3.00, and for the remaining days both men and women labourers were paid lower wages, which even went down to Rs. 1.00 per day.' (Agro-Economic Research Centre, Visva-Bharati (1972), Chapter V, pp. 38–40.)

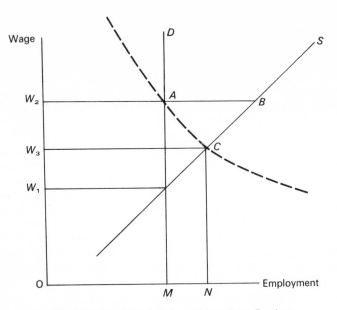

Fig. B.1. *The 'Crash Scheme' in a Poor Region*

Rs. 3 per day). This creates an excess supply of AB people. Whom to employ becomes an administrative decision and in both Bankura and Birbhum it seemed to have strong political aspects as well.[7] At wage rate W_2, the scheme is essentially doling out money, and it is not surprising that this creates the usual problems of a give away. Whether or not one accepts tales of corruption (these tales circulate in connection with virtually every project in West Bengal), it is clear that pressures in this direction are generated, and the problem is not really different from that of the pressures that make pure subsidies difficult to operate.

Would the managers of the project have an incentive for hiring people at a lower wage in the presence of excess supply? None is built into the

7. In Birbhum the more educated youth seems to have been favoured in a project that involved digging and creating an embankment by using labour-intensive techniques. The willingness of the educated youth to do this kind of manual work was much admired socially. Cf. 'As days went on, these young men took spade and shovels in their inexperienced hands and joined earth-work, leaving aside their education, their social status and the traditional do's and dont's ... It may be noted here that apart from a large number of graduates, there were quite a few holding post-graduate degrees and engineering diplomas.' (Subroto Chakravarty (1972), pp. 220–1.) Whether the educated were the right people to choose for this scheme was not, however, much discussed.

system. First, there are no cost—economy criteria proposed for the scheme. Second, it is not unusual in the Indian administrative set-up to judge success in terms of the size of the disbursement made rather than in terms of the *net* contribution. Third, through the stipulation that the cost of materials 'will have to be limited to 25 per cent of the cost of labour',[8] CSRE does, in fact, provide incentives for the project managers to pay higher rather than lower wages within the limits set. All these factors contribute to the tendency of the scheme to use less labour and to do less in redistributing income for the same amount of public expenditure. They also generate pressures on the administrative set-up charged with the arbitrary rationing operation.

Consider now an alternative system. If the project wages bill were restricted to the value given by W_2 wage rate and OM employment, e.g., to Rs. 100,000 per month (given by Rs. 100 wage to 1,000 persons), but (subject to the wages bill not exceeding this sum) the project managers could hire as many people as needed to eliminate the excess supply, what would happen? The demand for labour would now be given by the rectangular hyperbola AC, and the project managers would hire ON people at W_3 wage rate. There would be more work done, more people employed, more equal distribution of the funds and no corrupting pressures.[9] The allocation for material costs would remain unaffected.

A second aspect of the project that requires closer examination is the stipulation that people should be employed continuously for ten months. If this requirement is met (in practice, I am told that it is often violated), then again the income distributional benefits will be restricted to a comparatively small number of people (1,000 is an exceedingly small number for a district). Furthermore, it conflicts with the seasonal pattern of labour activity in agriculture. The question at issue is not merely the existence of non-seasonal unemployment, but – as argued in Chapter 8 – the economic incentive for members of peasant families to be involved in seasonal operations whether or not they are surplus in the production sense. The right to a share of the family output relates to one's contribution of labour, and even if the family output were to remain unchanged whether one shared the work of not, one would have an economic incentive to do so. It is also clear that opportunities for wage employment tend to expand remarkably in the busy seasons. The ten months' rule will create problems, unless the work schedule is very

8. CSRE, p. 4.
9. The middle-class educated job seekers might well be pruned out by this procedure, since they are attracted only by relatively higher wages, but jobs would go to people who are, by and large, much poorer.

cunningly timed with the proper discontinuities. Not surprisingly the rule is frequently broken and shorter term employment is quite common.

It is also worth commenting on the production aspect of the employment generated. To ensure that the projects do produce worthwhile capital accumulation, some kind of calculation of gains and losses from each employment project would seem to be necessary. A framework for this was discussed in Chapters 11 and 12. Even if the main concern of CSRE is with the income aspect, the productive contribution made by the project needs some systematic assessment.[10]

Furthermore, even in order to evaluate only the income aspect of CSRE, a more methodical analysis may be needed than is typically undertaken. When an unemployed person is employed in a project, he is not the only person to gain. Those on whom he was living when unemployed benefit as well. In the economic accounts presented in Chapter 11, the income aspect was split into the gain $(w - y)$ of the person getting the job and the gain $(y - m)$ of those supporting him, where w is the wage rate, y his consumption in the absence of the job and m his productive contribution to the family enterprise if he were not to be employed in this project. With surplus labour, $m = 0$, but even if m is positive, it will frequently be much less than y (see Chapters 4 and 6). A scheme aimed at employment as a vehicle of redistribution has to be concerned not merely with the immediately visible effects, but also with the effects that work through the complex economic and institutional structure.

B.3 Small and Marginal Farmers

'The first function of the agency (under SFDA)', we are assured, 'is to identify the small but potentially viable farmers in its area of operation.'[11] The typical case is that of a farmer with an average size of holding ranging 'from 2.5 to 5 acres in the case of irrigated or irrigable lands and up to 7.5 acres in the case of dry areas'.[12] To deserve support the farmer should not only be small and poor, but also 'potentially viable'.

No clear definition of potential viability has been offered anywhere in the literature related to the programme, and subject to the size definitions, 'each agency has been left to work out the norm for selecting the participants' (p. 4). Aside from the scope for arbitrariness and influenc-

10. See also R. Gupta (1971), Vyas (1972), and Visaria and Visaria (1973).
11. SFDA, p. 4.
12. SFDA, p. 4. 'In some projects such as those of Kerala and Mysore the lower limit has been adopted as 1 acre, since it is expected that with the intensity of cropping even a one-acre farm would reach viable standards' (p. 4).

ing that this lack of criteria involves, there is also the question of the underlying philosophy behind the approach. It seems to be something like the following. The small farmers need support and cannot stand on their own, but some of them are relatively closer to the viability line than others. By giving them a bit of a push, through credit, supply of inputs and services, etc. we can get them over to the other side of it. So, the argument runs, let us push these farmers up first.

If the object is to reduce the proportion of people below the viability line, this approach would indeed make some sense. If, however, the object is to help the neediest then it makes no sense whatsoever. The philosophy concentrates merely on the *number* below the viability borderline and is not really concerned with the *distribution* below that line.[13]

In defence of the approach it may be said that once some small farmers are pushed above the viability line, they do not need any further support, whereas the poorer farmers would continue to need support even if they were supported now. But is there such a dividing line? There is a fine gradation from extreme poverty to affluence; there is no identifiable point where one crosses the boundary. Even in terms of dependence on borrowing, this can occur at various income levels, and given the uncertainties of peasant life, all we can say is that the probability of such dependence will go down as one gets richer and has more resources. There is, furthermore, no substance in the statement that poorer farmers would continue to need support, whereas the potentially viable farmers, who are to be supported, will not need it later. Evidently, the poorer, non-potentially-viable farmers, who are denied support now on this ground, must do without it right now, and it is not clear in what sense they must be taken to be persistently dependent on support. The fact is that all farmers – indeed all men – can do with more support and – barring extreme cases of famine – can survive without it too. But the poorer farmers would seem to deserve support more strongly on egalitarian grounds. The philosophy of SFDA runs in precisely the opposite direction.

In practice, SFDA assistance has a further bias that may not be immediately obvious from the wording. It is not specified whether the

13. From this particular point of view it was perhaps a bit unfortunate that the focus of the important 'poverty debate' between P. Bardhan (1970), Minhas (1970), (1971), and Vaidyanathan (1972) was on the *number* below the poverty line, even though the debate drew attention to the pervasive problem of general poverty in India. A similar comment can be made about the use of the concept of 'income inadequacy' used in estimating the number of the 'working poor' in the Report of the ILO mission to Kenya (ILO (1972), pp. 60–3).

holding sizes mentioned are meant to be ownership holdings or operational holdings. In many cases ownership holdings are much smaller, but one's income will be influenced by one's operational holding. There is some evidence that SFDA assistance has frequently gone to farmers who operate holdings much larger than those stipulated in terms of ownership.

On the other hand, some negative factors make it difficult for many farmers to seek SFDA facilities. A high proportion of small farmers have land holdings fragmented into pieces lying in different areas and this is a major barrier to their ability to make proper use of the credit facilities in digging a tube-well or undertaking similar activities. Since SFDA is essentially a credit and marketing superstructure in addition to the existing agrarian framework, this kind of difficulty is bound to arise, and in effect it makes the SFDA benefits effectively available to a smaller number of farmers than envisaged. This is a technological limitation, since productive use of a well and other immovable capital assets depends not on one's total holding but on the size of each plot within this holding.[14]

These difficulties apply with no less force to MFAL programmes as well. 'The basic feature of this [MFAL] project', we are informed, 'is that agricultural labourers and marginal farmers would be enabled to have access to institutional credit facilities for undertaking various economic activities.'[15] Fragmentation prevents many potential users from benefiting from the facilities offered. To be able to pay back the loan for investing in, say, a dug-well, a certain minimal size of plot (as opposed to holding) is needed, and in practice this has been a substantial limitation.

The confusion between ownership holding and operational holding creates a bias similar to the one discussed in the case of SFDA. Further, a survey of the working of the project in the Bankura district indicates that a significant proportion of beneficiaries identified as 'marginal farmers' are engaged in other activities as well, such as trading, teaching, etc. This brings out another weakness of the SFDA and MFAL approach, viz., its concentration on the criterion of the size of the land owned. Class structure is a more complex phenomenon and one can own a small farm and still be relatively prosperous because of other sources of income. It is, of course, not the intention of the MFAL programme that these relatively

14. Minhas (1970) discusses the grave difficulties involved in any rural works programme unless it is accompanied by consolidation of holdings, and outlines a scheme for combining works programmes with consolidation and other institutional changes. In contrast SFDA goes to battle in the technological and institutional arena armed only with credit, marketing and custom services.
15. MFAL, p. 4.

prosperous people should benefit from it at the cost of the really marginal farmers or agricultural labourers, but the vagueness of the criteria for selection (other than the test of the size of the ownership holding),[16] together with the usual pressures generated on the administrative machinery, make such deflections difficult to avoid.[17] Since, furthermore, for many really marginal farmers, the ability to use credit facilities for investment is limited by fragmentation and other institutional and technological problems, the competition for MFAL facilities is frequently not severe, which makes it easier for the MFAL agency to take on farmers owning a marginal amount of land but not otherwise especially poor.

These inadequacies in the conception of SFDA and MFAL make them relatively weak vehicles for the relief of poverty and unemployment. The aim of encouraging capital formation by making credit easier for small and marginal farmers is, of course, entirely laudable, and if achieved would significantly alter the technology of cultivation by the poorer sections of the rural population and also lead to absorption of the underemployed labour force. But given the inability of these programmes to come to grips with the institutional and technological structure of the rural economy, not a great deal can be expected from them.

In addition to the problems already discussed, there is also the difficulty that neither the SFDA nor the MFAL agencies have much power over the institutions of credit and rural investment through which they are supposed to bring about the credit rearrangements. A distinction should be made between the agencies' function of subsidizing farmers, in which they do not need to go through some other institution, and their function of redirecting credit in which their role is that of a 'catalyst'. The ability of the SFDA and MFAL agencies to influence the established institutions of credit has not in fact, been uniformly great. Subsidization is the only thing that these agencies can do on their own, and this adds to the problems already discussed.

16. Since this monograph was written, the *Draft Fifth Five Year Plan* has been presented by the Government, and it recommends a substantial expansion of SFDA and MFAL merged together. But the criterion remains vague enough: 'The beneficiaries in these projects will be restricted to farmers with land holdings up to 2 hectares [5 acres] and agricultural labour' (2.88).
17. The following figures from a study of 85 'marginal farmer' households in the MFAL schemes in Hooghly District are of some interest: 'Out of 85 workers from the marginal farmers only 12 (14.12%) are exclusively confined to cultivation. There are 33 (38.82%) workers who have taken various secondary operations along with cultivation. Another set of 16 persons (18.82%) engaged in different occupations resort to cultivation only as a secondary occupation.' Agro-Economic Research Centre, Visva-Bharati (1972a).

B.4 Concluding Remarks

The recent Indian schemes to promote employment partly reflect increasing public concern with the phenomenon of rural poverty. The magnitude of this poverty — no matter which estimate one accepts — is, however, so large that even if the schemes all prove highly successful no dramatic impact can be readily expected. Just to get an idea of the order of the magnitudes involved, 46 projects under SFDA assisting 20,000 farmers each and 41 projects under MFAL assisting 50,000 farmers and labourers each, will altogether draw in a little over 3 million people by 1974, given a 100 per cent success rate. In three years the CSRE, by hiring 1,000 people in each district, could possibly give employment for 10 months each to somewhat under one million people. With their dependents these 4 million households may involve about 20 million people.[18] This is, of course, a large group, but it is still only a small fraction of the 154 million rural poor consuming less than Rs. 20 per month according to Minhas's (1970) estimate, and the estimates of others, e.g., Bardhan (1970) and Vaidyanathan (1972), yield much larger numbers of poor. And all of these 20 million do not, in fact, come from below the poverty line, as was noted in reviewing the CSRE, SFDA and MFAL programmes.

Further, the policy schemes seem to focus their attention on those close to the corresponding 'viability line'. The philosophy and the specific approach of the public employment programmes have been critically evaluated in this light, and their regressive character has been brought out.

Also the class composition of the beneficiaries is by no means as straightforward as it may at first appear. Through significant loopholes in the conception of the programmes, it has turned out that many among the poorest cannot benefit at all from these programmes, while some of the relatively better-off can be covered by them. The institutional framework of rural India makes these problems extremely real.

Finally, the schemes have suffered from an inadequacy of criteria for selecting projects or participants. The production aspect of employment was considered only in very general terms under CSRE and without much recognition of the institutional and technological features of rural India under SFDA and MFAL. Perhaps the biggest deficiency of these

18. Some of the benefits going to those employed will, of course, be passed on to others in the family (as discussed in § B.2), but some of these will be among the 20 million family members including dependants, and in the case of larger families, while the sharing will be wider, each beneficiary's gain will be very small indeed.

schemes lies in the absence of a systematic framework for evaluating the productive contributions of work programmes.[19]

19. Even the overall employment opportunities, as was explained in Chapter 9, depend on the output produced. Chapters 11–13 above were concerned with developing a framework for evaluating the economic impact of projects.

Appendix C | Labour Cost, Scale, and Technology in Indian Agriculture

C.1 Introduction

Despite considerable industrialization, about one half of the Indian national income at market prices still originates in agriculture, and about 70 per cent of the Indian labour force works in that sector. The question of technical choice in agriculture is, therefore, of fundamental importance for resource allocation and employment policy in the Indian economy.

In addition to the size of the agricultural sector, there are other reasons that make it particularly interesting to study the problem of choice of agricultural technology in India. While non-wage modes of employment are dominant in Indian agriculture, they exist side by side with substantial use of wage labour, and this contrast of alternative modes adds considerable richness to the picture of resource allocation in this sector.[1] The inter-farm differences in labour cost need special attention, particularly in view of what looks like the recent emergence of the modern capitalist farmer in Indian agriculture, even though there is some debate as to whether this epic hero is, in fact, emerging or not.[2] Second, there have been significant technological changes in Indian agriculture recently, e.g., the occurrence of a marked increase in the use of new high-yielding varieties of seeds and other features that characterize the so-called 'green revolution'.[3] Further, agricultural mechanization is beginning to make some headway in specific sections of the rural

1. See Sen (1962), Hanumantha Rao (1966), Saini (1971), and P. Bardhan (1973a).
2. See S. C. Gupta (1962), Thorner (1967), Rudra, Majid and Talib (1969), (1969a), (1970), Patnaik (1971), (1972), (1972a), and Chattopadhyay (1972), (1972a).
3. See, for example, Mukherjee (1970), Ladejinski (1970), Dharm Narain (1972), Schluter and Mellor (1972), and von Blanckenburg (1972).

economy,[4] and the movement raises important issues of technical choice and employment policy, related especially to labour cost.

C.2 Labour Cost and Productivity: Some Controversies

On the basis of the size class average data for the mid-fifties presented in the *Studies of the Economics of Farm Management*,[5] the following observations were isolated for comment in a paper of mine that proved to be very controversial.[6]

Observation I: When family labour employed in agriculture is given an 'imputed value' in terms of the ruling wage rate, much of Indian agriculture seems unremunerative.

Observation II: By and large, the 'profitability' of agriculture increases with the size of holding, 'profitability' being measured by the surplus (or deficit) of output over costs including the imputed value of labour.

Observation III: By and large, productivity per acre decreases with the size of holding.

It was argued in the same article that the procedure of valuing family labour at the market wage rate (used by the Farm Management Studies) overlooked the important feature of dualism in the labour market, and that the 'losses' incurred for smaller farms mainly reflected a confusion of concepts in applying to peasant farming the cost accounting procedures appropriate to capitalist farms. In so far as the smaller farms used cheaper family labour, there was nothing surprising in Observations II and III either. More labour would be applied per acre by such farms, given other things, and this would produce both larger output per acre (Observation III) and less profits, if family labour were to be valued at the market wage rate ignoring the 'wage gap' (Observation II).[7]

This labour-cost based explanation was contrasted in Sen (1964) with two other explanations of Observation III, viz., (a) that smaller farms were more fertile, and (b) that smaller farms had some technological advantages due to diseconomies of scale. While the latter seemed unpromising, the hypothesis of fertility difference appeared to have sub-

---

4. See, for example, Sarkar and Prahladachar (1966), B. Singh (1968), Sapre (1969), Hanumantha Rao (1972), (1972a), Raj (1972), and Sharma (1972). Also Appendix D below.

5. These studies, conducted by the Government of India, were initiated in 1954–5, and were originally confined to the states of Bombay, Madhya Pradesh, Madras, Punjab, Uttar Pradesh, and West Bengal The investigation was later extended to other states. See also *Farm Management in India: A Study based on Recent Investigations*, Government of India, New Delhi.

6. Sen (1962), p. 243.

7. Sen (1962), pp. 243–6.

stance both on empirical grounds and because of the plausibility of such an inverse relationship between size and fertility arising from population growth, subdivision and sales.[8]

However, since Observation III itself was based on data presented in terms of size-class *averages*, and not in terms of individual holdings, the question of there being an illusory element in this observation was also raised and it was argued that 'the inverse relationship is not yet something that can be taken as a well established fact'.[9] A lively debate has since taken place on this subject. It has examined the question of the statistical validity of Observation III as well as the correctness of the explanations offered.[10]

Having had the unenviable role of doing the initial poking at what has turned out to be a beehive, I shall take this opportunity of reviewing precisely where the matter seems to stand at this moment after the vigorous debating that has taken place. The question is of relevance to the relation between modes of employment and labour utilization discussed in Chapters 6–8.

There is first the question as to whether Observation III is, in fact, a statistical illusion arising from some kind of averaging bias. A. P. Rao (1967) provided some evidence to suggest that it might be so, and Ashok Rudra (1968) provided somewhat stronger evidence and a much stronger assertion that such was indeed the case. For twenty villages surveyed in Punjab, Haryana and Uttar Pradesh, Rudra saw no sign of an inverse relation between size and productivity per acre. There is, however, some uncertainty about Rudra's interpretation of his rank correlation tests. While the correlation was not significant in many of the cases, it was also true that a good many of his rank correlation coefficients were negative, and 'any overall test would give a significant verdict'.[11] Furthermore, Observation III was concerned with output per 'net' acre and not with output per 'gross' acre, whereas Rudra (1968) looked at the latter in his

---

8. It is a commonly observed phenomenon that *between* regions the more fertile tracts tend to produce a larger population and therefore greater subdivision of land. Also *within* a region the ability of the small farmer to survive and multiply depends on the fertility of the land he holds. See Sen (1964), pp. 325–5. See also Khusro (1964).

9. Sen (1964), p. 323.

10. See Hanumantha Rao (1963), (1966), Mazumdar (1963), (1965), Khusro (1964), R. Agarwala (1964), (1964a), K. Bardhan (1964), A. P. Rao (1967), Rudra (1968), (1968a), Saini (1969), (1969a), (1971), Bhagwati and Chakravarty (1969), Desai and Mazumdar (1970), Usha Rani (1971), Bhattacharya and Saini (1972), Patnaik (1972), and P. Bardhan (1973a), Srinivasan (1973), among others.

11. Bhattacharya and Saini (1972), p. A–63.

INDIAN AGRICULTURE 149

testing.[12] Since gross acreage measures the same land twice if it is double-cropped, one of the main avenues of greater use of labour for farms with cheaper labour cost finds no expression in the figures of productivity per gross acre.

Saini (1971) analysed 25 sets of disaggregated, farm-level data from nine states,[13] and fitted regressions of the form:

$$\log y = \alpha + \beta \log x \qquad (C.1)$$

where x = size of the operational holding

and y = value of output.

It is obvious that the inverse relationship requires that β be significantly less than unity. This turned out to be so for 18 cases out of 25. For four cases β was less than unity but not significantly so. Only in three cases was the estimated β greater than unity, though not significantly so; nor did the confidence intervals used by Saini exclude values of β less than unity. Thus Observation III would, on the whole, seem to be vindicated on the basis of disaggregated farm-level data as well.[14]

It is to be noted that Saini's data sets are based on information from different villages, whereas Rudra's fits were all for data from within particular villages. The distinction can be of some significance for the labour-cost-based explanation as well as for the fertility-based explanation. As far as the latter is concerned, it is obvious that some of the differences between the quality of land arising from differences in rainfall, irrigation, waterlogging, etc., would be eliminated if one analysed data for each village separately. Clearly, one would expect more bite in the fertility-based explanation in the case of farm data from different regions, and also from different villages within the same district, than within a given village.

While this may not be obvious, the same holds for the labour-cost-based explanation as well. In so far as the differences of labour cost reflect dual labour markets (see Chapter 6), the extent of dualism would

12. See Hanumantha Rao (1968). Also see Rudra (1968a).
13. Saini had data from the following 25 configurations: Andhra Pradesh (1957–8), (1958–9), (1959–60), Bihar (1958–9), Madhya Pradesh (1955–6), (1956–7), Madras (1954–5), (1955–6), Maharashtra (1955–6), (1956–7), Orissa (1957–8), (1958–9), (1959–60), Punjab (1955–6), (1956–7), Uttar Pradesh (1955–6), (1956–7), West Bengal (1955–6), (1956–7), and also for two further locations in Uttar Pradesh and Punjab, viz., Muzaffarnagar (1955–6), (1956–7), (1966–7), and Ferozepore (1955–6), (1956–7), (1967–8).
14. Earlier Hanumantha Rao (1966) had arrived at the same conclusion on the basis of disaggregated data from farms in Bombay and Andhra.

tend to be sharper across villages than within a given village. It has been observed that a substantial proportion of small cultivator households as well as non-cultivator wage-earner households are typically willing to accept employment 'within the village' but not outside.[15] Thus differences in labour supply conditions which may be partly ironed out within a village survive between villages. Therefore, from the point of view of the labour-cost-based explanation also, clearer inverse relation between size and productivity would be expected in farm data from different villages than from the same village.

Bhattacharya and Saini (1972) have analysed data from different villages in Muzaffarnagar in Uttar Pradesh and in Ferozepore in Punjab. On the whole, they confirmed the inverse relationship between size and productivity for Muzaffarnagar, but found the picture for Ferozepore to be relatively unclear.[16]

How much of the inverse relation between size and productivity survives in data from a given village remains, therefore, somewhat obscure, and much more empirical work will have to be done before the issue of inverse relation within a village is sorted out. However, at the wider level, the inverse relation would seem to be fairly well established, and corresponds to what one would expect in terms of general economic reasoning.

The inverse relation between size and productivity, as explained before, can arise either from differences in labour cost or from differences in land quality. The labour-cost hypothesis has, however, been recently attacked by Saini (1969), (1971). Saini fits a Cobb–Douglas production function to the data from the Farm Management Surveys for Uttar Pradesh and Punjab. Taking the marginal product of labour at the geometric mean level of inputs, he finds that the marginal product thus obtained exceeds the wage rate. 'Thus', concludes Saini, 'there appeared ample justification for the valuation of family labour at the ruling wage rate.'[17] However, this would seem to be a *non sequitur.* In order to check the labour-cost-based explanation one has to establish or reject *differences* in labour costs in different types of farms, and not simply compare the wage rate with the marginal product of the geometric mean farm. Furthermore, there are serious methodological objections to fitting a production function to a scatter with *different* factor ratios and then using that production function to compare the marginal product of each factor with an assumed *uniform* price of that factor.[18]

15. This is clear from the 25th round of the National Sample Survey (1970–1).
16. See also P. Bardhan (1973*a*).
17. Saini (1971), p. A–83.
18. See Rudra (1973).

Pranab Bardhan's (1973*a*) test of the labour-cost hypothesis is not based on taking the geometric mean level of inputs, and it is, therefore, of considerable interest that in one of his studies he too finds that for a cross-section of 67 farms in the paddy zone of the West Godavari district, the marginal product of family labour seems to exceed the wage rate. However, aside from other difficulties in such production function studies, there is also the problem that Bardhan does not include bullock labour or farm implements in the fitted production function. While leaving out these factors may be justifiable in order to avoid problems of multi-collinearity, the fact remains that some part of the marginal product attributed to labour may represent, as Bardhan himself points out, the contributions of complementary factors highly correlated with labour. The role of bullock labour is of particular importance in this context.

It would, thus, appear that the labour-cost-based explanation has not so far been falsified by any of the production function studies presented. It must, however, also be recorded that sufficient empirical testing of the explanation has not yet been done to enable us to confirm or reject the hypothesis with any confidence. In particular, the reasoning applied to the case of the inverse relation between size and productivity is essentially indirect, since size is treated as a proxy for the mode of employment. It should, however, be possible to relate labour use directly to the mode of employment both *within* each village and *between* villages. For reasons explained earlier, the labour-cost-based explanation would predict a clearer pattern relating labour use and the mode of employment in data for farms from different villages than for data from within a village.

It would be nice to be able to say that the debate on size and productivity has cleared up the empirical regularities as well as the validity of the alternative explanations. I am afraid neither of these two assertions can be made. Perhaps the only clear finding is that the size-productivity inverse relationship based on size-class average data is vindicated also by disaggregated inter-farm data from different villages in the same region considered together. But the picture is less clear for data within a village. This is, in any case, what one would expect on the basis of economic reasoning involving resource use and employment modes.

C.3 Choice of Modes of Production

In Chapter 7 a categorization of different types of farms was presented based on differences in property relations and employment modes. The differences in the use of wage labour catch only one particular aspect of that contrast. Consider a large wage-based capitalist farm on the one hand and a small share-cropped tenant farm on the other. While the wage cost may be significantly higher than the supply price of labour z in the crop-sharing farm, the real labour cost j in the latter need not be any lower than the wage rate w. It may be recalled that:

$$j = z/[\alpha + (1 - \alpha)h].\tag{6.1}$$

For a share-cropper α may be relatively small and the advantage of a lower z can well be wiped out (or even over-compensated) by a low α.[19]

There is also the question of the imperfection of the capital market. Since larger farmers have easier access to credit and may even get better terms,[20] they may be able to put in more resources into their land, and this factor in the context of the size—productivity relationship, will operate in the opposite direction from the labour cost differential. In the utilization of land, cheaper labour and dearer capital are to some extent competitive with each other, in the sense that one would encourage the use of more resources per acre of land while the other would discourage it. However, when it comes to the relative utilization of labour and capital goods, cheaper labour and dearer capital reinforce each other.

There are also significant differences in the ability to seize the available economic opportunities, which relates to the farmer's contacts with the world of modern innovation. The large farmers have an advantage in this, both because of a higher level of education, which seems to have a substantial role in Indian agriculture in the utilization of modern inputs,[21] and also because of the nature of the administrative set-up in public programmes involving agriculture, which makes it much easier for the larger farmers to make use of the available opportunities.[22]

In the progress of the so-called 'green revolution' in India, it is these non-labour advantages that seem so far to have dominated the field. There is much evidence that the major benefits from using the new varieties of seeds have gone largely to the relatively bigger farmers.[23] The large farmer does indeed have several advantages in the adoption of the new varieties. However, there is a basic asymmetry between these non-labour cost differentials, which favour the large farmer, and the labour cost advantages, which go in the opposite direction. The latter arise at

19. Even for the use of unpaid family labour, α and h may conceivably be significantly variable since a joint family can sometimes be quite large.
20. See, for example, Reserve Bank of India (1970).
21. See Chaudhuri (1968), (1969), (1971).
22. The recently introduced Small Farmers Development Agency (SFDA) and Marginal Farmers and Agricultural Labour (MFAL) schemes are attempts to counter this, though they are quite feeble in their effectiveness, as discussed in Appendix B.
23. See Frankel (1971). See also Lele and Mellor (1972).

least partly from the preferences and aspirations of the cultivators (see Chapter 6), whereas the former reflect institutional imperfections which can be remedied through suitable structural changes. It is, in this context, significant to note that when credit and other facilities have been made available to the smaller farmer his rate of adoption of the new varieties has not been any slower.[24] This is, of course, not surprising, since the disadvantages of the small farmer are almost entirely institutional, and the new varieties do make a substantial additional demand for labour,[25] so that the availability of cheaper labour is certainly an advantage.

In the discussion so far very little has been said about the economies or diseconomies of scale as such. Indeed, one of the main points of the labour-cost-based explanation of the inverse relation between size and productivity was to argue that 'if the explanation . . . is correct, the factor that makes a crucial difference is not size as such, which is incidental, but the system of farming, viz., whether it is wage based or family based'.[26] The distinction is of some importance for policy debates.[27] If the higher productivity per acre of the smaller farms arose from diseconomies of scale, that would amount not merely to an argument against capitalist farming but also to one against the co-operative mode of production. If, however, the difference arose from labour-cost gaps, then the relative advantage of co-operative farming would depend on its ability to use non-wage employment in an integrated communal set-up.[28]

It was argued in Appendix B that one of the problems in the operation of the SFDA and MFAL schemes arises from the fact that the small farmer frequently does not have a sufficiently large plot of land at one place to justify the investment of a tube-well.[29] This is an example of an economy of large scale which would seem to call for the use of co-operative arrangements for the utilization of ancillary inputs like tube-well water.[30]

24. See, for example, Schluter and Mellor (1972), and von Blanckenburg (1972).
25. See Shivamaggi (1969), Tripathy and Samal (1969), and Inukai (1970), among others.
26. Sen (1962), p. 246.
27. In the context of the size–productivity debate, Utsa Patnaik (1972a) argues in favour of measuring size by the value of output rather than by the acreage of land. In checking the scale advantages or disadvantages, this point is well taken. However, in so far as size is treated as a proxy for the underlying mode of production and for labour cost, the argument is less simple. The relative abundance of labour in relation to the available land is a relevant factor in this case.
28. See Chapter 3.
29. The problem is not confined to India. Nulty (1972) notes that in Pakistan the ownership of tube-wells is almost exclusively confined to farms of 10 acres or more.
30. It also suggests the case for land consolidation in the context of a rural works programme; see Minhas (1970).

Appendix D   A Study of Tractorization in India

D.1 Growth in the Use of Tractors

In 1951 there were only about 8,500 tractors in use in India. By 1966 the number had risen to around 54,000, and by 1969 it was well over 90,000. The sharp upward trend has accelerated further since then, and the Fourth Five Year Plan envisaged that by 1973–4 the installed capacity for the manufacture of tractors would amount to 68,000 *per year*. Since the demand for new tractors was by then expected to be around 100,000 per year, it was planned that 'the gap between demand and indigenous supply will be met by imports'.[1] The policy of encouragement of domestic tractor production also led to its delicensing in 1969, thereby giving it preferential treatment.[2]

Since tractors cost a lot of money and represent a capital-intensive and labour-saving form of investment, the recent change in public policy towards tractors is particularly worth examining. Despite the importance of the issue, however, it is not easy at this stage to do a detailed benefit–cost analysis of the kind discussed in Part V of this book, because a thorough examination of the available information reveals major gaps in the data on the impact of tractors on cultivation.

In § D.2 the literature on the impact of tractorization is reviewed. In § D.3 and § D.4 two important attempts at benefit–cost analysis of tractorization in India are critically evaluated in the light of the approach presented in this book. In § D.5 the policy issues are examined and the

1. *The Fourth Five Year Plan, 1969–74,* Government of India, New Delhi, 1969, pp. 115 and 135.
2. Since this monograph was written, the Government of India has published the *Draft Fifth Five Year Plan,* which envisages that 'the population of tractors in this country will move from 200,000 to 500,000 in the course of the Fifth Plan' (Vol. II, p. 14, 1.93).

relevance of our approach to technological decisions of this kind is illustrated.

D.2 Literature on the Impact of Tractorization on Employment and Output

The literature on tractorization reveals a remarkable heterogeneity of views even on purely factual questions. I shall briefly survey the main conclusions of the empirical studies.

Comparing the pattern of labour use in farms owning tractors and those not doing so in a sample from four districts of Punjab, viz., Bhatinda, Hissar, Ludhiana and Sangrur, B. Singh (1968) found that in producing wheat the tractor farms used 109 hours of male labour and 18 hours of female labour per acre, as against the other farms which used 161 hours of male labour and 13 hours of female labour on the average. This meant that the non-tractor farms used 38 per cent more labour than the tractorized farms. One difficulty in estimating the impact of tractor-ization from these data lies in the fact that the tractor farms differ from the non-tractor farms in other respects as well. For example, the average size of the tractor farms studied was 59 acres, whereas that of the other farms was only 21 acres.[3] In view of the discussion in § C.2 above, it can be argued that even in the absence of tractors the larger farms might have used less labour due to dual labour markets. There could also be differences in the quality of land.

This objection does not apply to the study of Sarkar and Prahladachar (1966). In the Dharwar district in Mysore 39 farms using 44 tractors in all were randomly selected and the farmers were questioned on the changes in permanent labour requirements as a consequence of tractori-zation. It appeared that there was a 17 per cent decrease in the perman-ent labour requirements as a result of tractorization. One difficulty in us-ing this study lies in the usual problems of recall encountered in the use of the questionnaire method. There is also the problem that the inform-ation relates not to the total use of labour (including family labour and casual hired labour) but only to the use of permanent labour.

In contrast with this study, Ashok Rudra (1971) reports that in his investigation of big farmers in Punjab, done jointly with Abdul Majid and B. D. Talib, it was found that tractors 'create demand for permanent servants and replace casual labour'.[4] Rudra points out that 'the most frequently observed combination of permanent servants and casual

3. B. Singh (1968), p. 84.
4. Rudra (1971), p. A–89. See also Rudra, Majid and Talib (1969), (1969a), (1970).

labour is one permanent servant and between 100 and 200 man-days of casual labour for non-mechanized farms; 0 permanent servant and between 100 and 200 man-days of casual labour for farms with pumps and tube-wells but no tractors; and 2 permanent servants and between 100 and 200 man-days of casual labour for tractorized farms'.[5] Rudra's conclusions were drawn presumably after correction for size variations.

Using data from *Studies in the Economics of Farm Management* relating to the Ferozepore district in the Punjab in 1968–9, Hanumantha Rao (1972*a*) studies data for 150 farms and relates, among other things, employment to a number of variables, of which one is a dummy variable representing whether the farmer owns a tractor or not. The coefficient, close to zero, for tractorization turns out to be not significant, and Hanumantha Rao seems inclined in the direction of regarding tractorization as not labour-displacing. He argues that 'the technological displacement of labour consequent on the use of tractor is roughly compensated by the rise in employment mainly as a result of the increase in yield associated with tractor-use'.[6] He also notes that in view of the complementarity between tractorization and irrigation and the use of high-yielding varieties, tractors may under certain circumstances expand employment.

Analysing the farm survey data of the Programme Evaluation Organization of the Planning Commission of India for 1967–8, 1968–9 and 1969–70 relating to the wheat belt of the Indo-Gangetic plain, Brian Lockwood (1972) finds that 'tractors are associated with a slight *increase* in hired labour'. His prediction, however, is that 'this situation may not last' when other operations not yet mechanized are put under machines, which 'seems inevitable' (p. A-122).

In a pilot study done in Haryana, R. K. Sharma (1972) compares tractor farms and non-tractor farms carefully chosen to be similar in respect of land holding and irrigation facilities. He finds that while farms with tractors require a somewhat larger amount of total labour, the rate of utilization (defined as labour used per cropped acre) is about 7 per cent higher for bullock farms than for tractor farms. There is greater labour use in tractor farms for harvesting, weeding and irrigation, but the labour requirement for ploughing is drastically cut by tractorization.

It would appear from all this that the precise impact of tractorization on employment is by no means clear.[7] There is also some lack of clarity regarding the impact of tractors on the value of output. Rudra (1973*b*)

5. Rudra (1971), p. A–94.
6. Hanumantha Rao (1972*a*), p. 10.
7. See also Bhatty and Siddiqui (1972).

notes that in his study of big farmers in Punjab it emerged that while pumps and tube-wells seemed to add to the output value per acre, 'there is no further increase, as a matter of fact there is probably a decrease, when tractors are also added'. In contrast, Hanumantha Rao (1972a), in his study of the Ferozepore Farm Management data referred to earlier, finds a significant positive impact. R. K. Sharma's (1972) conclusion goes in the same direction, though the effect of tractorization is not separated out from other differences between these farms, e.g., greater use of fertilizers.

In a very detailed study conducted in the Shahada taluka of Dhulia district in Maharashtra, Sapre (1969) also found a substantial increase in output value as a consequence of tractorization. He also provided a painstaking economic analysis of the case for the use of tractors. This study I would like to discuss presently, but a preliminary question on the relation between employment and output may be sorted out first.

It might appear that in view of the argument outlined in Chapter 9, and blessed in the form of eqn (9.1), a larger volume of output must imply a greater employment potential. There is somewhat stronger evidence in favour of the hypothesis that tractorization increases output per acre than in favour of the hypothesis that it increases employment within the farms. In view of (9.1), it might be held that the former is the more significant indicator of employment. Thus the employment effects of tractorization might be thought to be relatively favourable in view of the argument of Chapter 9. This is, however, not so. First, tractorization may be associated with a change in the mode of production and employment and the argument of Chapter 9, as explained there, applies only to wage-based employment. Second, while tractors may raise output per acre, in assessing the overall impact of tractorization on net output and on wage employment we must take account of the resource cost of achieving this increase in output. If these resources, instead of being invested in tractors, had been used in some other line, there would have been some increase in output as well. And the relevant question is whether the rise in output as a consequence of tractorization is *larger* than what could be achieved through some alternative use of the resources involved.

D.3 Sapre's Economic Evaluation of Tractorization
Sapre (1969) provides a benefit–cost analysis of tractorization, taking care to capture as many of the effects as possible. He uses two methods for calculating the profitability of tractors. One method 'compares the farm at two points of time, i.e., before and after the introduction of tractors and takes into consideration the added costs and added returns

caused by the relevant changes brought about by mechanization'.[8] 'If added returns more than balance added costs then one can conclude that tractors are profitable.'[9] This 'budgeting method' is contrasted with the 'substitution method'. Under the latter 'the bullock and human resources needed for operating the existing farm, i.e., the farm after mechanization but without tractors were hypothetically estimated'.[10] Then the costs of the two alternative techniques of producing the existing level of output were compared.

The two methods yielded conflicting results. The budgeting method indicated that tractors contributed negatively to net returns in the aggregate. Of the 76 farms studied 41 would have suffered economically from tractorization.[11] On the other hand, the substitution method indicated an overall net gain as a consequence of tractorization. Of the 76 farms, 59 were better off with tractors than producing the same output with more bullocks and more human labour.[12] Sapre asks, 'what is it then that makes a tractor a profitable proposition?' and answers that 'the extent to which a tractor displaces the resources on the farm is the key to the profitability of tractors'.[13] I intend to argue against this conclusion.

If both the estimates are accepted, the conclusion cannot be that tractors were profitable in any sense whatsoever. They would indicate only that tractorization would be a second-best solution *if* (i) output for some reason had to be increased to the level of the currently tractorized farms, and (ii) no other means of increasing output were available than the two alternatives of tractorization and increased use of bullocks and human labour. Clearly, the best solution would be not to increase the output of these farms above the level ruling before tractorization, if the choice permits three alternatives: (a) stick to the pre-tractor production pattern, (b) move to the tractorized production pattern, and (c) produce the output combination of the tractorized farm through increased use of bullocks and human labour. This is obvious since (a) is superior to (b) and (b) to (c), in view of Sapre's figures.

However, both estimates need not be taken seriously, and as Sapre himself points out, in the use of the budgeting method 'several items had to be left out' in calculating 'the added returns'.[14] This renders irrelevant the negative judgment yielded by the budgeting method, but of course it

8. Sapre (1969), p. 63.
9. Sapre (1969), p. 63.
10. Sapre (1969), p. 92.
11. Sapre (1969), pp. 76–8.
12. Sapre (1969), pp. 81–3.
13. Sapre (1969), p. 84.
14. Sapre (1969), p. 76.

does not vindicate the use of the substitution method. There is no particular sanctity attached to the current output structure of the tractorized farms, and the choice of the output level is also a part of the exercise. Nor is there any reason to confine the choice to two methods only, viz., tractors and bullocks, since there exist other methods of increasing output.

Perhaps the most important difficulty in interpreting Sapre's results from the policy point of view lies in the relevance of the prices used in the calculations. Sapre investigates market profitability[15] and hence he is justified in using market prices. But it is not really very interesting to ask whether tractors are profitable to the farmers acquiring them; presumably they are if the farmers continue to acquire them. The more interesting question concerns the correctness of the public policy of facilitating tractorization, and requires an examination of the justification of the government policy of 'encouraging the use of tractors by making credit available to the farmers on liberal terms for this purpose and by encouraging the production of tractors'.[16]

Table D.1

Selected Items in Sapre's (1969) Calculations of Profitability of Tractors Under the Substitution Approach

Tractor capacity H.P.	Sapre's 'profit' under the substitution approach (Rs.)	Wages saved for displaced labour per tractor (Rs.)	Interest on investment and insurance (Rs.)
14	1,858	1,921	682
28–30	2,550	2,211	1,266
35	1,888	2,465	1,641
48–50	1,293	2,202	1,816

It is very difficult to defend such a policy on the basis of Sapre's figures. Table D.1 presents some of the relevant items. It may be noted that even under the substitution approach the value of wages saved due

15. 'The important issue now is, therefore, whether it pays the farmer to introduce a tractor.' (Sapre (1969), p. l.)
16. Sapre (1969), p. 1. Sapre does not seem to discriminate sufficiently between the two types of questions and the ambiguity is caught by the query which motivates Sapre's investigation: 'Do tractors really displace enough resources so as to make it an economic proposition?' (p. 1).

to labour displaced in three cases out of four exceeds the figure for 'profits' arrived at by Sapre The question of the social valuation of labour in an economy like India is relevant in this context (see Chapters 12 and 13) and gains from tractorization may be largely illusory from the social point of view. Further Sapre uses an interest rate of 6.5 per cent 'because this was the rate at which loans were available from the Land Mortgage Bank in the District'.[17] But this is well below even the normal private rates of return and may be substantially less than the figures relevant for social benefit–cost analysis.[18] A strong overestimation of the saving of labour cost and a sharp underestimation of the cost of capital help to build up a figure of profits which cannot be the basis for public policy in this field.

On top of all this, the methodological limitation of the substitution approach remains. And the alternative method yields even a private loss, despite the underestimation of the capital cost of tractorization and the overestimation of the benefits in saving of labour costs. An economic case for tractorization cannot, therefore, be based on Sapre's findings.

D.4 Hanumantha Rao's Benefit–Cost Analysis

Hanumantha Rao (1973) has done a detailed study of tractorization in the Ferozepore district in Punjab. The evaluation has been done both from the point of view of private profitability and from that of social benefit–cost analysis. For 'small farms' of 10 acres, tractors seem to yield rather low private returns, but the position is quite different for 'large farms' of 50 acres. Rao concludes:

> The analysis in this paper suggests that the incentive for tractorization among large farms arises owing to the increasing requirements of bullock and human labour with the rise in the scale of operations as well as the rise in the costs of bullock and human labour. It would appear from this that if large farms are split into small family farms, the demand for tractors may decline significantly.[19]

That the same set of techniques of production may have varying relative profitabilities under different modes of production and employment is not surprising (see Chapters 7 and 13). Rao's result brings out the relevance of the existing structure of land holdings and of the possibility of land reform for tractorization.

17. Sapre (1969), P. 72.
18. Even if the social rate of discount is taken to be low, the higher social rate of return would require the use of a shadow price of investment p^I above the market price. See Chapters 10–13 and also UNIDO (1972).
19. Hanumantha Rao (1973), p. 17. The 'social' returns from tractorization as defined by Rao can also be seen to be quite low for small farms.

Given the pattern of land ownership, however, Rao finds that from the private as well as the social point of view, tractorization in large farms is beneficial. His conclusion is, therefore, not merely that large farms find tractors profitable, but also that given the institutional structure there is a social gain from the use of tractors in large farms. As far as private profitability is concerned, Rao's conclusion seems easier to accept than the result of his social benefit—cost analysis, and his methodology needs to be carefully examined.

The benefits of tractorization arise from three sources in the Rao calculations: (i) saving of labour costs, (ii) saving of bullock costs, and (iii) additional net output generated. The cost of tractorization consists of (i) capital cost, (ii) tractor fuel costs, (iii) tractor repair costs, and (iv) cost of hiring tractor drivers; the last three are flow costs. Rao considers divergence of private and social costs in two specific fields: (a) the overvaluation of labour cost by the market, and (b) the overvaluation of tractor fuel cost by the market. The former has been much discussed in this book, whereas the latter arises simply from the fact that Rao takes 'the shadow rate exchange' to be 33 per cent higher than the official rate, while the domestic market price of diesel oil is 214 per cent higher than its import price.[20] Correction of the former overvaluation tends to reduce the social return to tractorization given other things, whereas correcting the second overvaluation has precisely the opposite effect.[21] Thus the social return from tractorization, while on. the whole lower than the private return, is not all that much lower, according to Rao's analysis. Some of the relevant figures are presented in Table D.2 for the assumed labour coefficient 0.25, which is one of two alternative assumptions that Rao considers. Three alternative values of the ratio σ of the shadow price of labour to the market wage rate are considered.

Rao does not give the details of his calculations, nor the present value estimates. He does provide values of the benefit—cost ratios, but such *ratios* do not, as is well-known, give very much information.[22] The internal rates of return are also not, in general, very helpful,[23] but it is easily checked that in the study by Rao present value is a strictly diminishing function of the rate of discount so that at least the problem of

20. Since Rao's study was completed (and also since this book was written), the situation concerning oil prices has changed rather dramatically, with a negative impact on the profitability of tractors.
21. For other inputs and outputs the gap between foreign and domestic prices, due to such restrictions as the import duty, just about balances the undervaluation of foreign exchange in Rao's estimates.
22. See McKean (1958), or O. Eckstein (1961).
23. See UNIDO (1972).

Table D.2

*Internal Rates of Return from Tractorization in Large Farms:
Private and Social (Rao's Estimates)*

	Private rate (%)	Social rate (%)		
		$\sigma = 0.25$	$\sigma = 0.50$	$\sigma = 0.75$
A: No output change, only cost saving	12.50	4.75	9.25	13.50
B: Cost saving *plus* output rise due to tractorization	29.50	24.50	27.50	30.50

Note: σ = the assumed ratio of the shadow price of labour to the market wage rate.
Source: Hanumantha Rao (1973), Tables 5 and 6.

multiplicity of the internal rate of return does not arise.

Rao points out that 'as much as 88 per cent of the amount advanced to the farmers as tractor loans by the institutional sources was at 9 to 12 per cent interest rate' in Ferozepore in the period to which his data refer.[24] This range of interest rates ensures the private profitability of tractorization, but the social profitability – as defined by Rao – will depend on the acceptability of the output contribution of tractorization, on which there is indeed some considerable doubt, as we saw in § D.2.

If cost-saving is taken to be the main contribution of tractorization, then the social case for the use of tractors, seen in terms of Rao's study, will depend precisely on the valuation of the social cost of labour. The assumptions pertaining to the extent of market overvaluation, if any, in slack seasons as well as in peak seasons will have to be brought into the picture in precise terms.

One major drawback of the Rao study is its implicit assumption that the rate of discount equals the productivity of investment in each period. This permits Rao to work in terms of a shadow price of investment which exactly equals its market price. If, on the other hand, the appropriate social rate of discount is taken to be below the social contribution of investment (see Chapter 10), the shadow price of investment must be taken to be higher. This will, of course, reduce the social profitability of tractorization, and depending on the extent of the divergence, the resulting correction may change the economic case for tractorization quite

24. Hanumantha Rao (1973), p. 13.

substantially. The fact that some alternative forms of investment (e.g., minor irrigation) are supposed to yield extremely high rates of return is of obvious relevance to this question.[25] In the picture presented by Rao, the capital costs are incurred at one point of time whereas the returns all come later. This makes the results particularly sensitive to corrections of the price of investment.

D.5 Concluding Remarks

There is so much uncertainty about the impact of tractorization on agricultural output and employment that a definitive benefit–cost analysis of this important technological change cannot be done at this stage. One major source of controversy is the extent to which tractors increase yields, in addition to reducing labour and bullock costs. As was clear from examining Sapre's (1969) and Hanumantha Rao's (1973) important studies of the problem, the results of the social benefit–cost analysis depend heavily on the yield-increasing contribution of tractorization in addition to the cost-replacing aspects.

The evidence on the magnitude of yield increases resulting from the use of tractors is conflicting, as we saw in § D.2. In fact, in sharp contrast with Hanumantha Rao's (1973) conviction that tractorization leads to a substantial increase in yield per acre, based on his study of the Ferozepore district in 1968–9, Vashishtha (1972) argues on the basis of data from the same district for the same period: 'We do not find any evidence in support of the hypothesis that mechanization leads to higher employment and output per acre' (p. 19). Vashishtha's methodology is to examine the null hypothesis that the yield per acre of tractor and non-tractor farms is the same. While the unadjusted yield per acre of tractor farms turns out to be significantly higher than that of non-tractor farms, the mean yields after adjustment for variations in the use of seed, fertilizers and irrigation turn out to be virtually the same, and in Vashishtha's analysis 'seed-fertilizer and irrigation emerge as the main yield-increasing factors' (p. 19). If this analysis is accepted, then it is Case A in Table D.2 which will be relevant, and for that case the social acceptability of tractors even for large farms will depend crucially on the shadow price of labour, even in terms of Hanumantha Rao's own framework.

25. Rao himself notes that 'the case for or against tractorization does not depend on whether the social benefit–cost ratio is higher than the private benefit–cost ratio but on the relative (social) benefit–cost ratios of alternative projects for increasing output and employment' (p. 17). This remark points in the same direction as our concern with the shadow price of investment, even though it can be argued that since costs represent sacrificed benefits, the question of relative benefit–cost ratios should enter directly into the comparative size of benefits and costs of any project – under examination. See UNIDO (1972), and Chapters 11–13 above.

The cost of bullocks also poses a valuation problem of some import-ance. Bose and Clark (1970) have indicated some evidence for Pakistan which suggests that 'much of the food consumed by the draught animal population comes from wheat straw, rice straw and forage which has an insignificant opportunity cost'. If this is indeed so, then a valuation of the saving of the cost of bullocks done at market prices (as in Hanumantha Rao (1973)) will overestimate the cost-saving contribution of tractorization. On the other hand, it is also clear that with the growth of irrigation the opportunity of shifting the pattern of crops changes significantly, making bullock feed a more expensive item in terms of its opportunity cost.[26] Much depends on the precise pattern of land use and the irrigation opportunities.

The difficulties of a rigorous benefit–cost analysis of tractorization are obvious enough. The factual picture is unclear, e.g., the extent of the yield impact of tractorization has not yet been isolated from variations in other factors not complementary to tractor use for a sufficiently large number of cases. The valuation problems, especially of labour, invest-ment, foreign exchange and bullock fodder, are also complex.

Two results do seem to be clear enough, however. First, for large farms in such areas as the Ferozepore district in Punjab, the private profit-ability of tractorization is high and is certainly larger than the rate of interest for lending and borrowing relevant for large farmers. The rush for tractors and the pressure groups that this creates should come as no surprise,[27] even though a convincing social justification for making tractors and agricultural machinery 'the first charge on the nation's resources'[28] is yet to be produced. Second for small farms (10 acres or less) the social benefit–cost picture is certainly unfavourable to tractoriz-ation even with Hunamantha Rao's assumptions, and the corrections discussed in § D.4 will reduce the benefits vis-à-vis the costs of tractoriz-ation. The case for and against tractorization depends, therefore, on the pattern of land ownership and the possibility of land reform. The ambiguities, which I have tried to outline, in doing a social benefit–cost analysis of the use of tractors in large farms, do not in any way reduce the importance of this institutional question for the technological choice under examination. In view of the arguments presented in the text of this book, this should come as no surprise.

26. See Billings and Singh (1969), Parthasarathy (1971), and Raj (1972).

27. The combination of vested interests in the promotion of tractorization is quite remarkable, and Falcon (1970) has argued that 'large farmers, foreign and domestic industrialists, politicians and even aid agencies have vested interests in promoting various implements, including tractors' (p. 706).

28. The Fourth Five Year Plan: A Draft Outline, Planning Commission, Government of India, New Delhi, p. 173.

Bibliography

Agarwala, N. (1972), 'Disguised Unemployment, Unlimited Supply of Labour and the Wage Gap', *Indian Economic Journal*, vol. 19.

Agarwala, R. (1964), 'Size of Holdings and Productivity: A Comment', *Economic Weekly*, 11 April, vol. 16.

– (1964*a*), 'Size of Holdings and Productivity: Further Comments', *Economic Weekly*, 21 November, vol. 16.

Agricultural Economic Research Centre, Delhi (1971), *Primary Education in Rural India: Participation and Wastage*, Tata McGraw-Hill, New Delhi.

Agro-Economic Research Centre, Visva-Bharati (1972), *Study Relating to the Crash Scheme for Rural Employment in the District of Bankura, West Bengal*, Santiniketan.

– (1972*a*), *Study on the Problems of Marginal Farmers and Landless Agricultural Labourers in the District of Hooghly, West Bengal*, Santiniketan.

Anand, S. (1971), 'Rural–Urban Migration in India: An Econometric Study', mimeographed.

Appavadhanulu, V. (1971), 'Working Capital and Choice of Techniques', *Indian Economic Journal*, vol. 19.

Arrow, K. J. (1962), 'The Economic Implications of Learning by Doing', *Review of Economic Studies*, vol. 29.

– Chenery, H. B., Minhas, B. S., and Solow, R. M. (1961), 'Capital Labour Substitution and Economic Efficiency', *Review of Economic Studies*, vol. 43.

– and Kurz, M. (1970), *Public Investment, the Rate of Return and Optimal Fiscal Policy*, Johns Hopkins Press, Baltimore.

Asimakopulos, A. (1969), 'A Robinsonian Growth Model in One-Sector Notation', *Australian Economic Papers*, vol. 8.

Atkinson, A. B., and Stiglitz, J. E. (1969), 'A New View of Technological Change', *Economic Journal*, vol 79.

Bagchi, A. K. (1972), *Private Investment in India 1900–39*, Cambridge University Press, London.

Bardhan, K. (1964), 'Size of Holdings and Productivity: Further Comment', *Economic Weekly*, 22 August, vol. 16.

Bardhan, P. K. (1969), 'Equilibrium Growth in a Model of Economic Obsolescence of Machines', *Quarterly Journal of Economics*, vol. 83.

– (1970), 'on the Minimum Level of Living and the Rural Poor', *Indian Economic Review*, vol. 5.

– (1970*a*), 'The Green Revolution and Agricultural Labourers', *Economic and Political Weekly*, Special Number, vol. 5.

– (1970*b*), 'The Green Revolution and Agricultural Labourers: A Correction', *Economic and Political Weekly* 14 November, vol. 5.

– (1973), 'On the Incidence of Poverty in Rural India of the Sixties', *Economic and Political Weekly*, Annual Number, vol. 8.

– (1973*a*), 'Size, Productivity and Returns to Scale: An Analysis of Farm-Level Data in Indian Agriculture', *Journal of Political Economy,* vol. 81.

– and Srinivasan, T. N. (1971), 'Cropsharing Tenancy in Agriculture: A Theoretical and Empirical Analysis', *American Economic Review*, vol. 61.

Bator, F. P. (1957), 'On Capital Productivity, Input Allocation and Growth', *Quarterly Journal of Economics*, vol. 71.

Bauer, P. T. (1948), *The Rubber Industry*, Longmans, London.

– and Yamey, B. S. (1957), *The Economics of Underdeveloped Countries*, Cambridge University Press, London.

Baumol, W. J. (1952), *Welfare Economics and the Theory of the State*, Harvard University Press, Cambridge, Mass.

– (1968), 'On the Social Rate of Discount', *American Economic Review*, vol. 58.

Bergson, A. (1964), *The Economics of Soviet Planning*, Yale University Press, New Haven.

Bernal, J. D. (1969), *Science in History*, Penguin, Harmondsworth.

Berry, R. A., and Soligo, A. (1968), 'Rural–Urban Migration, Agricultural Output and the Supply Price of Labour in a Labour Surplus Economy', *Oxford Economic Papers*, vol. 20.

Bhaduri, A. (1966), 'The Concept of Marginal Productivity of Capital and the Wicksell Effect', *Oxford Economic Papers*, vol. 18.

– (1969), 'On the Significance of Recent Controversies in Capital Theory: A Marxian View', *Economic Journal*, vol. 79.

– (1973), 'Agricultural Backwardness under Semi-Feudalism', *Economic Journal*, vol. 83.

Bhagwati, J. N., and Chakravarty, S. (1969), 'Contributions to Indian Economic Analysis', *American Economic Review*, Supplement, vol. 59.

Bhalla, A. S. (1964), 'Investment Allocation and Technological Choice',

Economic Journal, vol. 74.
- (1965), 'Choosing Techniques: Hand-pounding *vs.* Machine-milling of Rice', *Oxford Economic Papers*, vol 17.
- (1970), 'The Role of Services in Employment Expansion', *International Labour Review*, vol 103.
Bhattacharya, N., and Saini, G. R. (1972), 'Farm Size and Productivity: A Fresh Look', *Economic and Political Weekly*, 24 June, vol. 7.
Bhatty, I. Z., and Siddiqui, H. Y. (1972), 'The Validity of Tractors as Capital Input in Farms of Different Sizes', *Margin*, Quarterly Journal of National Council of Applied Economic Research, New Delhi, vol. 4.
Billings, M. H., and Singh, A. (1969), 'Labour and the Green Revolution: The Experiences of Punjab', *Economic and Political Weekly*, vol. 4.
- (1970), 'Mechanization and the Wheat Revolution: Effect on Female Labour in Punjab', *Economic and Political Weekly*, vol. 5.
- (1970*a*), 'Mechanization and Rural Employment with Some Implications for Rural Income Distribution', *Economic and Political Weekly*, 27 June, vol. 5.
Blaug, M., Layard, R., and Woodhall, M. (1969), *The Causes of Graduate Unemployment in India*, Allen Lane the Penguin Press, London.
Bliss, C. J. (1968), 'On Putty-Clay', *Review of Economic Studies*, vol. 35.
- (1970), 'Comment on Garegnani', *Review of Economic Studies*, vol. 37.
Bloch, M. (1965), *Feudal Society*, tr. L. A. Manyon, vols. 1 and 2, Routledge, London.
Bose, S., and Dixit, A. (1969), 'Development Planning: A Theoretical Analysis', unpublished manuscript
Bose, S. R., and Clark, II, E. H. (1970), 'Some Basic Considerations of Agricultural Mechanization in West Pakistan', *Pakistan Development Review*, vol. 9.
Boserup, E. (1965), *The Conditions of Agricultural Growth*, Aldine, Chicago.
Bruno, M. (1969), 'Fundamental Duality Relations in the Pure Theory of Capital and Growth', *Review of Economic Studies*, vol. 36.
- and Burmeister, E., and Sheshinski, E. (1966), 'Nature and Implications of the Reswitching of Techniques', *Quarterly Journal of Economics*, vol. 80.
- (1968), 'The Badly Behaved Production Function: Comment', *Quarterly Journal of Economics*, Vol. 82.
Burmeister, E. (1974), 'Neo-Austrian and Alternative Approaches to Capital Theory', mimeographed, *Journal of Economic Literature*, forthcoming.
- and Dobell, A. R. (1970), *Mathematical Theories of Economic Growth*, Macmillan, New York.

Chakravarty, R. M. (1972), 'Limited Labour Supply in an Under-
developed Economy', *Indian Economic Journal*, vol. 19.
Chakravarty, S. (1969), *Capital and Development Planning*, M.I.T. Press,
Cambridge, Mass.
— and Lefeber, L. (1965), 'An Optimizing Planning Model', *Economic
Weekly*, Annual Number vol. 17.
Chakravarty, Subroto (1972), paper presented at the 1972 Annual Con-
ference of the Indian Economic Association.
Champernowne, D. (1954), 'The Production Function and the Theory of
Capital', *Review of Economic Studies*, vol. 21.
Chattopadhyay, P. (1972), 'Mode of Production in Indian Agriculture',
Economic and Political Weekly, 25 March, vol. 7.
— (1972*a*), 'Mode of Production in Indian Agriculture: An "Anti-
Kritik" ', *Economic and Political Weekly*, 30 December, vol. 7.
Chaudhri, D. P. (1968), 'Education and Agricultural Productivity in
India', unpublished Ph.D. dissertation, Delhi University.
— (1969), 'Education of Farmers and Productivity', in N. Pandit (ed.),
Measurement of Cost, Productivity and Efficiency in Education,
NCERT, New Delhi.
— (1971), 'Education in Production in Modernizing Agriculture in Asian
Under-developed Countries', in Japan Economic Research Centre,
Agriculture and Economic Development, Tokyo.
Chaudhuri, P. (1971), ed., *Aspects of Indian Economic Development*,
Allen and Unwin, London.
— (1972), ed., *Readings in Indian Agricultural Development*, Allen and
Unwin, London.
Chayanov, A. V. (1966), *The Theory of Peasant Economy*, ed. D.
Thorner, B. Kerblay, and R. E. F. Smith, Irwin, Homewood, Ill.
Chen, N., and Galenson, W. (1969), *The Chinese Economy Under Com-
munism*, Aldine, Chicago
Chenery, H. B. (1961), 'Comparative Advantage and Development
Policy', *American Economic Review*, vol. 51.
— and Clark, P. G. (1959), *Inter-industry Economics*, Wiley, New York.
Cheung, S. N. S. (1968), 'Private Property Rights and Sharecropping',
Journal of Political Economy, vol. 76.
— (1969), *The Theory of Share Tenancy*, University of Chicago Press.
Chopra, K. R. (1972), *Dualism and Investment Patterns*, Tata McGraw-
Hill, Bombay.
Clague, C. (1969), 'Capital–Labour Substitution in Developing
Countries', *Econometrica*, vol 37.
Cooper, C. (1972), 'The Choice between Alternative Mechanisms for
Setting up an Oil Refinery in a Developing Country: An Applica-
tion of Cost–Benefit Techniques to a Bargaining Situation',
mimeographed, Science Policy Research Unit, Sussex University.
— (1972*a*), 'Sectoral Capital Intensities', mimeographed, Science Policy
Research Unit, Sussex University.

Dandekar, V. M. (1962), 'Economic Theory and Agrarian Reform', *Oxford Economic Papers*, vol. 14.

— and Rath, N. (1971), *Poverty in India*, Indian School of Political Economy, Poona.

Das-Gupta, A. K. (1954), 'Keynesian Economics and Underdeveloped Countries', *Economic Weekly*, 26 January, vol. 6; reprinted in Das-Gupta (1965).

— (1956), 'Disguised Unemployment and Economic Development', *Economic Weekly*, 25 August, vol. 8; reprinted in Das-Gupta (1965).

— (1965), *Planning and Economic Growth*, Allen & Unwin, London.

Dasgupta, Ajit, and Pearce, D. W. (1972), *Cost—Benefit Analysis: Theory and Evidence*, Macmillan, London.

Dasgupta, P. (1972), 'A Comparative Analysis of the UNIDO *Guidelines* and the OECD *Manual*', *Bulletin of the Oxford Institute of Economics and Statistics*, vol. 34.

— and Stiglitz, J. E. (1973), 'Benefit—Cost Analysis and Trade Policies', *Journal of Political Economy*, vol. 81.

Dasgupta, S. (1972), 'Innovation and Yield Rates in Indian Agriculture', mimeographed, Institute of Economic Growth, Delhi.

Datta-Chaudhuri, M. (1967), 'Optimum Allocation of Investments and Transportation in a Two-Region Economy', in K. Shell (ed.), *Essays on the Theory of Optimal Economic Growth*, M. I. T. Press, Cambridge, Mass

— (1967a), 'Regional Specialization in Metallurgical and Metal-using Industries in India', *Indian Economic Review*, vol. 2.

— and Sen, A. K. (1970), 'Durgapur Fertilizer Project: An Economic Evaluation', *Indian Economic Review*, vol. 5.

Desai, M., and Mazumdar, D. (1970), 'A Test of the Hypothesis of Disguised Unemployment', *Economica*, vol. 37.

Dhar, P. N., and Lydall, H. F. (1961), *The Role of Small Enterprises in Indian Economic Development*, Asia Publishing House, Bombay.

Dharm Narain (1972), *Growth and Imbalances in Indian Agriculture*, Indian Society of Agricultural Statistics.

Diamond, P. A., and Mirrlees, J. A. (1971), 'Optimal Taxation and Public Production, I', *American Economic Review*, vol. 61.

Dixit, A. K. (1968), 'Optimal Development in the Labour Surplus Economy', *Review of Economic Studies*, vol. 35.

— (1971), 'Short-run Equilibrium and Shadow Prices in the Dual Economy', *Oxford Economic Papers*, vol. 23.

Dobb, M. H. (1948), *Soviet Economic Development Since 1917*, Routledge, London.

— (1955), *On Economic Theory and Socialism*, Routledge, London.

— (1956), 'Second Thoughts on Capital-Intensity', *Review of Economic Studies*, vol. 23

— (1960), *An Essay on Economic Growth and Planning*, Routledge, London.

Domar, E. D. (1966), 'The Soviet Collective Farm as a Producer Co-operative', *American Economic Review*, vol. 56.

Dorfman, R., Samuelson, P. A., and Solow, R. M. (1958), *Linear Programming and Economic Analysis*, McGraw-Hill, New York.

Dorner, P. (1972), *Land Reform and Economic Development*, Penguin, Harmondsworth.

Dumont, R. (1957), *Types of Rural Economy*, Methuen, New York.

Eckaus, R. S. (1955), 'The Factor-Proportions Problem in Under-developed Areas', *American Economic Review*, vol. 65.

– and Parikh, K. S. (1968), *Planning for Growth: Multisectoral, Intertemporal Models Applied to India*, M. I. T. Press, Cambridge, Mass.

Eckstein, A. (ed.) (1971), *Comparison of Economic Systems: Theoretical and Methodological Approaches*, University of California Press, Berkeley.

– Galenson, W., and Liu, T. (1968), *Economic Trends in Communist China*, Edinburgh University Press.

Eckstein, O. (1957), 'Investment Criteria for Economic Development and the Theory of Intertemporal Welfare Economics', *Quarterly Journal of Economics,* vol 71.

– (1961), 'A Survey of the Theory of Public Expenditure Criteria', in National Bureau of Economic Research, *Public Finance: Needs, Sources and Utilization*, Princeton University Press.

Education Commission, Government of India (1966), *Report of the Education Commission 1964–66*, New Delhi.

Elkan, W. (1973), *An Introduction to Development Economics*, Penguin, Harmondsworth.

Falcon, W. P. (1970), 'The Green Revolution: Generations of Problems', *American Journal of Agricultural Economics*, vol. 52.

Fei, J. C. H., and Ranis G. (1964), *Development of the Labor Surplus Economy: Theory and Policy*, Irwin, Homewood, Ill.

Feldstein, M. S. (1964), 'The Social Time Preference Discount Rate in Cost–Benefit Analysis', *Economic Journal*, vol. 74.

– (1972), 'Financing in the Evaluation of Public Expenditure', in Layard (1972).

Ferguson, C. E. (1969), *The Neo-classical Theory of Production and Distribution*, Cambridge University Press, London.

Findlay, R. (1962), 'Capital Theory and Development Planning', *Review of Economic Studies*, vol 29.

Finley, M. I. (1959), 'The Greeks and Their Slaves', *The Listener*, 10 September.

Fisher, F. M. (1965), 'Embodied Technical Change and the Existence of an Aggregate Capital Stock', *Review of Economic Studies*, vol. 32.

– (1969), 'The Existence of Aggregate Production Functions', *Econometrica*, vol. 37.
– (1971), 'The Existence of Aggregate Production Functions: Reply', *Econometrica*, vol 39
Frank, C. R. (1968), 'Urban Unemployment and Economic Growth in Africa', *Oxford Economic Papers*, vol. 20.
Frankel, F. R. (1971), *India's Green Revolution: Economic Gains and Political Costs*, Princeton University Press.
Freud, S. (1924), *A General Introduction to Psychoanalysis*, Boni and Liveright, Washington Press edition, 1960.

Gaiha, R. (1972), 'An Input Output Analysis of Labour Productivity in the Indian Economy', mimeographed, Institute of Economic Growth, Delhi.
Galenson, W., and Leibenstein, H. (1955), 'Investment Criteria, Productivity and Economic Development', *Quarterly Journal of Economics*, vol. 69
– and Pyatt, G. (1964), *The Quality of Labour and Economic Development in Certain Countries*, ILO, Geneva.
Garegnani, P. (1966), 'Switching of Techniques', *Quarterly Journal of Economics*, vol. 80.
– (1970), 'Heterogeneous Capital, the Production Function and the Theory of Distribution', *Review of Economic Studies*, vol. 37.
– (1970a), 'A Reply', *Review of Economic Studies*, vol. 37.
Georgescu-Roegen, N. (1960), 'Economic Theory and Agrarian Reforms', *Oxford Economic Papers*, vol. 12.
Ghosh, B. N. (1972), 'A Note on "Work Making" and "Work Stretching" Aspects of Disguised Unemployment', *Indian Economic Journal*, vol. 19.
Gintis, H. (1972), 'Alienation and Power', *Review of Radical Political Economics*, vol 4.
Guha, A. (1969), 'Accumulation, Innovation, and Growth under Conditions of Disguised Unemployment', *Oxford Economic Papers*, vol. 21.
Gupta, R. (1971), 'Rural Works Programme: Where It Has Gone Astray', *Economic and Political Weekly*, 15 May, vol. 6.
Gupta, S. C. (1962), 'New Trends of Growth', *Seminar*, No. 38.
Gupta, Satyadev (1972), 'Shadow Price of Labour', *Indian Economic Journal*, vol. 19.

Habakkuk, H. J. (1962), *American and British Technology in the Nineteenth Century*, Cambridge University Press, London.
– (1963), 'Second Thoughts on American and British Technology in the Nineteenth Century', *Business Archives and History*, vol. 3.
Hahn, F. H. (1966), 'Equilibrium Dynamics with Heterogeneous Capital Goods', *Quarterly Journal of Economics*, vol. 80.

– (1970), 'Some Adjustment Processes', *Econometrica*, vol. 38.
– and Matthews, R. C. O. (1964), 'The Theory of Economic Growth: A Survey', *Economic Journal*, vol. 74.
Hansen, B. (1966), 'Marginal Productivity Wage Theory and Subsistence Wage Theory in Egyptian Agriculture', *Journal of Development Studies*, vol. 2.
Harberger, A. C. (1971). 'On Measuring the Social Opportunity Cost of Labour', *International Labour Review*, vol. 103.
– (1972), *Project Evaluation: Collected Papers*, Macmillan, London.
Harcourt, G. C. (1969), 'Some Cambridge Controversies in the Theory of Capital', *Journal of Economic Literature*, vol. 7.
– (1972), *Some Cambridge Controversies in the Theory of Capital*, Cambridge University Press, London.
Harris, D. J. (1967), 'Inflation, Income Distribution and Capital Accumulation in a Two-Sector Model of Growth', *Economic Journal*, vol. 77.
Harris, J. R., and Todaro, M. P. (1969), 'Wages, Industrial Employment and Labour Productivity: The Kenyan Experience', *Eastern Africa Economic Review*, vol. 1.
– (1970), 'Migration, Unemployment and Development: A Two-sector Analysis', *American Economic Review*, vol. 60.
Harwitz, M. (1965), 'The Significance of an Epidemic', *Journal of Political Economy*, vol 73.
Hazari, B., and Krishnamurty, J. (1970), 'Employment Implications of India's Industrialization: Analysis in an Input–Output Framework', *Review of Economics and Statistics*, vol. 52.
Heal, G. (1973), *The Theory of Economic Planning*, North-Holland, Amsterdam.
Hewavitharana, B. (1971), 'Choice of Techniques in Ceylon', in E. A. G. Robinson and M. Kidron (eds.), *Economic Development in South Asia*, Macmillan, London.
Hicks, J. R. (1960), 'Thoughts on the Theory of Capital: The Corfu Conference', *Oxford Economic Papers*, vol. 12.
– (1965), *Capital and Growth*, Clarendon Press, Oxford.
– (1970), 'A Neo-Austrian Theory of Growth', *Economic Journal*, vol. 80.
– (1973), *Capital and Time*, Clarendon Press, Oxford.
Hirschman, A. O. (1958), *The Strategy of Economic Development*, Yale University Press New Haven.
– (1967), *Development Projects Observed*, Brookings, Washington.
Hoffman, C. (1967), *Work Incentive Practices and Policies in the People's Republic of China, 1953–65*, S. U. N. U. Press, New York.
Hopper, D. W. (1965), 'Allocation Efficiency in Traditional Indian Agriculture', *Journal of Farm Economics*, vol. 47.
Hornby, J. M. (1968), 'Investment and Trade Policy in the Dual Economy', *Economic Journal*, vol. 78.

Huang Chen *et al.* (1972), *China Tames Her Rivers*, Foreign Languages Press, Peking.
Hurwicz, L. (1971), 'Centralization and Decentralization in Economic Processes', in A. Eckstein (1971).
Hymer, S., and Resnick, S. (1969), 'A Model of an Agrarian Economy with Non-Agricultural Activities', *Review of Economic Studies*, vol. 36.

ILO (1961), *Employment Objectives in Economic Development*, Geneva.
− (1970), *Towards Full Employment: A Programme for Colombia*, Geneva. Led by D. Seers.
− (1971), *Matching Employment Opportunities and Expectations: A Programme of Action for Ceylon*, Geneva. Led by D. Seers.
− (1971a), *Concepts of Labour Force Utilization*, Geneva.
− (1972), *Employment, Incomes and Equality: A Strategy for Increasing Productive Employment in Kenya*, Geneva. Led by R. Jolly and H. W. Singer.
− (1972a), *Employment and Income Policies for Iran*, Geneva.
Inukai, I. (1970), 'Farm Mechanization, Output and Labor Input: A Case Study of Thailand', *International Labour Review*, vol. 101.
Ishikawa, S. (1962), 'Choice of Techniques in Mainland China', *The Developing Economies*, vol 1.
− (1970), *Agricultural Development Strategies in Asia: Case Studies in the Philippines and Thailand*, Asian Development Bank, Manila.
− (1967), *Economic Development in Asian Perspective*, Kinokuniya, Tokyo.
− (1973), 'A Note on the Choice of Technology in China', *Journal of Development Studies*, vol 9.
− and Ohkawa, K. (1972), 'Significance of Japan's Experience: Technological Changes in Agricultural Production and Changes in Agrarian Structure', in Japan Economic Research Centre, *Agriculture and Economic Development*, Tokyo.

Jayawardena, V. K. (1972), *The Rise of the Labor Movement in Ceylon*, Duke University Press, Durham, North Carolina.
Johansen, L. (1959), 'Substitution versus Fixed Production Coefficients in the Theory of Economic Growth: A synthesis', *Econometrica*, vol. 27.
− (1961), 'A Method for Separating the Effects of Capital Accumulation and Shifts in Production Function upon Growth in Labour Productivity', *Economic Journal*, vol. 71.
− (1972), *Production Functions*, North-Holland, Amsterdam.
Johnson, D. Gale (1950), 'Resource Allocation under Share Constraints', *Journal of Political Economy*, vol. 58.

Jolly, R., de Kadt, E., Singer, H., and Wilson, F. (1973), *Third World Employment: Problems and Strategy*, Penguin, Harmondsworth.

Jorgenson, D. W. (1961), 'The Development of a Dual Economy', *Economic Journal*, vol 71.

— (1966), 'The Embodiment Hypothesis', *Journal of Political Economy*, vol. 73.

— (1967), 'Surplus Agricultural Labour and the Development of a Dual Economy', *Oxford Economic Papers*, vol. 19.

— and Griliches, Z. (1967), 'The Explanation of Productivity Change', *Review of Economic Studies*, vol. 34.

— and Lau, L. J. (1969), 'An Economic Theory of Agricultural Household Behaviour', paper presented to the Fourth Far Eastern Meeting of the Econometric Society, Tokyo.

Joshi, H. (1972), 'World Prices as Shadow Prices: A Critique', *Bulletin of the Oxford Institute of Economics and Statistics*, vol. 34.

Joshi, V. (1972), 'The Rationale and Relevance of the Little–Mirrlees Criterion', *Bulletin of the Oxford Institute of Economics and Statistics*, vol. 34

Kahlon, A. S., and Gill, D. S. (1967), 'A Case for Mechanizing Selected Agricultural Operations in Punjab', *Agricultural Situation in India*, vol. 21.

Kahn, A. E. (1951), 'Investment Criteria in Development Programs', *Quarterly Journal of Economics*, vol 15.

Kaldor, N. (1957), 'A Model of Economic Growth', *Economic Journal*, vol. 67.

— and Mirrlees, J. A. (1962), 'A New Model of Economic Growth', *Review of Economic Studies*, vol. 29.

Kao, C. H. C., Anschel, K. R., and Eicher, C. K. (1964), 'Disguised Unemployment in Agriculture', in C. K. Eicher and L. Witt (eds.), *Agriculture in Economic Development*, McGraw-Hill, New York.

Karlin, S. (1959), *Mathematical Methods and Theory in Games, Programming and Economics*, vol. I, Addison-Wesley, Reading, Mass.

Keynes, J. M. (1936), *The General Theory of Employment, Interest and Money*, Macmillan, London.

Khusro, A. M. (1964), 'Returns to Scale in Indian Agriculture', *Indian Journal of Agricultural Economics*, vol. 19.

Kindleberger, C. P. (1958), *Economic Development*, McGraw-Hill, New York.

Knight, J. B. (1969), 'Earnings, Employment, Education and Income in Uganda', *Bulletin of the Oxford Institute of Economics and Statistics*, vol. 31.

Koopmans, T. C. (1957), *Three Essays on the State of Economic Science*, McGraw-Hill New York.

— and Montias, J. M. (1971), 'On the Description and Comparison of Economic Systems', in A. Eckstein (1971).

Krishnaji, N. (1971), 'Wages of Agricultural Labour', *Economic and Political Weekly*, 25 September, vol. 6.

Krishnamurty, J. (1972), 'Some Dimensions of the Urban Unemployment Problem', Working Paper 66, Delhi School of Economics.

– (1972*a*), 'Working Force in 1971 Census', *Economic and Political Weekly*, 15 January, vol. 7.

Kumar, D. (1970), 'Technical Change and Dualism within Agriculture in India', *Journal of Development Studies*, vol. 7.

Kuznets, S. (1966), *Modern Economic Growth: Rate, Structure and Spread,* Yale University Press, New Haven.

Ladejinsky, W. (1970), 'Ironies of India's Green Revolution', *Foreign Affairs*, vol. 48.

Lal, D. (1972), *Wells and Welfare*, OECD, Paris.

– (1972*a*), 'Poverty and Unemployment: A Question of Policy', *South Asian Review*, vol. 5.

Layard, R. (1972), *Cost–Benefit Analysis*, Penguin, Harmondsworth.

Lefeber, L. (1958), *Allocation in Space*, North-Holland, Amsterdam.

– (1968), 'Planning in a Surplus Labor Economy', *American Economic Review*, vol. 58.

– and Datta-Chaudhuri, M. (1971), *Regional Development Experiences and Prospects in South and Southeast Asia,* Mouton, Paris and The Hague.

Leibenstein, H. (1957), 'The Theory of Underemployment in Backward Economies', *Journal of Political Economy*, vol. 65.

– (1966), 'Allocative Efficiency *vs.* *x*-Efficiency', *American Economic Review*, vol. 56

Lele, U. J., and Mellor J. W. (1972), 'Jobs, Poverty and the Green Revolution', *International Affairs*.

Levhari, D. (1965), 'A Nonsubstitution Theorem and Switching of Techniques', *Quarterly Journal of Economics*, vol. 79.

– and Samuelson, P. A. (1966), 'The Nonswitching Theorem is False', *Quarterly Journal of Economics*, vol. 80.

Lewis, W. A. (1954), 'Economic Development with Unlimited Supplies of Labour', *Manchester School*, vol. 22.

– (1955), *The Theory of Economic Growth*, Irwin, Homewood, Ill.

– (1958), 'Unlimited Labour: Further Notes', *Manchester School*, vol. 32.

Little, I. M. D., and Mirrlees, J. A. (1969), *Manual of Industrial Project Analysis in Developing Countries*, vol. II, *Social Cost Benefit Analysis*, OECD, Paris

– (1972), 'A Reply to Some Criticisms of the OECD Manual', *Bulletin of the Oxford Institute of Economics and Statistics*, vol. 34.

Lockwood, B. (1972), 'Investment in Farm Machinery', *Economic and Political Weekly*, 30 September vol. 7.

Lu, C. L. (1971), 'The Local Industry and its Impact on Agricultural Development in China', *Asia Quarterly*, vol. 4.

Luce, R. D., and Raiffa, H. (1957), *Games and Decisions*, Wiley, New York.

Lutz, F. A., and Hague, D. C. (1961), *The Theory of Capital*, Macmillan, London.

Mahalanobis, P. C. (1969), 'The Asian Drama: An Indian View', *Economic and Political Weekly*, Special Number, vol. 4.

Mahbub-ul-Haq (1963), *The Strategy of Economic Planning*, Oxford University Press, London.

Malinvaud, E. (1967), 'Decentralized Procedures for Planning', in E. Malinvaud and M. O. L. Bacharach (eds.), *Activity Analysis in the Theory of Growth and Planning*, Macmillan, London.

Manne, A. (1967), *Investments for Capacity Expansion: Size, Location and Time-Phasing*, Allen & Unwin, London.

― and Rudra, A. (1965), 'A Consistency Model of India's Fourth Plan', *Sankhya*, vol. 27B.

Marglin, S. A. (1963). 'The Social Rate of Discount and the Optimal Rate of Investment', *Quarterly Journal of Economics*, vol. 77.

― (1963a), 'The Opportunity Costs of Public Investment', *Quarterly Journal of Economics*, vol 77.

― (1966), 'Industrial Development in the Labor Surplus Economy', mimeographed, Harvard University.

― (1967), *Public Investment Criteria*, Allen & Unwin, London.

Marschak, J. (1950), 'Rational Behavior, Uncertain Prospects and Measurable Utility', *Econometrica*, vol. 18; also 'Errata', *Econometrica*, vol. 18.

Marsden, K. (1970), 'Progressive Technologies for Developing Countries', *International Labour Review*, vol. 101.

Marshall, A. (1890), *Principles of Economics*, Macmillan, London.

Marx, K. (1875), *Critique of the Gotha Programme*; English translation in K. Marx and F. Engels, *Selected Works*, vol. II, Foreign Languages Publishing House Moscow.

― (1887), *Capital: A Critical Analysis of Capitalist Production*, Vol. I, ed. F. Engels, Sonnenschein, London.

Mathur, A. (1964), 'The Anatomy of Disguised Unemployment', *Oxford Economic Papers*, vol 16.

Mazumdar, D. (1959), 'Marginal Productivity Theory of Wages and Disguised Unemployment', *Review of Economic Studies*, vol. 26.

― (1963), 'On the Economics of Relative Efficiency of Small Farmers', *Economic Weekly*, Special Number, vol. 15.

― (1965), 'Size of Farm and Productivity: A Problem of Indian Peasant Agriculture,' *Economica*, vol. 32.

― (1973), 'Theory of Urban Unemployment in Less Developed Countries', mimeographed.

McIntosh, J. (1972), 'Some Notes on the Surrogate Production Function', *Review of Economic Studies*, vol. 39.

McKean, R. N. (1958), *Efficiency in Government through Systems Analysis*, Wiley, New York.

Meade, J. E. (1961), 'Mauritius: A Case Study in Malthusian Economics', *Economic Journal*, vol 71.

Mehra, S. (1966), 'Surplus Labour in Indian Agriculture', *Indian Economic Review*, vol. 1. Reprinted in Chaudhuri (1972).

Mehta, S. D. (1954), *The Cotton Mills of India*, Textile Association, Bombay.

Mellor, J. W. (1963), 'The Use and Productivity of Farm Family Labour in Early Stages of Agricultural Development', *Journal of Farm Economics*, vol. 45.

— and Stevens, R. D. (1956), 'The Average and Marginal Product of Farm Labour in Underdeveloped Countries', *Journal of Farm Economics*, vol. 38.

Minhas, B. S. (1970), 'Rural Poverty, Land Redistribution and Development Strategy', *Indian Economic Review*, vol. 5.

— (1971), 'Rural Poverty and the Minimal Level of Living: A Reply', *Indian Economic Review*, vol. 6.

Morishima, M. (1964), *Equilibrium, Stability and Growth*, Clarendon Press, Oxford.

— (1969), *Theory of Economic Growth*, Clarendon Press, Oxford.

Mukherjee, P. K. (1970), 'The HYV Programme: The Variables That Matter', *Economic and Political Weekly*, 28 March, vol. 5.

Myint, H. (1964), *The Economics of Developing Countries*, Hutchinson, London, fourth (revised) edition, 1973.

Myrdal, G. (1957), *Economic Theory and Underdeveloped Regions*, Duckworth, London.

— (1968), *Asian Drama*, Pantheon, New York.

National Council of Applied Economic Research (1972), 'Impact of Mechanization in Agriculture on Employment', mimeographed, New Delhi.

Newbery D. M. G. (1972), 'Public Policy in the Dual Economy', *Economic Journal*, vol 82

— (1973), 'The Choice of Rental Contract in Peasant Agriculture', mimeographed, Conference on Agriculture in Development Theory, Bellagio, May 1973; revised August 1973.

— (1973a), 'Cropsharing Tenancy in Agriculture: A Comment', mimeographed, Churchill College Cambridge.

Nicholls, W. H. (1960), *Southern Tradition and Regional Progress*, University of North Carolina Press, Chapel Hill.

Nordhaus, W. D. (1969), *Invention, Growth and Welfare*, M. I. T. Press Cambridge, Mass.

Nulty, L. (1972), *The Green Revolution in West Pakistan: Implications of Technological Change*, Praeger New York.

Nuti, D. M. (1970), 'Capitalism Socialism and Steady Growth', *Economic Journal*, vol 80
– (1970a), ' "Vulgar Economy" in the Theory of Income Distribution', *De Economist*, vol. 4.
Nurkse, R. (1953), *Problems of Capital Formation in Underdeveloped Countries*, Blackwell Oxford

Ohkawa, K. and Rosovsky, H. (1960), 'The Role of Agriculture in Modern Japanese Economic Development', *Economic Development and Cultural Change*, vol. 9.
Oshima, H. T. (1958), 'Underemployment in Backward Economies: An Empirical Comment', *Journal of Political Economy*, vol. 66.

Pack, H. and Bhalla, A. S. (1970), 'Labour Market Theory and the Extended Family System', mimeographed, Center for Economic Growth, Yale University.
– and Todaro, M. (1969), 'Technological Transfer, Labour Absorption and Economic Development', *Oxford Economic Papers*, vol. 21.
Paglin, S. (1965), 'Surplus Agricultural Labour and Development: Facts and Figures', *American Economic Review*, vol. 55.
Parikh, A. (1972), 'Employment Implications of Industrialization in Korea', mimeographed, University of East Anglia.
Parthasarathy, G. (1971), *Agricultural Development and Small Farmers: A Study of Andhra Pradesh*, Vikas Publications, Delhi.
Pasinetti, L. (1965), 'A New Theoretical Approach to the Problems of Economic Growth', in Pontificiae Academiae Scientiarum, *Scripta Varia*, North-Holland, Amsterdam.
– (1966), 'Changes in the Rate of Profit and Switching of Techniques', *Quarterly Journal of Economics*, vol. 80.
– (1969), 'Switching Techniques and the "Rate of Return" in Capital Theory', *Economic Journal*, vol. 79.
Patel, S. J. (1964), 'What is Holding Up Agricultural Growth?', *Economic Weekly*, Annual Number, vol 16.
Patnaik, U. (1971), 'Capitalist Development in Agriculture: A Note', *Economic and Political Weekly*, 25 September, vol. 6.
– (1972), 'On the Mode of Production in Indian Agriculture: A Reply', *Economic and Political Weekly*, 30 September, vol. 7.
– (1972a), 'Economics of Farm Size and Farm Scale', *Economic and Political Weekly*, Special Number vol. 7.
Pattanaik, P. K. (1972), 'Trade Distribution and Savings', mimeographed, Delhi School of Economics, Working Paper No. 96.
Perkins, D. H. (1969), *Agricultural Development in China: 1368–1968*, Aldine, Chicago.
Phelps, E. S. (1963), 'Substitution, Fixed Proportions, Growth and Distribution', *International Economic Review*, vol. 4.

– (1965), *Fiscal Neutrality Toward Economic Growth*, McGraw-Hill, New York.

Phelps Brown, E. H. (1962), *The Economics of Labour*, Yale University Press, New Haven.

Polak, J. J. (1943), 'Balance of Payments Problems of Countries Reconstructing with the Help of Foreign Loans', *Quarterly Journal of Economics*, vol. 57.

Pyatt, G. (1963), 'A Measure of Capital', *Review of Economic Studies*, vol. 30.

Rahman, A. (1963), 'Regional Allocation of Investment', *Quarterly Journal of Economics*, vol. 77.

Raj, K. N. (1957), *Employment Aspects of Planning in Underdeveloped Countries*, National Bank of Egypt, Cairo.

– (1960), *Some Economic Aspects of the Bhakra Nangal Project*, Asia Publishing House Bombay.

– (1972), 'The Mechanization of Agriculture in India and Sri Lanka (Ceylon)', *International Labour Review*, vol. 106.

Raj Krishna (1973), 'Unemployment in India', *Economic and Political Weekly*, 3 March, vol. 8.

Ranis, G. (1959), 'The Financing of Japanese Economic Development', *Economic History Review*, vol. 11.

Rao, A. P. (1967), 'Size of Holding and Productivity', *Economic and Political Weekly*, 11 November vol. 2.

Rao, C. H. Hanumantha (1963), 'Farm Size and Economies of Scale', *Economic Weekly*, vol 15.

– (1966), 'Alternative Explanations of the Inverse Relationship between Farm Size and Output per Acre in India', *Indian Economic Review*, vol. 1.

– (1971), 'Uncertainty, Entrepreneurship, and Sharecropping in India', *Journal of Political Economy*, vol. 79.

– (1972), 'Farm Mechanization in a Labour-Abundant Economy', *Economic and Political Weekly*, Annual Number, vol. 7.

– (1972*a*), 'Employment Implications of Green Revolution and Mechanization in Agriculture in Developing Countries: A Case Study of India', mimeographed presented at the International Economic Association Conference on the Place of Agriculture in the Development of Underdeveloped Countries.

– (1973), 'Investment in Farm Tractors in Punjab (India): Private versus Social Costs and Benefits', mimeographed, Institute of Economic Growth, Delhi

Rao, S. K. (1973), 'Measurement of Unemployment in Rural India', *Economic and Political Weekly*, vol. 8.

Rao, V. K. R. V. (1956), 'Investment, Employment and the Multiplier', in V. B. Singh (ed.), *Keynesian Economics*, People's Publishing House, Delhi.

Reddaway, W. B. (1962), *The Development of the Indian Economy*, Allen and Unwin, London.

Reserve Bank of India (1970), *Studies in Agricultural Credit*, Bombay.

Ricardo, D. (1815), *Essay on the Influence of a Low Price of Corn on the Profits of Stock*; reprinted in P. Sraffa (ed.), *Works and Correspondence of David Ricardo*, vol. 4, Cambridge University Press, 1951.

Ridker, R. G. and Lubell H. (1971), *Employment and Unemployment Problems of the Near East and South Asia*, Vikas Publications, Bombay.

Riskin, C. (1969), 'Local Industry and Choice of Techniques in Planning of Industrial Development in Mainland China', in UNIDO, *Planning for Advanced Skills and Technologies*, United Nations, New York.

— (1971), 'Small Industry and the Chinese Model of Development', *China Quarterly*, no. 46.

— (1973), 'Maoism and Motivation: A Discussion of Work Motivation in China', *Bulletin of Concerned Asian Scholars*.

Robinson, J. (1933), *The Economics of Imperfect Competition*, Macmillan, London.

— (1937), *Essays in the Theory of Employment*, Macmillan, London.

— (1954), 'The Production Function and the Theory of Capital', *Review of Economic Studies*, vol 21.

— (1956), *The Accumulation of Capital*, Macmillan, London.

— (1970), 'Capital Theory Up To Date', *Canadian Journal of Economics*, vol. 3.

— (1971), 'The Existence of Aggregate Production Functions: Comments', *Econometrica*, vol. 39.

— and Naqvi, K. A. (1967), 'The Badly Behaved Production Function', *Quarterly Journal of Economics*, vol. 81.

Robinson, W. C. (1969), 'Types of Disguised Rural Unemployment and Some Policy Implications', *Oxford Economic Papers*, vol. 21.

— (1971), 'The Economics of Work Sharing in Peasant Agriculture', *Economic Development and Cultural Change*, vol. 19.

Rosenberg, N. (1969), 'The Direction of Technological Change: Inducement Mechanism and Focusing Devices', *Economic Development and Cultural Change*, vol. 18.

Rosenstein-Rodan, P. N. (1943), 'Problems of Industrialization in Eastern and South-eastern Europe', *Economic Journal*, vol. 53.

— (1957), 'Disguised Unemployment and Underemployment in Agriculture', *Monthly Bulletin of Agricultural Economics and Statistics*, vol. 6.

Rudra, A. (1968), 'Farm Size and Yield per Acre', *Economic and Political Weekly*, vol. 3.

— (1968*a*), 'More on Returns to Scale in Indian Agriculture', *Economic and Political Weekly*, vol. 3.

– (1971), 'Employment Patterns in Large Farms of Punjab', *Economic and Political Weekly*, vol 6.

– (1973), 'Allocation Efficiency of Indian Farmers: Some Methodological Doubts', *Economic and Political Weekly*, 6 January, vol. 8.

– (1973a), 'Direct Estimation of Surplus Labour in Agriculture', *Economic and Political Weekly*, Annual Number, vol. 8.

– (1973b), 'Use of Shadow Prices in Project Evaluation', *Indian Economic Review*, vol. 8

– Majid, A., and Talib, B. D. (1969), (1969a), (1970), 'Big Farmers of Punjab', *Economic and Political Weekly*, vols. 4 and 5.

Rymes, T. K. (1971), *On Concepts of Capital and Technical Change*, Cambridge University Press, London.

Sahota, G. S. (1968), 'Efficiency of Resource Allocation in Indian Agriculture', *American Journal of Agricultural Economics*, vol. 50.

Saini, G. R. (1969), 'Farm Size, Productivity and Returns to Scale', *Economic and Political Weekly*, 18 June, vol. 4.

– (1969a), 'Resource-Use Efficiency in Agriculture', *Indian Journal of Agricultural Economics*, vol. 24.

– (1971), 'Holding Size, Productivity, and Some Related Aspects of Indian Agriculture', *Economic and Political Weekly*, 26 June, vol. 6.

Salter, W. E. G. (1960), *Productivity and Technical Change*, Cambridge University Press, London.

Samuelson, P. A. (1962), 'Parable and Realism in Capital Theory: The Surrogate Production Function', *Review of Economic Studies*, vol. 29.

Sanghvi, P. (1969), *Surplus Manpower in Agriculture and Economic Development*, Asia Publishing House, Bombay.

Sapre, S. G. (1969), *A Study of Tractor Cultivation in Shahada*, Gokhale Institute of Politics and Economics, Poona.

Sarkar, N. K. (1957), 'A Method of Estimating Surplus Labour in Peasant Agriculture in Overpopulated Underdeveloped Countries', *Journal of the Royal Statistical Society*, vol. 120.

Sarkar, K. K., and Prahladachar M. (1966), 'Mechanization as a Technological Change', *Indian Journal of Agricultural Economics*, vol. 21.

Sau, R. K. (1971), 'Resource Allocation in Indian Agriculture', *Economic and Political Weekly*, 25 September, vol. 6.

Schluter, M. G. G., and Mellor J. W. (1972), 'New Seed Varieties and the Small Farm', *Economic and Political Weekly*, vol. 7.

Schultz, T. (1964), *Transforming Traditional Agriculture*, Yale University Press, New Haven

– (1967), 'Significance of India's 1918–19 Losses of Agricultural Labour: A Reply', *Economic Journal*, vol. 77.

Scitovsky, T. (1952), 'Two Concepts of External Economies', *Journal of Political Economy*, vol 17.

Seers, D. (1970), 'Income Distribution and Employment', *Bulletin of the Institute of Development Studies*, vol. 2.

— (1970*a*), 'New Approaches Suggested by the Colombia Employment Programme', *International Labour Review*, vol. 102.

Sen, A. K. (1957), 'Some Notes on the Choice of Capital Intensity in Development Planning', *Quarterly Journal of Economics*, vol. 71.

— (1960), *Choice of Techniques*, Blackwell, Oxford. Also Sen (1968), 'Introduction to Third Edition', *Choice of Techniques*, 3rd ed.

— (1961), 'On Optimizing the Rate of Saving', *Economic Journal*, vol. 71.

— (1962), 'An Aspect of Indian Agriculture', *Economic Weekly*, Annual number, vol. 14.

— (1962*a*), 'On the Usefulness of Used Machines', *Review of Economics and Statistics*, vol 44.

— (1964), 'Size of Holdings and Productivity', *Economic Weekly*, Annual Number, vol. 16.

— (1964*a*), 'Working Capital in the Indian Economy: A Conceptual Framework and Some Estimates', in P. N. Rosenstein-Rodan (ed.), *Pricing and Fiscal Policies*, M.I.T. Press, Cambridge, Mass.

— (1966), 'Peasants and Dualism with or without Surplus Labour', *Journal of Political Economy*, vol. 74.

— (1966*a*), 'Labour Allocation in a Co-operative Enterprise', *Review of Economic Studies*, vol. 33.

— (1967), 'Surplus Labour in India: A Critique of Schultz's Statistical Test', *Economic Journal*, vol. 77; also 'A Rejoinder', *Economic Journal*, vol. 77.

— (1967*a*), 'Isolation, Assurance and the Social Rate of Discount', *Quarterly Journal of Economics*, vol. 81.

— (1968), see Sen (1960).

— (1970), *Collective Choice and Social Welfare*, Holden-Day, San Francisco, and Oliver & Boyd, Edinburgh.

— (1971), 'Aspects of Indian Education', Lal Bahadur Shastri Memorial Lectures for 1970; reprinted in Chaudhuri (1971).

— (1971*a*), 'The Methods of Evaluating the Economic Effects of Private Foreign Investment', UNCTAD, T/D/B/C.3/94/Add. 1.

— (1972), 'Control Areas and Accounting Prices: An Approach to Economic Evaluation', *Economic Journal*, vol. 82.

— (1972*a*), 'Levels of Technology in Agriculture and Employment', paper presented to the GOI—ILO Joint Workshop on Employment Generation, New Delhi, 2—7 August 1972.

— (1973), *On Economic Inequality*, Clarendon Press, Oxford.

— (1973*a*), 'Poverty, Inequality and Unemployment: Some Conceptual Issues in Measurement', *Economic and Political Weekly*, Special Number, vol. 8.

— (1974), 'On Some Debates on Capital Theory', *Economica*, vol. 41.

Sharma, R. K. (1972), *Economics of Tractor versus Bullock Cultivation*, Agricultural Economic Research Centre, Delhi.

Shell, K., and Stiglitz, J. E. (1967), 'The Allocation of Investment in a Dynamic Economy', *Quarterly Journal of Economics*, vol. 81.

Shinohara, M. (1962), *Growth and Cycles in the Japanese Economy*, Kinokuniya, Tokyo.

Shivamaggi, H. B. (1969), 'The Agricultural Labour Problem: Past Misconceptions and New Guidelines', *Economic and Political Weekly*, 29 March, vol 29.

Shonfield, A. (1960), *The Attack on World Poverty*, Chatto and Windus, London.

Singh, B. (1968), 'Economics of Tractor Cultivation: A Case Study', *Indian Journal of Agricultural Economics*, vol. 23.

Singh, S. (1972), 'Disguised Unemployment in Punjab Agriculture: 1906–7–1938–9', *Indian Economic Journal*, vol. 19.

Smith, M. A. M. (1972), 'Wage Differentials and Trade in Second Hand Machines', mimeographed, London School of Economics.

Solow, R. M. (1956), 'A Contribution to the Theory of Economic Growth', *Quarterly Journal of Economics*, vol. 70.

— (1956a), 'The Production Function and the Theory of Capital', *Review of Economic Studies*, vol 21.

— (1957), 'Technical Change and the Aggregate Production Function', *Review of Economics and Statistics*, vol. 39.

— (1960), 'Investment and Technical Progress', in K. J. Arrow, S. Karlin and P. Suppes (eds.), *Mathematical Methods in the Social Sciences 1959*, Stanford University Press.

— (1962), 'Substitution and Fixed Proportions in the Theory of Capital', *Review of Economic Studies*, vol. 29.

— (1963), 'Heterogeneous Capital and Smooth Production Functions: An Experimental Study', *Econometrica*, vol. 31.

Spaventa, L. (1959), 'Dualism in Economic Growth', *Banco Nationale del Levoro Quarterly Review*, vol 12.

— (1968), 'Realism without Parables in Capital Theory', Récherches récentes sur la fonction de production, Centre D'Etudes et de Récherches, Universitaire de Namur.

— (1970), 'Rate of Profit, Rate of Growth, and Capital Intensity in a Simple Production Model', *Oxford Economic Papers*, vol. 22.

Sraffa, P. (1960), *Production of Commodities by Means of Commodities*, Cambridge University Press, London.

Srinivasan, T. N. (1962), 'Investment Criteria and Choice of Techniques', *Yale Economic Essays*, vol 2.

— (1965), 'A Critique of the Optimizing Planning Model', *Economic Weekly*, Annual Number, vol. 17.

— (1968), 'Economic Prospects of High Yielding Varieties', *Indian Journal of Agricultural Economics*, vol. 23.

– (1971), 'The Green Revolution of the Wheat Revolution?', Discussion Paper No. 66 Indian Statistical Institute, Planning Unit, New Delhi.

– (1973), 'Farm Size and Productivity: Implications of Choice under Uncertainty', *Sankhya*, vol. 34.

Stern, N. H. (1972), 'Optimum Development in a Dual Economy', *Review of Economic Studies*, vol. 39.

Stewart, F. (1972), 'Choice of techniques in Developing Countries,' *Journal of Development Studies*, vol. 9.

– (1972*a*), 'The Choice of Techniques: A Case Study of the Manufacture of Cement Blocks in Kenya', mimeographed, Queen Elizabeth House, Oxford.

– (1972*b*), 'The Choice of Techniques: Maize Grinding in Kenya', mimeographed, Queen Elizabeth House, Oxford.

– (1973), 'Trade and Technology', in P. Streeten, ed., *Trade and Development Strategies for the 1970s*, Macmillan, London.

– and Streeten, P. (1972), 'Little–Mirrlees Methods and Project Appraisal', *Bulletin of the Oxford Institute of Economics and Statistics*, vol 34

Stigler, G. (1952), *The Theory of Price*, Macmillan, London.

Stiglitz, J. E. (1969), 'Rural–Urban Migration, Surplus Labour, and the Relationship between Urban and Rural Wages', *Eastern Africa Economic Review*, vol 1.

– (1972), 'Alternative Theory of Wage Determination and Unemployment in LDCs: I. The Labor Turnover Model', Cowles Foundation Discussion Paper No. 335, Yale University, New Haven.

– and Dasgupta, P. (1971), 'Differential Taxation, Public Production and Economic Efficiency', *Review of Economic Studies*, vol. 38.

Strassman, P. (1956), 'Economic Growth and Income Distribution', *Quarterly Journal of Economics*, vol. 70.

Swan, T. (1956), 'Economic Growth and Capital Accumulation', *Economic Record*, vol. 32.

– (1960), 'Growth Models: Of Golden Ages and Production Functions', in K. E. Berrill (ed.), *Economic Development with Special Reference to East Asia*, Macmillan, London.

Telang, M. A. (1954), 'Technique of Measuring Rural Unemployment', *Indian Journal of Agricultural Economics*, vol. 9.

Temin, P. (1966), 'Labour Scarcity and the Problem of American Industrial Efficiency in the 1850s', *Journal of Economic History*, vol. 26.

Thorbecke, E. (1973), 'The Employment Problem: A Critical Evaluation of Four ILO Comprehensive Country Reports', mimeographed, ILO, Geneva.

– and Stoutjesdijk, E. (1971), *Employment and Output*, OECD, Paris.

Thorner, D. (1964), *Agricultural Co-operation in India: A Field Report*, Asia Publishing House Bombay.

– (1967), articles in *The Statesman,* Calcutta, 1–4 November.
– and Thorner, D. (1962), *Land and Labour in India,* Asia Publishing House, Bombay.
Tinbergen, J. (1958), *The Design of Development,* Johns Hopkins Press, Baltimore.
Todaro, M. P. (1969), 'A Model of Labour Migration and Urban Unemployment in Less Developed Countries', *American Economic Review,* vol. 59.
Tripathy, R. N., and Samal B. (1969), 'Economics of High Yielding Varieties in IADP: A Study of Sambalpur in Orissa', *Economic and Political Weekly,* 25 October, vol. 4.
Turner, H. A., and Jackson D. A. S. (1970), 'On the Determination of the General Wage Level: A World Analysis', *Economic Journal,* vol. 80.
Turnham, D. (1970), *The Employment Problem in Less Developed Countries,* OECD, Paris.

UNCTAD (1972), 'Transfer of Technology', report to the third session of UNCTAD, mimeographed, Geneva.
UNIDO (1968), *Evaluation of Industrial Projects,* United Nations, New York.
(1972), *Guidelines for Project Evaluation,* United Nations, New York.
Uppal, J. S. (1969), 'Work Habits and Disguised Unemployment in Underdeveloped Countries: A Theoretical Analysis', *Oxford Economic Papers,* vol 21.
Usha Rani (1971), 'Size of Farm and Productivity', *Economic and Political Weekly,* vol 6.

Vaidyanathan, A. (1972), 'Some Aspects of Inequalities in Living Standards in Rural India', New Delhi, mimeographed.
Vashishtha, P. S. (1972), 'Impact of Farm Mechanization on Employment and Output: Some Preliminary Results', mimeographed, presented at the 12th Indian Econometric Conference, Kanpur.
Viner, J. (1957), 'Some Reflections on the Concept of "Disguised Unemployment" ', *Contribucoes a Analise do Desenvolvimento Economico.*
Visaria, P., and Visaria, L. (1973), 'Employment Planning for the Weaker Sections in Rural India', *Economic and Political Weekly,* Annual Number, vol. 8.
von Blanckenburg, P. (1972), 'Progressive Farmers in Mysore and Punjab', *Economic and Political Weekly,* 30 September, vol. 7.
von Neumann, J., and Morgenstern, O. (1947), *Theory of Games and Economic Behaviour,* Princeton University Press.
von Weizsäcker (1971), *Steady State Capital Theory,* Spring-Verlag, New York.

— (1972), 'Modern Capital Theory and the Concept of Exploitation', Working Paper No. 2, Institute of Mathematical Economics, Universität Bielefeld.

Vyas, V. S. (1972), 'Nature and Role of Rural Works Programme for Economic Development', mimeographed, Sardar Patel University, Vallabh Vidyanagar.

Vyas, V. S. (1972a), 'Institutional Change, Agricultural Production and Rural Poverty: Experience of Two Decades', mimeographed, Sardar Patel University, Vallabh Vidyanagar.

Ward, B. (1958), 'The Firm in Illyria: Market Syndicalism', *American Economic Review*, vol 48.

— (1971), 'Organization and Co-operative Economics: Some Approaches', in A. Eckstein (1971).

Weisskopf, T. E. (1967), 'A Programming Model for Import Substitution in India', *Sankhya*, vol 29B.

Wellisz, S. (1968), 'Dual Economies, Disguised Unemployment and the Unlimited Supply of Labour', *Economica*, 35.

Wheelwright, E. L., and McFarlane, B. (1970), *The Chinese Road to Socialism*, New York.

Winston, G. C. (1971), 'Capacity Utilization in Economic Development', *Economic Journal*, vol. 81.

Wong, J. (1971), 'Peasant Economic Behaviour: The Case of Traditional Agricultural Co-operation in China', *The Developing Economies*, vol. 9.

Wright, J. F. (1974), 'The Dynamics of Reswitching', mimeographed.

Yudelman, M., Butler, G., and Banerji, R. (1971), *Technological Change in Agriculture and Employment*, OECD, Paris.

Zarembka, P. (1972), *Toward a Theory of Economic Development*, Holden-Day, San Francisco.

Index of Names

Subject Index

191

Christopher Golden is an award-winning, *New York Times* bestselling author. He has collaborated on books, comics, videogames and scripts with other writers, including Mike Mignola, Amber Benson, and Charlaine Harris. He has also written novels for teens and young adults and, as an editor, has worked on several short story anthologies. Golden was born and raised in Massachusetts, where he still lives with his family.

You can discover more about the author at www.christophergolden.com

SNOWBLIND

Twelve years ago the small town of Coventry, Massachusetts was in the grasp of a particularly brutal winter. And then came the Great Storm. It hit hard. Not everyone saw the spring. Today the families, friends and lovers of the victims are still haunted by the ghosts of those they lost so suddenly. If only they could see them one more time, hold them close, tell them they love them. It was the deadliest winter in living memory. Until now. When a new storm strikes, it doesn't just bring snow and ice; it brings the people of Coventry exactly what they've been wishing for. And the realisation that their nightmare is only beginning . . .

CHRISTOPHER GOLDEN

SNOWBLIND

Complete and Unabridged

CHARNWOOD
Leicester

First published in Great Britain in 2014 by
Headline Publishing Group
A division of Hachette UK Ltd
London

First Charnwood Edition
published 2015
by arrangement with
Hachette UK Ltd
London

The moral right of the author has been asserted

All characters in this publication are fictitious and
any resemblance to real persons, living or dead,
is purely coincidental.

A catalogue record for this book is available
from the British Library.

ISBN 978–1–4448–2420–9

Published by
F. A. Thorpe (Publishing)
Anstey, Leicestershire

Set by Words & Graphics Ltd.
Anstey, Leicestershire
Printed and bound in Great Britain by
T. J. International Ltd., Padstow, Cornwall

This book is printed on acid-free paper

For Lily Grace Golden,
who brightens even the darkest days

1

Ella Santos stood on the sidewalk with a cigarette in her hand, watching the snow fall and feeling more alone than she ever had in her life. The storm seemed to loom around her, holding its breath and waiting for her to go back inside. For a couple of impossibly long minutes, no cars or plows appeared on the street. The bank and the boutique and the music store and the other restaurants on that stretch of Washington Street had all been closed up for hours, windows dark and abandoned. The city of Coventry had given itself over to the storm, and suddenly Ella felt foolish that she hadn't already gone home and crawled into bed with a mug of tea and an old movie.

She took a long drag on her cigarette and huddled deeper inside her down jacket before exhaling the smoke from her lungs. The only sound was the snow itself, falling so hard and fast that she could hear the strange shush of it accumulating. Ella shivered, and not entirely from the cold. Alone on the street, she might have been the last woman on Earth, the only human voice remaining but afraid to interrupt the quiet conversation between snow and sky.

A squeak of hinges and a burst of laughter came from behind her and she jumped, startled by two women emerging from the restaurant at her back. Quiet music — the lilt of an acoustic guitar — carried out to her as well, just before the door swung shut.

'Night, Ella,' one of the women said, pushing her blond hair out of her eyes. 'Thanks for staying open.'

Ella smiled, feeling foolish for the way she'd let the weird isolation out on the street get under her skin. As a kid she'd loved snowstorms, but as the adult owner of a restaurant, snow days were few and far between . . . and very bad for business.

'My pleasure,' she said, waving as the two women hurried across the street to their car, their shoes leaving tracks in the newfallen snow. 'I hope you enjoyed your meal. Get home safe.'

'You, too!' called the second woman, whose dress was entirely inappropriate for a snowstorm, even covered by her heavy jacket.

'Closing soon,' Ella replied.

The women had been inside the restaurant for just over an hour and at least an inch of snow covered their car. Instead of trying to clean it off they piled in, and now the windshield wipers kicked on, sweeping areas of the glass clean. The rear window remained covered with snow as they pulled from the curb. The driver would hardly be able to see a thing, but fortunately there weren't a lot of other cars on the road. Even the plows didn't seem to be making many appearances tonight.

Ella took another drag on her cigarette, letting the smoke warm her before she blew it out through her nostrils. She had started smoking one summer in high school when most of her girlfriends had taken up the habit. Now she hated it, knew it made her look weak and foolish instead of cool and sexy, but she'd tried to quit half-a-dozen times and always started up again.

A loud bang and scrape announced the arrival of a plow several blocks distant and she turned to watch its grinding progress, the upper halves of its headlights peering over the giant metal blade.

The restaurant door swung open again and she turned to see her bartender, Ben Hemming, poking his head out. His blue eyes blinked against the sudden gust that drove snow into his face.

'You okay, boss?'

Ella smiled, reaching up to wipe snow from her eyelashes. 'Just thinking. Things wrapping up in there?'

'Near enough,' Ben replied.

If he thought she had a screw loose, standing out there in a storm that was fast becoming a blizzard, he hid it well. *Maybe it is a little crazy*, Ella thought. But as isolated as it made her feel, she liked the pure white calm of it all.

'Time?' she asked.

'Quarter after eight,' Ben replied, snowflakes adding to the premature white in his hair.

'All right,' she said, tossing the cigarette to the snowy sidewalk and grinding it out with her bootheel. 'Last call. We'll close up at eight thirty.'

'Thanks,' Ben said. He started to duck back inside, then hesitated. 'You sure you're okay?'

Ella bent to pick up the crushed, damp cigarette butt. 'Always.'

3

Ben didn't recognize the lie or at least didn't challenge it. He let the door swing shut, in a hurry to start closing out tabs. Ella couldn't blame him; Ben had a pretty wife and a new baby at home and he didn't want to leave them alone in the storm. Nobody was waiting for Ella back at her little house on Cherry Road. For her, there was no rush.

As she pulled on the ornate door handle a massive gust of wind slammed it tight again. It felt as if the storm fought against her, but she forced the door open and slipped inside. She turned as the door swung shut and caught a glimpse of the plow going by. In its headlights she saw just how thick and fast the snow was falling. Then the door slammed and she flinched. The blizzard had arrived.

The Vault had two big fireplaces, which had been roaring all through dinner and had now begun to die down. The early evening had been fairly busy despite the storm. Now, only three tables were occupied, but the family at one and the older couple at another were in the process of gathering their things and slipping on jackets and scarves and gloves. The trio of twenty-something guys at the last table seemed in no hurry, sipping their coffees while one worked slowly at his tiramisu.

Four people were at the bar — all of them regulars who would go now that Ben had doubtless announced last call. In the far corner, where she had live music Thursdays through Saturdays, TJ Farrelly sat on a stool with his fat-bellied acoustic guitar, playing an old Dave

4

Matthews song. It made Ella smile. As long as somebody was there to hear, TJ would keep playing. Sometimes he would play after all the customers were gone, entertaining the staff while they swept up and cashed out.

Snow melting in her hair, trickling icily down her neck, Ella went into the ladies' room to flush her cigarette butt, promising herself she wouldn't smoke again tonight. She glanced in the mirror and laughed softly at her reflection, reaching up to brush the snow out of her hair and off the shoulders of her coat.

As she left the bathroom, the small window set high on the wall began to rattle in its frame and she thought she could actually feel the building sway. The restaurant was sturdy — once upon a time it had been a bank — but the walls shook and the draft that whipped around her made the bathroom door close with a bang.

It almost felt as if the storm had come in after her.

★ ★ ★

TJ watched Ella cross the restaurant and exchange a quiet word with the last group of diners at The Vault, three guys who seemed intent on camping overnight at the table if only someone would keep the coffee coming. TJ thought it was funny how the career drinkers at the bar would happily slide off their stools, tip the bartender, and head home, but the guys reminiscing over coffee were reluctant.

Old friends, TJ figured. *High-school buddies*

5

who haven't seen each other in a while. He would have asked them, but he felt fairly certain. TJ had always been observant; he had a knack for figuring people out, though Ella tended to puzzle him. The restaurant was basically her life. TJ figured it was normal for someone to be that wrapped up in an endeavor like this, where the financial margins were slim and the risk of ruin was pretty sizable. But Ella was thirty-two years old and single, not to mention considerably attractive, with long legs and chocolate-brown eyes and a mouth he'd thought more than once about kissing. There had to be someone she trusted enough to manage the restaurant a couple of times a week so that she could do something for herself — go to a movie or a concert or, for once, eat somewhere other than in her office in the back room of her own restaurant.

As if summoned by his ruminating about her, Ella came his way, a drink in one hand. In the other she carried her blue down jacket, which dripped with melting snow. The storm had wreaked havoc with her wavy, shoulder-length hair, but TJ thought the disheveled look worked for her.

He cut off the song he'd been singing even as she dumped her jacket onto the four-top table closest to him and sank into a chair. Sipping the drink — he guessed Captain Morgan and Coke — she put her feet up on the chair across from her. The back fireplace crackled off to her left and he saw that she was enjoying the heat.

'Play you something, Ella?' he said.

She pulled a mock-sad face. 'You put away your harmonica.'

TJ reached into his backpack. 'Anything for you.'

Sometimes she liked him to do sad, old Neil Young songs and sometimes more upbeat Dave Matthews stuff, full of heartache and irony. He considered Blues Traveler, but the night was winding down early and it felt later than it was, so something melancholy felt appropriate. Only after he had launched into 'Sugar Mountain' by Neil Young did he recognize the sadness in Ella's eyes and realize it might have been a mistake. But as he sang he watched her settle into the song the way she settled into her drink and he could see that both had somehow made her feel better, and he was glad. TJ knew he couldn't make Ella happy — only she could do that — but he sure as hell didn't want to make her sad.

He loved playing at The Vault. Music had never earned him enough to live on, but he didn't think he could get through a day without laying his hands on a guitar. His father had forced him to learn a trade, which was how TJ had ended up with an electrician's license, and he was grateful to the old man for pushing him. But even when he wasn't playing music he could hear it in his head, feel invisible guitar strings under his fingers. That was the trick with a restaurant audience, he'd found. They didn't clap much, but as long as he was playing for himself, he didn't need their applause.

Tonight, though, he found himself playing for Ella.

7

'That what you had in mind?' he asked when he'd hit the last note.

'Perfect,' she said. 'I wish you could sing me to sleep some nights.'

'Anytime.'

Ella smirked and glanced away. 'Flirt.'

'Sorry. Can't help it, I'm afraid. My father was an incorrigible flirt. It's in the DNA. No cure.'

She laughed softly and shook her head. 'Oh, well . . . in that case you're forgiven.'

The last of the stragglers were heading for the door and the staff had started to set up for the next day. Ella glanced toward the kitchen, probably thinking she ought to be overseeing the activity back there. TJ wanted to remind her that the chef and his people knew what they were doing — it was all washing dishes and prepping for tomorrow — but he kept his mouth shut. It was none of his business.

'I guess we all ought to be heading home, huh?' Ella said, glancing at the trio of coffee drinkers as they finally made their exit.

'Not me. I told my mother I'd crash at her place tonight.'

Ella leaned back in her chair, took a sip of her drink, and gave him a dubious look. 'Your mother?'

TJ shrugged, his hands idly toying with notes on his guitar. 'She's an old lady — though she'd punch me if she heard me say it. If the power goes out, I don't want her to be afraid, y'know?'

'That's really sweet.'

'Nah. I'm her son. It's what you do.'

'Not what all sons do,' Ella said, getting up

8

from the table. 'You're a good guy, TJ.'

She kept her glass with her — she wouldn't have left it on the table for anyone else to pick up — and started to the kitchen.

'You should get going,' Ella said. 'Bring your mom in for dinner some night. My treat.'

'I'll do that,' he replied. 'But I'm not in a rush. She's not expecting me for a while yet and she's only gonna want me to watch the Food Network with her or something. You mind if I keep playing till it's time to lock up?'

Ella glanced back at him. 'As long as you want to play, you'll never hear me telling you to stop.'

She hurried away to the kitchen. TJ smiled as he watched her go, wondering if he might not be the only flirt in The Vault tonight.

★ ★ ★

Allie Schapiro stood vigilant by her microwave oven, listening to the kernels pop inside. The microwave gods had a cruel sense of humor, putting the little button labeled POPCORN right on the front of the machine. After burning bags of popcorn over and over she had finally learned that just pressing the button and walking away led to scorched kernels and that horrid smell. So while the movie played on in the living room — she had refused to let Niko pause it for her — she listened to the popping until the intervals began to seem like pauses, and then she took it out.

Opening the steaming bag, she found the corn popped to perfection, the buttery scent wafting through the kitchen. Allie gave her microwave nemesis a smirk and a soft 'hah,' and then separated the popcorn into two plastic buckets she'd retrieved from a cabinet.

When she returned to the living room, Marty McFly was eluding Biff on a skateboard in 1955. *Back to the Future* was one of Allie's favorite movies and she'd been shocked to discover that Niko and his daughter, Miri, had never seen it.

'That smells good,' Niko said. Beside him on the sofa, eleven-year-old Miri shushed him, totally under the movie's spell. Her copper eyes were bright, framed by a lovely tangle of curly brown hair.

Allie's kids — sons Jake and Isaac — lay on their bellies on the floor, chins propped on their hands, staring at the giant flatscreen. At twelve, Jacob was two years older than Isaac, but they were similar enough that people sometimes mistook them for twins. Allie didn't see it, really. Jake had darker hair and nearly always wore a serious expression, while Isaac never lacked a grin . . . not to mention that he was four inches shorter than his older brother. She figured it was something in the way they connected, the way they sometimes spoke at the same time, each filling in missing words in some tale they were concocting. And, like their mom, they loved movies.

She set one of the buckets between them and Jake grabbed it immediately and pulled it in front of himself.

'Jacob,' she said, not quite sternly. 'Share.'

He didn't look up, just slid the bucket back to

the space between them. Isaac had never taken his eyes off the television. When Biff crashed his car into the back of a manure truck and ended up buried in shit, both boys laughed. So did Allie. Watching this movie was like coming home in some strange way, and sharing it with Niko and his daughter tonight was something special, the two families together.

Strange, but wonderful.

She settled onto the sofa on Niko's left and tucked her legs beneath her, handing him the popcorn.

'Thanks, love,' he said, kissing her cheek as he dug out a fistful, then held out the bucket to Miri.

The little girl seemed entranced by the movie, but Allie had long since gotten the impression that Miri noticed all sorts of things when she didn't seem to be paying attention. *Not so little a girl*, Allie thought. At eleven years old, Mirjeta Ristani was a hell of a lot more sophisticated than Allie had been at that age.

Now Miri glanced up at her father, took note of the kiss that had just occurred, and smiled at Allie.

'Thanks, Ms. Schapiro.'

'We're not at school, Miri. You can call me Allie.'

Miri nodded and dug into the popcorn, noncommittal on the subject of calling her former teacher by her first name. The boys, of course, had no problem calling Niko 'Niko,' but that familiarity did not mean that they accepted him just yet.

11

This night had been planned for weeks as the beginning of an effort to change that. The boys' father had been killed seven years past, in combat in Afghanistan, and for a long time she'd resisted the urgings of her friends to date again. When she'd finally given in, she had gone on a brief flurry of awful first dates and exactly three disappointing second ones. After the last of these, she'd been sitting alone at a table in Krueger's Flatbread and had just started to laugh. She had covered her mouth, hiding her grin and stifling her laughter until it subsided, and only then had she realized that she had begun to cry.

Niko had been eating at the bar with Miri, then in the fourth grade. They knew her, of course — the year before, she'd been Miri's teacher, and Allie had certainly noticed Niko. It would have been impossible not to, handsome as he was with his regal, sculpted features, olive skin, and eyes the same copper as his daughter's. And here she was making a public spectacle of herself. Hideously embarrassed, Allie had risen and made a beeline for the exit, smiling politely as she passed them at the bar.

'Ms. Schapiro,' Niko had said, in that silky voice that made her pause.

'Mr. Ristani,' she had managed.

He had not smiled, not attempted to placate her. Instead, he had said three words that had alternately infuriated and inspired her for more than a week afterward.

He had said, 'Laughter is better.'

Troubled, she had mumbled something and

departed and for a week had avoided even looking at Miri in the halls at Trumbull Middle School. And then she had dug through the school phonebook and called him out of the blue on a Friday night and asked him if he remembered what he had said to her in the restaurant. It had surprised her that he did.

'I wanted to thank you,' she said. 'And to tell you that I agree.'

They had been dating for more than a year. Darkly handsome, kind-hearted, and staggeringly good in bed, he was everything she could have hoped for. Her mother ought to have been ecstatic that Allie had found a man who loved her. The woman had always wanted her to date a doctor. But, as she had made very clear, she had meant a Jewish doctor, not an Albanian one. Fortunately, Allie had stopped giving a crap what other people thought of her choices on the day she became a widow.

Things weren't quite so simple for the boys, or for Miri. It was for their sake that she and Niko had kept their relationship fairly quiet, wanting to spare their children the gossip at school and to save Miri from being interrogated by her mother, Niko's ex-wife, Angela. Tensions still lingered between Niko and Angela, who was a nurse at the hospital where he worked.

'Hey,' Niko said, giving her a nudge. He searched her eyes. 'I thought this was your favorite movie.'

Allie took a handful of popcorn from the bucket on his lap. 'One of them.'

'You seem far away.'

'No,' she said, smiling. 'I'm here.'

She kissed his cheek out of reflex, just a bit of reassurance that all was well, and saw that Miri had been watching the exchange closely. Allie arched a querulous eyebrow and Miri gave her a shy smile and returned her attention to the movie.

A gleeful flutter touched her heart; Miri was onboard! Several of her friends had told her that she needed to focus on her relationship with Niko, that the kids would just have to deal with it because eventually they'd all be grown up and off to college and she couldn't let their needs dictate her life. But she wanted Miri to like her, to feel comfortable with her, and she wanted — no, needed — Jake and Isaac to feel the same about Niko. If she and her handsome man had any chance at a future, it had to include their children.

Tonight had been the beginning of an effort in that direction, carefully planned. Dinner and a movie, in and of themselves, were not a big deal. But the night would end with Miri and Niko sleeping over, with Miri in the spare room and Niko in Allie's bed. She had to fight back her own awkwardness at the thought of it so that the kids would not read it in her face and think she and Niko had anything to feel awkward about.

Forcing her anxieties away, she tried to focus on the movie and realized that Jake had been watching her. Like Miri, he had caught her little snuggle and kiss with Niko, but Jake's face was unreadable. She smiled at him and he gave her the too-cool nod that had become his universal

14

response of late and turned back to the TV.

Come on, woman, she thought. *Breathe.*

The boys hadn't balked at the idea of Niko and Miri staying over, and Miri seemed at ease. It was all going to be fine. The storm raged outside and they were all cozy and warm here in the house. In a little while, when the movie was over, she'd make hot chocolate and take out the cookies she'd baked earlier. Things were going perfectly.

That's what worries me, she thought.

But she nestled herself against Niko and he slipped his arm around her on one side and Miri on the other, and she let herself get lost in the movie again.

When Jake glanced back at them, Allie had a moment of unease, wondering if her cuddling with Niko was bothering him. After a moment, she realized that Jake wasn't even looking at her and Niko. He was sneaking glances at Miri. Lovely Miri, just a year behind him in school. The girl caught him looking and Jake smiled at her. Miri gave him a half shrug, raising her eyebrows as if to say, *What are you looking at?* Jake rolled his eyes and looked back at the television, and Allie saw a sly, shy little smile appear on Miri's lips for just an instant before vanishing as if it had never been there at all.

Oh, my, she thought. *No wonder they don't mind hanging out together.*

Jake and Miri were crushing on each other, and neither of them had any idea that the other felt the same. Allie smiled. It was adorable and complicated, all at the same time, but for now

15

she would choose to focus on the adorable part.

The wind gusted hard enough to rattle the windows in their frames and snow pelted the glass. The lights flickered and the television screen dimmed for a moment.

'Oh, no,' Miri said.

'We'd better not lose power,' Isaac said.

Jake kept his chin in his hands, now. 'I kind of like it, actually. Candles and blankets.'

Miri shivered. 'But it'll be so cold.'

'We'll be all right, love,' Niko assured her.

'Well,' Isaac muttered, 'I guess as long as it doesn't go out before the movie's over.'

As if he'd given the storm a dare, another gust slammed the house and again the lights flickered. This time, they went out.

★ ★ ★

Joe Keenan took it slow across the bridge that spanned the Merrimack. The wind off the river whipped snow against his windshield and he gripped the wheel tightly. The snow fell so hard that his wipers could barely keep up with it. Where they didn't reach, a fresh inch had built up on the glass in just the past half hour of his shift. He wanted to turn on the light bar on top of his patrol car, but they weren't supposed to hit the blues without reason, and he didn't want to give anyone reason to bust his balls. Not with six days remaining until he completed his rookie year. The phrase made it sound like baseball, but in your first year on the Coventry PD you were fair game for everything from gentle hazing to

16

practical jokes, and you took the fall for fuckups that weren't rightly yours.

A gust of wind buffeted the car so hard that the steering wheel jerked in his hands.

'Son of a bitch,' he said under his breath, wishing he were home with his wife, Donna, watching a movie or even one of her bizarre reality shows.

Not a chance, though. On nights like this, a handful of more-established cops would call in sick — they'd even have a debate about whose turn it was — and every rookie would be out in the damn storm, responding to calls about power lines being down or elderly folks who'd slipped in their driveways, trying to keep up with the shoveling so the sixteen inches of ice and snow that had been predicted wouldn't freeze like concrete.

Bent over the wheel to peer out through his windshield, speedometer dropping under twenty miles per hour, he mentally corrected himself. He'd lived in Coventry his whole life, and in his experience there *were* no nights like this. His parents and aunt and uncles talked about the Blizzard of '78 with this weird combination of fear and reverence and even fondness, but this storm was starting to rage seriously. Apparently, back in 1978 the blizzard had stalled, the conditions just right to keep it spinning on top of the greater Boston area for days. Tonight's blizzard wasn't likely to hang around that long, but if the sexy, doe-eyed weather girl from channel 5 had been right this morning, it would be remembered with some fear and reverence of its own.

Keenan turned on the heater. He hated to run it because something had broken off or been jammed inside and the blowing air caused an annoying clicking sound, not to mention that some drunk kid had puked in the back the week before and the smell lingered no matter what efforts were made to clean the seat and floor. The heat only made it worse.

'This is bullshit,' he whispered, as if someone might overhear, and he glanced at his own blue eyes in the rearview mirror for reassurance. His mirror image agreed with him.

He flicked on his right-turn signal, though nobody was on the road to notice. Coming off the bridge, he saw the gleam of the Heavenly Donuts sign and felt a little spark of happiness in his chest. He desperately needed a coffee. He'd park and sip it for a few minutes and drain away the tension that had built up from all the time he'd spent with a white-knuckle grip on the steering wheel. He hated driving in storms.

So maybe you don't. Tuck away in a parking lot for an hour. Who'll notice, out in this? And it was true. If he got a call and had to respond, he could do that. But an hour of rest with a big hot cup of Heavenly's coffee would make him more alert and better able to do his job — at least that was what he told himself. Trying to peer through the clear parts of the windshield and the hypnotic swipe of the wipers had him halfway to falling asleep as it was.

The lure of coffee drew him into the parking lot and almost immediately he started having

18

second thoughts. There hadn't been a plow by in a while; there had to be three inches of snow in the lot and more was falling by the minute. What if he fell asleep and got snowed into the lot? Better to keep moving.

Still . . . a café mocha would be bliss.

He ran one big hand over his bristly blond buzz cut, hesitating only a second before he slid the cruiser into the drive-through lane, frowning as he spotted a single truck parked in the lot, more than half a foot of snow already accumulated on top of it. Rolling down his window, he waited at the big menu board. A terrible feeling washed over him. Something was wrong, here.

'Hello?' he called.

No answer. Not even static. Troubled, he took his foot off the brake and let the patrol car roll around the corner of the building, tapping the accelerator. But it was only as he rolled up to the window and saw the gloomy shadows inside that he understood the crisis at hand: Heavenly Donuts had closed up early because of the storm. There would be no coffee.

Bummed, Keenan started mentally mapping out his distance to other coffee shops. Coventry had a Starbucks and three Dunkin' Donuts, but the nearest of the four was miles away and there was no guarantee that they wouldn't all have shut down as well. Not that he could blame them: there weren't many customers braving the streets tonight.

With a sigh, he pulled out of the lot, figuring he might as well drive over to the nearest

Dunkin', especially considering how quiet his radio had become. During the evening commute he'd responded to five different accidents. It was a part of living in New England he had never understood. These people saw snow every winter, but somehow every summer they seemed to forget how to drive in it.

Now, though, going on ten P.M., pretty much everyone was home safe and sound except for an unfortunate handful, like plow drivers and rookie cops.

Driving along South Main Street, Keenan realized he'd screwed up, so distracted by the unfulfilled desire for coffee that he'd forgotten to clean off the windshield. The wipers were starting to stick, so he hit the lights and started to pull over to the curb, the swirling blue making strange ghosts in the storm and tinting the flakes on the glass.

With a loud crump, the car struck something that rocked it violently to the left. He slammed on the brakes, arms rigid on the wheel, so tense that he was unable to muster a single profanity. His heart thundered in his chest and he felt it in his eardrums and temples — worried for a moment that he might be having a heart attack and thinking about cutting back his Oreo intake — and then the car skidded to a shuddering halt and he exhaled.

He slammed the patrol car into Park.

'Motherfucker,' he said, just to assure himself that his capacity for profanity had not suffered any injury.

Popping the door, he climbed out and took in

the strange, silent landscape of Coventry under siege by winter. Power lines hung low and heavy. Shop windows were caked with blowing snow. Drifts had begun to form. The blue glow from his light bar spun all around, painting it all in ghostly shapes that waxed and waned without a whisper.

Boots crunching in the snow, Keenan stepped back and scanned the driver's side for damage. Finding nothing amiss, he made his way around the front and was happy to see both headlights in working order. Since the moment of impact he'd been running through a catalog of things he might have hit — parked car, dog, deer, person — but he didn't think it had been any of those. The wet snow had crusted thickly on his windshield, but the wipers were still clearing enough of a span that he would have seen anything as large as that. His headlights and the streetlamps might not cut very deeply into the storm, but they were still working.

Still, he'd hit *something*, and as he came around to the passenger's side, he saw that he had the dent to prove it. He searched the street and glanced over at the sidewalk but saw no sign of whatever it had been. Following his tire tracks thirty feet back the way he'd come, he saw no other tracks. No prints. No blood in the snow or evidence that there had been anything at all. It was easy to make out where the impact had occurred by studying the way the tire tracks jagged so abruptly to the left.

'What the hell?' he muttered.

Keenan walked back to the car, confounded

21

by the dent. How could he have hit something when there had been nothing to hit? He crouched by the car and wiped off the snowflakes that had started to adhere to the dent. He'd catch hell for this and would never be able to explain it, but he wasn't going to solve the puzzle by freezing his ass off while the storm whited out any evidence.

As he started back around the front of the car, still bathed in those blue lights, a thought occurred to him. What if he hadn't hit anything after all? What if something had hit *him?*

Keenan gritted his teeth against the cold and shook his head. It was a stupid idea and the semantics didn't make a damn bit of difference. Even if a bear had come hurtling out of the storm and crashed into his car as he drove by, there would be some evidence of its presence. Blood. Fur. Tracks.

Unless the bear had wings, it hadn't been a bear.

2

Pulling into the parking lot at Harpwell's Garage, Doug Manning heard his stomach growl. The smell of Chinese food filled his car and he felt immensely grateful that the family that ran the Jade Panda lived above their restaurant, and so had stayed open as the snowfall totals mounted and the wind drove it into drifts. He hadn't been as lucky finding an open liquor store, but he figured the guys had enough beer to last the night, and if not there were assorted, quarter-full bottles of booze in Timmy's office.

Most people played it safe, stocked up on essentials at the supermarket and hunkered down for the storm with a movie or board games. Doug's wife had wanted him to do exactly that, but the guys who worked at the garage had been planning to get together for the Bruins game tonight, and if he had tried to back out because of a little snow — or a lot — he'd never have heard the end of it. So there'd be beer and Chinese and a lot of bitching about their wives. The Bruins were playing in Florida, the lucky bastards, so the storm wouldn't have any impact on the game.

Doug parked and climbed out of his restored Mustang. Three steps from the car, blinking snowflakes out of his eyes, he slipped and bobbled the huge brown paper bag filled with steaming Chinese food. He clutched the bag, closing his eyes, and when he opened them a second later he was amazed to find himself still standing, bag still safe in his arms.

Heart pounding, he gave a little laugh. Timmy Harpwell paid a decent wage and Doug liked his job, but other than that, Doug and luck didn't get along very well. There were people, his older brother included, who considered him a fuckup and there were a lot of days he would have agreed. If he'd dumped a hundred and fifty bucks' worth of Chinese food in the parking lot, he'd have been better off climbing back into the Mustang and heading home to Cherie. The guys would have given him no end of shit. At least with Cherie he knew he could smile and apologize and make her a drink and she'd forgive him eventually. If he listened to her bitch enough, he might even find some makeup sex at the end of the rainbow.

But he hadn't fucked up this time. No apologies would be necessary.

Careful as hell, he made his way across the snowy lot to the door. No matter how many inches fell, they'd have no problem getting out in the morning. Timmy Harpwell had a plow on his truck; tomorrow he'd be clearing senior citizens' driveways and making a ton of cash, and that meant his own parking lot would be the first pavement he cleared. Doug might even be home before Cherie woke up in the morning. He could picture her bright orange hair spread across the pillow and imagine sliding in beside her, waking her with a kiss, and had to fight the temptation to just drop off the Chinese food and head home. Timmy Harpwell liked to hold court, and he didn't employ guys who weren't interested in kissing the ring now and again.

Half Korean, on his mother's side, with her black hair and eyes so brown they might as well have been black, Doug had dealt with plenty of racist shit growing up in Coventry, both casual and malicious. Most of the malicious stuff had gone away when he'd topped six feet and two hundred pounds, but the casual, aren't-we-buddies-just-busting-each-other's-balls racism would never go away. He'd learned early on that if he wanted to keep working at Harpwell's, he had to take whatever shit was dished out and try to find some way to give it back. The minute he showed how much it bothered him, or let on that he'd rather spend time with his wife than the boys at the garage, Timmy would stop giving him even part-time work, and he and Cherie couldn't afford that.

Doug banged in through the door and snow blew in behind him as it whisked shut. The front office was empty so he made a beeline for the back room. There were nine guys sprawled on stained sofas and chairs arranged around the giant TV. Doug had missed half of the second period, but he'd lost a game of rock-paper-scissors with Franco over who would pick up the food. They had both been hired last year and were the two lowest guys on the totem pole, which meant they always got the scut work, but Doug didn't mind.

'All hail the conquering hero!' he announced

as he entered, carrying the huge bag. 'And nobody touch my fried dumplings.'

Most of the guys cheered and raised their beers, a couple of them rising to help him sort out the food. Not Timmy Harpwell, though. Sitting there with his carefully sculpted beard scruff and his perfect hair, the boss just snickered, shot a glance at Zack Koines, and shook his head.

'Don't worry, Dougie,' Timmy said. 'Nobody's gonna touch your little dumplings.'

'I'd like to touch your wife's dumplings, though,' Koines muttered.

'Oh fuck, Zack, you didn't just,' Timmy said.

'Oh, I fucking did.'

The guys all laughed and Doug gave a dry chuckle, pretending he hadn't taken offense, that it was all a big joke. He could feel the grin on his face and knew the guys would read it wrong, would think he was smiling instead of getting ready to tear out Koines's throat.

Instead he laughed a bit louder.

'If that junkie Filipino hooker hadn't shown up at your front door,' Doug said, 'maybe you'd still have a wife of your own to go home to. Shit, your wife might even have let you stay if the hooker hadn't been so fucking ugly. She musta taken one look at that bitch and thought, 'You'd rather fuck this than me?' No wonder she — '

'Doug!' Timmy Harpwell snapped.

'What? We're all fucking jokers here, right?' Doug said, throwing his arms wide, gesturing to the others. 'Just having a few beers, busting each other's balls. Zack goes on twenty-four/seven

26

about how much he wants to bang my wife, but he's just kidding, right? It's a big joke, I know. I just thought it might be funny to put it all in perspective.'

'Jesus,' Franco whispered.

Doug glanced around, but none of the guys would meet his gaze. None of them except Timmy and Koines, both of whom were staring at him.

Koines started for him but Timmy halted him with a gesture, then turned back to Doug.

'You're fired,' the boss said. 'Get the fuck out.'

Heart slamming in his chest, fists clenching and unclenching, Doug laughed again. 'Are you kidding me? For that? We're always busting each other's — '

'Don't,' Timmy said. 'Let's not pretend.'

Fury made Doug shake but he knew there was no argument to be made, and if he went after Koines he'd only end up out in the lot, bleeding in the snow. So he threw up his hands.

'Fine. You win. But your management style sucks, man.' He turned and started for the table where he'd set the bag of Chinese food.

'Leave it,' Timmy said.

'I put my twenty bucks in. My food's in there.'

Timmy stared at him but said nothing. None of the guys dared to speak up for him.

Stomach growling, Doug gave a slow nod, then turned and headed back out into the front office. As he reached the door he heard Koines call out behind him.

'Asshole,' the son of a bitch said. 'And you're a shitty mechanic, too.'

27

Doug pushed open the door and stepped out into the storm, the wind and snow crashing into him. His skin felt so hot that he imagined he could feel the snow steaming as it touched him.

Cherie, he thought.

But he couldn't go home to her now. Couldn't bear to tell her he'd lost his job. He fished his keys out of his pocket and headed for the Mustang, hoping that the Jade Panda would still be open and he could silence his growling belly with some food, then drown it in whiskey.

He started up the Mustang and hit the gas, roaring out of the lot, tires slushing through inches of snow.

Fucking storm. Fucking Koines, he thought. But he knew what Cherie would say: *Your stupid mouth.*

★ ★ ★

TJ Farrelly packed away his guitar in the hard-shell case he had been using since the age of fourteen. His parents had wanted him to use a soft case, a canvas thing that he could wear like a backpack, but in his mind those were for hippies who had to hitchhike from one gig to the next. The hard-shell case was old-fashioned, but he couldn't help feeling that a proper musician — someone who loved his guitar — wouldn't treat it like a backpack full of dirty shirts and spare socks. He did have a backpack, in which he carried a selection of harmonicas and the neck gear that went with them, but his guitar was precious to him. Its tone might as well have been the sound of his own voice.

'Wow,' Ella said from across the restaurant. 'TJ, come have a look at this.'

He snapped the guitar case closed and glanced over at her. She stood at the front door of the restaurant, the door open just a crack. Snowflakes danced in past her, wind rustling her hair, and a pang of regret hit him hard. Ella hadn't even turned around to look at him, but still she was beautiful. They had been friendly for ages, but tonight — sitting around talking as, one by one, the rest of the staff finished prepping for the next day and headed out into the storm — TJ had felt a connection to Ella that he could not explain.

They had sat together while the logs burned down in the fireplace; he strummed and sang a few songs, faltering in the middle and jumping to some other tune. He could play in front of crowds and he could play for himself, but when The Vault's cook had gone out the door and left them intimately alone, he'd felt self-conscious about playing just for her. His fingers jumped around on the neck of the guitar, the pick sweeping the strings, and he'd moved from song to song like some ADHD kid who couldn't just leave the radio on one station.

'It's pretty bad out there, huh?' he asked as he moved across the restaurant toward her.

Ella didn't turn around. 'It's crazy. We must be getting three inches an hour.'

The wind howled through the narrow opening of the door. TJ saw the door judder in her grasp. He went to join her and she let the wind force the door open wider. The two of them stood there looking out at the street together.

'You weren't kidding,' he said.

The snow blanketed everything, save in places where the wind had scoured it nearly to the pavement, creating huge drifts that crested like ocean waves in the middle of the street. Whatever work the plows had done the storm had undone. From the looks of things, it had been a while since anyone had even attempted to clear the road. There were tracks that cut through it, though. Someone in a truck had gone past in the last half hour or so and not gotten stuck. But Ella drove a Camry.

'You going to be okay getting home?' he asked. 'I've got my Jeep. I could drive you.'

She turned to him and TJ became abruptly aware of how close they were standing. Only a few inches separated them. Ella shivered as a fresh gust buffeted them and more snow danced across the threshold of The Vault. Outside, the storm raged, but here they were just on the edge of shelter, somehow daring and yet still protected.

'I've been thinking I might just sleep here. In my office. I've got a blanket in there and some cushions. If I try to go home I might get stuck, but even if I make it, I've got to worry about getting back here in the morning.'

TJ might have told her she couldn't be sure she would even open tomorrow, that the storm looked fierce enough that the whole region was likely to shut down for the day. But her lips glistened in the light above the restaurant's doorway and her eyes were a bright, burnished copper.

A snowflake landed on the lashes of her left eye and he couldn't breathe.

They leaned in, but she paused, glancing down and away. 'You need to go. It keeps up like this, even that old Jeep won't get you home.'

'Ella, I — '

'You told your mother you'd be there.'

TJ smiled, hanging his head in defeat. But only for a second.

'Something's going on here,' he said, gazing at her until she had to look up and meet his eyes. 'This is one of those moments . . . I can feel it.'

'You can feel it?' she said, cocking her head.

He struggled for a second, not knowing how to continue. Then he reached up and brushed away a stray lock of hair that hung across her eyes and she shivered again, their gazes locked.

'I don't play a lot of the songs I've written. I guess I'm a little afraid to share them. But you know my song 'Stars Fall'?'

She nodded. 'I love that song.'

'One night in high school I slept over my friend Willie's house. Me and Willie and another friend, Aaron, had spent the day together, and it had been a *great* day. Maybe the greatest day, back then. Willie wanted us to stay over, to take sleeping bags and steal beer from the fridge in the garage and go and camp in the woods by Kenoza Lake. I got permission but after Aaron called home he said his mother wouldn't let him sleep over. We all knew he was lying.'

'He didn't want to camp out or he didn't want to drink?' Ella asked, letting the door swing closed, the two of them even more intimate now, just inside with the storm screaming beyond the door.

TJ shrugged. 'Maybe both. Thing is, that night cemented something for me and Willie. We didn't see a bear or meet a bunch of girls or find secret treasure or anything. But we lay out all night by the lake and watched the stars. We talked all night about our families and about girls and about the future. I can still remember it vividly, but that's because *it felt* vivid, even then. After that night, Willie and I were inseparable.'

'Were?' Ella asked.

A familiar grief ignited within him. 'Iraq. He didn't come home.'

'I'm sorry.'

For a moment, TJ said nothing. Then he reached out and took her hand, meeting her gaze again. 'Things were never the same with Aaron after that night. He was still our friend, but he hadn't been there, y'know?'

Ella let out a breath and gave a tiny nod. 'I think I do.'

'I don't want to be Aaron,' he said.

'What . . . ' she said, laughing softly. 'What about your mother?'

'The drifts are so bad out there, I'm not even sure the Jeep could make it,' TJ said. 'I'll call her and explain. She'll understand.'

Ella smiled. 'Let me rebuild the fire, then. And you'd better get that guitar out again.'

TJ grinned and bent toward her, hesitated for

a second, and then brushed his lips across hers. No need to rush. They had all night.

Ella locked the door to keep the storm at bay.

Later, as she poked at the logs in the fireplace and the wood began to blaze with light and heat, he played 'Falling Slowly' by the Frames, the one Ella was always asking for.

And the power went out.

★   ★   ★

Martha Farrelly loved her son, but sometimes it frustrated her that he treated her like an old lady. Sure, she'd been a late bloomer as a mother — she'd been forty-five when she gave birth to TJ — but she thought she was in excellent shape for a woman of seventy-one. She did yoga, went to the gym three times a week, and knew her way around a computer just as well as her son did, though that wasn't saying much.

The only reason she'd asked him to stay over tonight was that she was worried about getting out of the driveway in the morning. She had a man who plowed her little patch of pavement, but after even a moderate snowfall he tended to take his time, clearing the way for his bigger customers first. In a blizzard like this, there was no telling when he would show up, and Martha had a lot on her agenda for tomorrow, starting with her favorite yoga class at seven A.M. If the plowman didn't show up, she wanted TJ there to dig her out, but he thought she was afraid of the storm.

Silly boy, she thought. At her age, there wasn't

much that frightened her. Certainly not a snowstorm, no matter how many inches might fall. Her refrigerator and cabinets were full and she didn't eat much anyway. If she ended up snowed in for a few days, it would just give her a chance to do some reading.

When he'd called to say that he had gotten held up at the restaurant and the roads were looking ugly, she'd been a little perturbed, but any worry over missing her morning yoga session was outweighed by the unusual hesitancy in his voice. As uncommon as it was, she knew that quaver all too well — how could she not, after raising him? He'd met a girl. Yoga or no yoga, Martha was not about to stand in the way of her son getting himself a new girlfriend. One of these days, she hoped to have grandchildren.

He was a good man, her TJ. Called her every few days even when his work kept him busy and never forgot her birthday or missed taking her to brunch on Mother's Day. He didn't visit often, but Martha didn't mind that so much; she had a life of her own, and she understood in a way that a lot of her friends never seemed to. They were always complaining about their children and grandchildren not making enough time for them, somehow forgetting that they had raised those children to go off and have good lives of their own, to raise good children and to *do* good for others. She and TJ had dinner together every three or four weeks and once in a while they met up for a movie, and those times were lovely, but she never wanted him to see her as needy . . . as an old lady who needed someone to take care of her.

'Old, my bony ass,' she muttered to herself, and then chuckled. If she was muttering to herself about her behind being bony, she might be on the elderly side after all. But she didn't have to like it, and she didn't intend to surrender to it, either.

The fellow doing the weather this week on channel 5 had sounded so ominous talking about this storm that it had made her a little nervous. The regular guy, Harvey something, was on vacation — and he'd sure picked the right week to be away — and Martha would have felt more confident in the forecast if he had been doing the predicting. Regardless, the storm was shaping up to be just as nasty as advertised.

Martha sat in the soft, floral-upholstered reclining chair in her living room, flipping TV channels with her remote. The dance show she liked had ended at ten o'clock and she'd spent three-quarters of an hour dissatisfied with everything else she found, watching bits and pieces of half-a-dozen different movies and snippets of reality shows that tried to lure her in. She felt a certain horrific fascination with those shows but could not bring herself to sit through an entire episode. She felt sure that if she ever did, her humanity and intelligence would be lost forever. A bit melodramatic, she knew, but still somehow true.

Irritated, she changed the channel again, searching for anything that didn't seem vapid. Not that she would be awake much longer — she would doubtless fall asleep in the chair the way she did nearly every night — but she wasn't ready to succumb to sleep just yet.

When she clicked over to a Clint Eastwood movie she gave the remote a breather. Eastwood was just about the only legitimate old-time movie star left on the planet and she had always liked looking at him. Even as he aged he was still interesting to watch.

Within minutes, her eyelids grew heavy and her head slowly lolled to one side. Half aware, Martha shifted to get more comfortable, listening to Eastwood's throaty growl.

The phone jerked her awake. It jangled a tinny melody that she preferred to an old-fashioned ring — usually. This late at night it was intrusive and much too cheerful. Frowning, Martha rose and hurried as best she could into the kitchen, thinking it must be TJ, checking up on her, but by the time she picked it up, there was nothing on the other end. Hitting the 'Flash' button several times, she could not raise a dial tone. The storm had knocked out the telephone line.

She'd gotten off her chair for nothing.

Standing in the kitchen, she thought about going up to bed rather than falling asleep in front of the TV. Instead, she wetted her lips with her tongue and went to the cabinet in search of the bag of Oreos she kept for just such moments. She imagined the cookies behind a special display case marked IN CASE OF EMERGENCY BREAK GLASS and smiled.

She made herself a cup of tea, nibbling on a couple of cookies as the water came to a boil, then letting the bag steep in the hot water long

36

enough to make the tea nice and strong. As she fished out another Oreo, a knock came at her front door. Martha jumped, startled by the sound, then glanced with a frown at the clock on the microwave. It was 10:51 P.M. What could this possibly be about?

Hurriedly discarding the used tea bag, she left her cup sitting on the counter, steam rising into the chilly air, and headed back through the living room to the front door. She knotted her eyebrows and peered at the darkened windows. Snow had accumulated on the screens and made little piles on the sills just beyond the glass. She tried to imagine who might be out and have reason to knock so late, and then she halted, five steps from the door, thinking about downed power lines and ruptured gas mains. Could there be some kind of evacuation?

The knock came again, and she thought of the phone call. Exhaling, laughing at her nervousness, she realized the only logical answer: TJ must have tried to call to check on her and then when the line went dead he'd come out into this crazy storm, worried about her.

'You know,' she said as she unlocked the door and then pulled it inward, snow flying in her face, 'I really *can* take care of myself.'

But, in truth, she could not.

And it was not her son at the door.

★   ★   ★

Cherie Manning was pissed. The power had been out for over an hour, and the way the storm

37

had been slamming the house, she knew it would not be coming back before morning — and maybe not for a while after that. One of the trees in the backyard had already fallen over, a huge branch smashing against the cellar bulkhead. Another few feet and it might have shattered windows or even the wall.

'And where the hell is Doug?' she said into her cell phone. 'Out drinking with the rest of the grease monkeys.'

Curled up on the sofa with a thick blanket, talking with her best friend, Angela, she watched the way the candlelight played across the glass of the windows. She knew there were drafts in the little house she and Doug had bought in the fall, thinking it was time to start a family, but the way the flames flickered, it seemed like something was open somewhere.

'Did you call him?' Angela asked.

Cherie rolled her eyes. She didn't want to be a bitch, but sometimes Angela could be so dense.

'Five times. He's not picking up.'

'Come on, Cherie. You know how guys are. He's drinking with his buddies and watching the game. He probably left his phone in his jacket or something. Or he's not getting reception because of the storm. I tried you twice before I could even get a call through. Cell service is all screwed up tonight.'

'Maybe,' Cherie allowed.

'You know Doug's not half as bad as some of these guys,' Angela went on. 'At least you know he's not with some hooker — '

'Do I?' Cherie said.

38

'Oh, please! Yes, you do! He might not always have the most common sense but the big doofus loves you and that's got to count for something.'

Cherie smiled and shifted under her blanket, watching the candles flicker, thinking of times she and Doug had lit candles even when there wasn't a blackout.

'It does,' she admitted. 'It counts for a lot. I just don't like being home alone in the dark. And I wish he'd stand up to Timmy Harpwell. The guy is such an — '

'Asshole,' Angela chimed in.

'I was going to say 'idiot,' but 'asshole' works for me.'

They both laughed. Cherie had been feeling sorry for herself, home alone in the storm. She wished now that when Doug had told her he would be out late, she had asked Angela to come over. But, of course, absurdly petite as she was — the girl still had the same body she'd had at twelve — she might have just blown away.

Barks erupted from beneath the coffee table and she jumped, heart hammering in her chest. Her little terrier bolted from beneath the table in a blur of reddish gold fur, yipping his head off.

'Oh, you little prick!' Cherie said, one hand over her chest, feeling the rapid thunder of her racing heart as she caught her breath.

'What's going on?' Angela asked.

'Brady's having a fit.'

The dog stood in front of the front door, barking and sniffing. He turned to look at her and then erupted in another round of lunatic barks, edging closer to the door.

'What's he barking at?' Angela asked.

'No idea,' Cherie said, throwing back the blanket and sitting up.

She wore an old, faded green Coventry High T-shirt and plaid flannel pajama pants. Her red hair up in a ponytail and no makeup at all, she was not prepared for visitors, so she prayed that this wasn't Doug bringing one of the guys home from the garage. She could see it now, one of his buddies too drunk to drive in the blizzard, ending up sleeping on her sofa.

'Ange, honey, let me go. I think this might be Doug.'

'If it's not, call me back. I'm bored.'

'At least you still have power,' Cherie said, walking to the door. 'I'll talk to you later.'

They said their good nights and Cherie ended the call. Brady kept barking, his nails scritch-scratching against the small rectangle of tiles by the front door. Cherie unlocked the door and opened it, hugging herself against the frigid air that swept in. Even the streetlights were out, but she could see there was no car in the driveway or on the street in front of the house.

Barking, Brady darted past her legs and squeezed out through the six-inch gap she'd opened.

'Dammit,' Cherie snapped. 'Come back here, you spaz!'

But there was no stopping the little dog. Brady rocketed down the steps and into the snow. It was so deep that he was practically lost, jumping and barking and spinning in circles as the wind swept brutally across the yard.

40

'Shit,' she whispered. 'Brady, please, come on! Get inside!'

For a moment she held out hope, but the dog just kept barking. She sighed, getting more irritated by the moment, and slipped her feet into the boots she'd kicked off by the door earlier in the day. Still clutching her cell phone, she stepped out into the storm, realizing immediately that it had been a mistake to come out — even for a minute — without a jacket.

The cold bit into her alabaster skin and her teeth chattered.

'Come on, baby,' she said, descending the few steps to reach the dog.

It seemed like at least a foot had fallen already and she winced as the driving snow pelted her face. The cold sank its teeth into her, digging all the way down to her bones. Cherie started across the lawn, boots sinking deeply into the heavy, wet snow. The wind struck her so hard that she staggered, trying to keep her balance, and as it whipped past her ears she almost thought she could hear a voice, a hushed whisper.

Brady paused his barking, cocking his head, ears at attention. He seemed to be staring at her as he took a snow-shuffling step backward. Flakes had built up on his snout and now the wind drove against the little dog hard enough to ruffle his fur.

The wind whispered to her again and this time Cherie turned, eyes narrowed against the storm. In the blinding whiteness she could make out the warm lights inside her house, and that just pissed her off more. She spun on the dog, took a step

41

toward him, and Brady erupted into a fresh round of barking. Cherie knew all his tones, just as a mother knows the difference in cries of hunger or panic or pain in her infant, but these were new to her, a plaintive, frantic barking that tugged at her heartstrings. If not for the storm she would have wanted to grab the dog up and snuggle with him, give him comfort. Right now, she just wanted to kick his ass.

'That's it!' she said, slogging toward him, turning her face away from the stinging brutality of the storm.

The dog barked fiercely, backing up, trying to elude her. When she was nearly upon him, he turned to try to run, but could not move quickly in the deepening snow, and Cherie snatched him into her arms.

'Come on, you little shit,' she cooed lovingly, pressing his small body against her chest. 'Let's get in . . . '

The whisper came again, carried on the wind, a low susurrus that insinuated itself into her ears like the soft, chuffing laughter of mischievous children playing hide-and-seek. This time she heard it more clearly and she strained to listen, thinking there must be words in that whisper, that someone must be nearby. Perhaps lost or injured in the storm.

'Hello?' she called, turning toward the bushes that ran along the front of the house. The storm stole her voice away, carrying it off to be a whisper in someone else's ear, and her bright orange hair blew across her eyes.

Screw it, she thought, turning into the gale

and slogging back to the front stairs. Somehow she had come a good twenty feet from the door without realizing it. Snow had begun to rime the fabric of her clothes and to cling to her cheeks and eyelashes.

Just as she reached the steps, Brady began to whine and tremble and then at last to growl. Cherie glanced round, wondering if he'd heard the whisper, too, and while she was turned away the dog twisted in her grasp and gave her a vicious bite to the hand, his teeth breaking the skin and digging in. Crying out in pain, she let go and the dog dropped to the snow, tumbled and righted himself, and then ran off into the storm so quickly that it was almost as if he had vanished.

In shock, she stood there and stared at the place where he had disappeared into the blizzard, wondering what she was supposed to do now. The temptation to just leave him out there was great, but if anything happened to him, she would never forgive herself.

'Son of a bitch.'

She had to go in and warm up, put on some layers and a winter coat, hat, and gloves. But first she had to see to her hand, which was throbbing, the bite wound burning. For a long moment she could only stare at the punctures where Brady's teeth had torn her flesh, and then her gaze tracked down to the sprinkle of her blood dripping into the snow, the crimson splashes quickly being whited out again.

How did I get here? she thought. *How did I get to this night, home alone?*

Sighing, she held her injured hand against her shirt and turned to mount the steps. As she did, she realized that the wind had mostly died, as if the storm held its breath . . . or as if something stood between her and the worst of the gale.

It whispered and it took hold of her throat with long, frozen talons. Another yanked her hair and her head snapped backward. In the sky she saw more of them, falling from the sky with the ice and snow, driven by the wind. They twisted and slunk through the storm, turning the wind to their favor.

Frigid fingers cut deeper than Brady's teeth.

As they lifted her and she felt her feet leave the ground, one unlaced boot slipping off and tumbling into the snow, Cherie began to cry.

Her tears turned to ice on her cheeks.

3

'Mr. Manning, you should not go out there,' said the Chinese waiter. 'You too drunk to drive good even without this storm. You should stay. Free food and drinks. Well, maybe free coffee. We all staying tonight. We have pillows and blankets.'

Doug ruminated on that one for a blurry, boozy moment. Several waitresses had gathered to observe the waiter's attempts to get him to stay and he couldn't tell from their expressions whether they hoped he would or they'd rather he hit the road. If the manager of the Jade Panda was worried enough to make his staff sleep in the restaurant, maybe it was a mistake to try to drive in the blizzard.

'It's only seven or eight miles,' he said, hearing the sloppy slurring on some words and cursing himself for that last whiskey. Or the last three.

You should stay, a voice said in the back of his mind. A surprisingly clear, sober, nonslurred voice. *Don't be stupid*.

'I . . . I can't. Cherie, my wife, she's expecting me.'

'You call her,' said the waiter.

Peng, Doug remembered. *His name is Peng. Actually Chinese, unlike most of the other random Asians on the staff. White people don't know the difference.*

'The phone is not working but you have cell phone, yes?' Peng asked.

45

Doug nodded, reaching into his pocket. So drunk that when he did, he felt himself slip off-balance and staggered a step and thought to himself, *You are so fuckin' drunk*. But not so drunk that he couldn't open up his contacts list and call HOME. Only after he'd stared at the screen for what seemed like forever, swaying on his feet, did he understand why the call was not going through.

No signal.

He shook his head, mind made up now. Stuffing the phone back into his pocket, swaying a little, he turned to the waiter — what the hell was his name again? He'd just known it.

'I gotta go,' he said.

The waiter started to argue but Doug was already headed for the door. He slammed out into the night, rocked by the blizzard, the cold so sharp that it instantly numbed his face. The Mustang was halfway across the lot, next to the post that held up the Jade Panda sign, but the sign was almost entirely obscured. Beneath the dim light cast by the lampposts, the true strength of the blizzard was visible . . . thick, heavy snow falling at a clip like he'd never seen before.

Cherie would be waiting for him. She would be worried. In the morning, she would be massively pissed off at him for getting fired, even though he'd done it standing up for her honor. But he couldn't let her spend the night alone without any way of knowing if he was still alive. They fought like hell and she could be a total bitch at times and she took too many pills and he was worried about that, but she was his wife and he loved her. Couldn't imagine being with anyone else.

He had to get home.

Getting out of the parking lot was a bitch. The Mustang's tires slewed and spun and he ended up going right over the curb to get into the street, but once he was on the road and moving, he was all right.

Driving too fast. Way too drunk. In the middle of a blizzard New England would talk about for a decade.

But all right.

Until the warmth of the car's heater began to settle into his bones and the hypnotic swipe of the windshield wipers eased their gentle rhythm into the beat of his heart, and his eyelids began to feel heavy. So heavy.

Until he came to the end of Monument Street, where the choices were left or right, but the only thing that lay straight ahead was acres of snow-laden trees.

Doug snapped his eyes open in time to hit the brakes, but the tires found no purchase and the snowbank came up too fast and then he was through it and down the hill and the hood was buckled around a tree and his forehead was bleeding and the windshield was cracked where his skull had struck it.

He heard a tire spinning as the cold began to seep in, began to settle and accumulate quickly on the glass around him.

Half conscious, he thought he saw a face out there, beyond the spider-webbing of cracks in the windshield, but he knew he must be

47

imagining it. The only thing outside the ruined Mustang was the storm.

The engine ticked as it cooled.

Doug closed his eyes.

* * *

More than half the city had lost power. Everyone had hunkered down to wait out the blizzard, and that seemed to include the hookers and meth-heads on Copper Hill, the city's worst neighborhood. Joe Keenan hadn't received a single call about gunshots or domestic violence tonight, but even if he had, he wasn't sure he would have been able to respond. The side streets were thick with snow, and if he got stuck in a drift somewhere he'd never hear the end of it.

Now he cruised along Winchester Street, noting the candlelight glow inside the old Victorians and Federal Colonials. Old-growth trees, weighted with snow, hung their branches over the road to form a surreal white tunnel. One of those old oaks had come down and taken the power line with it. Keenan rolled up in his patrol car, headlights washing over the figures in orange jackets, swaddled in hats and scarves and stomping their feet to keep warm as they cut into the splintered tree while others were dealing with the fallen power lines.

Thirteen lines down so far, Keenan thought. *Gonna be a long night.*

Tens of thousands were without power in Coventry alone, and these poor bastards were going to be working around the clock out here in the storm until every bulb was burning again. Right now they would be focused on cutting off power to the fallen lines — most of the cleanup and repair would have to wait until morning — so it surprised him to see them taking apart the massive fallen oak.

Keenan put on his blues, the lights dancing around the car, mixing with the red and orange emergency lights of the workers' vehicles and making strange, unnatural colors. One of the workers approached the car. Keenan figured him for a foreman, considering that he seemed focused mostly on drinking from a huge thermos while the others tried not to electrocute themselves.

'How's it going?' Keenan asked.

'Slow as molasses.' The tall man took a sip from his thermos and then wiped the back of his glove across his thick, white mustache. 'No easy way to do this even in the best conditions. But this is just nuts.'

'Why not wait till morning?'

The foreman shrugged. 'Guess they figure it's gonna snow half the day tomorrow anyway, so we might as well get started.'

'I don't know how you guys are keeping up with the downed lines,' Keenan said. 'I've responded to calls about three of 'em already. They've all had the juice cut off pretty damn quick after we locate them, but just getting to them must a bitch, considering what a bang-up job Public Works is doing with the plowing.'

The foreman laughed, rolling his head back

with a snort of disdain. 'Those fucking guys. Don't get me started. You know they're all somewhere drinking whiskey and laying bets on who'll take down the most mailboxes.'

Keenan chuckled. 'You're not kidding. I saw three of the trucks in the BJ's parking lot.'

He didn't begrudge the plow drivers their breaks. They would be cleaning up after the storm for a long time. And he understood the temptation to take it easy, knowing how few people would be out on the road tonight. *But I'm out here*, Officer Keenan thought. *And I'm not the only one.*

'You getting a lot of calls tonight?' the foreman asked.

'Enough,' Keenan said. It had been quiet at first, but in the past two hours the calls had come more frequently, all of them concerning downed power lines.

'Well, stay safe.'

Officer Keenan wished the man the same and rolled up his window, tapping the accelerator. He felt the tires spin for a second, kicking up snow before they found purchase. His fingers ached just from the grip he had been keeping on the wheel since he'd started his shift and he wanted his soft, warm bed. More than that, he wanted this night to be over.

A burst of static came over the radio and the dispatcher's voice filled the car. 'Coventry Control to Car Four.'

Keenan picked up the radio. 'Car Four, Winchester Street.'

'Car Four, we have a call from a Jill Wexler,

50

Seventy-five Kestrel Drive. Her fifteen-year-old-son, Gavin, went sledding with two others. The boys were sleeping over the Wexlers' and snuck out. The woman thinks they went out to the viaduct behind Whittier Elementary. The father — Mr. Wexler — is out looking for them.'

'Car Four responding,' Keenan said.

He hit the pedal and the car slewed a bit until he righted it, keeping the nose straight ahead. If the kids and Mr. Wexler were out behind the Whittier school, all would be well, but if they weren't, the dispatcher would send a BOLO to all cars with descriptions of the missing. Normally the department wouldn't react so swiftly, but in the middle of a storm like this they were more concerned with safety than protocol.

The fastest way to the Whittier school would normally be up French Farm Road, but it was so steep and narrow and the side streets such a mess that he was sure he would have trouble getting to the top. Instead he took a longer route, past the Greenwood condo development and along the curving slope of Greenwood Avenue, which took him on a long climb to the parking lot for the baseball field behind the school.

A two-foot-high snow wall had been left by the plows, blocking in the parking lot. Keenan swore and pulled over, flicking the blues back on and killing the ignition. He peered into the storm, barely able to see twenty feet across the snow-blanketed field. The wind rocked his car and he thought again of his warm bed.

Then he remembered Mrs. Wexler, waiting at home for her husband and son, and the parents

51

of the two other boys out there — *idiots*, he thought, but teenage boys all had a little idiot in them — and he got out of the car. Pulling his hat down around his ears and slipping his hands into heavy gloves, he slammed the door and climbed over the wall of snow, blue lights swirling around him.

He was breathing heavily before he'd made it fifteen yards, laboring through snow already calf-deep and struggling to see where he was going. Thick flakes slipped down inside his collar. The wind knocked him around and snow stung his cheeks, but every six or seven steps he'd feel a lull in the wind and the thickness of the blizzard would diminish just enough for him to make sure he was on the right track.

Whittier Elementary sat on the bald crest of a hill, ringed by trees. Wind sheared across the top of the hill, slicing over the baseball field, but Keenan kept going, promising himself an enormous coffee as soon as he could lay hands on one . . . and after he had smacked Gavin Wexler and his two idiot friends in the head.

'Stupid kids,' he whispered, bending into the storm.

He paused to orient himself and felt the ache of the cold settle into his fingers. The school was to his right. In a momentary lull, he saw the black stripes of the power lines that marched across the hill behind the school, and turned left toward the far corner of the field. A chain-link fence was supposed to keep kids away from the viaduct that ran down the hill in that corner, but in the winter it was the greatest place to sled.

Young Joe Keenan had been there with his own idiot friends dozens of times, but they'd never done it in a blizzard at one thirty in the morning.

A voice came to him on the wind and he looked up, peering through the snow at nothing. The cold cut deeply despite his jacket and hat and gloves, but he forged ahead, wondering if the raging wind and whipping snow had played a trick on him, if the sound he'd heard had come from some other direction. Half-a-dozen steps more, and he found his answer — a dark silhouette staggering toward him, straight ahead.

'Hey!' Officer Keenan shouted. 'This way!'

Stupid. The guy was already heading this way. But maybe he needed to know he wasn't alone.

He heard the voice again, though it sounded different this time. A soft, chuffing whisper. Yet it confused him because it came not from ahead but behind and to his left. The wind drove harder, thickening the white curtain in front of him and obscuring his view of the figure in the snow.

The storm playing tricks on me, Keenan thought.

But then the whisper came again, so close it seemed to be right at his ear, and he felt something snag on his jacket and turned with a shout, reaching for his gun — stupid because he had gloves on.

He stared into the storm, not breathing, heart booming inside his chest, waiting for a lull in the gale. When it came and the snow fell straight down for once instead of whipping sideways, he saw nothing. No one was there. And yet that

53

whisper lingered in his mind so vividly that his heart still thundered and he took short, nervous breaths. His thoughts rushed back to earlier in his shift and whatever had made the dent in his car.

'Hello?' a voice called.

Spinning around, he saw that the silhouetted figure had come nearer. Keenan saw a bulky green jacket with a hood, but the face was in darkness until he swung his flashlight up. The blizzard played havoc with the beam, but he could make out the man's basic features and the frantic terror in his eyes.

'Sir, I'm a police officer. Are you hurt?'

Keenan flashed the light in his eyes again, waved it back and forth, and wondered if the guy was in shock.

'Are you Mr. Wexler?' he asked.

The guy blinked. He looked around as if he'd lost something and then fixed his gaze on Officer Keenan.

'I'm okay. It's the boys. You've gotta help the boys,' Wexler said, his voice rising from numbed to frantic in the space of a handful of words.

Wexler grabbed Keenan by the wrist but the officer yanked his arm away.

'Please, sir, just show me where they are.'

The man nodded his head and then just kept nodding it as he turned back the way he'd come.

'This way,' he said. 'Hurry. I thought . . . my cell phone didn't work, maybe the storm, and I thought I'd have to go all the way home and then . . . please!'

Wexler struggled through the storm and

54

Officer Keenan followed, more certain with every step that they were headed for the chain-link fence at the corner of the ball field that led down onto the viaduct . . . to the narrow slope that Keenan and his friends had grown up referring to as Meatball Hill, after the time Frankie Matos had gone flying off the side and into the trees and torn up his knee so badly it looked like a raw meatball. That was both the danger and the allure of the place. If you screwed up and went off the side, the viaduct dropped off at a rough angle for a good ten feet, all covered with trees.

They reached the fence and Wexler started to climb over.

Keenan grabbed his arm. 'No, Mr. Wexler. You need to stay up here and watch for more help to come.'

Whatever waited for him at the bottom of Meatball Hill, Keenan figured if he needed to call it in, it would help to have Wexler at the top to flag EMTs or other officers as they arrived.

Taking a deep breath, the icy chill drawn inside him, he scaled the gate at the top of the viaduct, balanced precariously a moment, and then dropped down on the other side. When he landed in the snow he went down on one knee, grabbing hold of the chain link to keep from falling. This sort of thing had been a lot easier when he was fourteen.

Keenan tried to peer down the narrow hill. Through the maelstrom of white he vaguely made out the electrical towers that marched across the shoulder of the hill below, where the

55

viaduct leveled out. Meatball Hill was about eighty feet in length — not as long as his memory had imagined but just as steep as he'd recalled. The deep snow around his feet was trampled by the bootprints of several kids and the viaduct was striped with the paths of sleds.

The sleds, he thought, frowning as he remembered the other dangerous element of Meatball Hill — the gate at the bottom. The fence down there was a twin to the one at the top, chain link with a double-door gate, framed with metal piping. In order to sled down the viaduct, you had to be willing to bail out at the bottom and let your sled hit the gate, but Keenan remembered staying on too long several times, so that his momentum took him skidding along the snow into the fence.

'Shit,' he whispered to himself, his hands and face growing numb. Then he raised his voice to be heard over the storm. 'Did one of them hit the fence, Mr. Wexler? Are there injuries?'

'Yes,' Wexler replied, his voice strangely clear amid the roar of the blizzard. 'It's Gavin. And not just . . . '

Keenan had whipped off his glove and slipped out his radio. As soon as he hit the button a burst of static filled the air. A squeal came from the radio, loud enough to blot out anything else Wexler might have said.

'Coventry Central, this is Car Four,' he said. 'Come in.'

He started down the hill, listening to the radio hiss and pop, but he'd taken only five steps when he realized that Wexler had stopped in

56

midsentence and hadn't said more. Worried that the guy might be collapsing in shock, Keenan turned to check on him, but saw no sign of the man.

'Mr. Wexler?' the officer called as he struggled back to the gate.

He peered into the storm and shouted the man's name again, scanning the frozen baseball field — or as much of it as the storm allowed him to see. A fresh burst of static came from his radio and Keenan jumped, startled. He lifted the radio and hailed Dispatch again, even as he stared into the driving snow. There was nowhere for Wexler to have gone. Nowhere he could have gone, at least not fast enough that Keenan wouldn't have spotted him.

'Wexler!' he shouted.

No answer.

Until one came, but this was not the voice of a grown man. A younger voice, frantic and plaintive, cried out from the bottom of the viaduct, calling for help. Keenan swore, glanced once more at the void in the storm where Wexler had just vanished, and turned to stumble, march, and slide down the steep slope of Meatball Hill.

The radio kept crackling. He tried calling in again and heard a snippet of words among the static but nothing he could make out clearly. The storm was interfering with everything.

Twenty feet from the fence, snow frosting his coat and sticking to his face, Keenan barely made out a pair of figures on the ground.

'Hello?' he called.

'Here!' a voice came back. 'Right here!'

Exhausted from fighting against the brutal wind, Keenan staggered toward the two boys, one of whom knelt in the snow, cradling the other in his lap. The upright boy was a skinny little guy whose eyebrows were rimed with snow. He wore a wool peacoat and a scarf pulled up to cover the bottom of his chin and he gazed at Keenan with pleading eyes.

'Help him!'

Keenan stood over them, studying the unconscious boy, whose head lolled alarmingly to one side.

'What happened?'

'He tried to help Gavin,' the skinny kid said, his voice cracking with emotion.

Keenan frowned. 'Neither of you is Gavin Wexler?'

'I'm Marc Stern. This is Charlie Newell,' the kid said. 'Gavin's . . . ' His face crumpled into grief and horror. 'Gavin's over there.' He nodded toward the gate, only another ten feet away.

Keenan stumbled over and nearly tripped on a small figure in a gray-and-blue winter coat that lay mostly covered beneath at least an inch of snow. Even as he bent to brush some of the snow away, he smelled the stink of burnt flesh and he froze.

'No!' skinny Marc Stern cried. 'Don't touch him! It might not be safe!'

Keenan backed away, glancing around to take in the scene, and then he heard a spark and a pop and he understood it all. He craned his head back to look up at the power lines that ran perpendicular to the viaduct, crossing the path just on the other side of the fence at the bottom of Meatball Hill. A long black line hung from one of the towers, and about fifteen feet to his left it draped across the top of the fence.

A sizzle and hiss reached him and he saw a little shower of sparks come off the fence where the power line had fallen on it.

He didn't want a better look at Gavin Wexler's burnt corpse, and he didn't have time for one. He hurried back to the other boys and dropped to the snow beside Charlie. He felt the boy's wrist for a pulse but it was weak if there at all, so he checked Charlie's neck and found his heart still beating.

Keenan glanced up at Marc. 'So, Gavin hit the fence. Did he grab it, use it to help himself up?'

Marc nodded vigorously. 'He couldn't even scream. We saw him standing there and we didn't know what was happening because he was so quiet and then his gloves caught fire and we could smell, like, burning hair, and Charlie went to try to pull him off the fence and I screamed for him not to and . . . and . . . '

'It's okay,' Keenan lied, glancing at the skinny kid. 'It's gonna be okay.'

The kid didn't bother to argue. It had been a stupid thing to say and they both knew it. Gavin had been electrocuted to death. His flesh had been smoking. His gloves and probably other things had caught fire. Now they were out here in the blizzard at two in the morning and Charlie had a slow, flickering heartbeat. He'd been electrocuted, too, trying to save his buddy. There wasn't a damn thing okay about it.

'Charlie,' Keenan said, leaning in. 'Charlie, can you hear me?'

He hit the call button on the radio again and static squealed, echoing off the trees and the storm.

'Coventry Central, come in!' he called. 'Coventry Central, please respond!'

Nothing but static.

Charlie started to twitch and jerk. Marc cried out, pulling his hands away as if afraid he was somehow responsible. The unconscious kid seized and spasmed and began to groan and all Keenan could think about was the boy's heart. He'd felt a flutter when he'd checked Charlie's pulse and Keenan figured he'd had a heart attack, and maybe this was another one.

'Back up!' Keenan said, shuffling over beside Charlie on his knees as Marc retreated.

Should've covered him with my coat, he thought, as if that would've prevented whatever this was.

Keenan grabbed Charlie's flailing arm, then put weight on his collarbone, trying to hold him down to keep the kid from hurting himself. He twitched once and then lay still; the seizure had stopped. It took Keenan only a second to realize that the seizure was not the only thing that had ceased — the rise and fall of Charlie's chest had gone still.

Cursing, Keenan checked the kid's pulse again, but couldn't find one. A calm not unlike the numbness the blizzard caused began to spread through him. Keenan wished for EMTs. He wished for a portable defibrillator. All he had was a terrified, skinny little frostbitten teenage boy and his own two big, fumbling hands. He made sure Charlie's airway was clear and then started chest compressions, damning himself for every second he'd delayed, talking to Mr. Wexler and checking on Gavin's corpse.

'Come on, come on,' Keenan said, talking as much to himself as to the quieted heart of Charlie Newell.

Wexler, he thought, remembering the man's fumbling, shocked attempts at communication. Somehow he'd run off so fast that he'd vanished into the blizzard, but had he gone far?

'Mr. Wexler!' Officer Keenan screamed. 'Can you hear me up there? Are you still here?'

No reply. He wondered if Wexler had gotten his act together enough to fetch EMTs or just call 911. Surely that was what he'd intended to do before Keenan had run into him.

'Come on, Charlie,' skinny Marc pleaded.

But despite the rests between repetitions of chest compressions, Keenan's arms were getting tired fast. The storm worked against him, as if the wind did not want this boy's heart to beat again.

'Wexler!' Keenan cried.

He caught Marc staring at him and they locked eyes a moment. Keenan paused in his compressions, pulled out his cell phone, and tossed it to the kid, who fumbled it with his frozen hands and let it fall to the snow.

'Call 911!' Keenan said.

'I tried. Me and Mr. Wexler both did. Our phones — '

61

'Try mine!'

Nodding, Marc worked off one snowy glove and tried to use Keenan's phone to call 911.

'A couple of bars!' Marc cried.

'Make the call!' Keenan said, between compressions.

In moments, he heard Marc announcing their location and then repeating it several times, trying to communicate, tears of frustration springing to his eyes as he desperately tried to tell the dispatcher where they were and what they needed.

More than a minute passed and Keenan's arms were growing tired. Charlie had not so much as twitched. His pulse had not fluttered. His skin had begun to grow even colder than before. A long sigh escaped Joe Keenan's lips and he shuddered as he sat back on his haunches, gazing at the frostbitten, frozen features of Charlie Newell, who had died right in front of him. Charlie Newell, whose life he had failed to save.

'Do something,' skinny Marc said, but without much fire. It was a hollow plea. The boy knew there was nothing to be done.

Marc began to sob, hugging himself. Keenan could only watch him. The wind shifted for a moment and he smelled the aroma of Gavin Wexler's burnt flesh still in the air.

The snow kept falling.

Keenan knew he had to leave the dead boys behind. He had to take skinny Marc with him, go back up the hill, over the fence, and make it to his car. He hoped the car radio would be working better than his handheld. Marc had gotten through to 911 but Keenan felt pretty dubious that the dispatcher had been able to hear half of what the kid had told her before the call had been cut off.

He just wanted to take a minute, in the cold and the storm, as the snow began to accumulate on his clothes and the still form of Charlie Newell. Keenan fought back tears as the icy wind assaulted him.

Charlie Newell, he thought, and knew he'd never forget the name.

The kid who'd died at his feet. The kid he hadn't been able to save.

4

Allie Schapiro lay in bed with Niko, watching him sleep. The candle on her nightstand had burned down nearly to the bottom and begun to dim, but the flame endured. In the flicker and gutter of the candlelight, he looked so handsome that her heart swelled and she could barely breathe. The windows rattled in their frames and the storm blew so hard that the house shook with its fury. She'd never taken the wind chimes off the back deck when winter arrived and now she strained to listen for their frantic music. Earlier she had heard the chimes clearly but now they had been silenced; the wind had blown them down.

Beneath the comforter she was warm, so she knew that the goose bumps that kept prickling her flesh came not from the cold but from the memory of making love with Niko earlier in the night. Just the thought sent a delicious shiver through her that hardened her nipples and ignited a fresh yearning at her core. She reached out under the covers and ran a hand along his thigh.

Gazing at him, her heart so full, she slid her hand out from beneath the comforter and touched his face, caressing the contours and shadows of his deep-olive skin and feeling the stubble on his chin. He had long, beautiful eyelashes that she envied.

As she studied him, Niko opened his eyes. A tired smile touched his lips.

'You should be sleeping,' he said.

Allie cupped his cheek with her hand, bent in, and brushed his lips with hers.

'It was a good night, wasn't it?' she said.

'The beginning or the end?'

She glanced away, blushing a little, surprised that he could make her feel shy after all that they had shared, and all that they had done together.

'Both,' she admitted. 'But I meant earlier, with the kids.'

Under the sheets, Niko placed a hand on the curve of her hip, trailing his fingers along her skin.

'It was perfect, Allie. Dinner was wonderful. And it was great to see the kids relax around each other, and with the two of us together. It all seemed so . . . normal.'

'Normal is nice,' she said.

'Normal is *very* nice,' Niko replied.

Once the power had gone out, Jake and Isaac had insisted that they had to eat all the ice cream in the freezer to keep it from melting, even though they'd had no idea how long they would be without electricity. Another night Allie would have refused, but she had not wanted to disrupt the playful atmosphere. While she and Niko had poured glasses of Shiraz and watched the storm through the slider that led to the deck, the kids had sat at the kitchen table and polished off whatever had been left of three different pints of Ben & Jerry's. Fortunately, even that sugar had not kept them awake terribly late. Without lights or television, they were all asleep by eleven o'clock. Allie and Niko had given it forty minutes to make sure they weren't going to stir and then he had taken her to bed.

Skittish and paranoid, worried that one of the kids would come to the door and find it locked and *know* what was going on inside, it had taken her a while to relax. Niko had been patient with her, had used his hands and his tongue and his words to wonderful effect, and in time she had forgotten all about Jake and Isaac and Miri. Other than Isaac, they were old enough to know what it meant for an adult couple to sleep in the same bed — or what it could mean. Niko assured her that they wouldn't want to think about it, and she hoped he was right.

'You know what this means,' he said now, still tracing his fingers along her leg, and then moving his hand up, slipping it beneath the soft cotton of her T-shirt.

'No.' She searched his dark eyes. 'What does it mean?'

'We can't pretend this is just dating anymore,' he said, his voice a low rumble. 'We're all here together. A couple. With the kids under one roof, it feels like a family. They may not put labels on it, but they'll feel it.'

Allie smiled, becoming shy again. The night had given them both a glimpse into what life would be like in the future, with all their children together in one house, and maybe another child that would be theirs together.

'What about school?' she asked. 'People are going to talk. And what about Angie? You know she's going to be a total bitch when she — '

'She's already a bitch,' Niko said. 'If she tries to make life difficult, I'll handle it. I just didn't want to deal with the fallout until I knew what this was.'

'So what is it, then?' she ventured, gazing boldly into his eyes.

'This?' he said. 'This is the real thing.'

★ ★ ★

Cradled in dreams of summer, Jake tried to cling to sleep. But he heard his name whispered again and again and felt himself being jostled and even before he opened his eyes he knew Isaac must have had a nightmare. He reached out and slapped his brother's hands away.

'Go back to sleep,' he murmured.

'Jake, please . . . get up,' Isaac whined. 'I'm scared. Jake, come *on*.'

More than anything, it was the way Isaac's voice broke on that last word that made Jake open his eyes. The brothers had shared a room ever since Isaac had been big enough to sleep in a bed instead of a crib and there had been many times when his little brother had woken him after a nightmare, needing to pee but afraid to go out into the hallway by himself. More than a year ago, Jake had stopped accompanying Isaac into the corridor, forcing him to brave the trip on his own, but after the first couple of times Isaac had stopped asking; but even on the worst of those evenings, when the nightmares had been particularly terrifying, Jake had never heard this tone in his brother's voice.

Something was *wrong*.

'Jake, they're out there.'

Troubled, Jake rubbed sleep from his eyes and looked up at his brother. The power was still out so he didn't have the familiar glow of his clock to tell him just how late it was, but not a hint of daylight showed outside the windows and the blizzard still raged, so he knew it wasn't even close to morning.

'What are you talking about?'

Isaac tugged on his shirt, urgency in his blue eyes. 'Come see.'

Huffing his frustration, Jake threw back his covers and dragged himself out of bed.

'I heard scratching at the window,' Isaac began. 'I know you'll say it's just the tree and that's what I thought first, too. It creeped me out but I knew it was the branches. The wind's so strong and I knew it was just scratch-scratch, y'know? Only then I started really listening to the wind and it was mostly going in the other direction and the scratching kept going and so I looked up and . . . I saw something.'

His voice dropped low, quiet and scared.

'Like what?' Jake asked, yawning, shuffling across the floor in his socks. He always wore socks to bed; they made him feel safe.

'Like a face,' Isaac said, unwilling to look at him.

'Oh, bullshit,' Jake muttered. 'Ike, you know better than that.'

'Don't swear,' Isaac said, concerned about the profanity despite his fear. It always got under his

68

skin when Jake cursed, which was half the reason Jake did so.

Jake went to the window but could barely see anything through the snow that had accumulated on the screen. A tiny drift had formed on the sill, building up against the outside of the glass. No way Isaac could have seen anything through this, he thought, although as he looked more closely he realized that the visible part of the screen — between the snow-clotted portion below and the shade that blocked the upper half of the window — was only frosted with snow. He could make out the storm outside and saw that it had begun at last to wane. The wind had lessened and the snow fell more or less straight down instead of being driven sideways.

'I don't see anything,' he said.

He almost added that he was going back to bed, but then he saw that Isaac wouldn't come any closer to the glass and he understood that his brother would not let him sleep until he had been more thoroughly reassured.

Jake tugged on the shade and it rattled upward. With a soft cry, Isaac jumped back from the window, staring as if he expected that same face to be staring in at them.

'Nothing,' Jake said. 'There's nothing out there, Isaac. Now go back to bed.'

Dissatisfied, Isaac stared at the carpet. 'I won't be able to fall asleep.'

'I don't care,' Jake said curtly. 'Seriously. You just lie there if you have to, but there's nothing out there, little brother. Don't wake me up again.'

He went back and flopped into his bed, dragging the covers over himself as Isaac stood there and kept staring at the window.

'Go to bed, Ike.'

★ ★ ★

Isaac said nothing. He glanced over at Jake once, twice, a third time, but it was clear that his big brother had no intention of doing anything. And maybe there was nothing to be done, nothing out there in the storm at all, but he knew what he had seen, and whatever was or wasn't there now, something had been there before. He'd seen that face.

Mustering up his courage, holding his breath, Isaac went to the window and looked out into the falling snow, searching the stormy sky for any sign of the owner of the white eyes that had peered through his window. He looked into the snow-laden branches of the tree that stood off to the right, but he saw no sign of anyone hiding among those bare, skeletal sticks.

Then he glanced down at the yard and saw them — a trio of figures darting around in the falling snow, several feet off the ground, as if they were dancing on the wind. They seemed to vanish and reappear with each gust, hiding behind the veil of falling snow and then emerging once more.

Isaac sucked in a shuddery breath, pressing his forehead to the cold glass. His heart sped up again as he was breathing in tiny gasps. His throat felt as if it was closing up and his lips went dry. It couldn't be real — had to still be a dream — but if he was dreaming, how could he feel the damp, icy cold of the window against his skin? He'd had to pee since he had climbed out of bed and now the urge became terrible.

'Jake,' he whispered, afraid that somehow they would hear him.

'Whaaaat?' his brother said, groaning, without turning over in bed.

Isaac began to tremble. He'd thought they might vanish completely but they were still out there. His breath frosted the glass and he felt like crying.

'There are monsters in the yard.'

'Go to *bed*, Isaac. There's no such thing as monsters.'

His eyes welled with tears. *Yes, there are,* he wanted to say. But he knew the tone in Jake's voice. Sometimes they were best friends — they did everything together — and sometimes Jake treated him like they were worst enemies, like everything Isaac said or did, even breathing the same air, was stupid and babyish. Isaac wasn't stupid and he wasn't a baby anymore and when Jake treated him that way he usually just gave it right back to him . . . but it hurt so much. Tonight, none of that mattered. Tonight, Jake had to listen.

'Come look,' Isaac said.

'Go to bed.'

'Jake — '

'I'm not kidding, Ike. I already told you. No monsters. No faces at the stupid window. You heard a branch or just the snow hitting the glass.

Go to sleep or I swear to God I'm going to pound you.'

Isaac thought about screaming, considered going across the hall to wake Miri. He could go to his mother's room but Niko was there and it made him nervous, thinking about bothering them. And the longer he looked out the window, watching those figures slipping through the storm, the more he thought they weren't just dancing . . . they were playing. There were four of them now, and if they were playing, maybe they weren't monsters after all. Not really.

The snow had built up on the screen so much that he could not see very well and the frost of his breath on the glass had made it worse. Isaac pulled back and wiped at the condensation, then bent to peer outside again.

They were gone.

He blinked and looked again, craning his neck left and right to see if they had gone into a neighbor's yard. It surprised him to realize that he was a little sad, and he unlocked the window and forced it open. The storm had swelled the frame and he had to work at it, the wood squealing a little.

'Ike, what the hell?' Jake murmured. 'Close the damn window.'

Isaac ignored him, reached out and tapped some of the snow off the screen. He leaned on the windowsill and pressed his face against the screen as the wind gusted past him and the frigid cold invaded his bedroom. The sheer blue curtains billowed to either side but he ignored them, scanning the night and the storm.

'Goddammit!' Jake snapped. Isaac heard him whip back his covers and climb out of bed, heard him grunting as he stormed across the short distance between them. 'It's freezing out there!'

'Well, duh,' Isaac said, still searching the yards on either side and across the street, forcing the screen a little, trying to get a better look around. 'It's a freakin' blizzard.'

'Isaac,' Jake said, his voice full of menace.

Jake grabbed his brother's arm. Isaac tugged uselessly at his grip, turning toward him as that familiar fraternal anger blazed up.

'Let go!'

'You had a bad dream,' Jake insisted. 'And if you saw anything outside that wasn't just your imagination, it was Mr. Pappas walking his dog. Nobody else would be walking around out there in the middle of the night.'

'It wasn't Mr. Pappas,' Isaac said softly, glaring at him.

'Then who — ' Jake began, but his words cut off.

His gaze had shifted. Isaac saw that Jake wasn't looking at him anymore but staring past him, at the window, and the terror blooming on his face made Isaac spin toward the window just in time to see the blue-white figures rushing through the storm, long arms reaching forward, long fingers and hands and forearms sliding through the screen as if it weren't there at all, sifting through in a spray of ice crystals and shadows.

Frozen fingers clutched at him, cut his skin, turned his bones to rigid ice, and then they

73

pulled. Isaac hit the screen face-first, his arms coming after. His back scraped the underside of the open window and he flailed his arms, trying to grab hold. A hand grabbed his ankle and only then did he hear the screaming. His own voice, and his brother's.

The tug on his ankle lasted only a moment, long enough for him to be twisted around, to glance back inside his room and see Jake grasping at empty air, screaming his name.

And then he was falling.

* * *

Allie burst into Jake and Isaac's room with Niko and Miri only steps behind. She staggered to a halt, staring at the horrid tableau before her. Jake stood beside the window, tears in his eyes and a scream dying on his lips. The window was open but the screen had fallen out. Snow whipped into the room, not much but enough that she could see prints on the carpet where Isaac had been standing moments before. The snow was already melting, the prints disappearing.

'Oh my god,' she heard Niko say behind her.

Then she heard herself shrieking the same words as she rushed to the window and looked out, praying she would not see the thing she feared most. But there Isaac lay, twenty-five feet below and not moving.

Jake said something but Allie could not hear him. She turned and bolted for the door, felt Niko try to take her arm and heard his soothing voice but tore free of him and ran out and down the stairs. She flung the front door open, hearing their footfalls behind her but not slowing, not waiting. Barefoot, bare-legged, she plunged into the knee-deep snow and forged a path to the place where Isaac had fallen, telling herself with every step that the snow had broken his fall, that it was so deep and soft it would have been a gentle landing.

The window screen stuck out of the snow like a cleaver jutting from a butcher's block.

Numb, she came upon Isaac and saw right away that it had not been a gentle landing. Her baby boy had broken when he fell. His left leg and his neck were turned at impossible angles. His face was turned up toward her and she saw the panic and fear etched there and felt a cry of grief rip her up inside as it forced its way from her lips.

She dropped into the snow and picked him up, cradling him as she had done on so many nights when he had a fever as an infant. Isaac had been a sickly boy.

'Mom, please!' Jake pleaded behind her. 'Come back inside! The ice men will get you! Please!'

Allie barely heard him.

Then Niko was there, one hand on her shoulder, and she glanced back and saw Jake and beautiful Miri standing together in the open doorway, crying and shivering, each also broken in his own way. Allie laid her head back against Niko's chest and released a sob that became a wail.

'We need help,' Niko said. 'I hear a plow over

on Salem Street. The phones aren't working and I can't get a signal on my cell. I'm going to run and flag the guy down. He'll have a radio. He'll . . . '

The words trailed off. Allie had heard them but wasn't listening, didn't care, couldn't feel anything other than the grief that tore and gnawed and ripped at the cavity inside her chest where her heart had been.

Niko ran back into the house and she heard him talking quickly with Jake and Miri, heard something about shoes and pants and frostbite. Niko rushed out again moments or full minutes later, she could not be sure. Jake called to her, still begging her to come inside.

But Allie could only sit and watch the snow begin to accumulate in the hollows of Isaac's eyes. The wind had dropped to almost nothing, turning the blizzard into a gentle snowfall, and the night had begun to lighten to a gray dawn, all of Coventry covered in ice and snow.

Miri called out to her father, crying for him to come back.

But he never would.

TWELVE YEARS LATER

5

Doug Manning sat at the table in the corner farthest from the door, close enough to the bathrooms to catch the faint scent of stale urine. Chick's Roast Beef had gone downhill over the past few years but he wasn't going to bitch about it. Everything in Coventry — hell, the whole country — had gone downhill. The talking heads on TV said the economy was improving, but most of the guys he knew were still scared shitless that their jobs might evaporate out from underneath them. Either that or they were already unemployed.

Doug himself was just barely hanging on.

The bell above the door jangled and he looked up to see a middle-aged mom headed for the counter with a pair of boys maybe six and eight. The brats stuck their tongues out at each other and raced around their mother, using her legs as a barricade against direct assault. The boys drove her nuts while she tried to order for them and he saw her irritation growing. As she rolled her eyes in frustration she glanced down at them and, despite her pique, gave them a tired smile. It hit him hard, that smile, reminded him far too much of Cherie.

'Anything else?' the Puerto Rican girl behind the counter asked.

'Yeah.' The mother sighed. 'You can tell me why everyone in this town is so edgy today.'

'Bad weather,' the girl said.

'It's a snowstorm. Probably not much of one,' the mother replied. 'Big deal.'

The counter girl cocked her head as if she were waiting for a punch line too long in coming.

'Logan, stop that!' the mother snapped.

Then she lifted a hand to her temple, exhaling with embarrassment. 'Sorry. Just one of those days. The guy at the gas station was super rude. Then this lady dropped her purse and I went to help her and she practically barked at me that she could do it herself. And don't get me started about the way people drive. If it's gonna turn into an icy mess later, so be it, but right now it's just a few flakes. I mean, it's New England, after all. It's not your first snowstorm.'

The woman shook her head and that faint, Cherie-like smile returned. At some point her brats had frozen in place just to listen to her.

'Oh my god, they've done it to me, haven't they? I've become one of the angry snow-day people.'

'It's okay. We all have those days,' the counter girl said, fixing her baseball cap over her ponytail. 'You sure you don't want something else?'

'Rum and Coke?' the mother said with a soft laugh.

'Best I can do is ice cream.'

'Did she say ice cream?' one of the kids piped up.

'Hush,' the mother said. Then she fixed her gaze on the counter girl. 'Seriously, why are people so edgy today?'

'Are you not from around here?'

'Rhode Island, originally. Why?'

The counter girl gave a nod. 'You remember the blizzard ten or twelve years ago? Like a million feet of snow, no school for days?'

'I guess,' the woman said, grabbing her younger son by the arm and steering him away from the older one. 'You guys got hit harder up here than we did, but I watched it on TV. Bad storm, sure, but this is no blizzard. No reason for people to get worked up about it.'

'I'm with you,' the counter girl said. 'But I was only seven when it hit, so I don't remember it well. Older people in Coventry get antsy every damn winter. A bunch of people died in that blizzard — like eighteen. I guess it just haunts them a little.'

Doug's chest hurt and he realized he'd been holding his breath.

A little? he wanted to say. *Haunts them a little?*

But how could this girl with her nose ring and streaks of purple in her hair know that his wife had been one of those eighteen? That he could have stayed home and kept Cherie company in the blizzard but instead had chosen to hang with the guys and ended up drunk with his car in a ditch? That every snowfall reminded him that he hadn't been there for his wife when she'd needed him most? She couldn't, obviously . . . but still he wanted to snap at her.

The bell over the door rang again and he glanced over to see Franco and Baxter coming in. He sat up straighter, his pulse quickening. He should have been relieved that they'd arrived — he had to be at work in a little more than an hour — but he didn't think he would ever be happy to see these two.

He spared a last glance at the stressed-out mom, realizing she didn't look like Cherie at all. Twelve years had passed since the night his wife had died and he still saw her in the faces of women he passed on the street. Still dreamed about her. Still loved her. These days, his life didn't have any room for love. It was all about work and trying to figure out if he could live with the things he'd done. Most days the answer was yes.

'Dougie Doug, what's happening?' Franco said as he slid into the booth.

'You guys hit traffic or something?' Doug asked.

Baxter dropped into the booth beside Franco. He leaned back, cocking his head and studying Doug with those ice-blue eyes, his tattoos a silent declaration of war to anyone around him.

'You in a hurry?' Baxter asked, the question tinged with irritation and menace.

'I got work.'

Baxter nodded toward the front counter of the diner. 'You gotta eat, right?'

'Yeah, I guess,' Doug said.

'You fucking guess,' Baxter said, sneering. He leaned across the table and dropped his voice to a cruelly intimate whisper. 'Don't be a little bitch, Doug.'

'Baxter — ' Franco started.

'Shush,' Baxter said, keeping his eyes fixed on

Doug. 'When Franco said we oughta bring you in, I only went along with it because we both grew up on Copper Hill. You were a hardass little kid, man. I remember the day Benny Hayes stripped off Julie what's-her-face's shirt on the basketball court. What were you, twelve? Benny had two years and thirty pounds on you, easy, and you beat him bloody. Kid lost a couple of teeth and any chance of ever being respected by the neighborhood again.

'Now, I figure you were playing white knight, rescuing the damsel in distress even if the damsel was a tiny-titted China girl with a mouthful of braces. Maybe it was an Asian thing. But you had fuckin' steel that day, man. And the white-knight shit . . . that's what it was. Shit. We were *all* stealing from the White Hen back then, and the night I stole that Caddy, you were my fucking lookout. You were with me, Kelly, and the Deeley brothers that whole night, man, riding around in a stolen car, drinking stolen beers, smoking stolen cigarettes.'

Baxter dropped back against his seat. He took a wad of cash from his jacket pocket and threw it onto the table.

'So go get your lunch, Dougie. I don't want you late for work. But let's stop pretending you're some kind of saint.'

Doug's heart pounded. He glanced at Franco but knew there was no help coming from that direction. Taller and leaner but jacked from years of lifting free weights, and quick as the devil, Franco probably could have taken Baxter if it came to fisticuffs. But something about Baxter made people uneasy and therefore compliant. It had always been that way, but never more so than now. With his prison tats and those cold eyes, Baxter was the alpha dog in pretty much any room he entered.

'I'm no saint,' Doug said quietly, glancing over his shoulder to make sure nobody was looking at them. A couple of old townies were two tables down, drinking coffee with their scarves still on. The mom had picked up her order and left with her boys in tow. He turned back to Baxter and Franco. 'But this is bigger than stealing condoms and cigarettes from the goddamn White Hen.'

Baxter smiled. 'We're grown-ups now, Dougie. Stakes are higher. I know you're out of practice. Hell, I've seen how out of practice you are. And I know it's been twenty years since you took something didn't belong to you. But I told you when we brought you in . . . you're either in or you're out.'

Doug stared at him for a few seconds and then he laughed. 'For Christ's sake, all I did was bust your balls because you were late.'

Franco scratched at his goatee and looked out the window.

Baxter just shook his head. 'It ain't what you said. It's the vibe that's burning off you, today and every other time we've gotten together. You're about to crawl out of your skin, man.'

'Doug,' Franco said, finally speaking. His prior silence made the single word stop the rest of the conversation dead. 'You and me, we worked together off and on, yeah? But we were never friends. That hasn't changed. I like you well

84

enough, but you and me don't have the history you got with Baxter. I suggested we bring you in because you had the access and you had the need. You were squirrelly right off the bat, but me and Baxter, we figured you'd calm down once you got a little money in your pocket. So far, that hasn't happened.'

No longer smiling, Baxter leaned in again. 'What we're saying is, chill the fuck out or we cut you loose.'

Something fluttered in Doug's gut and he wasn't sure if it was fear or anger. *Hunger, probably*, he thought. The guys were right, he definitely had the need. He might be the first guy Timmy Harpwell brought in when he needed an extra mechanic, but he was also the first guy kicked to the curb when business took a downturn. The last two years he'd been picking up a couple of days a week at Harpwell's Garage, money under the table so he could collect unemployment. He'd looked for other, more reliable work, but there were too many idle hands and hardly any jobs.

The fluttering in his gut halted and an icy knot took its place.

'I told you I'm in. Damn right I need it,' he said, glancing from Baxter to Franco. 'I just don't think it's real smart to be having lunch together at fucking Chick's Roast Beef in the town where we're doing shit we don't want to get caught doing. One of you gets picked up, I don't want to be a Known Associate. You see what I'm saying.'

Baxter exhaled, sitting back for a moment

before he looked at Franco.

'White Knight has a point.'

Franco nodded, then gave a shrug. 'Next time we get together at night? At Dougie's place?'

'That works,' Baxter said, turning to Doug with a smile. 'We'll come in the back door. I'll bring the beer if you get the food.'

The idea of these guys coming to his house after dark to plot more of the small-time heists they'd been living off the past couple of months made his skin crawl. But it made sense, especially since the alternative was spy shit that none of them had the brains for.

'Sounds good,' he said, keeping his tone level and wondering if he could ever get his own eyes to look as cold as Baxter's.

Wondering if that was something to wish for or something to dread.

The bell above the door rang again. Doug glanced up at the big man who stepped into the diner and froze, unable to breathe. The guy nodded in recognition and Doug found himself just able to return the nod, watching as the new arrival brushed a few snowflakes from the lapels of his wool coat. His paralysis broke the moment the man reached the counter, talking happily to the counter girl, musing aloud about the relationship between Chick's onion rings and his cholesterol.

Doug knew the big guy. They'd played football together at Coventry High years ago. Got shitfaced together at a few parties junior and senior year. They'd both dated Victoria Allen at some point, though the chronology escaped him.

Local boys, Doug thought, *but only one of us made good.*

'Meeting adjourned,' Doug said quietly, sliding to the edge of his seat.

Baxter grabbed his wrist, the grip strong, but maybe not strong enough. *Yeah,* Doug thought. *Could be I've been going about this all wrong.*

'Where the fuck do you think you're — ' Baxter began.

Doug shut him down with a glare. Maybe his eyes were cold after all. 'Call me later and we'll pick another place,' he said quietly, and then lowered his voice further: 'Somewhere without cops.'

Franco, idiot that he was, actually turned fully around and gave Detective Joe Keenan the once-over. Doug wanted to put his face through the plate glass window beside the booth. Something inside Doug had broken when Cherie died. He'd been sleepwalking, just moving with the current of his life. But the last couple of months with these guys, cloning the keys from the most well-to-do customers at the garage, smart enough not to hit anyone whose car he worked on personally, doing a little quiet, very rewarding bit of burglary . . . something was waking up in him, too. Maybe not the thing that had died along with Cherie — his hope, he guessed — but something with a little ambition and not a lot of patience.

Doug got up from the booth and left them sitting there. They'd already drawn the cop's attention and he didn't want to say another word to either one of them about their next job, whether the cop would hear them or not.

'Manning,' the cop said, looking him up and down.

'Keenan,' Doug replied. 'Heard you're a detective now. That entitle you to extra doughnuts?'

Detective Keenan smiled. 'Actually, it does.'

Doug grinned. 'Looks it.'

The cop shot him the finger. 'Fuck you.'

'You don't need to say it, Joe. I can read sign language.'

Keenan laughed. 'How's things?'

'Been better,' Doug replied, a thin smile forming on his lips. 'But I'm still breathing, so life can't be all bad.'

'Some days I wonder,' the cop said.

'I'll see you around,' Doug said, heading for the door.

The bell rang when he pushed it open. As he glanced back he saw Keenan looking over at the table where Franco and Baxter still sat.

'Yeah. Drive safe,' Keenan replied.

The wind smacked the door shut behind him as Doug stepped out into the bleak January mess. Light snow fell and he blinked several flakes from his eyes as he dug out his keys, swearing under his breath. He climbed into his old Audi — a battered piece of shit everywhere but under the hood, where it gleamed — and started it up. As he backed out of his parking space, he glanced at the diner windows but couldn't see inside. Slamming it into Drive, he tore out of the tiny lot, tires gripping the road despite the slickness of the wet snow.

He smacked the wheel with an open palm. 'Fuck!'

Keenan didn't have psychic powers or anything, but Baxter had done time and one look at Franco and you knew he was up to no good. The cop would be filing the moment away for future reference, and it pissed Doug off. If he'd sunk low enough to turn into a two-bit thief — and he had — he was going to have to insist on a little bit of discipline from these pricks.

He'd been haunted for twelve years, damning himself for not going straight home after Timmy had fired him that night. If he had, Cherie might be alive today. He'd been in his own kind of jail. He'd be damned if he'd end up inside a real prison now that he was starting to see a little light.

As the engine roared and the wipers skidded back and forth on the windshield, Doug told himself that stealing from rich assholes didn't make him a bad guy, just a desperate motherfucker who no longer cared about the rules.

He told himself that a lot.

★ ★ ★

Keenan ordered a cheesesteak sub and onion rings, knowing that the grease would sit in his stomach later and not caring. He needed comfort food today. Truth be told, what he needed was a six-pack of MGD and maybe a few more besides, but he'd realized a long time ago that drinking to forget only gave him more bad memories. These days, when the snow came down hard and he started thinking about the Wexler family and about Charlie Newell, he just let it come. He'd seen worse things in the past twelve years than the electrocuted corpse of Gavin Wexler and he'd watched other people die; little Charlie Newell had just been the first. People thought he'd worked and studied so hard to become a detective because he had ambition, but he had them fooled. He just didn't want to be the first guy on the scene anymore. Not ever, if he could help it.

The crazy thing was that when he had nightmares, they were mostly about Gavin Wexler's father, who'd been there one second and gone the next, like a gust of wind had carried him off. In Joe Keenan's dreams he would be searching for Wexler — sometimes in a storm but at others in the woods or along some downtown alley — and he'd have the total conviction that the guy was there, just out of sight, that if Keenan turned at just the right moment he'd find Wexler. That certainty grew more and more heightened until he woke up. Even in his dreams, he never did find Carl Wexler.

'You okay?' asked the girl behind the counter.

The ring in her nose wasn't his style, but otherwise Keenan figured she was pretty enough. He tried not to let himself think in those terms about girls that young, but the purple streaks in her hair intrigued him. Of course, his wife would've preferred he not think that way about anyone but her, but she was realistic — guys

90

always looked. So did women, Keenan knew, but he and Donna both pretended otherwise.

Detective Keenan gave her a lopsided grin and rubbed a hand across his blond buzz cut. 'Just a few cobwebs in the brain today.'

'Snow does that to everyone around here,' the girl said.

'Yeah. I guess it does.'

She handed the order slip for his sub to the irritated-looking cook in the back and then went to get some frozen onion rings to dump into the fryer. As bad as they were for him, he loved to hear them sizzle. The owner — not Chick, who'd been dead for a quarter century, but a Brazilian named Maurice — used some brilliant concoction of herbs and spices that made those onion rings the town's best-kept secret.

Keenan always joked with Donna that they were his personal crack and perhaps one day his doom. Donna didn't think it was funny. They had two little boys she'd have to raise on her own if her husband committed suicide-by-onion-ring. He made light of it when Donna teased him but he had no intention of going anywhere. He'd watched Jill Wexler at her son's funeral, still hoping her husband would reappear as suddenly as he'd vanished. He had never seen anyone so alone.

Perusing the offerings in the soda case — trying to force himself to believe that flavored water tasted as good as grape soda — he glanced at the two guys sitting in the back of the diner. The tall, skinny, olive-skinned guy might be Italian or Latino. He ID'd the other guy as Pete

91

Baxter. Any cop in town would have known Baxter right off, and not just because of the spiderweb tattooed on his neck or the ugly black tattoo on his left forearm, which looked more like a sea lion but was supposed to be a cat.

Cocaine seemed almost quaint these days, but Baxter had a deep and abiding love for powder, the more the better. From what Keenan remembered, the guy had been arrested half-a-dozen times or more for petty theft, burglary, and a variety of other charges, but had somehow managed to avoid doing any real time until Coventry PD had caught him with enough coke to charge him with possession with intent to distribute. Nobody actually figured Baxter for a serious dealer. He'd sell off half the coke to pay for procuring it, set a startling amount aside for himself, and then give the rest away to family and friends like he was Santa Claus.

Pete Baxter was the kind of guy Detective Keenan's grandfather Leo would have called a turd. And maybe that was true. Maybe Baxter was just a piece of shit that Keenan could ignore until he committed another crime. But the few times he'd seen the guy, Baxter had made him antsy. Cocaine didn't have the same effect as meth, but Baxter always seemed like a runner, crouched on the starting line and ready to bolt. Only for him, the starting gun would be permission to lash out, to hurt people, to inflict pain and suffering. The cocaine might have been his way of tamping down the jittery, violent thing inside him or it might have been his attempt to find the courage to unleash it, but that thing was there inside Pete Baxter. Most of the cops he'd ever heard talk about Baxter thought he was a joke — just another lowlife — but Keenan thought he was a savage, looking out at the world through a human mask.

So what was Dougie Manning doing having lunch with Pete Baxter and friend? Chances were they knew each other. The city of Coventry had quite a sprawl, but most of the people of any given generation seemed to cross paths in one way or another. Coventry was the kind of place where just as many people grew up and stayed in town to raise their families as left to start new lives elsewhere. There were plenty of people proud to be Coventry townies. Still, he didn't like it. Maybe it wouldn't have bothered him so much if the idiots had even eaten lunch.

The table where Baxter and his friend sat was clean. Not so much as a stray smear of ketchup. They hadn't eaten, hadn't ordered, and Doug Manning had taken off pretty much the second that Keenan had come in. People who got together around a table and didn't make it a point to eat weren't having lunch — they were having a business meeting.

Baxter and his friend had a quick, muttered conversation and then Baxter slid out of the booth, glancing up at the menu board. Apparently he'd finally realized how stupid they looked just sitting there. The cute counter girl bagged Keenan's greasy lunch and rang it up while Baxter tried hard not to look at him. Keenan thanked her as he paid, but then he hesitated, waiting as Baxter started to order.

'Gimme one buffalo-chicken sub and a six-inch tuna — '

Keenan's radio crackled with static, a little squawk that included his name.

'Detective Keenan, please respond,' the dispatcher said.

He turned away from the counter, slipping the radio from its sheath on his belt. The greasy aroma steaming up from the brown paper bag in his hand made his stomach rumble with pleasure as he fumbled with it. All eyes were on him as he pushed out the door and into the falling snow, including Baxter's. He hated the vibe he got off the guy, but he couldn't arrest him for crimes he hadn't committed yet.

'This is Keenan,' he answered as he moved toward his car. 'Go ahead.'

'Detective, we've got an assault on a woman, 107 Capen Street, apartment 3B. Officers are on the scene but request a detective.'

'On my way,' he said, then clipped the radio to his belt and dug out his keys.

He'd have to eat and drive, but he'd been on the job so long that he'd become pretty good at it. Keenan's real concern as he drove away was Doug Manning and what he was doing hanging out with a turd like Baxter. They had never exactly been friends back in the Stone Age, but the detective had always thought of Doug as a decent guy. Cocky but well meaning. It might not be today, but eventually that savage thing inside Baxter was going to rip its way out and anybody in the bastard's vicinity was going to get hurt.

Keenan hoped Doug wasn't going to be one of them.

★   ★   ★

At least once a week, Jake Schapiro's mother reminded him that her friends and colleagues thought his occupation ghoulish. Most of the time, he succeeded in ignoring her, primarily because he felt sure that when the subject of his career arose, she would be the first among her particular group of hens to look down her nose at his chosen profession. When she did succeed in rattling him, they always ended up talking about Isaac and he hated having that conversation with her. It had been twelve years, he would tell her, just let it go. But neither of them believed that Jake had put the pain of his brother's death behind him. He mourned in his way and his mother in hers, and neither approved of the other's chosen method of grief therapy.

At least his didn't involve a bottle.

Jake focused his camera on the nightstand. The drawer had not been pushed in properly, so it sat at an angle, one corner of its shallow depth peeking out. Something about it seemed off to him. Except for the shattered lamp and overturned chair, the bed in disarray, and the other obvious signs of struggle, the place seemed the domain of a woman who liked things clean and orderly.

He snapped a photo of the nightstand, the flash illuminating the scene starkly white. When

95

he blinked, the image of his little brother broken and dead in the deep snow — flakes still accumulating on his face — flickered through his mind. The night of Isaac's death he had watched the crime-scene photographer at his work for several minutes until his mother had realized it and pulled him away, covering his eyes.

She'd been too late. Every time he used this equipment he saw Isaac's face with each brilliant flash of the camera and wondered if things would have been different that night if only he'd paid more attention to his little brother's fear.

'Are you gonna be much longer?'

Startled, Jake turned to find Harley Talbot looming behind him. At six foot five and built like a truck, Harley looked like a star linebacker because that's what he'd been in college, but he'd never had any interest in being anything but a cop. In the uniform he looked especially imposing, but Jake knew him too well to be intimidated by him, police officer or not.

'Almost done,' Jake said.

'So damn slow.'

'Bite me.'

Harley smiled. Jake knew he did his damnedest not to smile on the job because it gave him a sweetness that undermined any sort of menace or intimidation. Harley tried to save his smile for the multitude of women who paid him attention whenever they hit up the local bars and restaurants. Coventry didn't have much by way of night life, but what little there was had welcomed the new cop in town with open arms.

'Keenan's gonna be here in a few minutes,' Harley said, smile vanishing, voice low. 'Sooner you're both done, the sooner we're out of here. Simple assault, Jacob. Snap a couple more shots and let's take off.'

Jake glanced at the bedroom door but the corridor outside was empty. Harley's partner, an aging cop named Ted Finch, had been taking the statement from the victim out in the tiny living room when Jake had arrived. No one would overhear them.

'You sure it's that simple?' Jake asked.

Harley raised a brow. 'You aren't?'

'Not sure,' Jake said, glancing at the nightstand again. 'Anyway, you're the cop. Just a couple more pictures.'

Jake moved into the corner of the room to take an establishing shot of the room from that angle. Harley stepped out of the frame, leaving only the twisted bedspread and sheets, which hung like drapes on one side of the bed. The pillows were askew. The lamp had been thrown and shattered, maybe after striking the bureau.

He frowned. The drawers of the bureau were all shut tightly.

So what? he thought. *Nobody does anything the same way every time.*

In his mind's eye, though, he saw the drawers and cabinets in the kitchen. The struggle hadn't gotten that far. The overturned chair was in the living room, where a shelf of knickknacks had been shattered — things that had clearly had sentimental value to the victim.

Something didn't fit, but he couldn't put his

finger on it. Instead he took a step nearer and focused more clearly on the bed from this angle. A small spray of blood had scattered droplets on the dangling sheets and he wanted to get a clear picture of it. Would the police have a lab analyze the blood to see if it had come from the victim or the assailant? In a murder or rape, sure, but what about assault and attempted rape? He figured they had to, but even after a couple of years at this job, he didn't know as much about police work as he pretended to while talking to girls in bars.

He had to compete with Harley somehow.

Looking through the camera's viewfinder, he noticed something else. Snapping the picture, he zoomed in and took another, then walked to the bed and got down on one knee.

'What are you doing, Jacob?' Harley warned.

'Yes, Jacob, what are you doing?'

Jake glanced up sharply. Detective Keenan had come into the room just behind Harley and they made a comical picture. With his Irish face and blue eyes, the detective reminded Jake a little of the actor Daniel Craig. His big hands and the slight crook in his nose that showed it had once been broken suggested he might once have been a boxer, and he was not a small man, but next to Harley the detective seemed diminished.

'Doing your job for you, I think,' Jake replied.

The look that rippled across Keenan's face made Jake blink. His balls didn't exactly shrink up inside his body, but they certainly did not approve. The detective's light tone and the way he'd entered the room had allowed Jake to forget for a second just how serious Keenan was about his job.

Keenan stepped around Harley and moved deeper into the room, taking in the crime scene with a sweeping glance.

'You want to explain that?' he asked without looking at Jake.

'Just instinct and observation. I get a different perspective sometimes through the camera. The nightstand drawer is kind of cockeyed, which I know sounds stupid . . .'

He trailed off. It did sound stupid. But had he just seen Keenan take visual note of the same thing?

'Go on,' the detective said.

Jake pointed to the spot where the mussed sheets draped to the floor. 'Under there.'

Keenan went down on one knee and picked up the edge of the hanging sheets to reveal the small white pill-bottle cap that Jake had spotted in the shadows there. The detective left the cap where it was — he wouldn't pick it up without donning latex gloves for fear of contaminating evidence.

'Talbot, gimme your flashlight,' Keenan said.

Harley handed it over and the detective used the light to search under the bed before clicking it off and handing it back. Keenan brushed off the knees of his trousers as he stood and turned a contemplative eye on Jake.

'No bottle,' Jake said.

'Nope,' Keenan agreed.

Pulling a latex glove onto his left hand, the detective went to the nightstand and tried to

99

open it. The drawer stuck but with a bit of jostling he got it to slide open. It was empty.

'Talbot, have you been into the bathroom?' Keenan asked.

'Took a look, yeah.'

'Anything out of place?'

'No,' Jake said, cutting in. 'And I took pictures. But I didn't — '

Keenan nodded. 'But you didn't open the medicine cabinet.'

'No,' Jake said. 'I didn't.'

Harley crossed his arms, his body practically blocking their view of the open door. 'So it's a drug thing. We go into the bathroom again, we're going to find the medicine cabinet empty. Some pill-head came in and beat the lady up for her meds?'

'Not just her own prescriptions — ' Detective Keenan started.

'I get it, Detective,' Harley interrupted. 'She's a pill-head, too. She had a bunch of illegal scrips, maybe was selling them, and some guy knew it and cleaned her out. Probably someone she knows.'

Jake and Detective Keenan both looked at him.

Harley laughed and shook his head. 'You two think you're Holmes and friggin' Watson. Can we just finish this shit up and go? I go off duty in twenty minutes and I need a cocoa.'

'Cocoa,' Jake repeated.

Harley glowered at him. 'When it snows, I like cocoa. A little whipped cream, too. You got something to say about it?'

100

Detective Keenan outranked him but didn't say a word. Neither did Jake.

'I thought not,' Harley said. Scowling, he turned and left the room. Jake laughed and started packing away his camera.

'You're pretty smart, kid,' Keenan said, sounding for a moment like he'd stepped out of some 1940s gangster movie.

'Harley doesn't think so,' Jake replied with a laugh.

'Ever think about becoming a cop yourself?'

Images of that night flickered through Jake's mind again. Isaac's broken body, the falling snow, the flash of a camera . . . those had been real, tangible things. Awful things, yes, but they had been solid and true and grimly understandable. The bright flashes had taken away the shadows — all except for the sad hollows around his dead brother's eyes. That had been a reality that twelve-year-old Jake could understand. The more he had talked about the things that Isaac claimed to have seen out in the snow, only to have cops and shrinks think he'd imagined it or was making it up, the less he felt willing to admit what he had seen. *A face at the window. Icy hands coming through the screen . . .*

Until eventually he had begun to realize that the cops and the shrinks had to be right. They had to be. His little brother's imagination and his own grief had gotten the better of him.

But even now, a dozen years later, the camera gave him comfort. Pictures made it real. The flash chased the shadows away and left only the tangible world. If the camera couldn't see

101

something, it wasn't real.

'I'd make a terrible cop,' Jake said at last, as he slung his camera bag over his shoulder. 'Besides, I only do this so I can afford to take the pictures I care about.'

Keenan fished out his phone. No crime-scene tech had shown up and he needed some fingerprinting done. Whoever had been sent out had probably been delayed by the storm, but Keenan didn't need Jake to tell him that.

'Be sure to invite me to your first gallery opening,' the detective said.

Jake couldn't tell if he was being sarcastic. He didn't like to talk about what his mother called his 'nice pictures.' She thought his paying job was ghoulish and wished that he could make a living as a different sort of photographer. So did Jake.

'I'll do that,' he said, and headed out the door.

On his way out he took another look at the victim. In the bedroom they'd been making light of the situation, but when she glanced at him and he saw her face again — the swelling, the dried blood on her lips — he felt bad about that. Addict or not, she deserved sympathy. At twenty-four, he knew far too many people who used drugs or alcohol to try to forget the things that haunted them. Coventry had more than its fair share of bad memories.

He went down the stairs and out into the storm, nodding to the cop guarding the door. Normally there would have been neighbors and other spectators gathered outside but the snow fell thickly now, a white silence that spread across the city. The forecast called for about eight inches, turning to rain at the end. It would be a hell of a mess tomorrow, but this afternoon and tonight it was beautiful.

Jake hurried to his car, anxious to get out his personal camera. He'd first truly fallen in love with the camera in high school, taking pictures of ominous thunderheads from his back porch, finding beauty in the churning clouds and the way the blue sky had been so quickly blotted out. Now his real art — photography that he had indeed shown in a few galleries, not that he'd ever tell Keenan that — was photographing storms of all kinds. Trees bending in a gale, rain on glass, shafts of light spearing through black clouds. Snowstorms provided the most beautiful and haunting images of all.

But his favorite photographs were not of the storms themselves. The ones about which he felt the most passionate, and perhaps not coincidentally the ones he had sold for quite a bit of money, were pictures of the mornings after. When the sky had cleared and the sun had returned and, despite whatever damage the storm had left behind, everything looked clean and pure and somehow renewed . . .

He never saw Isaac in the snap of the lens when he took those pictures.

Those were the moments he lived for.

6

A knock at the door got Allie Schapiro up out of her chair. She'd been sitting beside a window in her living room, reading by the wan gray daylight that filtered through the storm and drinking a glass of red wine. One finger holding her place in the book, she went out into the little foyer and put her hand on the doorknob.

'Who's there?' she called.

TJ Farrelly identified himself and she pulled open the door. Scruffy and blond, midforties, he stood on the stoop in the swirl of snow and greeted her with a kind smile and tired eyes. His hair was too long and he needed a shave, but that unkempt quality made him more handsome instead of less.

'Oh, thank God,' she said. 'And thank *you* so much for coming out today.'

Allie stood back to let TJ enter. He stamped snow off his boots on the little rug in the foyer and his eyes found the book in her hand.

'Sorry to interrupt your reading.'

'Oh, not at all,' she said with a nervous laugh, closing the door. 'Honestly, I kept rereading the same section over and over. I haven't been able to focus on it at all.'

TJ adjusted the heavy tool belt on his waist in that unconscious, get-the-job-done way she had always loved to see in men. It gave an aura of confidence that was contagious.

'No worries, Ms. Schapiro,' he said. 'I'll take care of you.'

Though he seemed a bit wary of her, Allie gave a little inward chuckle at the sexy-handyman clichés that popped into her mind. As a younger woman she would have blushed, but once she had passed fifty something had changed in her. Yes, she kept her hair dyed an attractive auburn and had it styled regularly, and she chose her clothes carefully, but those were things she did for herself and not for others. She no longer cared quite as much about what other people thought. Once it had bothered her that she had a reputation as being a bit of an uptight bitch. People ought to have understood, given the losses in her life, or that was the way she'd rationalized it. Now she understood that life was all about loss, that everyone suffered in his own way. She just wasn't ever going to be able to be the kind of person who pretended to be happy when she wasn't.

'Please, TJ,' she said, 'I'm not your daughter's teacher anymore. You can call me Allie.'

The man looked surprised. 'All right, Allie. Lead the way.'

She picked up the heavy-duty flashlight from the little table in the foyer and clicked it on. TJ unclipped a small but powerful light of his own from his belt and followed her down the short hall to the kitchen, through the cellar door, and down the steps into the basement. Even less of that gray light filtered through small box windows close to the ceiling, the glass rectangles half covered by the newfallen snow outside, making the flashlights helpful but not entirely necessary. Not until nightfall, at least.

'The fuse box is over there,' she said, shining her flashlight on it.

'Gotcha.' He went over and opened the panel, moving the light over the circuit breakers.

'It really does mean the world, you coming out in the storm.'

'I couldn't leave you in the dark,' he said, almost casually clicking the breakers and snapping them back into place. 'Not with the snow . . .'

He trailed off, pausing as if rooted to the spot, one hand on the metal door of the fuse box. The flashlight wavered in his hand.

Allie's chest hurt. She had forgotten to breathe.

'I'm sorry,' he said, turning toward her, the beams of their flashlights throwing ovals of illumination on opposite walls.

She wet her lips. 'It's okay. After all this time I'd better be able to talk about a little snow without letting it get the better of me. Besides, you lost someone in the storm, too. I'm sure you're happy to talk about your mother, to remember her.'

'Most of the time,' TJ allowed. 'Though for some reason it's harder to talk about her when it snows. It always feels wrong, somehow.'

'I know the feeling. But it's okay. If you and I can't understand each other, who could?'

He didn't quite manage to smile, but nodded and turned his light back to the electrical panel.

Allie had first met TJ at a memorial for those

killed or lost in that blizzard on the one-year anniversary of the storm. At that point, he and his wife, Ella, had been married less than a month and already had a little girl at home. Many years later, at a parent-teacher conference, Ella had lightheartedly revealed that their daughter, Grace, had been conceived during that storm.

So at least one good thing came out of it, TJ had said.

The couple had exchanged an ugly sort of look, then. One she had seen all too often in her years as a teacher. That particular look never boded well for marriages. Allie had thought then and still believed that it would be a shame if the Farrellys' relationship hit the skids. Pint-size Grace — copper-eyed and tiny and always buzzing with positive energy — had two parents who obviously loved her very much. A separation or divorce would dim or destroy the little girl's smile, and it saddened Allie to think of it. The Farrellys were a nice family, but over the past few years she and the rest of the staff at the Trumbull School had seen a lot of nice families buckle under the stresses of the times.

Allie knew a little something about the ruination of nice families. After the death of her husband she had thought she would never find happiness again, and then she'd met Niko Ristani and she had allowed herself to believe, had built a little nest in her heart for hope to grow and take flight. The storm had taken all that away from her, had killed her Isaac and had swallowed Niko up, never to be seen again. How a grown man could vanish from the face of the Earth in the twenty-first century boggled her mind, but it had happened. And Niko wasn't the only one.

Something popped on the electrical panel and TJ swore, jumping back. Thin tendrils of black smoke rose behind one of the breakers with a sizzling, snapping sound.

'Oh no!' she said, focusing her flashlight on the panel for a moment before TJ's body blocked the beam.

'Son of a bitch.' He growled, throwing switches and shining his own flash across the board. 'You have a fire extinguisher?'

'Under the kitchen sink.'

'Get it!'

Allie ran, her mind awhirl with fear of her house burning down, wondering if she would have time to fetch the photo albums on the floor of her bedroom closet, the only things in the house she thought she could not live without. All those pictures of Isaac and Jake when they were young — the only pictures there would ever be of Isaac. Losing those . . . She couldn't even conceive of it.

Moments later she hustled back down into the cellar, her flashlight beam bouncing on the steps before her, with no recollection at all of actually fetching the fire extinguisher.

'I've got — '

'We're good,' TJ interrupted.

Allie stood at the bottom of the cellar steps, her heart thumping in her chest. She watched him for a second as he used his flashlight to

108

examine the wiring that went into and came out of the electrical box.

'My house isn't burning down?' she said.

'Not at the moment. At least I don't think so,' he said, turning toward her. 'But I can't promise it won't. I guess you know the wiring in this house is pretty ancient. Truth is, you need to get all the wiring replaced. What's here is not really meant to meet modern needs and even if it could, the breakers can't meet the strain.'

Her heart sank further with every word and she felt a little sick. 'I can't afford all that.'

'You might have to figure out a way, Allie. I'm sorry. Could be it won't cost as much as you think it will, but look — that's a conversation for another day. Right now we need to get your electricity running and that's something I can do. The main breaker is totally fried, which is why the whole house was affected. I can replace that and the damaged wiring — I've got everything I need in the truck — and be out of here in a couple of hours, max. It won't solve your problems long term but at least it'll give you light and heat for tonight.'

The mention of heat made her blink. Allie wore a thick, green wool sweater with a little hood and deep pockets. When it had begun to get cold she had slipped it on, assuming that the heat wouldn't be off for very long. But if TJ hadn't been able to fix it, she would have had to find somewhere else to spend the night, and she really had nowhere to go. It wasn't that she had no friends — her friends Mark and Charles would have let her sleep at their place, and her best teacher-friend, Phoebe Ridgley, would have loved the chance at a girls' night — but Allie didn't like to sleep away from home. And she didn't like going out in a storm.

TJ was right: somehow she was going to have to put together the money to rewire the house. But at least she didn't have to figure it all out today.

'Thanks so much,' she said, hoping he felt her sincerity. 'I'm so grateful that you were willing to come out on a Saturday. What a life-saver.'

'My pleasure,' he said, hiking up his belt as he approached, then passed her and started up the stairs. 'It's what I do.'

Allie heard the defeated edge to his voice, a tinge of sadness. Over the years since they had first met, she had been fortunate enough to see him perform at The Vault several times and thought he had a wonderful singing voice and a lovely way with the guitar.

'If you mean rescuing no-longer-quite-damsels in distress, then okay,' she replied. 'But I hope you're not giving up the music.'

TJ stopped on the steps, bent slightly to crane back down toward her. 'If we can't get customers into the restaurant, there's no money to pay either of us. Waiters and cooks come first. I've got to make money elsewhere, but in this economy, even being an electrician isn't pulling in the income it used to.'

'I'm sorry to hear that,' she said quietly.

He chuckled darkly. 'Me too. But don't be sorry you called. I can use the work. And anyway, Ella closed the restaurant for the storm.

We don't share space very well these days, so I'm just grateful to be out of the house.'

TJ hustled up the stairs. Allie stood in the dim basement, flashlight hanging at her side, searching for some words that might bring him comfort. For long minutes she waited while he fetched what he needed from his truck, and by the time he returned she still had not been able to think of anything she might say that could help him. For a couple of minutes she watched him work and then she excused herself to go back upstairs, intending to get stuck back in the book she was reading.

Whatever solace TJ Farrelly sought, he would have to find it on his own. She had racked her brain until she had realized the truth: she had none to give.

* * *

Late that afternoon TJ drove home with his hands so tight on the wheel that his knuckles hurt. He never shied away from going out in a storm, never let inclement weather keep him from his destination. Not since the night he'd left his mother home alone after he'd promised to see her through the blizzard. He had never learned what it was that had made her wander out into the night and had learned to live with the fact that he'd never know, but he still had nightmares about the morning the police had brought him to the morgue to identify her body. The corpse had been wide-eyed and rigid and bleached pale by the nine days that had passed

111

before an old woman who worked at Saint James rectory had seen his mother's arm sticking out of the melting snowbank that had been plowed up against the side of the building.

TJ would rather end up in a snowbank himself than let the weather keep him away from people who were waiting for him — people he loved. And he did still love Ella, no matter how tense things had become. No matter that they sometimes snapped at each other when they spoke, as if they were angry at the words leaving their lips instead of the way their life together had begun to fray.

Fray, he thought now, reaching out to turn the windshield wipers up to high. *We've been fraying for years. This isn't fraying, it's unraveling.*

The wipers thumped their insistent rhythm, not clearing as much of the glass as he wanted. Rolling down the window, he reached out and bent forward as he drove, digging his fingers into the now-slushy buildup at the edge of the wipers' span, scraping it away. Headlights loomed ahead and he sat up straighter, raising the window as he nudged the car to the right to give a wide berth to the plow headed in the other direction.

As he hit the button to raise the window he realized that the darkness of the storm had given way to nightfall. At this time of year, evening didn't even have the courtesy to wait for afternoon to end before moving in, but with a thick blanket of storm like this, the day never properly arrived. Now it was over before it had really begun.

He turned his truck onto Calewood Drive, snow slushing around the tires, and came in view of his home. Once upon a time the warm yellow light of the lamppost would have gladdened his heart but tonight the sight weighed him down. It hardly ever felt like home to him anymore. Instead it was a boxing ring, frozen in the held-breath moment before either of the fighters had thrown their first punch. And when that punch came . . . man, he knew it was going to be a doozy.

Pulling into the driveway, he killed the engine and climbed out of the truck. He hadn't made it halfway up the front walk before the front door opened, the light from within silhouetting his daughter, Grace, who stood with one hand on her hip. With her slender build, long legs, and wavy brown hair, she looked like a miniature version of her mother.

'Get in here, mister!' the eleven-year-old playfully demanded. 'This beef stew I made isn't gonna eat itself.'

'I don't know about that,' TJ said as he mounted the front steps. 'You never know with monster beef.'

Grace backed up to let him in, frowning. 'That doesn't even make sense.'

'Sure it does,' he said, stamping the snow off his boots, taking in the familiar messy sprawl of the living room and the rich aromas of cooking stew. 'Monster beef could come back to life. The little bits could attack each other right in the pot.'

His little girl rolled her eyes. 'Not only does

113

that not make sense, it's really gross.'

'I'm a guy,' TJ said, unlacing his boots and pulling them off. 'Guys are gross.'

'That's for sure,' Grace agreed.

She began to giggle as he scooped her up and dropped her on the sofa, nuzzling and biting her belly and then, as she tried to free herself, locking his teeth on her forearm in true monster fashion. As a baby, Grace had cried every time they put her into her car seat, making any road trip a fresh descent into parental hell. That had ceased as soon as she grew old enough to talk and be distracted in the car, and otherwise she had been almost uncannily well behaved, so sweet and good-natured and polite that other parents always begged for their secret. Nobody ever wanted to believe their answer, which was that they had simply been lucky.

Now Grace was eleven and things were starting to change, not just her body but her relationships with her parents, too. Grace had grown old enough to challenge them, to push their buttons for no reason other than to discover the results of having pushed them. She had started to pay more attention to the way she dressed and the way she wore her hair. The whole thing unsettled the hell out of TJ. His pride in her seemed constantly at odds with his desire not to lose the purity of the relationship they'd had all her life up till now. They had a little while still, he thought, before the real battles over boys and makeup and dating would begin, but he knew that time with his little girl was fleeting, so he tried to make the most of it.

Of late it had been growing more difficult. Grace felt the tension between her parents and it created a distance that TJ wanted very badly to bridge. When he and Grace were alone, they could just be Dad and Gracie again, and he knew the same must be true of Grace and Ella. But when the three of them were together there was a kind of stiffness to their interactions, a wary uncertainty that TJ hated.

Maybe that's the secret, he thought. *No more family.*

Growling, he pulled Grace's arms away from her body and saw that the struggle had bared her abdomen. With a laugh he ducked in and began to blow raspberries on her belly. Grace squealed and tried to twist free, her right knee catching him under the chin. His jaws clacked together and he fell back off the couch, landing on his butt. He sat with one hand on his chin like a boxer unsure as to how he'd ended up on the mat. His jaw throbbed and he gave a low moan.

Grace tried to stifle her giggles out of deference to his pain but when he glanced up at her he couldn't help giving a small laugh, which got her giggling even worse and then they were both laughing.

Out of the corner of his eye, TJ saw Ella step into the room, her dark, lustrous hair drawn back into a ponytail. She wore an open, indulgent smile full of such love that he wanted to cry for all the days they'd wasted on petty hurts and harsh words.

'All right, you goofballs, come and eat,' Ella said. She pointed at TJ. 'Wash your hands first.'

'I think my jaw is broken,' TJ said, faking a muffled drawl.

'Serves you right, horsing around like that. She's too big to be wrestling with you,' Ella chided him, but he could see she didn't mean it.

'Not my little girl.'

TJ rose and passed the sofa, headed for the bathroom. He picked up a cushion and whacked Grace with it, inducing another fit of giggles.

'No fair!' Grace yelled. 'No cookies for you.'

TJ froze, then slowly turned to look at Ella. 'There are cookies?'

'Mom's making them,' Grace said. 'She promised.'

'You know Gracie likes me to bake when it snows,' Ella said.

TJ gave her a hesitant smile. He opened his mouth to speak but no words came out, and perhaps that was for the best. In that moment, with the wind rattling the windows in their frames and the snow swirling beyond the glass, their little family unit remained intact. It felt as if they had somehow been transported back to a time before they had let their lives fall into a pattern of discontent and recrimination.

'What?' Ella asked, searching his face, not entirely trusting his smile.

'Just thank you,' he replied. 'That's all.'

For once, her smile seemed to reach her milk-chocolate eyes, but her expression quickly turned serious. She nodded, acknowledging all the things that TJ wasn't saying . . . all the things neither of them would say tonight. A moment had arrived that was full of potential, and neither of them would ruin it.

'You're welcome,' she said, turning away. 'Now come on. Wash your hands so we can eat!'

Grace leaped from the sofa. 'I call first dibs on cookies!'

'We haven't even had the stew yet,' TJ reminded her.

Grace rolled her eyes and waved away this observation. 'Psshht,' she said. 'You can have first dibs on stew.'

TJ laughed and shook his head as he exited the room. While he was in the bathroom washing his hands he heard bowls and silverware clinking and cabinets opening and closing as Ella and Grace set the table.

Shutting off the tap, he caught a glimpse of himself in the mirror. He wore his blond hair a bit shorter these days and perhaps his face had thinned, and there were circles under his eyes that hadn't been there even a few years earlier, but he had grown accustomed to seeing a sort of forlorn quality to his eyes that seemed absent at the moment.

He exhaled, feeling the stress easing out of him.

'Come on, Daddy,' Grace called from the kitchen. 'You can't have cookies if you don't eat your stew.'

TJ smiled at his reflection in the mirror.

It was going to be a good night.

★ ★ ★

Jake Schapiro stepped back into his family room, drying his hands with a dish towel.

'It's been a while since I made dinner for someone,' he said.

Harley Talbot sat cross-legged on the carpet with Jake's photography portfolio open on his lap. The normally unwieldy portfolio looked like little more than a notebook in the hands of the gigantic cop.

One eyebrow arched, Harley regarded Jake sincerely. 'Just so we're clear, I don't fool around on a first date.'

Jake threw the dish towel at him. 'You're not my type.'

Harley caught the towel before it hit him and tossed it onto the coffee table. 'Seriously, man, what *is* your type? Every time we hang out, you ask me about who I've been seeing but you never have an answer yourself. Are you really that boring?'

'That's why I made friends with you, Harl. I wanted to live vicariously through your love life.'

'Damn, but you are the king of evasive answers.' Harley tapped the open portfolio with one huge finger. 'You got talent, man. Between the crime-scene stuff, your photo blog, and taking pictures for the *Gazette*, you've got like three jobs. These pictures you take for yourself . . . they're beautiful. I don't claim to be some kind of art critic, but these storm photos are pretty unique. And you know your way around a kitchen, which women love. So what's the deal?'

Jake stuffed his hands into his pockets. 'You liked the chicken, huh?'

'Shit yeah,' Harley said, grabbing his Sam Adams from the coffee table and taking a swig. 'I don't know how you cook it without burning that Parmesan crust right off, and the risotto was like eating a little piece of heaven — '

Jake laughed. 'Oh my god, you did not just say that. How do you ever get women to pay attention to you for more than five minutes?'

Harley leaned back against the couch and took another swig of beer. 'Come on, man. Just look at me.'

'Well, maybe that's it,' Jake said. 'I don't look like you.'

'Granted, you're kind of skinny, but you have your nerdy charm.'

'Hey, now. I'm not a nerd, man. Hipster, maybe.'

'Fine,' Harley said. 'Hipster charm.'

'Thank you,' Jake replied. 'Meanwhile, I'm getting another beer.'

He went back into the kitchen and fetched a Corona from the fridge, cutting himself a slice of the lime that he'd left out on the granite counter. Even just a room away from Harley, the house seemed to reassert the abandoned sort of quiet that had compelled him to buy it in the first place. Now, more than two years after he'd moved in, the rambling old farmhouse still needed almost as much fixing up as it had when he'd taken possession. The only room that he'd managed to get into pretty much the condition he'd envisioned was the kitchen, but even here there was the matter of the old window and the dead radiator beneath it. Both had to come out,

119

but he was putting it off until he could afford to replace all the windows. Until then it would remain a house of winter drafts and half-renovated rooms, a work in progress. But Jake figured that he himself was a work in progress, so maybe it really was the perfect home for him after all.

Jake squeezed lime into the neck of the Corona bottle and left the twisted slice on the counter, heading back to the family room.

Family room, he thought. Why did he keep referring to the space that way? He wasn't in any rush to have a family. Not that he wanted to be alone forever, but he liked the solitary quality of his life out here on the outskirts of Coventry. Still, he supposed it had been too long since he'd had company other than Harley or the few friends he still kept in touch with from high school. Work had sort of consumed him. Harley had underestimated at three jobs. Jake also sold his photos online for everything from calendars to book covers to greeting cards. He still couldn't ask a lot for such uses, but the more popular his work became, the higher he could push his asking price.

'What do you think?' he asked as he rejoined Harley. 'You up for a movie? I was thinking *L.A. Confidential*, 'cause you said you hadn't seen it. That's a gem, man. Russell Crowe, Kevin Spacey, Guy Pearce, Kim Basinger . . . but it seems like it's practically forgotten.'

Harley had moved to the big easy chair at one end of the coffee table. He'd closed the portfolio and sat sipping his beer, head cocked, gazing out the window at the snow falling. The storm had warmed a little, so the flakes that hit the glass made a wet ticking noise. Not quite sleet, but getting there.

'Sorry, man. I've got an early shift. Probably going to be a mess in the morning with downed lines and such. Soon as I finish this beer I should head home.'

'Says Officer Drink-'n'-Drive.'

'I had three beers in three friggin' hours.'

'I know,' Jake said. 'It's pitiful how you nurse those things. Big guy like you.'

Harley chuckled, the sound a deep rumble in his chest, as Jake sat down on the sofa and took a long swig of his Corona. His gaze wandered to the window and he found himself staring at the frame and sash and sill, hating how dry the wood was and vowing to repaint in the spring if he couldn't afford to replace them altogether. The wind gusted outside and the resulting draft made him shiver, as if the storm had reached right into the house and traced its fingers along the back of his neck. There were half-a-dozen blankets scattered around the family room thanks to that draft. Most of the time he found it just a part of the house's charm, but not in a storm.

Not with the snow falling outside.

'You never answered my question,' Harley said.

Jake didn't pretend that he hadn't heard or didn't understand the reference.

'You've had three girlfriends since I've known you,' Jake said. 'It seems easy for you, jumping in and out of relationships like that. You start one up, get all intense, and then it falls apart for one reason or another.'

Harley shrugged. 'You find out things about each other or you just realize you don't like the woman as much as you thought. Or she doesn't like you. That's the way it goes, man. Trial and error.'

Jake nodded. 'I guess. But it seems effortless for you. For me . . . I don't know, it's just too much damn work. Yeah, it's nice to have someone. Have things to look forward to. And I'm gonna go out on a limb and say I like sex. Sex makes me the kind of happy that I usually only manage to be in dreams.'

As soon as the words were out of his mouth he glanced at Harley, thinking his friend would mock him, but Harley's intelligent eyes were wide and thoughtful.

'Anyway,' Jake went on, 'I had a couple of long-term girlfriends in high school and maybe three relationships since.'

'But?' Harley asked.

Jake tried to find the words. Glancing around the room, he spotted the boxes of new hardwood flooring in the corner and something clicked in him.

'This house,' he started. 'You've been in most of the rooms and I'm sure you've seen the pattern. The stairs are new but the railing needs replacing. The back bedroom has half a new floor. The bathroom down here has all new fixtures but the tile for the floor is in boxes.'

'I've been meaning to talk to you about that. It's kind of weird having to stand on broken-down cardboard boxes while I piss.'

Jake raised a hand. 'There you go. I like the project, y'know. I bought this place so I could work on it, but why can't I finish anything?'

'Maybe — '

'Rhetorical question. I know why.'

'And?' Harley asked, draining the last of his beer.

'I think I love the idea of the house more than I love the house. When it's all fixed up — when it's what I imagine it's supposed to be — what happens then?'

Harley leaned forward in the creaking chair, set his empty Sam Adams bottle on the coffee table, and pointed at him.

'You're saying that's why your relationships don't work? You can't be bothered to work at making them better because you're worried they'll disappoint you in the end?'

Jake sipped his beer, mulling it over.

'It sounds shitty when you say it like that, but yeah. I guess that's what I'm saying.'

'That's pitiful,' Harley said.

Jake laughed out loud. 'Asshole.'

There was one girl Jake had felt different about, but they'd been closer to best friends than boyfriend and girlfriend. Really, Miri Ristani was the only person he had ever felt understood him after Isaac died. They had understood each other, really. After all, they had been together that night, and Miri's father had been among those who had gone missing in the blizzard and turned up dead days later when the snow started to melt. He and Miri had both lost people they

123

loved to the storm. And when Jake talked about the figures that Isaac had seen out in the snow, the hands that had dragged Isaac out the window — dragged him to his death — Miri had really seemed to believe him.

At least back then she had. They'd been kids, of course, and the older they'd gotten, the less either one of them felt comfortable talking concretely about that night and the more they were both willing to just nod and go along when people talked about the many tragic accidents that storm had caused.

Jake had stopped talking about what he'd seen. Part of him had even stopped believing the evidence of his own eyes . . . but he had never really forgotten, and sometimes he dreamed that he stood at an open window watching terrible, slender, icy figures dancing in the falling snow. In his nightmares they knew he was watching — he felt it — and he waited as if frozen for the moment they would turn and look his way.

Miri had understood, even after they had stopped talking about it. But she had left Coventry soon after her high school graduation five years earlier and never looked back. Never even sent him a letter. Jake missed her, but even if she showed up on his doorstep with a six-pack and threw herself on his mercy, he didn't think he could forgive her.

He and Harley had become good friends, but Jake wasn't ready to talk to him about Isaac . . . or about Miri.

Harley stood. 'All right. I'm done psychoanalyzing you for tonight,' he said in a terrible

German accent. 'At our next session, we will discuss your resentment toward your parents.'

'Can't wait,' Jake said, rising to see him out.

They said their good nights, Harley promising a rain check on *L.A. Confidential*. They had bonded over a mutual love of movies, good food, and New England Patriots football. Jake hated the boozy, frat-house-swagger mentality that a lot of football fans had. He was happy to have a friend who would have a few beers and yell at the TV with him while they watched the game, but didn't need to get drunk and bump chests at every touchdown. In the year or so that they'd been hanging out together, Harley had fast become one of his closest friends. He felt comfortable with the guy, and that was uncommon for him.

As Harley went out to his car, using an arm to wipe thick, wet snow from his windshield, Jake stood in the open door and watched the storm churn and eddy across his property. The trees were heavily burdened but they still bent with the wind. With the snow turning to sleet there wouldn't be much more accumulation, but the roads would be frozen and treacherous tonight, and tomorrow's commute would be a total mess.

'Hey!' he called. 'Watch it driving home, okay?'

Harley had opened the car door and now he paused before climbing in, bathed in the yellow light inside the big old Buick.

'Don't worry, Mom. I'll be careful.'

The massive policeman folded himself into the front seat and yanked the door shut. A moment later the Buick's engine growled to life and Harley began to back out of the driveway. The headlights washed over the house and yard, illuminating the tree line at the edge of the property for a few brief moments.

In among the trees stood a human silhouette, a small man or a child lost in the storm. A dark outline, immobile, watching his house.

'What the hell?' Jake said, taking a step out onto his front stoop before he realized he had only socks on his feet.

Wetness soaked through the cloth and he stepped back inside the open door, taking his eyes off the silhouette for a brief moment. When he glanced back up, Harley's taillights were vanishing up the road and the woods were too dark for him to tell the difference between one tree trunk and another, or discern whether the silhouette he'd seen had been a person at all, or just a trick of the shadows.

In spite of the wet snow that whipped at his face and arms and dampened his clothes, he stood inside the open door and squinted into the storm, watching the trees for some hint of motion that could not be explained by the urgings of the wind.

Giving up at last, the chill sinking deeply into his bones, he turned to go back inside. A gust blew against the door and for just a moment he thought he might have heard a voice on the wind, saying his name.

He froze there with the door three inches from closed, his hand unmoving on the knob.

Then he laughed softly and shook his head.

Over the years he had often thought that one day he would be able to endure a snowstorm without being haunted by the memory of his brother's death. He still hoped that would be the case, but it was clear that the day hadn't yet arrived. The storm seemed to resist as he closed the door, shutting it out. The dead bolt made a heavy, satisfying thunk as he turned the lock, and Jake found that he liked that sound.

He liked it very much.

7

In the gun safe on the top shelf of Doug Manning's closet, snug beside his Glock 19 and two small ammunition boxes, there lay a key ring. Each of the seven keys bore a set of initials written in black Sharpie marker, indicating the name of the person whose front door could be opened by that key. Whenever a customer at Harpwell's Garage had been foolish enough to leave his house key on the ring while his vehicle was being worked on overnight, Doug took the key to Jameson Hardware after hours and had a duplicate made. He had copied a dozen keys so far, and he, Franco, and Baxter had already used five of them to gain entry to houses and steal whatever valuables they could lay their hands on.

After the job was finished he would always stop and toss the duplicate key down a storm drain, so the keys that could tie him directly to crimes already committed were gone. The remaining seven — certainly enough that he would not have to make any new ones for a while — sat in the gun safe, calling to him. Each one was a crime yet to be committed, a betrayal of the faith he'd once had in himself. Just having them in the house, storing them next to his gun, turned his mood black and put his teeth on edge.

I'm not a bad guy, he thought. But he could not escape the truth, that the gun and the keys made him feel nearly as sinister by their mere presence as did the knowledge of his crimes.

I'm not a bad guy.

Doug lay on his bed fully clothed, the room bathed in the blue light from his flatscreen television. According to the onscreen guide, this channel was meant to be showing a mixed-martial-arts tournament but instead he'd turned it on to find a celebrity poker game. None of the so-called celebrities interested him but he had left it on because he had never been very good at poker and thought he might learn something. Instead he found himself barely able to pay attention. His thoughts were drawn to that top shelf in the closet. He could practically feel the key ring in there, as if it gave off some unpleasant vibration.

Every day he tried to forget about those keys and every night he could think of little else. Yes, he had thrown away the ones they had used, but eventually the burglary investigations would crisscross at Harpwell's Garage. Unless every cop in Coventry was painfully stupid, they would figure out how the burglars were getting in without forced entry and start putting two and two together, tracking places where all the rich assholes could have had their keys stolen or copied. Doug had been careful to establish alibis for three out of the five robberies so far, but none of them would stand up to close scrutiny. He'd also taken four of the twelve total keys during shifts when he wasn't working — wasn't even supposed to be there. He'd gone in to pick up his pay and hung around shooting the shit with some of the other mechanics . . . been smart about it.

The cops would consider him, of course, but they wouldn't be sure. It helped that he had no criminal record. Once they started sniffing around, though, his little life of crime would come to a screeching halt. Doug had told Franco and Baxter that from the beginning.

The keys, though . . . they could trip him up. If the cops got a warrant and found that key ring, they might not be able to connect them to previous thefts but it probably wouldn't take them long to identify them as copies of house keys of Harpwell's customers. There had to be a better place to hide them but try as he might, he couldn't think of anywhere he could be certain they would remain hidden. A safe deposit box might work, but it would be damn inconvenient and someone was bound to notice him going in and out of the bank. If he stuck them in a jar and buried it in the yard, he would still have to dig them up every time he needed a key.

The keys were a problem.

How the hell did you get into this? he asked himself.

His head hurt, but not nearly as much as his back. He lay in bed, propped on a pillow, barely even seeing the so-called celebrities as they announced what charities they were playing poker for — as if they didn't really need the money themselves. A vein in his temple throbbed in time with his pulsing awareness of the key ring and how fucking stupid he'd been to get involved with Baxter and Franco. With work scarce and money even scarcer, he had persuaded himself that he was far cleverer than he actually was. Desperation, he had found, could be very convincing.

As for the crimes themselves, Doug waffled between guilt and a cynical sort of pride. The pride always made him feel even guiltier. The people he'd robbed might be rich and some of them might even be assholes, but he hadn't been raised to take things that didn't belong to him. Most people dropping off a car for service at Harpwell's left only their car keys, but some customers — usually men — would hand over the keys and then go jump into another vehicle with their wives or girlfriends, knowing that the spouse or partner or roommate had her own set and, after all, it was only for a night or two. For some reason these guys pissed him off, not because what they'd done was stupid but because of the carefree arrogance of their stupidity. In a way, stealing from them was doing them a favor, teaching them a valuable lesson.

The keys practically screamed at him from inside the metal box up in the closet. Wasn't he just as stupid as those rich guys, having the damn things in his house?

'Fuck!'

He jumped up from the bed, turned toward the closet, and immediately staggered and groaned as pain lanced through his back and neck. Swearing profusely under his breath, he leaned against the wall. The pain ran like an electrical current across his shoulders and down the musculature of his back and he ground his

131

teeth together, acutely aware — as he was anytime the pain seized him — of how alone he was. There had been women in his life in the past twelve years and he had genuinely cared for some of them. But none of them had eclipsed Cherie. From the day they'd met, he had always felt that she was too good for him. He had defined himself — who he was and what he was capable of — by his reflection in her eyes. If he could be half the man she wanted to believe he was, that would have been enough.

Now it just didn't seem to matter much anymore. Who did he have to worry about disappointing? No one. All he had was his pain and his guilt and the pills that made them go away.

The pill bottle sat waiting on his nightstand, as it always did. The original injury dated back years, to a fall he'd taken at the garage. Over time he had reinjured it so that he no longer seemed to have a single day without pain . . . without pills. It had gotten so bad that local doctors wouldn't even prescribe for him anymore and he had to go out of town. Lately, Franco had been hooking him up. Half the money he had gotten from the burglaries had gone to pills, but what choice did he have? He had to have something to dull the pain.

Dry swallowing two pills, he recapped the bottle and just stood for a second, letting the muscles in his neck relax a little. When he found he could breathe without pain, he walked gingerly over to his closet and looked at the rectangular gray gun safe that sat on the top shelf among piles of loosely folded T-shirts. The keys were just adding to his anxiety, which only tensed him up and made his back pain worse. One way or another, he had to get the keys out of his house. Now that he'd decided upon the task, it seemed important to do it immediately, snow or no snow.

'Screw it,' he whispered to his empty house.

Doug punched in the five-digit code. The safe gave a long beep, almost as if it were deciding whether to cooperate, and then popped open with a clunk of the locking mechanism. As he reached in, his fingers grazed the handle of his Glock, causing his pulse to quicken. There were so many things a gun would solve, but Doug had never been enough of a coward to ever seriously consider suicide. His life hadn't turned out as he'd hoped, but he was still above ground. He might not like who he had become, might still burn with the guilt of not being there when Cherie needed him, but he didn't hate himself enough to think a violent exit would be preferable to his current life. It turned out that there were many things he was willing to do to resolve his problems, but that wasn't one of them.

He touched the key ring, snatched up the keys, and pulled them from the safe. For a second he stared down at his half-closed hand, studied the jagged teeth of the visible keys, wondering if he could do this. Baxter and Franco would be very unhappy with him — more than unhappy, they'd probably hurt him badly. If he really wanted out of the jobs they were planning, the smart thing to do would be to give them the keys and tell them to leave him out of their plans from now on. But then the keys would still lead the cops back to Harpwell's Garage. He would be questioned, and once he had turned his back on them he couldn't be sure about Baxter and Franco covering for him.

'Shit,' he whispered, feeling the jagged weight of the keys in his grasp.

His decision had already been made. He had to get rid of the keys.

As he reached up to close the safe, the doorbell rang. He twisted around and stared in the direction of the front door as if he could see it through walls and floors. Barely breathing, half paralyzed, he clutched the keys and turned to glance out the window to confirm that the storm still raged outside. The snow had turned mostly to sleet and it pelted the glass in a harsh chorus. Who the hell would dare this weather to pay him a late-night visit?

The cops were definitely a possibility, here to question him or even arrest him. Baxter and Franco were another possibility. Either way, a late-night visit in an ice-and-snow storm did not bode well. Doug wetted his lips with his tongue; his throat and mouth were feeling very dry. What was he supposed to do with the keys in his hand? There was nowhere he could really hide them, which left him with only one practical choice. He put the keys back into the safe, closed the door, and relocked it.

Whoever was at the front door began to knock loudly, a series of raps followed by a long pause.

He stood and listened. Then the doorbell came again and he thought he heard a distant voice, perhaps female, so faint that it might have been his imagination. He narrowed his eyes, paranoia turning to curiosity.

The house went silent. In that moment the idea of a surprise visitor seemed somehow preferable to letting whoever it was walk away without his ever knowing who it had been. He would be wondering — and fretting — about it for days.

Doug strode out of his bedroom and pounded down the steps. The sidelights on either side of the front door were veiled by gauzy curtains Cherie had picked out when they'd first moved into the house, so he couldn't see outside. As he approached the door he had every intention of opening it, but he hesitated as he reached for the knob. The outdoor lights were off and the only noise was the skitter of sleet on the panes of the sidelight windows.

'Who is it?' he called, but too quietly.

The doorbell did not ring again, nor did anyone knock, but he had the unsettling sense that his visitor had not left, was instead waiting outside in the freezing rain.

'Hello?' he called again. 'Who's there?'

Wary, thinking again of the keys upstairs and what they might mean, and studying the dark, gauze-veiled sidelights, he forced himself to reach out and twist the dead bolt open.

When he heard the voice again there could be no mistake. His visitor was a woman. She still sounded far away but he heard the shriek of the storm around the house — the whole house shuddered with it — and he figured the wind had carried her words away.

'Doug?' she said, standing just on the other side of the door.

His first thought — a crazy, impossible dream of a thought — was that Cherie had come home. Though he had watched them lower her casket into the earth, he could not deny the sureness that came over him that somehow she had come back.

A shiver of fear ran up his back, his heart rejecting the impossible, even as he smiled excitedly and turned the knob, tugging the door open. It blew inward with such force that he nearly lost his grip on the knob. The wind blasted him and sleet spattered the tile of the foyer, wet slush immediately building up on the small rug in front of the threshold.

For a second or two, Doug didn't recognize the woman who stood on the front stoop. She held a burgundy umbrella that dripped all around the edges. Her long coat was black, and the wet slush had begun to build up into a layer of wet ice on the fabric where the umbrella could not cover her. Wide hazel eyes gazed out from beneath black bangs, somehow both pleading and joyful. Her long hair framed her face, and it was due partly to this change in style that he did not know her at first.

'Hey,' she said softly, and for a second longer she sounded uncannily like Cherie. But of course it was Cherie that his heart had hoped for.

Doug blinked. 'Angela?'

One corner of her mouth lifted in a shy smile. 'Hey,' she said again. And then she shrugged, giving him an apologetic look. 'Do you think I could come in? It's kind of nasty out here.'

'Shit, yes, of course,' he said, reaching out and taking her hand to guide her in from the storm. 'I'm sorry. I just wasn't expecting anyone and I was half asleep and then I wasn't sure if I'd heard a knock or not. And now I'm babbling like a friggin' idiot.'

As she closed her umbrella, Angela Ristani smiled sweetly at him and he felt as if he were in some kind of alternate reality. Other than occasionally at the supermarket or in line at Carter's Ice Cream, he hadn't seen her since they had broken up, more than two years earlier. Somehow, in the time that had passed, Angela had become even more beautiful. There had always been an edge to her, a harshness that Doug figured maybe nurses just had to adopt in order to survive in their profession.

'You're not an idiot, Doug,' she said, setting her umbrella on the tile floor.

Angela's black, heavy wool greatcoat was nearly soaked through. The sleet that had accumulated on the cloth was quickly melting, some of it dripping onto the throw rug. Doug pulled himself away from her gaze long enough to shut the door and then turned back to her. For a second it seemed like she'd brought the winter inside with her — as if closing the door hadn't been enough — and then the chill passed and the warmth of the radiators struggled to make up for the infusion of cold air.

'It's good to see you,' she said, still smiling and searching his eyes. 'Really good.'

Doug gave a nervous laugh. 'You too, Angie. Really. But also a little strange. Kind of bizarre, you just showing up on my doorstep in the middle of a storm.'

She looked stricken. 'You don't want me here?'

Something in her voice, some plaintive quality, made him look at her more closely. Her beauty had never been in doubt, not even when he had ended things with her. But Angela Ristani had too many rough edges, some of them merely abrasive but some of them sharp enough to draw blood. She had been Cherie's closest friend, but Doug had met Angela first. They had met at a little Irish pub downtown called the Peddlar's Daughter, both of them approaching the bar to put in orders on a crowded night. They'd joked about being beer-gophers for their friends, and soon enough they had abandoned the people they'd come in with and gone off to huddle in a corner. Angie had been a flirt and a bit of a bitch, confident and brassy, and when he asked for her phone number she had done something he would never forget: she had arched an eyebrow and her smile had been a kind of challenge.

'I could give you my number,' she had said that night, 'or you could just take me home.'

After that one night together, he had learned that Angela had a boyfriend and soon their entanglement had become a friendship. It was Angie who had introduced him to Cherie. Years

138

after the storm that had killed his wife and her ex-husband, they'd crossed paths in the Peddlar's Daughter again, and found some solace in each other. For months they had tried to fuck all the grief and anger out of their hearts until Doug began to believe that they had each been only half successful, leaving him with all his grief and her with all her anger.

In the months they had spent together she had never really opened up to him. Her daughter had moved away somewhere but Angela never talked about her. In the end it was her emotional distance that had eroded the relationship to a point where it could no longer be saved. With her dark eyes and high cheekbones, and with a tall, slender figure that drew plenty of attention, she never failed to distract him with her beauty. In bed she always seemed hungry, not sexually insatiable but dissatisfied in some other way. Some nights he'd made her come again and again until at last he was too exhausted to continue, and every time she would kiss him and stroke his chest and then cuddle up close to him as if it were his heat she wanted more than his heart or his cock.

Now all those defenses seemed stripped away. She wore a smile so open that her happiness shone through and he just didn't know what to make of it.

'It's not that I don't want you here,' he said. 'You're welcome anytime.'

'But?' she asked, challenging him, almost pouty. The Angela he knew was more likely to claw than to pout.

139

He laughed softly. 'Shit, it's just weird, okay? Come on, you've gotta see that. You show up at my door, soaking wet. No phone call, no text. And we didn't end on the best of terms.' Doug sat on the bottom step and studied her. 'Come on, Angie. What is it? You didn't come over here just because you suddenly decided you missed me.'

Unbuttoning her coat, she glanced shyly away from him.

'Help me with this?' she asked.

Doug rose from the steps and grabbed the heavy coat by its collar as she slipped out of it.

'Thing is, Doug,' she said, 'I did come over here because I missed you. But you're right about one thing.'

Half turned toward him, she lifted her gaze and he saw that her mascara had started to run in the storm, turning her expression vulnerable and tragic and wild, all at the same time.

'I *am* soaking wet.'

She reached behind his neck and pulled him down to meet her kiss. Her lips only brushed his at first and she let out a breath as if she'd been holding it for ages, shuddering into his arms. Her kiss turned hungry, but this was a yearning, loving hunger instead of the sorrowful, bottomless hunger he had seen in her before.

'Oh my god,' she whispered, nuzzling his throat, pressing her body hard against his. 'I've missed you so much.'

When he tried to speak, Angela silenced him with her mouth. After that he kept mostly silent, at least in terms of words.

* * *

Whenever Ella Santos made love to her husband the rest of the world vanished around them. Tonight she sat astride him, rising and falling in a slow, deliberate rhythm that made her drunk with arousal. Sometimes, especially after they'd been fighting, she wanted him to dominate her completely, to make it rough and fast and primal, so that they both felt that she was all his. Other times she wanted the other side of the coin and she took control, making love to him so exquisitely that they shuddered with each delicious moment of connection.

Ella traced the contours of his face, her heart suffused with a mixture of love and regret that she saw reflected in his eyes. Making love with TJ, she felt herself plugged in to a simpler time between them when all he had to do was pick up his guitar and she would see how he really felt about her and about their future together. Their pattern had changed in recent years. Agitated by stress factors they could not control, one or both of them would say something hurtful, something that could be forgiven but not forgotten, and those cruel things would plant seeds of discontent and anger.

Only with TJ inside her, the two of them desperately searching for the past in each other's eyes, could she find the happiness she had once felt. Only by making love to him did her thoughts clear enough for her to recognize that there was a path back to that happiness for them, but it lay forward.

141

'Ella . . . ' He reached up to caress her breasts, to run his thumbs over her nipples and pinch them gently, making her shiver.

His hips rose to meet her, his urgency growing even as she felt the crest rising within her, carrying her toward bliss. She studied his eyes and wished that he would always look at her that way.

'This is how it should be,' she said breathlessly. 'You listening, honey? This, right here . . . we've got to find a way to . . . to bottle it. Hold on to it.'

She glimpsed a fleeting sadness in him and then, face flushed, TJ smiled.

'We could just never stop,' he suggested, thrusting suddenly upward.

Ella shivered with pleasure and bent lower over him, her hair brushing his face, suddenly weak with need and pleasure. Her legs began to shake as her orgasm approached and she gripped his shoulders fiercely, both wanting to reach her climax and wanting to hold back and savor this crest.

'Good idea,' she managed. 'Just do this . . . forever.'

Forever. No more fighting. No more tension. Just this feeling of unity.

TJ went rigid, trapping her on top of him. They came together, which hadn't happened in a very long time. Panting, smiling, nuzzling into each other, they sank down on the bed and tangled themselves up, limbs purposefully wound together. Aftershocks of pleasure rolled through Ella and she grabbed the back of TJ's head and kissed him deeply, then laid her head on his chest and ran her fingers through the blond curls there.

'You're right, you know,' TJ said quietly. 'We've got to hold on to this.'

For long, wary seconds, she did not reply. Then at last she managed to speak.

'How do we do that? We haven't had much luck so far.'

'We start like this,' he said. 'Just talking about it. We owe it to Grace.'

'We owe it to each other, too. I do love you, you know?'

TJ shifted onto his side in bed, extricating himself from her so that they were face-to-face on the same pillow. Ella ran her hand over the scruff along his jaw that he never quite allowed to turn into a beard. She searched his gaze, heart pounding, wondering whether it was too late for them. If their relationship fell apart it would be due to neglect, and they would both be to blame.

'I love you, too,' TJ assured her. 'But where do we go from here? We keep blaming each other — '

'For everything,' she agreed.

The economy had begun to recover a little, but not quickly or vigorously enough to save them financially. Not yet, anyway. Ella had done everything she could to keep The Vault from going under, changing the menu and the marketing, but the restaurant was still barely paying for itself. She hadn't drawn a salary in years. They'd been living off whatever TJ could earn as an electrician and musician. If he hadn't inherited their little house from his mother, there would have been no way for them to afford rent or a mortgage. It did feel as if their prospects were brightening, but she didn't know if it would happen quickly enough to keep them above water.

'We can't gamble on this,' Ella said. 'All the bullshit and blame — they're habits now. Maybe we need someone . . . a referee.'

'A therapist?' TJ asked. 'You'd do that?'

'Would you?'

Ella said a silent prayer of thanks and hope. She didn't know if they could make this moment of calm understanding last, but she certainly intended to try.

'I think we should — ' she began.

Down the hall, Grace began to scream.

Jerking away from TJ, Ella scrambled from the bed. Her legs tangled in the sheets and she fell to the floor, whacking her elbow on the hardwood. She cried out as she tore free, looked up and saw TJ pulling on a pair of sweatpants he'd discarded by the bed. He called out their daughter's name and Ella echoed him.

'A nightmare?' TJ asked.

Ella tore the sheet off the bed and wrapped it around herself, rushing out of their bedroom behind him.

'I don't think so,' she said.

A mother knows her baby's cries, even when the baby in question isn't really a baby anymore. This fearful, panicked scream had been born from more than any bad dream. They ran down the short upstairs hall, past the bathroom, and

144

charged through Grace's open bedroom door, TJ in the lead.

Ella ran in behind him and went straight to their daughter. Grace knelt on her bed, pressed into the corner between the headboard and the wall with a pillow clutched against her like a shield. Her eyes were wide with terror. She spared them only a single glance, her focus locked on an empty spot at the foot of the bed.

'What is it, Gracie?' TJ asked, turning right and left, searching for some threat to his girl.

When Ella took Grace in her arms the girl stopped screaming, but still could not help staring at that spot at the end of her bed.

'What happened?' Ella said quietly. 'What frightened you, kiddo?'

Grace blinked, shook her head as if waking, and turned to stare at her mother.

'An old lady,' the little girl said. 'Right in my room, down at the end of the bed. A *ghost* lady.'

Frigid fingers danced along Ella's spine and she shivered, glancing at TJ. There were only the three of them in the room, that much could not be argued. But instead of turning to look back at Ella and Grace, TJ could not tear his gaze from the window on the far wall from Grace's bed, which stood open a couple of narrow inches.

'Did you leave that open?' Ella asked.

Snow had swirled in and built a thin, ridged layer of white on the sill. It had begun to turn to sleet, a thousand icy little pinpricks on the window glass.

'No,' TJ said, turning to her. 'I don't think so.'

Ella didn't think she had, either.

145

'Ssshhh,' she whispered to Grace, holding her daughter tightly. 'It's okay. It was just a bad dream. You're okay now.'

One of us must have opened it and not remembered, she thought.

She held the girl close but her eyes were on TJ. He stood frowning at the open window for several seconds longer and then at last he walked over, swept the snow from the sill to the floor, and shut it tightly.

The wind and the sleet continued.

One of us must *have.*

8

Detective Keenan rolled through the red light at Winter and Main without bothering to turn on the siren. It was after one A.M. and the roads were abandoned except for the plows, whose drivers were trying to scrape the sleet and snow from the street. The coming day promised to be even colder, and if the slush froze solid before they could get it off the pavement, the streets would be even more treacherous.

The engine purred as he guided his unmarked to the next intersection, then turned left along the river. The blue lights built into the grille of the vehicle threw gliding blue phantoms onto the snowbanks around the car. The tires splattered the slush to either side as he drove but he kept his hands tight on the wheel, ready to act if he hit an ice patch.

Another winter, another friggin' snowstorm, he thought.

But this wasn't just another storm. The sleet had made sure of that. He remembered worse, of course — both snowstorms and ice storms — but this one had turned out to be pretty bad, and very weird. The department had received more than a dozen calls from folks who claimed to have seen ghosts. Detective Keenan figured they were either cranks or nutjobs and had said as much when the dispatcher had called him several hours before to see if he would drive up nearly to the state line to talk to a woman who had asked for him by name but not given her own. Keenan had declined; he'd been off duty, and there was no reason the woman couldn't give her statement to a uniformed officer and wait until tomorrow for a detective to investigate her ghost story.

Insane, he thought now, driving along Riverside Road, the water churning by on his right. *A little snow and people go batshit crazy.*

'You're one of them,' he said aloud, his voice filling the quiet of the car.

It was true enough. During most snowstorms in the past dozen years, people in Coventry had gotten . . . twitchy. There were always frantic calls about missing kids who turned out to have gone sledding or — with the older ones — were out drinking with friends. Joe Keenan had been through enough of these that he'd become almost numb to the skittishness that came over so many Coventry folks in the winter-time.

Tonight felt different.

Ghost stories *were* different. As unsettled as the town always grew during a storm, this was a new development. A dozen calls, each with a story. He could still recall with anxious clarity the sound it had made that night twelve years ago when he had hit something in the blizzard with his car. The dent had been there for months before the police department's mechanics had gotten it fixed. And he remembered the deaths of Charlie Newell and Gavin Wexler, and the way the Wexler kid's father had been there one second and gone the next. Lost in the storm.

148

Detective Keenan thought the people who had been unnerved by snowstorms for the past dozen years needed to move on, but tonight people — too many people — were talking about ghosts, and it freaked him out a little.

Stupid, he thought.

Maybe it was, but he kept his hands tight on the wheel and surveyed the road ahead with great care.

The wipers scraped the icy windshield and freezing rain pelted the roof. Nothing came out of the storm to smash into his car and he sure as hell didn't see any ghosts. But then he hadn't come out tonight because of ghost stories. He had made it clear to Trisha, the dispatcher who'd called, that he wasn't responding to crazy complaints unless the captain on duty ordered him to do it. That call had never come, but twenty minutes ago he had received a different one — a call that had gotten him out of his chair and moving so quickly that he'd left the TV on, only realizing it when he was in the car, headed for the river.

Now the icy water churned past on his right, visible through the trees that grew along its banks in this part of Coventry. To Joe Keenan, the best thing about the city had always been its eclectic nature. If you wanted a busy downtown or a modern suburb or a remote rural farmhouse, you had to only drive a couple of miles and you could find it, all within the city limits. That also meant that the Coventry PD saw all kinds of crime and had to be equipped to handle everything from meth dealers to petty theft and breaking up high-school parties. None of those things would have persuaded him to put in overtime tonight. But there were things that even the most hardened cynic could not ignore.

Up ahead, red-and-blue lights swirled in the darkness, reflecting off the newfallen snow and the droplets of sleet that still slashed down from the sky. Detective Keenan slowed his car and pulled in behind a darkened Coventry PD patrol vehicle. He made sure not to box in the ambulance that sat waiting for a passenger. Cursing the wind and the tiny daggers of sleet, he climbed out of the car and opened the battered black umbrella that he kept on the floor in the backseat. Some of its spokes had torn through the fabric but it did the job.

Detective Keenan walked through the trees, greeted by uniformed officers with a wave or a grim word. A group of police officers had gathered at the river's edge. Beyond them, a silver Mercedes lay on its roof, halfway into the river. The current dragged at the front end, which was almost entirely submerged, and he wondered idly if the current would be strong enough to pluck the car from the bank and swallow it entirely.

A loud beeping echoed along the riverbank and he glanced farther south, where a tow truck had pulled over and was now reversing through a narrow gap in the trees often used by local fishermen. The beeping came from the tow truck, that backing-up alarm that he had always found more irritating than helpful.

150

The group standing by the river included cops both in and out of uniform, paramedics, and Al Dyson from the county medical examiner's office. Two men in hip waders were thigh deep in the icy river, checking out the car, neither of them stupid enough to stand downriver from the vehicle, just in case the current dislodged it.

Callie Weiss saw him first. She tapped her partner on the arm and they both peeled away from the group to greet him.

'Detective,' Callie said. She was a slim brunette with a Roman nose and full lips who spent her off hours at a dojo and her summer weekends at Warrior Camp. Callie Weiss might be only a few inches over five feet but Keenan knew she could have kicked his ass without breaking a sweat.

Her partner, a big ginger guy called Ross, seemed to sneer at the sky. 'Nice night for it, huh?'

The freezing rain pelted Keenan's umbrella but he was glad to have it. Callie and Ross wore waterproof jackets and the hats that would keep the worst of it away, but he knew that the rain must have gone down their necks and soaked through their pants and shoes by now. It would be a shitty night for all of them, and it was just getting started.

'Paint me a picture,' Detective Keenan said.

'This picture isn't clear enough?' Ross asked. Keenan shot him a dark look and turned to his partner.

'The car is registered to Christopher Stroud,' Callie said. 'Home for the Strouds is Falcon

151

Ridge Road. Officers sent to the residence found a family friend house-and-cat sitting for them, said they were on a ski weekend in New Hampshire and were due back tonight.'

Detective Keenan glanced at the Mercedes. He'd taken note of the ski rack before but hadn't paid enough attention. The car had gone into the river upside down, tearing the rack right off the roof. At least two pairs of skis had been torn off, left scattered along the bank, but one pair of skis remained locked to the ruined rack, shorter than the others. Kids' skis.

A tight knot formed in his gut and he started for the car, stood behind it and tried to see through the night-black glass of the rear windshield.

'What've we got?'

Callie and Ross had followed. He felt them just over his shoulder, watching him the way he watched the two guys in waders who were peering in through the shattered driver's side window.

'We broke the passenger window,' one of the guys said. 'Car was filling up. Water would've dragged it off the bank. This way it flows right through.'

'People,' Detective Keenan said, hearing the sharp, cold edge in his voice and not caring. 'I meant people.'

Now that he'd shifted his position he had a better angle and he saw at least one body inside, hanging upside down by the seat belt.

'Driver is presumably Christopher Stroud,' Callie Weiss said, coming to stand beside him on

152

the bank. 'Safe to assume the passenger is his wife, Melissa.'

A clanking noise made Detective Keenan look up. The tow-truck driver had backed as close to the water as he dared and now he stood at the back of the truck with the hook and chain in his hand. With the flick of a switch, he set the electric winch moving, unfurling lengths of cable until he had it long enough to secure to the car.

Keenan barely took note of the tow driver or the winch. He stood waiting. Listening. After a few seconds he turned to look at Callie.

'What about the kid?'

'Kid?' Ross asked.

Detective Keenan stared at him. The umbrella sagged in his grip and he let it slip down to hang loosely beside him, upside down just like the car. He glanced at Callie and then turned to look at the other cops and the paramedics and even Al Dyson from the ME's office. They were just waiting for the tow truck to haul the Mercedes out of the water so they could bag and tag the bodies of Mr. and Mrs. Stroud. Detective Keenan had been called out to survey the scene, make sure it was just an accident, a happy couple who'd foolishly chosen to drive home in this weather, a little too fast around a corner, a date with the Merrimack River.

'The goddamn kid!' Keenan snapped. He pointed at the ski rack. 'The kid who belongs to these skis. Or didn't the cat-sitter tell you the Strouds had a kid?'

Callie Weiss had gone pale, staring at the car

153

and the river and then forcing herself to meet Keenan's gaze.

'I don't know if . . . I mean, I wasn't the one who . . . '

The tow-truck driver had hooked up the car. As he walked back to the winch controls, Detective Keenan felt a strange, dark certainty come over him. He barked at the others to get out of the way, waved the waders back from the car, and then stood to watch while the Mercedes was dragged from the river, sliding on its roof in the snow, hundreds of gallons of water pouring out of the broken windows.

The two guys in waders sloshed toward the car but Detective Keenan beat them to it. Abandoning his umbrella, he dropped to his knees in the slush. Water soaking through his pants, he bent to shine his flashlight within. The Strouds had drowned. Mr. Stroud hung limply from his seat belt, the deflated air bag a dead white balloon. He'd sustained a massive contusion to the side of his head, likely when the car had rolled. It was probably his head that had broken the driver's side window; chances were that he had died before the car had even gone under water.

His wife had managed to get her seat belt undone but it hadn't saved her. Upside down, she lay in a tumble of limbs on the inverted ceiling of the car. Melissa Stroud's eyes were wide and staring as if they saw into another world and water had pooled in her gaping mouth. Keenan had seen too many corpses in his life, but there seemed something especially obscene about Mrs. Stroud.

The backseat of the car was empty. He'd barely noticed before but the rear passenger window was broken, just like the front one.

'Did you do that?' he asked the two waders, pointing to the window.

'No,' the talkative one replied. 'The back of the car was mostly above water when we got here.'

It made sense, of course. The windows were likely to shatter when a car rolled. The fact that the rear windshield and the front passenger window hadn't broken in the crash was more of an anomaly than the rear passenger window breaking.

He shifted his flashlight around, examining the backseat. The beam halted on the door latch and he frowned. Keenan used his flashlight to brush away loose shards of safety glass and pushed himself through the broken window, taking a closer look.

'Blood,' he said, flashing the light around for a moment longer before pulling out of the car.

'The kid, you think?' Ross asked.

Detective Keenan shot him a hard look, then turned to Callie. 'Get me information. Now. I want a description of the Stroud child within five minutes. Name, gender, height, weight, identifying marks. I want a photograph in fifteen minutes or less. And at some point between the two, I want as many people on this site as you can muster. We're going up and down the river, full-on search party.'

'You don't want to wait till morning?' Ross

asked, glancing dubiously at the riverbank. 'If the body snagged on the shore, it's not going anywhere till dawn. If it's still floating we're not going to find it tonight anyway.'

Keenan felt his fists clench. He swallowed hard and begged himself not to punch the guy. Bile rose in the back of his throat and he thought of Charlie Newell and Gavin Wexler — other kids he had not been able to save.

'And what if this kid's alive?' he asked, staring at Ross. Stepping back, he spread his arms, addressing the rest of the gathered men and women. 'The back of the car was not submerged. Rear window was broken. There's blood on the handle. Someone who was in the backseat and who sustained injuries in the crash tried to get out with that handle before climbing out the window.'

He shone his light up and down the riverbank.

'Whoever owns those smaller skis might be in the river, yeah,' he went on. 'But the way it looks, we have to assume that the kid wandered away from the crash, probably looking for help. We are going to be that help.'

People were scrambling. The guy from the ME's office did his job, supervising the recovery of the bodies of Christopher and Melissa Stroud from their vehicle. Everyone else was refocused on the task of finding the missing child. Maps came out and zones were marked off, but several officers had already spread out to search the immediate vicinity of the crash. Phone calls would be made. If the kid had been picked up by another car or shown up at a hospital, they would know soon enough.

Keenan stood staring at the river, hoping. He wondered why Jake Schapiro hadn't shown up with his camera. It might be helpful later to have photos of the site and the inside of the car before the small army of searchers arrived to trample the area.

'Zachary,' a voice said behind him.

He turned to see Callie Weiss holding a police radio as if it might ward him away.

'Zachary Stroud,' she said. 'Ten years old. Goes to Whittier Elementary. A picture's on the way. We should be able to get it to everyone shortly.'

Detective Keenan could not speak. Could barely breathe. He only nodded and then returned his attention to the river. Cars were approaching. He heard their engines and knew that the search was about to begin. Nobody else would be out in the middle of the night in this weather. The chief wouldn't be among them yet, but he wouldn't be that far behind. Chief Romano would take charge. Keenan would be relieved; he wanted to be out there searching in the dark and freezing rain.

Zachary Stroud, he thought, setting the name firmly in his mind.

Another boy lost in the storm.

'No,' he muttered to himself. 'Not again.'

He wouldn't let it happen again.

9

Ella came awake on Sunday morning with sunlight streaming through the windows in her bedroom. They had left the curtains open last night and now she had to turn her face away from the brightness, burrowing into her pillow's cool shadows. The memory of the night before returned to her slowly. Furrowing her brow, she wiped sleep from her eyes and flopped onto her back.

After Grace's bad dreams, she and TJ had first insisted that their daughter try to go back to sleep on her own. She was eleven years old, after all, not a baby anymore. But when for the third time an anxious Grace had appeared at their bedside, Ella had gone back to her daughter's room and they had climbed into bed together. This had been their pattern for years when Grace was troubled or ill. Most of the time it seemed preferable to letting her get into the habit of sleeping with her parents, but there had been nights when Ella cursed TJ for his firm resistance to letting Grace drift off between them. She understood his reluctance to set a precedent, but at three o'clock in the morning, when she'd had only small snatches of broken sleep, Ella didn't give a crap about precedent.

During the night she had tried to depart Grace's bed several times, only to have the girl stir and call for her to come back. Finally, after hours without any decent sleep, she had slipped from beneath Grace's covers and shuffled back to her room. TJ had sprawled across their bed, claiming most of it for himself, and she'd had to shake and poke him to get him to move over. This morning, her eyes burned and her head felt heavy, as if she'd had too much to drink the night before. Of TJ there was no sign save a tangle of sheets and bedspread that had been twisted up and hung off the bed on his side.

Groaning, Ella sat up and swung her legs out of bed. She dragged on a pair of yoga pants and rose, going to the window and squinting against the bright sunshine. The storm had been fierce yesterday, but now the sky was nearly cloudless. The yard and driveway were covered with a thick layer of snow capped by a gleaming crust of ice. The plows had been through, evidenced by the white ridges on either side of the road, but given how much frozen mess remained, it had been many hours since the last one went by.

What a shame, she thought. Grace would want to play in the snow today, would insist that Ella, and possibly TJ, accompany her outside. But Ella thought her daughter was going to get bored very quickly when she realized this snow was no good for sledding or snowballs or for building snowmen.

Still tired, she managed to trudge into the corridor and downstairs to the kitchen. A glance into the living room did not turn up Grace as she had expected. The TV wasn't on. Nor was Grace in the kitchen; instead, she found her husband at the counter with a mixing bowl and a mess.

'Morning,' she said. 'What're you up to?'

TJ gave her an open smile, no hesitation or reservation. She felt tentative herself. Making love with him last night had given her hope for the first time in a long while that their relationship could be healed, but one night could not erase the injuries they had inflicted upon each other in the past few years. Looking at him now, though, she wondered if she wasn't making it more difficult than it had to be.

'Banana pancakes!' he said happily, digging into a corner cabinet. 'And, if you'll give me a minute, coffee.'

He pulled out a couple of pods for the big Keurig on the countertop.

Maybe it actually is this easy, she thought. Her mother had always said that all men ever really needed to be happy was food, sex, and peace at home. Ella had thought about that many times over the years of her marriage, but watching TJ now, she felt that she was having a minor epiphany. Could it be that those three things were all *she* needed to be happy as well?

'Grace is still sleeping?' Ella asked.

'She was when I came down,' he replied. 'It's a good thing, too. Maybe she's had some nicer dreams to wash away the scary ones.'

'You're awfully cheery this morning,' she said as TJ popped the first pod into the coffeemaker and slipped a mug into place.

He glanced up at her, a flash of regret in his eyes. 'Sorry. I know you're probably exhausted from being up with Gracie, but ... I don't know.' He shrugged. 'Nightmares aside, it was a good night, wasn't it?'

'It was,' she agreed, 'though maybe ... incomplete. We might need a redo.'

He smiled the same rakish grin that had first stirred her twelve years before.

'That can be arranged.'

TJ set the pan on the stove and turned on the gas flame. While the pan heated up, he chopped up a banana and then whisked the batter for a few seconds. Ella just watched him, looking for signs of strain behind his demeanor. The tension between them had abated but not vanished and she knew he still felt it. But at least he was trying.

A for effort, babe. A for effort.

And if TJ was willing to make the effort, could she do any less?

'What do you think that was all about?' she asked, fetching orange juice from the fridge. 'The ghost thing, I mean.'

'Bad dreams,' he said.

'Sure,' Ella replied, getting a small glass from the cabinet to the left of the stove. 'But she's never had one like this. I just hope ... '

TJ poured dollops of pancake batter onto the hot pan, doling it carefully with a wooden spoon. When he'd made the third one, he glanced up at her.

'What do you hope?'

Ella finished pouring her juice, then shrugged. 'I don't know. Sometimes nightmares come from stress in your life. I just hope things haven't been so tense around here that we've been planting those seeds in her mind and they're coming out like this.'

This sobered him. 'I'd never want that.'

Ella put the juice bottle away and then turned to him. 'Me either.'

TJ touched her face and she felt a delicious ripple pass through her, a memory of the night before. Ella slid her arms around him and tilted her head back to accept his kiss. Their lips met and she inhaled his breath, giving him her own, mingling themselves in that way that had always seemed so intimate to her.

When he pulled back, she winced in disgust. 'I'm sorry,' she said. 'I need to brush my teeth.'

He laughed. 'Yeah, you do. But that's love, honey. Morning breath can't kill it.'

She whacked his arm and then as if to test the theory she kissed him again, though more chastely.

'You're burning the pancakes,' a voice said.

Startled, they both jumped a little and turned toward the kitchen entrance. Grace stood there in her pink New England Patriots T-shirt and a pair of loose cotton pajama pants that were covered in penguins. The clothes were hers, but something about her seemed different. She stood almost at attention, head tilted back with an air of dignified disapproval that might have been comical if that disapproval hadn't seemed aimed at her parents.

'Grace?' Ella said.

'Hey, Gracie, I'm glad you're awake,' TJ said cheerily. 'Want banana pancakes?'

'Not those, TJ,' the little girl said. 'You're burning them.'

The first time she'd said it, neither of her parents had really registered the words. Now TJ swore and hurried to the stove, using his fingers to flip the pancakes over; he'd been too busy kissing Ella to get the spatula from the drawer. Ella saw that Grace was right: the pancakes had burned a dark brown on one side. This batch would end up in the sink disposal. The good news was that he hadn't gotten to the stage of adding banana slices.

Suddenly Ella heard an echo of her daughter's words and realized what had sounded so wrong to her.

'Since when do you call your parents by their first names?' Grace ignored her, instead watching her father scrape the burnt pancakes off the pan. TJ cleaned it off as best he could and then set it back down on the burner.

'No, no,' Grace said, huffing as she approached the stove. 'You're just going to get that burnt flavor in the next batch. You've got to clean it first.'

The little girl took the pan from her father and ran water into it over the sink. The hot pan hissed and steamed when the water struck it.

'Careful!' TJ said. 'You should really let me do that, Gracie. I know you want to help, but — '

As he reached for the pan, she turned her back to block him, finishing the job and making short work of it. Ella and TJ just watched as she turned and gave her father a look that seemed to say *there, that's how it's done*, and then set the pan back on the burner.

'There,' Grace said, reaching up to tug at some unruly locks of her hair, tucking them tightly behind her ears. 'Don't put the banana in too early and you'll be fine.'

What the fuck was that? Ella thought.

'Grace,' she said sternly.

The little girl turned to study her gravely, as if Ella were some new and unwelcome discovery. Grace had always been a little sassy with her, and Ella knew that lots of girls reached the point where they tried to act more maturely and to distance themselves from their parents and the children they had once been, but this went way beyond anything she'd ever expected . . . and it had arrived in her daughter's behavioral repertoire at least two years before Ella had thought it might.

'Yes, Mother?' Grace said at last.

Mother?

'Don't call your father by his first name.'

Grace smiled. 'Of course,' she said, turning to her father. 'Sorry about that, Dad.'

As her parents watched, Grace Farrelly turned and left the room. 'I'm going to watch some TV,' she said. 'Please let me know when the pancakes are ready. I'll have three or four, I think. I'm starving.'

Ella realized that her mouth had been hanging open for several seconds before she turned to stare at her husband.

'Where did *that* come from?' she muttered.

'Not a clue,' TJ said.

Her husband remained staring at the kitchen

164

entrance, as if thinking that Grace might return and take a laughing bow to let them in on the joke. But Ella felt pretty certain it hadn't been a joke at all.

It sure as hell hadn't been funny.

★ ★ ★

In his years on the Coventry Police Department, Joe Keenan had seen the ugliest facets of human behavior — rape and murder and addiction, suicide pacts, parents prostituting their kids in exchange for drugs — but every once in a while he was reminded of the basic decency of his community. As dawn gave way to morning, the sunlight making the frozen hardpack glisten like diamonds, he paused and leaned against a tree, exhausted and out of breath, and watched people moving through the woods around him. There were police officers, on duty and off, and there were also firefighters and EMTs and city workers and ordinary volunteers who had responded to a summons in the middle of the night and gone without sleep to beat the bushes in search of a little lost boy who'd become an orphan overnight.

None of them wanted to believe that Zachary Stroud had drowned in the river. For hours, as the storm wound down from snow to sleet to rain to a morning of dissipating clouds, they had searched behind and in the branches of every tree, checked every depression in the ground, and followed the riverbank looking for footprints in the wet soil there. Police cars

165

cruised the neighborhoods just inland from the river. Now that dawn had arrived, some officers had begun canvassing door-to-door on the nearest streets.

'Falling down on the job, Detective?' a deep voice said.

Keenan glanced to his right, toward the deep, rushing whisper of the river, and saw Harley Talbot approaching. Officer Talbot must have been off duty because he was out of uniform, clad instead in a blue cable-knit collared sweater, jeans, and boots.

'I know you're screwing with me, Harley, but today's not the day,' Detective Keenan said.

'I've got you, man,' Harley said. 'You've been out here all night and we haven't found a damn thing. Gotta be demoralizing. But don't lose hope, Detective. Nobody's giving up yet.'

Detective Keenan nodded. 'Why is that, do you think? I mean . . . if we haven't found the kid by now . . . '

He let the words trail off but the question was clear. The search would continue all day long. Dogs had been brought in overnight but with all the newfallen snow they had not been able to get a scent to follow.

'Not that big a riddle,' Harley said, veiled in the golden early-morning light, almost ghostly. 'They don't want to believe the worst. Holding on to hope when most people would give up . . . that's faith, man. Everyone knows how this is gonna end, but they hold on because giving up the search means giving up hope, and nobody's ready for that.'

Keenan inhaled, cold morning air filling his lungs. His eyes burned with exhaustion and his limbs felt leaden from slogging along a mile or more of wooded riverside, but he could go on. They had to keep looking.

'I'm with you, Harley,' Detective Keenan said. 'Though I have to tell you, it takes more than hope to keep going. It takes coffee. If I don't get a massive caffeine injection I'm not going to be any good to anybody.'

Harley grinned. 'Shit, Detective, that's easy. Head out to the corner of Riverside and Harrison. Got a food truck there. The owner's giving away free coffee to all the searchers. It's no Starbucks, but it'll pick you up.'

Detective Keenan thanked him and headed west. The stretch of woods he had found himself in was maybe four hundred yards from river to road, not far at all, but it took him nearly fifteen minutes of moving through underbrush and around trees to reach the pavement. As he did, his cell phone rang.

The food truck was parked as promised. Lights were on inside the truck, though the sun had come out. Half-a-dozen people were standing or sitting near the big open window on the side of the truck, including two women who sat cross-legged on the snow, too tired to care if the dampness soaked through their clothes.

'Joe Keenan,' he said, phone to his ear.

'It's Sam.'

'Lieutenant Duquette,' Keenan said. 'I hope you're calling with good news.'

'I'm afraid not,' the lieutenant replied. 'We've

got more searchers coming in, but just no sign of the boy.'

Keenan eyed the food truck longingly, craving the coffee so powerfully that his need for it unnerved him. But this conversation could not be avoided.

'You sound defeated,' Detective Keenan said. 'This isn't over, Lieutenant.'

'We've scoured the river's edge and the woods,' Duquette replied. 'If the Stroud boy was out there, we'd have found him. He's in the river, Joe. You know it and I know it.'

Keenan's heart turned to ice. He flashed back to Charlie Newell dying in his arms.

'I know nothing of the kind.'

'Detective — '

'You're not abandoning the search,' Keenan said quickly.

'Don't be an idiot,' the lieutenant said. 'The media would be so far up the mayor's ass that they'd be camped out in his colon. He'd take it out on the chief and we'd all pay the price. We've got to keep it going a couple of days, but I'm telling you we're not going to find anything. You're not a rookie, Joe. You know this. Unless the kid was snatched — '

'I'm not saying he was snatched. But if he wandered away, could be somebody picked him up — '

'In the middle of that storm?'

'There were people out in it. The Strouds were out in it.'

'And they're dead.'

'Not everyone who was driving in the storm

168

finished the night upside down in the river, Lieutenant. All due respect.'

Seconds ticked by. Detective Keenan felt the sun warming him, heard the wet snow slipping off branches and footsteps clomping through the snowy woods. Voices called to one another hopefully, just as Harley Talbot had said. There were so many people in Coventry who were hurting, just like the rest of the country, people who were still weathering years of a struggling economy. But the people out searching didn't care about their own troubles this morning.

'My search for this kid isn't for show,' Keenan said quietly, the phone tight against his ear. 'We've got people searching the banks downstream for miles. I'm not discounting the idea that Zachary Stroud ended up drowning, but I'm not going to just assume it either, not when the only evidence we have indicates that he got out of the car on dry land, or near enough to it.'

He heard the lieutenant sigh on the other end of the line. 'We're both tired, Joe. I'm not asking you to stop searching. But we've known each other a long time and I know you take things like this pretty hard. I'm just trying to prepare you, that's all.'

Keenan froze. Lieutenant Duquette trying to protect the feelings of one of his detectives? *Wonders never cease*, he thought. But then he realized that the sympathy might not be so benevolent.

'Yeah, I do take it hard if a child dies on our watch,' Keenan said. 'I don't think you can be human and not be affected by something like

169

that. But if you're questioning my ability to do the job — '

'What are you talking about?'

'I just want to assure you that I'm fine. I'm up to it. All I need is caffeine. We're going to find this kid, Sam.'

'I hope like hell that we do, Detective. But you can't spend the next two days out there looking for him. You have other work to do.'

'I'm not chasing down ghost stories,' Keenan snapped, heart racing. 'You want to spend time on nutjobs who saw UFOs or fairies, you can send uniforms to take their statements. I've got a few open robberies that you and I both know we're never going to solve with the evidence I've got, and that assault case from yesterday, which turned out to be the woman's ex ransacking her place for drugs. That guy's already in custody, as of yesterday afternoon. Given that, do you really want to pull me off the search for a kid who escaped the car his parents died in?'

'I'm not pulling you off the search,' Lieutenant Duquette said. 'But you need to be practical. I can keep you out of the detectives' rotation today and maybe tomorrow. But if something else comes up that I need you for, you're going to have to do your job.'

'That's exactly what I'm doing.'

The lieutenant sighed loudly again.

'Word's going on to the media about the Strouds. There'll be pictures of Zachary on TV and online all day. If someone picked him up, even if the kid can't remember his own name, they'll know it by dinnertime for sure. But I'll

170

tell you what's worrying me.'

'What's that?'

'If someone picked the kid up, why haven't they called us already? If he's injured, why haven't they shown up at the hospital?'

Detective Keenan had no answer for that. The same questions had been gnawing at his gut all night and had only grown worse as morning arrived.

'If Zachary Stroud's alive,' the lieutenant went on, 'chances are he's still out there somewhere. I hope you find him, Joe. And I sure as hell hope you find him hiding in some bushes somewhere instead of at the bottom of the river.'

'So do I.'

'Call me the minute you find anything,' Lieutenant Duquette said. 'I'm keeping the chief informed.'

The call ended before Keenan could reply. Not that he had anything more to say. Sam Duquette was a good man and a good cop, though he could be one hell of a ballbuster at times. Like everyone, his nerves were frayed. Bad enough this family had to suffer such a crushing tragedy, but if the boy was alive and they couldn't find him, the Coventry police would look completely inept. Detective Keenan wasn't much worried about the city's reputation, but his higher-ups had to be.

Slipping his cell phone into his pocket, he crossed the street and headed for the food truck. His craving for coffee — for anything other than finding Zachary Stroud alive — had vanished, but if he didn't get some caffeine into his body, his addiction would punish him with a splitting headache, and he couldn't afford that. He needed to be awake and alert, not just to search for the boy but to figure out what to do if the search became a mystery. He didn't believe the boy had gone into the river, but if he wasn't in the woods and hadn't wandered into one of the surrounding neighborhoods, then where had he gone? People didn't just vanish.

The thought made him freeze, standing in front of the food truck, drawing curious glances.

Sometimes people do vanish, he thought, remembering Carl Wexler. *Sometimes they do.*

⋆ ⋆ ⋆

Jake Schapiro dreams of his dead brother. They're watching TV in the living room, some ancient episode of SpongeBob that they've seen a thousand times before. Their mom sits in her chair in the corner, correcting school papers and telling them stories about the crazy kids in her class. She never names the kids, always starts her tales with 'one of the girls' or 'one of the boys,' but Jake and Isaac can usually figure out whom she's talking about.

Mom looks tired tonight. Even more so than usual, and that's saying something considering how little sleep she gets during the school year. Summers aren't really vacations so much as opportunities for Allie Schapiro to catch up on her sleep. Teachers and the children of teachers understand the dynamic better than other people, understand how much work it is to go in and face the kids every day, keep them thinking and keep them entertained and try to inspire them to give a damn about their futures. She earns those bags under her eyes. Truth is, Jake doesn't mind those bags. A couple of the boys in his class have told him they think his mom is hot, so anything that makes her look older and less attractive is okay with him. Even as he thinks this, he knows it's unkind, but he can't help it.

A commercial comes on. Isaac jumps up and zooms around the room in that irritating way he's been doing since he could walk. He sings a song he knows only because it's on Jake's iPod.

'Isaac, is all of your homework done?' Mom asks.

Jake smiles. He has math practice questions to do but intends to dash them off in homeroom. He relishes the knowledge that Mom won't ask him — he never gives her reason to worry about his schoolwork — but Isaac is a little ADHD and when he starts acting like a little spaz, she worries.

The little goofball rushes from the room, arms out like he's an airplane, totally lost in his own brain. Isaac-world, they sometimes call it.

'Isaac?' Mom calls.

Jake rolls his eyes. He doesn't much care about SpongeBob these days, but he just wants them both to chill.

'Ike!' he shouts.

There's a pause, like his little brother has skipped a beat. Like the way the TV sometimes seems to freeze and become pixelated and then

173

catch up with the sound and image of whatever Jake might be watching.

Out of the corner of his eye, Jake sees Isaac come back into the room. He continues to make his airplane buzz for a couple of seconds and then interrupts himself. 'Yes?'

'Did you do your homework?' Jake asks, not looking at him.

Wake up, Jakey.

Isaac's voice sounds strange, suddenly. Like it's a whisper in his ear instead of coming from across the room. Jake frowns.

'I'm not asleep, dumbass.'

'Hey!' Mom snaps. 'Watch that. You know I don't like when you two speak that way to — '

Wake up, Jakey. Please, wake up.

'My homework's all done,' Isaac says, in a whiny sort of why-don't-you-leave-me-alone voice.

'I wish mine was,' Mom mutters.

Reluctantly, because it's easier to think of himself instead of someone else — even his mother — Jake turns to his brother, thinking that he'll make nice with Isaac and the two of them can go upstairs and watch TV or read comics or something in order to give their mother some quiet time to work.

Jake cannot breathe. His heart races and a scream begins to build in his chest, right in the middle where he thinks his heart must be.

'What?' Isaac demands, pouting angrily and crossing his arms. 'Why are you looking at me like that?'

The scream bursts from his lips in a wordless babble of terror. Jake scrambles, falls from his

174

chair, and then lurches to the other side of the room, taking cover beside his mother's chair. He's screaming and crying at the same time, shouting out words that his mother doesn't even realize he knows, calling out to God in the same breath as he mutters ohfuck ohfuck ohfuck.

Then the pain of it hits him, the grief, the terrible sadness beneath his fear.

'What happened to you?' he cries.

'Stop it,' Isaac says. 'You're scaring me.'

But Isaac is blue-white and rigid in death. His eyes have collapsed into his head and there is ice in his hair and frost on his skin.

'Stop it, Jake,' the little dead boy says.

Jake keeps screaming, and somehow in his ear he hears the whisper — the other Isaac voice — speak again.

Please, Jake. You've gotta wake up.

* * *

He woke with a cry, gasping for air as if somehow in sleep he had been suffocating. In his bed, snow falling outside, he lay wide-eyed and stared up at the ceiling, trying to steady his pulse and his nerves and forcing himself not to fall back to sleep too quickly for fear that he would drift back into the same dream.

Jake often dreamed about Isaac. Sometimes they were sweet dreams that broke his heart as he woke, remembering the tree fort they'd built in their backyard and the way that — though Isaac had driven him crazy sometimes — Jake had always loved sharing his room with his

175

brother. Together in the dark, when they were supposed to be trying to fall asleep, they would share their secrets and talk to each other with a kindness and joint sense of aspiration that they never would have while awake.

And sometimes the dreams were nightmares.

He thought about his mother. For the first time in a while, he wondered how often she dreamed of Isaac and how often she had nightmares about searching for Niko Ristani. As far as Jake knew, his mother had never fallen for anyone after Niko's death. He wasn't sure she would ever allow herself to be in love again. Instead she spent her days teaching school and her nights drinking too much wine, and Jake thought that was a tragedy. He wanted his mother to be happy. She deserved that.

A scratching at the window made him shiver. Snow and ice against the glass — he told himself it had to be that. Not the things he didn't like to think about, didn't usually allow himself to remember. Not the things that slipped their icy hands right through the screen and dragged little children to their deaths.

'Get it out of your head,' he said to himself, a whisper in the dark.

Please, Jake. I'm afraid.

The words rose as if from his dreams, just as much inside his head as his own voice. Twisting under the covers, shoving himself against the wall, he turned to face the rest of the room.

Isaac stood six feet away, just as icy blue and dead as he'd been in the dream.

Jake screamed . . .

. . . And started awake, gasping.

'Holy shit,' he muttered. 'Ohfuck ohfuck.'

He sat up in bed, morning sunlight streaming in through the windows, melting snow and ice dripping from the roof outside, falling past his window. *Just a dream*, he reassured himself. *A dream within a dream*. He laughed uneasily but he was unconvinced, glancing around the sun-soaked bedroom in search of dead boys in the shadows.

The cobwebs of dreams were still in his head and it took him several long moments and deep breaths to dispel them. He felt the chill in the room and the softness of the sheets. He rubbed his eyes, waking further, and became aware of the cottony film inside his mouth. *Morning breath*. Dragon breath, his mom had called it when he and Isaac were little. That was definitely not the kind of detail that usually populated his dreams.

'Okay,' he said. 'Not a dream.'

Needing to relieve his bladder, Jake threw his sheets back and started to climb out of bed.

'Is it really you?' a small voice asked.

Jake froze. Heart pounding, he turned to look at the open doorway to his bedroom. In the hallway just outside the room stood a small boy who was *not* his brother, Isaac. Perhaps ten — the same age Isaac had been at the time of his death — the boy had dark blond hair and impossibly blue eyes. His face was smeared with dirt and his nose and mouth were caked with

177

dried blood, swollen and on the way to a serious bruising. He had no jacket and his clothes were torn and dirty.

'Jake?' the little boy said, his voice resonating in the bedroom, a plaintive sound that put the strangest thoughts into his head.

'What are you doing, kid?' Jake asked, grabbing the jeans he'd left crumpled on the floor and sliding into them. 'You can't just come into somebody's — '

'Is it really you?' the boy interrupted. He stepped into the room, flinching from the bright sunlight.

A shiver went through Jake. *Surreal.* Maybe his nightmares were just lingering, but the kid's voice sounded familiar.

'What are you doing in here, kid?' he asked. 'You can't just walk into somebody's house. And what happened to your face?'

His memory flashed back to the night before. He'd thought he had seen someone at the edge of the woods during the storm. Standing before him was an explanation.

'How did you — ' he started.

'Jake, please,' the boy said, his upper lip quivering as tears began to spill from his eyes. 'Is it really you? Don't you . . . don't you *know* me?'

All the breath went out of Jake. The winter chill in the house sank to his bones. That voice.

'No way . . . ' Jake said. 'No fucking way. Who put you up to this, kid? Tell me right now and you won't be in trouble. You tell me — '

The little boy — this blond boy with the unfamiliar face but the voice Jake remembered

178

too well — shushed him.

'Please,' the boy said, glancing around nervously. He came deeper into the room, approaching Jake's spot by the bed. 'It's going to be okay. If you keep it secret, if you hide me when the time comes, it will all be okay. We can be together again.'

'Isaac?' Jake whispered.

The little boy put out his arms like airplane wings. He smiled at Jake, wiping at his tears.

'Buzz buzz, Jakey,' he said.

Jake staggered backward a step, shaking his head, his breath coming in small, hitching gasps. *No*, he thought. *No, no*.

The kid put out his arms, reaching upward as if he expected a hug . . . as if this impossible creature, this dead boy speaking from the mouth of a stranger, thought that his brother would embrace him.

Shaking, Jake moved aside. The hurt in the boy's brilliant blue eyes should have stung Jake's heart. Instead it stoked his fear. That hurt could not be a dream.

'Jake — '

'No!'

He bolted around the kid and raced out the door. Words tumbled through his mind. *Ghostdemonzombie*. And then another: *dream*. He went down the steps of the old farmhouse two at a time, flung open the front door, and hurtled himself out into the ice-encrusted snow-pack in jeans and a T-shirt, his feet bare. Sometimes, if he was falling asleep while driving, he would slap himself in the face. He did it now,

179

standing there freezing, and the sting of his palm brought him into vivid reality.

'Wake up!' he shouted, feeling brittle reality crumbling around him, remembering the way it had felt that night twelve years earlier, when it had happened to him the first time. This couldn't be real. It couldn't. 'Wake up!'

Turning, he saw the little boy through the open door — coming down the stairs, pursuing him, lips pouting, tears on his cheeks.

'Jake,' the boy said, the name a tremulous plea. 'You've got to be quiet or they'll get us. They'll get us *both*.'

10

Doug Manning woke slowly, breathing in the scent of the woman in his bed. A smile crept across his features even before he opened his eyes to find himself spooning behind Angela Ristani, the two of them burrowed beneath flannel sheets and a thick down comforter. He nestled himself more tightly behind her, pressing his face into her hair and enjoying the touch of his bare skin against hers, the softness at the curve of her ass meeting his growing hardness.

'Well, well,' she said, her voice raspy as she came sleepily awake. 'Good morning to you, too.'

She stretched, pressing back against him, and then turned to face him, black hair fanned out on the white pillow. Even with her smeared makeup and the years that were creeping up on them both, she looked beautiful.

'Looks like that wasn't a dream I had last night,' he said.

Angela gazed into his eyes, seeking something that Doug hoped she would find.

'No dream, buster. I'm real. And I hope you thought it was a good dream.'

'Are you kidding? I wouldn't ever have wanted to wake up.'

He touched her face, pushed his fingers through her hair, and then kissed her. She responded with a passion that startled him, cleaving to him and moaning lightly. He felt as if she were opening beside him, as if she had been bound up with tension and uncertainty that fled in that moment of surrender. Emotional, not sexual, and that was what surprised him most. The Angela Ristani he knew, his late wife's best friend, the woman with whom he'd shared a torrid, volatile relationship, had been full of sharp and cynical edges. All that hardness seemed absent now.

Doug whispered to her, urgent words. Primal things. Amazement and wonder. He slid a hand along her leg and then lifted it, resting her knee on his hip as he opened her more fully, his fingers tracing along the inside of her thighs. She shivered and gave a little gasp as he touched her, and he felt the familiar animal need rising within him.

'Wait,' she said, pushing his hand away.

He blinked as if waking for a second time. She withdrew from him slightly, closing her legs, and kissed him once before drawing back so that they were face-to-face, but each on their own pillow island.

'Are you going to want me to leave?' Angela asked. 'Y'know . . . after?'

Doug ran his hand over the curve of her hip. 'You can stay forever as far as I'm concerned.'

She smacked his chest. 'Don't do that. I'm asking a serious question.'

'Okay, okay. Serious question deserves a serious answer.'

He glanced at the window, where the morning sun shone brightly. A small drift of snow had formed in one corner and clung to the screen, but it was all melting now. Icicles dripped water, shrinking. It was going to be one of those days when the whole world seemed to have quieted down. *Winter wonderland*, he thought. The kind of day that was best when shared. Did he want her to go?

'I don't have to work today,' he said. 'I'd like to spend the day with you, in or out of bed.'

She kissed him, then pulled back to reveal an exuberant grin. Throwing back the covers, she sprang from the bed, picked up her panties and slipped them on, then grabbed the T-shirt he had been wearing the night before.

'Where are you going?' he asked, starting to climb out of bed as well.

'No, no. You stay there,' she said, slipping on his T-shirt.

Angela picked up the remote control from the nightstand and tossed it onto the bed.

'Watch TV or something. A morning like this . . . it's a time to spend cocooned inside. Making love and watching old movies and eating in bed.' She went to leave but paused just inside the bedroom door, smiling playfully. 'Scrambled eggs with Tabasco and bacon on the side, right?'

Doug laughed. Suddenly the morning seemed just as surreal as the night before.

'You're making me breakfast in bed?'

'Unless you're not hungry.'

His stomach growled at the mere suggestion. 'Breakfast would be amazing.'

'Coming right up, then. Don't move a muscle.'

Angela darted into the hall and he heard her light footfalls on the stairs as she went down to

183

the kitchen. Doug stared after her for several long seconds, happily befuddled. Whatever had gotten into her, he was pretty sure he could get used to it. Not that he wanted to jump back into a relationship with her, but she had definitely changed. The Angela Ristani he thought he knew would have scoffed at the idea of making him breakfast in bed — once upon a time she had teased the hell out of Cherie for just that sort of romantic gesture — but this morning she acted like she'd suddenly woken up from a cynical dream to discover that she was actually kind of sweet.

And how does she know about the Tabasco? He tried to remember if they'd ever had breakfast together, but even if they had, was Angie the kind of woman who would remember what her boyfriend liked for breakfast? Maybe, but he would never have guessed it.

Doug picked up the remote and turned on the TV. Channel 5 had always had the best newscast in Boston — people who seemed real, like you'd bump into them on the street and they'd say hello. He'd remained loyal to the station for as long as he could remember paying attention to the news.

Naked, relishing the feel of the flannel against his skin, he propped himself up on a pile of pillows and relaxed with the talking heads of channel 5. The scent of Angela remained in the pillows and the musk of the sex they'd had the night before lingered as well. If the shyly smiling woman who'd just gone down to spoil him with breakfast in bed was indicative of some new leaf

184

she had turned over, Doug believed he could get used to having Angie back in his life.

Wistful, the familiar ache returning to his heart, he thought of Cherie. In truth, he would always think of Cherie. He knew that. And it wasn't just because Cherie and Angela had been best friends. No matter who came into his life, even if he married again, he would always be in love with Cherie. But twelve years of cycling between loneliness and superficial relationships had been long enough. He deserved something good in his life.

'Don't get ahead of yourself, man,' he whispered to the room.

It's just sex and breakfast so far.

The *so far* made him smile. Time would tell. It always did.

A frown creased his brow. He'd been only half paying attention to the television but now he sat up a little higher. The gorgeous brunette who did the morning weather — hugely pregnant, as she seemed always to be — had just brought up the screen with the five-day forecast.

'Right around thirty degrees Monday and a couple of degrees cooler on Tuesday, but it'll feel warmer thanks to the sunshine we'll be getting. There'll be plenty of melting as well, just in time for what could be some huge snowfall on Tuesday night leading into Wednesday. We're looking at some massive totals, folks, along with potential blizzard conditions north and west of Boston. It's too early for really accurate numbers, but . . . '

Doug stared at the screen as the map of the

greater Boston area appeared, showing the snowfall projections. The swath of color that included the Merrimack Valley indicated a possible fourteen to eighteen inches.

The smile that spread across Doug's face was entirely different from the one he had shown to Angela just a few minutes earlier. It came with a nervous tremor in his stomach, and his pulse quickened.

On the nights that he had met with Franco and Baxter to plan their petty little burglaries or to case a property before a break-in, they'd talked idly about an ice storm that had shut down southern New Hampshire for a week . . . and about the blizzard that had taken Cherie Manning's life. During a storm like that, people lost their power. Many lost their heat. Some — mostly those who could afford it — got out early and set up in a hotel for the night, enjoying being catered to.

They'd talked about a storm when most house phones and burglar alarms wouldn't work. When cell phone service would be unreliable at best, thanks to all the people trying to make sure their loved ones were all right. A night when even if the alarms went off the cops wouldn't be able to make it out to the crime scenes. They already had the guns and the masks, and Doug and Franco knew a guy who would loan them some big-ass snowmobiles and not ask questions as long as he got a cut.

In his gun safe, Doug had keys to four of the most expensive houses in Coventry.

Another tremor went through him and his

smile faded. The idea scared the shit out of him, made him queasy, but he had no intention of letting his fear get the better of him. He had played by the rules for most of his life, and what had it gotten him? A part-time job, and not even that when things got lean at Harpwell's. An empty little house that his wife had inherited from her mother. An empty fridge. Old friends who behaved awkwardly around him because they felt sorry for him.

As crazy as it sounded, even to him, stealing from people was the first thing he had ever done that made him feel as if he was in control of his life. If the government couldn't fix the economy enough for him to get a fair shake, a full-time job with a fair wage, then he would take what he felt he was due.

The smell of frying bacon wafted up to him and he felt a flicker of regret. This thing with Angela seemed promising. Based on the way the morning was going, it certainly didn't feel like a one-night stand. Doug thought it would be nice to have someone in his life who looked at him the way she did, but the timing left something to be desired. He didn't want her to feel that he was blowing her off, but he would need to get on the phone to Franco and Baxter as soon as possible. Things needed to be set in motion.

All they needed to fulfill their ambitions was the right storm, and it looked like it was on its way.

Coventry wouldn't know what hit it.

⋆ ⋆ ⋆

The little boy sat in Jake Schapiro's kitchen, a plate of French toast in front of him. Jake had cleaned the blood off his face, thinking it was likely that the kid's nose was broken, though the very mention of a doctor — or of leaving this house at all — caused such a panic in the kid that Jake didn't dare mention it again. At least not yet.

He'd given the kid clean, dry socks as well as a T-shirt and sweatshirt that floated on him, but at least he was warmer and cleaner than when he'd arrived. The question of just how he'd arrived — how he'd gotten in without breaking locks or windows — remained a puzzler. The kid claimed he'd come in through a second-story window that had been open mere inches and Jake was too baffled to debate the point. There were bigger mysteries here.

As Jake watched, the kid ate hungrily and washed down each bite with a sip of hot chocolate. Isaac had often done the same. As the kid wolfed his breakfast, Jake tried to convince himself it wasn't his little brother sitting in that chair. That should've been easy: his brother would have been twenty-two now, if he hadn't already been dead for a dozen years. And this kid didn't look anything like Isaac.

It's just not possible. Jake repeated this in his mind like a mantra. He leaned against the kitchen counter and watched the kid from a distance, studying his every word and gesture for echoes of Isaac. He felt cast adrift, not only floating on an undulating sea of fear and uncertainty but unable to decide which way he ought to hope the wind blew him.

The little boy hummed happily to himself while he ate, almost imperceptibly dancing in his chair. This meal gave him such pleasure.

Isaac had done that as well.

Stop it, he thought. *You're thinking crazy thoughts. It can't be him.*

You saw him dead.

But as Jake watched the boy sipping hot chocolate in between bites of French toast, he knew the truth. He could *feel* his brother in the room with him. And although — except for in a crackly old family video — he hadn't heard Isaac's voice since that horrible night, he recognized it. Every time the boy spoke, Jake felt the world tilt beneath him a little. It felt like he was watching an expertly dubbed foreign film, where the words fit the movements of the lips but the voice somehow did not match the character.

'Thank you,' the kid said now, glancing up at Jake as he took a sip of hot chocolate. 'I was so hungry. It was hard to even remember what it felt like to . . .'

The little boy trailed off.

Jake leaned against the counter, trying to keep the urge to freak out under control. It bubbled just beneath the surface but he managed to keep a leash on it.

'What it felt like to what?'

'To eat,' the kid said. 'I remember wanting to, and what my favorite foods were. But I couldn't remember what anything tasted like. Isn't that weird?'

189

'Yeah,' Jake said, his mouth going dry. 'Pretty weird.'

Weirdness abounded.

'What were your favorites?' he asked.

The kid narrowed his brilliant blue eyes and then seemed to surrender a little of himself. 'You're testing me. I know. I understand.'

A tiny shard of guilt lodged itself in Jake's heart, but he ignored it, watching the boy. Not pulling his gaze away.

'Burgers and milk shakes at Skip's,' the boy said, sticking a forkful of French toast into his mouth and talking as he chewed. 'Apple Jacks. Chicken pot pie. The blintzes Mom makes at Hanukkah.'

Jake flinched. Allie Schapiro hadn't made blintzes during the holidays in all the years since Isaac had died. They had been a thing between mother and younger son; Jake had never liked them.

He stared at the kid, who was practically swaddled in the New England Patriots sweatshirt that Jake had loaned him. With the sleeves pushed up so that his hands were free, swimming inside the voluminous sweatshirt, he looked like some kind of refugee. And maybe that was precisely what he was.

I can't deal with this alone, Jake thought. *I need perspective.*

The kid glanced at him in alarm, as though he had read Jake's mind.

'You can't tell anyone I'm here,' the boy said quickly, his French toast forgotten. He shifted his chair and it squeaked on the floor. Whatever

190

else he was, the kid was tangible. Solid flesh and blood.

'Explain that to me,' Jake said. 'Why not?'

The kid glanced away. 'If they know I'm here, they'll come for me. I just . . . I want to stay with you.'

'You talked about them before. But you haven't said who they are.'

The boy shuddered. His lower lip pushed out, not in a childish pout but on the verge of tears. It hit Jake in the gut. He thought of all the times he had cried in the months after Isaac's death, promising that if God would just give his little brother back, he would be so much kinder to him.

'No, hey,' Jake said, moving away from the counter at last.

He slid into a chair across from the boy, but Isaac looked away.

Isaac. He had thought of the boy as Isaac. Emotion roiled inside him, a swirl of hope and fear and wonder and sorrow that made him feel sick and elated all at once.

'It's okay,' Jake said. 'You've been through something. I'm not sure what I really believe, but I believe that much. We don't have to talk about this now. It can keep a little while.'

The boy lifted his gaze, his eyes full of hope. 'You promise?'

'I do. For now, I do.'

When the kid went right back to hungrily demolishing his French toast, Jake could only smile. Why, he wondered, was it so easy to pray to God for miracles but so hard to accept one when it had been granted?

Was that truly what had happened? Had he been granted a miracle? And what did it mean for life and death . . . and afterlife? The kid that sat across from him with a frothy hot-chocolate mustache had to be some kind of ghost, but he was tangible and solid and *alive*.

'Are you . . . reincarnated?' Jake said.

Isaac gave a shrug. 'I don't know what that means.'

'You know my brother . . . you know that *you* died?'

The boy's face fell. He slouched in his chair a little and nodded, pushing away his plate. He'd lost his appetite.

'You have Isaac's voice but not his face. Were you just . . . dead for a while . . . and then you were born again to a different family?'

Isaac's eyes lit up — and it seemed okay, somehow, to start thinking of them as Isaac's eyes.

'That's it,' the boy said, tapping the table. 'That's what happened. Is that re-in . . . '

'Reincarnated. Yeah.'

Jake fell silent. He had more questions, like how old the boy had been when he realized that he had lived another life. Had he always had his old memories or had they come to him gradually? Jake let out a breath of amazement, trying to wrap his head around the whole thing.

Isaac started twisting up the paper napkin Jake had given him. It frayed a little and he began to tear it apart.

'You can't tell anyone, Jake. Especially not Mom.'

'Why not?'

Isaac looked up at him, his eyes suddenly older, tired, and weighted down with difficult knowledge.

'Most people wouldn't believe you,' Isaac said. 'They'd think you were crazy, right? And even if they did believe you . . . it's just got to be our secret. It's not safe for either of us if you tell.'

He said 'tell' the way that little boys always did, as in 'I'm going to *tell*.'

'What about Mom?' Jake asked. 'Why can't I — '

'I want her to know,' Isaac interrupted. 'More than anything. I want to see her. That would be . . . ' He began to well up with tears again. 'But not yet, okay? She thinks I'm dead, just like you did. We need to think about it, figure out the best way to talk to her about it. I'm afraid if we just, y'know, spring it on her, she might have a heart attack or something.'

Jake hesitated, but one look at the emotion filling the boy's face made his decision easy.

'Okay. We wait.'

★ ★ ★

Two hours later, Jake sat on the couch, struggling with the promises he'd made. Isaac's small body lay curled next to him, totally conked out. The kid slept the same way he'd eaten breakfast — as if he hadn't done it in years. They had talked and talked, both about their childhood together and about Jake's life now. The conversation had never for a moment lost

193

the dreamlike sheen that had surrounded them from the moment of their first encounter that morning. Despite the persuasiveness of the kid's voice and memories and solidity, Jake kept waiting for someone to jump out and tell him he'd been punked. As a child he'd been fascinated by magicians, loved watching them and trying to figure out the trick. This felt much the same.

Isaac snored lightly. His mouth hung open and a tiny string of drool lay across his cheek. He looked as if he could sleep forever.

Jake glanced at the television, marveling at the cartoon images on Nickelodeon. Talking to Isaac had been surreal enough, but after they'd spoken for a while, the kid had asked if they could watch something. Sitting there on the couch watching cartoons with his dead brother as if there was nothing extraordinary about it . . . that had been the most surreal moment of all.

He didn't want to get up. Didn't know what he'd do with himself. How could he have a normal conversation with anyone right now?

Isaac's dirty sneakers were pushed up against his thigh. Jake felt the pressure, the confirmation of reality. But as he sat there with the soft snoring of the reincarnated boy for company, he could not help but begin to wonder about the nature of reality. Back in high school, one of his friends had suffered a serious psychotic break, thought that aliens were monitoring his every conversation and that the entire government was a vast, conspiratorial network of collaborators serving alien overlords. The jokes had been nonstop, but Jake had never thought it was funny. He knew the little psycho — Jeff Tanner — pretty well. He'd seen the fear and confusion and paranoia in Tanner's eyes. With therapy and serious drugs, Tanner had recovered.

The question, as Jake now saw it, was whether or not his brain had gone 'full Tanner,' as the kids at Coventry High had often said when someone started acting crazy or belligerent.

Jake looked at the sleeping boy beside him and smiled. Isaac's nose remained swollen from whatever had bloodied him that morning, but he still looked pretty adorable, snoozing away and drooling. If this was a psychotic break, it was an incredibly detailed bit of imagination.

A thought struck him and he rose from the couch. Isaac slept on undisturbed as Jake strode into the little dining room. Like so many rooms in the house, this one was unfinished. Capped wires jutted from the ceiling where a chandelier belonged. The walls had been painted an antique-rose hue but he'd left the plates off the outlets. The floors needed to be done, and the table and chairs were much too obviously a set he'd picked up from a yard sale.

His camera sat with some of his equipment on the scratched and uneven table. Jake grabbed the camera and left the still-unfinished room. Perhaps, he had begun to think, it was not meant to be a dining room. Time would tell.

Returning to the couch, he raised the camera and studied the boy who might be Isaac through the viewfinder. He snapped a picture and then three more in quick succession, afraid that the tiny noises would wake the boy, but Isaac did not stir. Tapping the button on the back of the camera, he scanned back through the photos he'd taken. Isaac showed up in all of them, looking no different from the way he looked to the naked eye. He wasn't a vampire, at least, but as for a figment of the imagination, Jake could not be certain. If all this was some psychotic episode, what did the camera prove?

Nothing.

He set his camera on the coffee table and picked up the remote control, settling back onto the couch, careful not to rouse Isaac. After a storm he usually liked to be outside taking pictures. Today would have been the perfect day for it, warm sun melting ice and snow all over town, but instead the gauzy drapes were drawn to keep out prying eyes. Isaac had pleaded with him and Jake had thought it a small concession. The kid had obviously suffered some kind of trauma. He would speak about it when he felt comfortable enough. Until then, Jake just had to keep from going nuts.

Aiming the remote, he started surfing channels in search of a movie or one of the home-improvement shows he always thought would inspire him to complete some of his projects around the house. He bounced through a couple of news stations as well and landed on a flick with a young Denzel Washington before he froze and started back through the channels.

Hurrying through the news stations he had seen a photograph of a boy, a familiar face, for it belonged to the kid sleeping on the couch beside

196

him. A terrible car accident in the middle of the storm, a Mercedes upside down, half submerged on the edge of the Merrimack River. Husband and wife dead. Police searching for their son, Zachary Stroud.

Isaac had been reborn as Zachary Stroud.

Local police and volunteers were searching for him. The state police were putting divers into the river, though the current might have carried the boy miles beneath the frozen surface, at least according to the news anchor.

Only the current hadn't carried the boy anywhere. He was asleep on Jake's couch.

A terrible paralysis gripped him. Jake stared at the television, not wanting to look at Isaac — at Zachary Stroud — not wanting to think about all the people searching for this boy. Divers in the river. Relatives who'd already lost the boy's parents and didn't know the kid was alive. Alive and safe. Snoring on Jake Schapiro's couch.

He should call. He knew that.

But the ache in his heart would not let him.

He had just gotten Isaac back. Somehow, through means he would never have believed possible the day before, his brother had returned to him. Now he had to think about what to do — the *right* thing to do. Reincarnated somehow, Isaac was here with him. If he called the police, if he handed the boy over without telling their mother, without giving her the chance to speak to her dead son, it would be an unimaginable betrayal.

Jake simply couldn't do it.

Isaac doesn't want you to, he told himself. *He*

197

doesn't want anyone to know he's here.

But it was more complicated than that, wasn't it? Rationalizations wouldn't cut it. Even if this kid was Isaac, he was also, somehow, Zachary Stroud.

'Jesus,' Jake whispered.

Not a prayer, but nonetheless a plea. He had to talk to someone, but who would believe him? Who would listen to this crazy-ass story and not try to interfere? Whom could he trust? He racked his brain but couldn't come up with anyone he dared share his story with.

Then he glanced at Isaac, sleeping so peacefully, and it hit him. There was one person he could call, one who would understand, maybe the only person in the world who might believe him. Someone who no longer had any connection with Coventry and would be too far away to interfere.

Jake rose from the couch and went to the kitchen, opening the drawer where he kept the phone book. Beneath it were all sorts of business cards, take-out menus, and scraps of paper going back a long while. He found a torn blue scrap upon which he'd hastily scrawled a cell phone number he'd acquired six months before.

It won't work, he thought. *She'll have a new one by now.*

But he picked the phone up off the kitchen counter and dialed the number, then stood and listened to it ring and ring.

★ ★ ★

198

In the moments before sunrise, even the forgotten corners of Seattle took on a glow that suggested their best days were still ahead. Miri Ristani jogged past the silent hulk of the Brimstone Brewery, her breath fogging the crisp winter-morning air, her heart keeping rhythm with her feet as she ran. Four years earlier, when her wanderings had first washed her up on the proverbial shores of the haven that Seattle had become for her, the old Brimstone Brewery had been a brick eyesore of boarded windows and rusted pipes. Now it was being refurbished as a nightclub with upper floors dedicated to studio space for artists and musicians, just another way in which the passing days seemed to be scouring the rust off the face of the whole Georgetown neighborhood of Seattle. One of the oldest neighborhoods in the city, it was somehow also one of the newest. Its rebirth had not yet arrived, but it was gestating nicely.

Miri ran with a steady, even gait, breathing the winter air, understanding with every step that her friends were frustrated by these early-morning runs. Bad enough to be out alone so early in the summer months, they would say — had often said — but to run the streets of Seattle before dawn by herself, a woman alone, was just asking for trouble. She raced past a bagel shop, the smell of coffee spreading up and down the block, then crossed to the other side of the street to avoid roadwork. The storefronts were familiar territory to her by now, a florist, a karate school, a tiny Chinese restaurant, a Laundromat . . . and sprinkled among them, plenty of abandoned shops with soaped windows and drooping For Lease signs. The neighborhood might be improving in spite of the economy, but it still had a long way to go.

Still, she wasn't afraid to be out in the dark alone. In the years since her high school graduation, Miri had walked far more dangerous streets and come through unscathed. Alone never bothered her. Alone, in fact, had become her sanctuary. Five years earlier she had hit the road, put Massachusetts behind her, and not stopped until she hit the Pacific Ocean, which seemed like it might be just far enough away from her mother in order for her to breathe.

On mornings like this, just breathing was enough.

As she rounded a corner past a pub that still reeked of last night's beer, she saw the sun coming up over the tops of the buildings to the east. Its reflection flared in a hundred storefront windows and she felt as if she were entering some brilliant hall of mirrors. This early on a Sunday morning the only people on the street were workers headed home from the night shift and people like Miri, who knew that half the beauty had already spilled out of a day by the time nine o'clock rolled around.

She relished her isolation. Breathed it in. Blessed the spirit of winter.

Felt her cell phone buzz against her abdomen.

Just the vibration threw off her stride. She considering ignoring the call, but at half past seven on a Sunday morning it could only be something urgent, so she slipped the phone from its clip and glanced at the screen as she darted around a tree that grew up out of the sidewalk.

Call from . . . JAKE.

The contact listing on her phone didn't have a last name for Jake, but she didn't need clarification. There were other guys in her life with the same name but the rest of them needed modifiers, either last names or Jake-From-Philosophy or Jake-From-the-Gym or Jake-From-Oklahoma.

Miri held the vibrating phone by her hip as she ran on another half-dozen paces. The idea of talking to Jake opened up so many questions in her mind, little windows that offered views of parts of her heart she wasn't sure she felt like seeing again. Six months had passed since she'd last spoken to Jake, six months since she'd had contact with anyone from home. This early in the morning he could only be calling about something terrible or something wonderful. He'd know she would be awake — if anyone truly knew her, Jake was that someone — but courtesy would keep him from dialing the phone unless it was urgent.

The dread that clutched at her nearly stopped her in her tracks but she managed to take a deep breath and keep going. She exhaled, phone still vibrating in her hand.

Maybe he's getting married, she thought, *calling to tell me he's engaged.*

But Miri didn't think so. She thought it must have something to do with her mother, that the bitch-queen Angie Ristani had finally drunk herself to death or ended up in jail for slapping a

201

cop or inadvertently killed one of the patients she was supposed to be nursing back to health. Miri hadn't spoken to her mother in two years and had no interest in hearing about her now.

Not even if she's dead. Not even if she's dying, and needs you?

'Fuck,' Miri whispered.

She slowed her run, the rhythm of her heart now as off-kilter as her stride, and answered the call.

'Hello?' she said, coming to a halt.

Silence greeted her. The line sounded flat and empty. She glanced at her phone and saw that the call had ended. Jake had either given up or been shunted to voice mail. Breathing, feeling the winter chill creeping in now that her muscles were at rest, she watched the phone and waited for it to tell her there was a voice message. A full minute passed before she decided that Jake had simply hung up.

With a glance to make sure she wouldn't bump into anyone, Miri started walking toward home. Her heart still beat its running rhythm and her arms and legs felt good, ready to work, but her phone seemed an anchor in her hand.

At the intersection with Carpenter Street she turned left instead of right, toward home. Four shifts a week, in between classes at the university and the tutoring she did to help pay for school, Miri worked at a café and performance space called Mocha, which would have been cooler if it hadn't been across the street from a hair salon. There was nothing hipster about blue-haired old ladies.

Still, she loved Mocha and the friends she'd made while working there. Right now she wanted coffee as much for warmth as for the companionship it would bring. Most of the time she preferred being alone, felt her soul expand in isolation, her understanding of the world growing. But not today.

Swearing quietly, she glanced at her phone and went to the Recent Calls screen. Her thumb hovered over JAKE. She didn't have to call him back — if it was something important he would call again — but her heart held a certain amount of guilt where Jake Schapiro was concerned. When she'd left Coventry, she'd left him as well. Sometimes she felt like it was good to be rid of him, healthy to put behind her a relationship that had been poisoned by mutual grief more than a decade before. Other times she missed him and resented him for being the one person from Coventry she hadn't been able to forget.

The phone buzzed in her hand.

This time she didn't hesitate.

'It's awful early,' she said, glancing ahead at the welcoming sight of the stylized, steaming coffee cup on the sign in front of Mocha, a block away. 'Tell me it's good news.'

No sound came through the phone. Even the telltale hollowness of an open line was absent. The call was just as flat and dead as the first one had been. *Must be dropping calls*, she thought, and was about to hit the red button to end the call when someone spoke.

'*Miri*.'

She froze, phone clutched to her ear. The

203

Mocha sign seemed a thousand miles away. Winter seemed to sense an opening, sliding into the space between clothing and flesh and then somehow between flesh and bone. When she inhaled, she felt the frost in her lungs.

The voice did not belong to Jake.

'*Miri, honey?*'

Impossible.

'Daddy?'

Niko Ristani had wandered off in a blizzard in search of help and ended up frozen to death. Her father had been dead twelve years, but there could be no question — it was his voice on the phone.

'*Come home, Miri. I need you here. Jake and Allie need you, too.*'

The February morning had made her skin so cold that her hot tears stung her face.

'Daddy,' she whispered, staring at the Mocha sign ahead but feeling as if the ground had suddenly slanted, as if she had slipped sideways out of the world. 'Is it really you?'

'*The storm is coming back to Coventry, Miri. Everyone we loved is in danger. I want to help them but the only way I can do that is through you.*'

A hiss of static burst from the phone, a wail and shush that might have been interference or might have been wind and ice.

'I don't understand,' she said softly. 'What kind of — '

'*Miri,*' he said, his voice almost lost in the static.

The line went dead. Numb, not breathing, she

204

looked at the phone. Two words were on the screen — CALL FAILED — but there were two other words echoing in her mind, the last words she thought she had made out amid that hiss before the call had been cut off.

Come home.

11

The lunchtime crowd that Sunday at The Vault could have been charitably described as thin. The plows had finished up their work in midmorning and the sun had done a perfect job of melting whatever ice remained on the roads. The temperature had risen above forty degrees — warm for February — and narrow little streams of snowmelt ran along the drifts and into sewer gratings. The warm-up would not last very long, especially with a more troubling storm just days away, but for the moment Coventry was a winter wonderland. People should have been out taking advantage of it, but there were fewer than fifteen customers inside The Vault.

Halfway through playing an obscure old tune by The National, TJ glanced at the clock. He hit a wrong note and sang over it, hoping nobody noticed. The hands of the clock were crawling toward one P.M. and he knew Ella must be thinking the same thing he was — where were the Faithful? They never used the phrase at the restaurant, but at home that was how they always referred to the people who rolled in between twelve and one, after the eleven o'clock Mass had gotten out. Without the Faithful, there wasn't much point in opening for lunch on Sundays.

As he sang and played he glanced around the restaurant again. He spotted Mrs. Bridges and

Mr. McFarland, a pair of single oldsters who had become regulars for Sunday lunch. At their age, he figured, they didn't call each other boyfriend and girlfriend, but Ella had told him they'd both lost spouses to cancer and seemed to have a very nice thing going on Sundays — Mass, and then lunch at The Vault. Their presence reassured him that there hadn't been some church boycott of the restaurant, but that was cold comfort.

He finished the song to a smattering of polite applause from the table nearest the corner where he always set up. Everyone else in the place seemed to think the music must be coming from speakers somewhere. Up until the economy had bottomed out, Ella had done a robust Sunday-brunch business. Sometimes TJ had played and at other times he had arranged for various local musicians to come in. Jazz, blues, folk, and holiday music when the Christmas season rolled around. But people without jobs didn't go out for Sunday brunch and that wasn't going to change even if Michael Jackson and Whitney Houston got out of their graves to serenade them over Belgian waffles.

TJ glanced around and spotted his coffee on top of his amplifier. What the hell he'd been thinking by leaving it there he had no idea, but he retrieved it and took a sip. It had cooled too much to taste very good but he took another long sip anyway, then set the mug on the floor.

When he looked up, Grace had appeared beside him. She leaned against the wall, sipping pink lemonade and looking as adorable as always in black boots, leggings, a green top, and a white down vest with a faux-fur fringe on the hood. At home she still seemed like his little girl but out in public she liked to adopt a more sophisticated air. If this was what eleven years old brought, the idea of fifteen terrified him.

'Hi, sweetie,' he said, strumming the guitar and adjusting the tuning. 'Did you have lunch?'

'Pot pie,' Grace replied, her nostrils flaring in distaste. 'It's dreadful.'

'You love the pot pie,' he said, bristling a bit. She'd been behaving oddly since breakfast. 'I hope you didn't say that to your mother.'

Grace fixed a disapproving frown upon him. 'Of course not. That would be rude.'

'Good. I don't know what's gotten into you today, but — '

'Why do you do this?'

A shiver passed through him. He couldn't have said why, but he certainly didn't like the way she looked at him.

'Do what?'

He knew he ought to be playing another song, but it wasn't as if the dozen people in the restaurant were paying much attention.

Grace gestured toward empty tables. 'This. I just don't know why you bother.'

'Hey. That's enough of that.' He clicked off his microphone and gave her a withering look. 'You know exactly why I'm here.'

'Enlighten me.'

Enlighten her? He wanted to slap her face. If he had been the kind of man who would ever strike a child, he'd have done just that. On the other hand, he couldn't deny that in the middle

208

of his anger was a tiny spot of pride. What eleven-year-old used the word *enlighten* in a sentence? Grace could probably even spell it properly. Had Ella had that kind of vocabulary in the fourth grade? TJ surely hadn't.

He took her arm, not hard enough to hurt but firmly enough to let her know he meant business. Her lips made a thin line but she did not complain or try to pull away as he drew her nearer, lowering his voice to a whisper.

'I get it, okay?' he said. 'Things have been tense. Maybe your mom and I have been at each other's throats a little, but we love each other and we love you. If we're fighting, that doesn't mean you have to choose sides and it damn well doesn't mean you have to act out to get attention.'

'I'm not acting out.'

'You're being rude and condescending to your parents and you're only eleven years old. That's not okay. Wouldn't be okay if you were twenty or forty, either. We're doing our best for you and for us as a family.'

TJ glanced around to make sure no one had taken an interest in the whispers being traded in the corner. 'They're lean times, kid, but not so lean that you didn't get the whole outfit you've got on for Christmas. I'm here playing because live music is something we can offer that most local restaurants can't afford right now. We can't afford to have anyone else do it, so here I am.'

'It's supposed to bring in customers,' Grace said, her eyes gleaming in the sunlight coming in the window behind them, the same rich

209

chocolate brown as her mother's.

'Exactly,' TJ said.

'Does it seem to you that it's working?' the little girl said, sighing as if she were a teacher about to give up on her student.

TJ flinched. Another ripple went through him but this wasn't anger; it felt more like embarrassment. He worked his jaw, tamping down the urge to snap at her.

'We're doing everything we know how to do,' he whispered. 'It'll turn around.'

The Vault had cut back its hours so that it was closed on Mondays and Tuesdays and open for lunch only on the weekends. The landlord had cut the rent considerably, knowing that the chances of getting another restaurant into the space in difficult times were slim.

'Will it?' Grace asked, sipping her pink lemonade.

'I just said it would,' TJ barked.

A clink of silverware brought him around. He blinked and saw that half-a-dozen heads had turned and some of the customers were observing them now. He swore inwardly. Most of these people were regulars. They couldn't afford to scare even one of them away.

'Listen,' he said, bending to get his coffee mug. 'Do me a favor, all right? Go and get your dad a fresh cup of coffee.'

He held the cup out to her. For a moment Grace looked at it with disdain that bordered on a sneer and then, reluctantly, she took it from him with her free hand.

'Sure,' she said, starting to turn away.

TJ clicked his microphone back on.

'But . . . Dad?'

He glanced at her.

'She doesn't appreciate it,' Grace said, tossing her head to get her hair out of her eyes. 'You realize that, don't you? You're like the band that kept playing while the *Titanic* went down. You're doing all you can to keep her dream alive, but she never spares a moment to wonder what happened to *your* dreams.'

The microphone probably hadn't picked up what Grace had said, but it would catch his voice for sure. It took him a second or two of numb astonishment to react, and then he reached up to click the mic off again, but Grace was already walking away.

'This place is *doomed*,' she said.

She smiled, then, but it didn't reach her eyes. They were grim and knowing, not cruel but brutally cold.

That is not an eleven-year-old, he thought. And then he gave a dry, humorless laugh, knowing that must be what every parent thought at one point or another.

As he started into another song, his anger turned to worry. The ugliness between him and Ella had begun to tear their daughter up inside. What she'd said had some truth in it, and that hurt, but it hurt far worse for him to think of what they were doing to her childhood.

Something had to change, for Grace's sake. He hoped that his marriage could be healed, but he thought the status quo would be even worse for Grace's psyche than divorce.

211

He watched his daughter go up to the bar and offer up his coffee mug for a refill. Leaning against the bar, back arched in a confident, almost defiant pose, she looked over at him and gave a little shrug and toss of her head, as if to say, *Sorry, Dad, it's just tough love.* When the bartender, Herbie, had poured a fresh cup of coffee, Grace touched his hand and mouthed a thank-you. Everything about the gesture — the look in her eyes, the way she stood, the small, knowing, confident smile — gave off the aura of a grown woman, not a child.

TJ lost his place in the song and faked it, repeating an earlier verse.

Nobody seemed to notice. *Or maybe it's just that nobody cares.* He didn't like to think that, but Grace's callous pragmatism had rubbed off on him.

As she came back to him with the coffee, he watched her poise and gait.

Who the hell are you?

The thought startled and saddened him, haunting him for the rest of the set. It felt to him as if, when he wasn't looking, some grown-up girl had replaced his baby. It happened to every father. He'd known the day would come but had never suspected it would be so soon, and now he was blindsided.

His little girl was gone.

★　★　★

Doug Manning stood near the foot of his bed, trying to pull on a blue cotton hooded sweater

212

while conducting a phone conversation.

'Yeah, I'm watching NECN right now,' he said quietly, switching the cell from one ear to the other as he dragged the sweater over his head. 'They just did the weather. Looks like it's gonna hit us on Wednesday, twenty inches or more. Slow-moving. It's a monster.'

A chill went through him that he knew a lot of people in Coventry would share. Watching the computer model of the storm churning in from the west, all he could think about was blinding snow, a city buried in paralyzing drifts of white, and the frostbitten cheeks of his wife when they'd finally found her and brought him in to identify her corpse.

This storm would be different, though. Instead of destroying his life it would help him build a new one.

'Looks like this is it,' Franco said on the other end of the line.

'Looks like,' Doug replied.

'Are you up to it? Second thoughts? You lose your nerve in the middle of this thing and me and Baxter maybe end up in jail. I can't take the risk.'

Doug tamped down the anger rising in him. 'You kick a dog enough and he can't help biting you, man. I've been kicked enough over the years. I'm ready to start biting, and I'm gonna sink my teeth in deep.'

'What the hell you talkin' about, man?'

'I'm ready, that's all. I'm not going to screw this up. If the plan goes south it's going to be one of you guys who blew it.'

213

Franco grunted. 'Better not let Baxter hear you talking like that. You'll get him paranoid about working with you.'

'Fuck Baxter. It's happening this week, during this storm. I have one chance at really turning things around and I'll do it alone if it comes to that. I ain't doing this for fun and I sure as hell ain't doing it for you and Baxter.'

Franco went quiet. A few seconds of silence passed between them while the sports guy reported on the Celtics' latest winning streak.

'I don't think of you as a friend,' Franco said at last.

'Feeling's mutual.'

'No, listen up. I think of you as a tool — '

'Franco — '

'A tool is useful as long as it works,' Franco went on. 'You don't want to see your place in this, I can't be responsible for what happens.'

Doug laughed softly, but loud enough for Franco to hear him over the phone.

'I'm no master criminal, that's true,' he said, with a glance at the bedroom door to make sure that Angela hadn't come back upstairs. 'But this is my plan. My goddamned idea. Never mind that I'm the one who got us the house keys; I'm the one whose ass is on the line. Somehow I managed to give you the impression that I'm some kind of pussy, maybe because I haven't been ripping people off since my cradle days the way you and Baxter have. But this is my gig, man. The keys are mine. The life I've been living since I lost my wife . . . if I'm gambling my life and my house and my freedom, that doesn't feel

214

like a lot of risk to me. So we're either in this together, all of us, or I try to pull it off myself. You want to trade bullets over it, let's go and do it. Otherwise, stop pushing me. You want me to bare my throat to you like we're some dog pack, but it's not gonna happen, Franco.'

Again, Franco hesitated. The anger churning inside Doug started to cool and harden into grim confidence when he heard that silence on the line. He felt good, really good, for the first time in so long. While Angela had gone downstairs to make them some lunch, he'd taken a shower and shaved and pulled on clean clothes. Watching the weather forecast had filled him with a peculiar excitement, a dreadful anticipation.

'You going to say all this to Baxter when we meet tomorrow?' Franco asked.

'I am.'

'All right, Dougie. We'll see how that goes. You might regret asking to meet in the damn woods instead of somewhere public where he'd be less likely to snap your neck.'

'I guess we'll find out,' Doug replied.

He ended the call without saying good-bye and tossed the phone onto the bed. He felt powerful somehow. Energized.

'Well, *that* was interesting.'

Doug looked up to see Angela standing in the doorway with a tray of grilled cheese sandwiches and coffee, which were just about all his kitchen had to offer at the moment.

He blew out a long breath. 'How much of that did you hear?'

She arched an eyebrow. 'Enough to know

215

you've been a bad boy.'

Doug picked up the remote and clicked off the TV, trying to interpret her facial expression.

'You don't seem all that troubled.'

Angela slid the lunch tray onto the low bureau. She started to speak and then her smile faltered and a terrible sadness seemed to descend upon her. Powerful emotion made her voice crack when she tried to speak, and she waved a hand in front of her face, mustering control of herself.

'Sorry,' she said, forcing a smile.

Doug took a step toward her, hands up, wanting to comfort her. 'I didn't mean for you to hear any of that, and I'm sorry, but I can't apologize for any of it.'

With her sad smile, she put a hand on his chest, grabbing a fistful of his sweater. 'I'm not looking for apologies and I'm not gonna judge you. The world owes *you* an apology, babe.'

Doug stared at her, having trouble processing her acceptance. They'd had a brief, torrid relationship several years ago. Angela had been just as broken and needy as he'd been and they'd abused each other emotionally, each forgiving the other. By nature she was loud and a bit crass and rough in the manner of young beasts who don't know their own strength.

'Who the hell *are* you?' he asked.

Angela stepped in close to him, pressed her body against his and her lips to the softness of his throat.

'I'm the woman who's not running away.'

'What I can't figure out is why.'

With a soft kiss, she pushed him backward until he struck the bed and sat down, and then she straddled him playfully. They were both fully clothed and she made no effort to undress him or herself, just touched his face and gazed into his eyes with something like love. She couldn't love him; Doug felt sure of that. They didn't know each other well enough. But something in her eyes made his mouth go dry.

'You may be up to no good, but you're a good man,' she said, almost in a whisper, more vulnerable than he had ever seen her before. 'I don't like the idea of you doing something criminal mostly because it makes me afraid for you. I know you're not some killer or rapist and you're not going to really hurt anyone. You're stealing from someone, right?'

He knew he ought to keep his mouth shut. A crazy thought struck him: could her showing up have been something other than serendipity? Had Baxter somehow sent her? Or the cops?

Her eyes put the lie to that.

'Yeah. Something like that,' he confessed, drawing in a deep breath, feeling something inside him that he didn't quite understand.

Why was he telling her the truth? He'd never been the kind of guy who turned into a fool in a woman's presence. Only Cherie had ever had that effect on him. He thought of Jack Nicholson, of a famous line in one of his movies that he'd always told Cherie applied to the two of them: *You make me want to be a better man.*

'And you're not going to take anything from someone they can't afford to lose?'

217

'No.'

She smiled. 'Told you.'

Doug slid his fingers into her hair, bent to kiss her, and stopped.

'You're just going to trust my word? You're so sure I'm a good man?'

Angela's only answer was a kiss.

'Listen,' she said, adjusting herself on his lap, rocking a little bit as she straddled him, rubbing denim against denim. 'This thing that happened last night and this morning . . . I think it's going pretty well, don't you?'

'Is that a trick question?' he asked, enjoying the friction.

She grinned. 'Me too. And I'm not ready to let it end. I don't want to freak you out but I called my boss from downstairs and told her I'm taking a week of my accumulated vacation time from the hospital, starting now. We had something, once upon a time . . . the beginning of something, anyway. And I want to see if we can make it grow again.'

Doug's pulse had begun to race. He let out a shuddery breath and pushed against her, grabbing her ass and pulling her more tightly to him.

'*Something*'s growing,' he said.

'Hey,' she said, giving him a little slap on the arm that made him laugh and wince at the same time. 'I'm serious.'

'I know you are,' he said, stroking her hair. 'And I'm not gonna lie. It's a little fast. Kind of abrupt. What we had before . . . it didn't feel like romance to me, y'know? It felt like two people

218

trying to save each other from drowning.'

Angela kissed him gently, breathing words into his mouth.

'This feels different, doesn't it? From before?'

'Completely,' he said, pulling her down onto the bed.

They made love again, lunch entirely forgotten, and if Doug forgot himself amid the passion and whispered his dead wife's name into her ear, Angela seemed not to notice, or not to mind.

★　★　★

Officer Harley Talbot hated the stereotype of the doughnut-eating cop, which meant that every time he pulled into the Heavenly Donuts parking lot he felt as if he were somehow betraying his fellow police. Not that most cops shared his concerns. A morning never passed at the Coventry police station without a couple of dozen doughnuts being put out on the table in the break room and then slowly devoured, usually by men. Even now, female officers had to work their butts off to be treated equally by their superiors, and one of the ways they did that was by staying fit, working harder, and making more arrests.

Harley appreciated that in so many ways. He knew what it was like to hold oneself to higher standards than those around you. His size and the unusual darkness of his skin caused people to make assumptions about him and he proved them wrong through his actions and words. It came in handy, being able to intimidate the hell out of most people just by looking their way without a smile on his face. But it could be tiresome as hell. The last thing he needed was another assumption being made about him. But Heavy D, as some of his brothers and sisters in blue called the doughnut shop, made the best damn cup of cocoa in town. And he loved his cocoa.

He'd been out all night looking for Zachary Stroud and had been ordered home shortly after sunrise. Four hours' sleep and a shower later and now he was in uniform and headed back to the river to rejoin the search.

Pulling into the parking lot of Heavenly Donuts, he slouched a little in his seat, barely conscious of it, then parked his patrol car up against a snowbank in the back. They had a drive-through, but he'd developed a nice rapport with the staff, and when he had a few minutes he liked to see them in person. When he went in and chatted with the owner, Rick Newell, or one of his employees, he always got an extra helping of whipped cream on his cocoa.

Harley worked hard to keep fit and treated his body right, but a man couldn't resist a little extra whipped cream. He was only human, after all.

As he strode to the doughnut shop, shoes squelching in the dirty slush, the door slammed open and a young guy hustled out and nearly collided with him.

'Whoa,' Harley said, grabbing the guy's shoulders and nudging him back to arm's length. 'Watch it, man.'

The guy looked up and Harley blinked in surprised recognition. Nat Kresky went to the local community college and worked at Heavenly Donuts to pay his way. He still lived with his parents but covered the minimal tuition with his savings and what he made slinging coffee. Harley had never seen Nat without a smile on his face — the kid always piled on the whipped cream for him — but this afternoon, Nat looked lost in despair and confusion.

'Sorry,' Nat mumbled, and tried to go around.

Harley grabbed his arm. 'Nat, what's the matter? Something happen?'

Ordinary human concern had prompted the question, but so had cop instincts. Harley believed his were pretty good, and something told him this kid wasn't upset just about a girlfriend dumping him or bad news at home. He didn't know Nat well, but they'd talked enough for him to see how far off the rails his troubles had sent him.

When Nat looked at him, though, Harley wondered if maybe he didn't know the kid at all.

'I'm fine, Officer. Sorry, but . . . I'm fine.'

He tried to pull away but Harley held him without effort.

' 'Officer'?' Harley said.

'Sorry,' Nat replied, glancing down at his name tag. 'Officer Talbot. Can I *go* now?'

Harley released him but blocked his way. 'What's up with you, Nat? You hit your head? You okay?'

'I'm not okay,' the kid spat, shooting an angry glance back at the door of the shop. 'I just got

221

fired 'cause I don't know how to work the stupid machines!'

Harley's insides gave a little twist. Getting fired was the least of Nat's troubles.

'Nat, what's my name?'

'What, did I pronounce it wrong?' the kid whined, glancing away with the petulance of a middle-schooler. 'Officer Talbot.'

'You don't know me?'

A change came over the kid instantly, like a wave passing through his body, an alarm bell that had just gone off in his head and echoed inside him. His eyes went dull and crafty.

'Course I do.'

Harley didn't believe him. 'What is it, then? My first name?'

Nat hesitated, caught.

'You screwed up at work 'cause you couldn't remember how to work the machines. That's what you're saying, right?' Harley asked. 'There's not much to them, and Mr. Newell's a good guy, so I'm figuring it had to do with the cash register, screwing up orders, the kind of stuff you've been doing here for years.'

Nat's lower lip quivered. 'He thought I was on drugs, all right? They all thought I was on drugs! He should know I'd never . . . '

The kid silenced himself, turning away. 'Just leave me alone, okay? I'm going home. I just need sleep.'

Harley shifted to intercept him, not letting him leave.

'It's more than that, Nat, and I can tell you know it. You don't even recognize me and we see each other three or four times a week right inside the shop. Something's goin' on in your head. Hop in the car and I'll run you over to the hospital. You need a doc to check you out, make sure it's not serious.'

Nat wouldn't look him in the eye. 'I'm just going home. I'll get my dad to take me.'

Again he tried to pass by and this time Harley grabbed his arm harder. He pointed toward the cruiser he'd parked in back.

'Get in,' he said. 'You wanna go home first, that's fine. I'll take you there. No way I'm going to let you drive. It's either me or I call you an ambulance.'

Nat's lips were pressed into a thin, angry line. Harley had expected the kid to stamp his foot, but finally he started for the patrol car.

'Fine,' Nat huffed. 'But this is stupid.'

Harley followed, hoping the kid was right. But you didn't suffer the kind of memory loss Nat was showing signs of without having something wrong with you, some trauma or an aneurysm or something.

As he got the kid into the backseat, he spared one last, regretful glance at Heavenly Donuts. He had a terrible feeling he wasn't going to get his cocoa today.

12

Recent years had brought some unseasonably mild winters, but this had not been one of them. The cold weather had swept down from Canada in early November and never really abated for more than a day or so. There were times when the sun shone brightly enough to chase the chill away for a few hours. Now, late afternoon brought on the early arrival of darkness that had always made Joe Keenan want to hole up inside his house with a book and a few logs burning in the fireplace. In early February, spring seemed somehow further away than ever.

He leaned against the hood of his unmarked, drinking weak coffee that tasted like it had been strained through a brown paper bag, and watched the industrious local-media people setting up lights for the live shots they would do during the five o'clock news. They'd be getting under way anytime now, and the reporters were choosing their shots, figuring out the best places to stand in order to have police or volunteer searchers — or at least the icy river — in the background.

Keenan knew what they'd be reporting: nothing. No headway had been made in the search for Zachary Stroud, which had been going on for nearly fifteen hours without a single lead beyond the initial discovery of the boy's blood inside the car. The vehicle itself had been

224

removed long ago, as had the corpses of Zachary Stroud's parents. Searchers had combed the woods by the river and begun a door-to-door canvass, hoping to find someone who had seen the boy wandering in last night's storm or even this morning — maybe wet, maybe bleeding.

The Coventry Harbor Master had come out and taken a look at the river, confirming what Keenan had already guessed: while the current ran strong under the frozen surface, there was too much ice for them to attempt to drag the river in search of a body. State-police divers had gone into the water in midmorning, picking places up and down the bank to enter and search beneath the ice, but to no avail. Keenan didn't believe the boy had fallen into the river, but even if he had, the chances of their finding his body down there were slim.

He sipped his lukewarm, paper-bag-tasting coffee and watched the last of the sun sliding behind the roof-and-treetops on the western cityscape. Going without sleep had become just part of the job over the years, but that didn't mean he didn't get tired. His eyes burned and his body felt like he had suddenly found himself on a planet with heavier gravity, every step a slog. Since last night his only fuel had been crappy coffee and a slice of cold pizza, but he had passed beyond hunger by now.

A rookie in uniform tramped through the trees to the line of cars where Keenan rested. The detective tried to remember his name.

'Taking five?' Keenan asked.

'Maybe ten,' the rookie replied. He seemed

troubled and distracted, shifting around as he poured himself a Styrofoam cup of crappy coffee from the little snack table some volunteers had set up. 'What about you?'

'My brain is fried,' Detective Keenan said. 'Tired as I am, I might see Bigfoot out there.'

Instead of the chuckle Keenan had expected, the rookie gave him a dark look. 'You're giving up on the kid?'

The detective bristled. 'Who said anything about giving up?'

'A lot of the searchers are saying there's no way he could've survived in the storm last night, or he drowned, or whatever,' the rookie said.

Something about his tone made Keenan take a closer look at the man. His name tag identified him as Marco Torres. Short, muscular, black hair buzzed close to his scalp, he'd been with the Coventry PD just a few months, but apparently he thought that gave him the experience to needle a detective.

'It's weird,' Keenan said. 'You say that, but it doesn't sound like you believe it.'

What it really sounded like, to Keenan, was a test of faith, like Torres had thrown out that comment to see if the detective would agree with him, like a girlfriend commenting on the beauty of another woman just to gauge her guy's response.

'I don't know what to believe,' Officer Torres said, turning away as he sipped his coffee. 'I just hope we find him soon, or that he's got somewhere warm to spend the night. Nobody should have to die alone, out in the cold, especially not a child.'

Though he agreed, something about the guy's tone still troubled Keenan. He studied the rookie from behind, trying to decipher what it was about Torres that set him on edge.

The sound of tires on gravel made Detective Keenan turn. In the gloaming of the day, light fading, a familiar, unmarked Crown Victoria pulled onto the shoulder and stopped. The engine shut off, ticking as it cooled. Keenan didn't have to be able to see through the tinted windows to know who was behind the wheel and his belief was confirmed when the door popped open and Lieutenant Duquette emerged. The fiftyish man had a rounded belly, a walrus mustache, and a balding pate, and he wore round little glasses that reminded Keenan of the aging actor in the diabetes commercials that were always on TV.

'Torres,' Keenan said.

The rookie turned around just as the lieutenant approached them, hitching up his belt. Lieutenant Duquette glanced at Torres but then turned his entire attention on Keenan.

'You look like shit, Joe.'

Keenan nodded. 'Thank you, sir.'

'I'm not kidding. You've been out here too long. It's taking a toll. You should rein things in a little, go home and get some sleep.'

'I don't look much better than this on my best day, Lieutenant.'

'I'm not asking, Detective.'

Keenan frowned. He was aware of Officer Torres watching them but this seemed very personal and he had no idea why that might be.

'What's changed?' he asked.

The lieutenant arched an eyebrow. 'I don't take your meaning.'

'You tried to get me to pull back on the search this morning and here you are, in person. Sorry, but I just want to know if there's been a break in the case I don't know about, because it seems to me we've still got a missing kid.'

Lieutenant Duquette shot a glance at Torres. 'Give us some breathing room, would you, Officer? But don't go far. I'll need you momentarily.'

'Yes, sir,' Torres replied, taking his coffee off in the direction of the lieutenant's Crown Vic because his other choices were toward the river or toward the media.

When Torres had excused himself, the lieutenant took a step closer to Keenan, invading the detective's personal space with his belly and his 'stache and his bad breath.

'The Stroud boy must be in the river,' Lieutenant Duquette said. 'We've gone house to house on all of the adjacent streets, combed the woods, checked the hospitals, put out a call for help through the media . . . it doesn't take a detective to realize there's only one logical explanation.'

The last bit had been meant as a jab, Keenan knew. He felt it, but didn't let it show.

'The divers found nothing,' he said, dumping out the rest of his paper-bag coffee. 'There are other possibilities. And there is zero evidence that the kid went into the water. None. Maybe you don't believe he's still out there, but I do.

Zachary Stroud was injured in the accident and wandered off. Maybe he hit his head and he's confused. Maybe he asked the wrong person for help and got abducted. Hell, maybe the crash was no accident and the whole thing was set up to snatch the kid.'

'That's ridiculous.'

'But not impossible,' Keenan insisted, his irritation burning some of the exhaustion out of him.

The lieutenant sighed and it was like the sound of a whale venting from its blowhole. Stroking his mustache, Duquette looked around and then turned back to Keenan, lowering his voice to a conspiratorial tone.

'The search isn't coming up with anything, Joe. We've done all we can on the ground. The divers will be back in the water tomorrow but we're cutting back on the man power out here. We'll keep leading searches for a couple of days on a smaller scale, but if we still haven't found him by then, the river gets the blame.'

Detective Keenan knew better than to argue any further. The decision had been made, and as much as he hated it, he understood.

'All right,' he said. 'I've got two more days.'

The lieutenant's eyes narrowed and he tapped one finger to Keenan's chest.

'Go home, Joe. You're no good to this kid if you can't even think straight,' the lieutenant said. He turned and called to Torres to return to them. 'I'm going to make sure you get home in one piece. I don't want you behind the wheel on so little sleep.'

'I'm fine, Lieutenant — '

'No, Joe. You're not. You're going home. Unless you want to tell me what makes you so damned special?'

'What?' Keenan said, unable to hide his anger. 'When have I ever — '

'Do you honestly think all of these other police officers and the volunteers — some of them firefighters and EMTs and veterans — do you really think they need you here to tell them what to do?'

Detective Keenan faltered, exhaling, feeling all the anger bleeding out of him. Much as he hated to admit it, the lieutenant had him.

'Of course not,' he said.

Lieutenant Duquette nodded, then cleared his throat as he turned back to the rookie.

'Officer Torres, I'm worried about Detective Keenan falling asleep behind the wheel. Run him home, would you?'

Minutes later, Keenan sat in the passenger side of his own car as Torres chauffeured him. Another officer would swing by and pick Torres up afterward. The nighttime rushed in around them, somehow managing to make the car's headlights seem altogether brighter.

They rode in silence for a while before Torres piped up.

'Ugly storm coming,' the rookie said. 'Weatherman says it could be as bad as the Big One.'

'So I hear.'

Silence, save for the purr of the engine and the tires on pavement and the occasional burst of police-radio static.

'I don't know how you kept it together after that night,' Torres said, his voice flat, carefully neutral.

Detective Keenan turned slowly to look at him.

Torres flexed his fingers on the steering wheel and shifted in his seat, feeling Keenan's displeasure.

'I'm just saying,' Torres went on. 'It had to be traumatic for you, those two boys being electrocuted, one of them dying right in front of you. Then the father just vanishes. It has to change you, something like that. I only wondered if it made you care more in a case like this, or care less, and just work harder so you don't have to add to the guilt you're already — '

'Who the fuck do you think you are?' Keenan shouted.

'Sorry. I didn't mean anything. I just heard about — '

'You've been with the department what, six months?'

Expressionless, Torres gripped the wheel and kept his eyes forward. 'Something like that.'

'And you think you've earned the right to ask me questions like that?' Keenan said, fuming, slowing his breathing, trying to get a handle on his anger. His pain. 'You don't know me, Torres. Don't ever talk to me about the storm again, or about anything I might think or feel. Just do your job and I'll try my best to keep you from being shot in the back of the head by some meth-head because you've got no common sense and you've alienated your fellow officers.'

231

'Detective, I — '

'Shut it.'

Torres complied, but for only a minute or two. When he took the turn onto Detective Keenan's street, just blocks from his house, the rookie made the mistake of speaking up again.

'You're not going to give up, are you?' Torres asked hopefully, as if he'd never asked a more important question in his life. 'Just tell me that much.'

'Hell no,' Keenan said, still fuming. He shook his head in frustration.

The tires skidded in sand as Torres braked in front of Keenan's house. Detective Keenan popped the door and got out, sticking out his hands for the keys, which Torres promptly turned over.

'The higher-ups want us to move on already, but I intend to find that kid,' Keenan said. 'Alive.'

Torres slammed the door to Keenan's car, then leaned on the roof. For all his deference before, his expression had turned defiant.

'I only ask because of the bang-up job you're doing so far,' Torres said, biting off the words. 'Your track record of bringing missing kids home alive kind of sucks.'

Keenan snapped, all rational thought driven out of him. He circled around the front of the car, keys gripped in his right fist, anger boiling in his head and heart.

'You son of a bitch,' he sneered. 'How fucking dare you?'

He issued no threats. Threats were for people

who still saw a path other than violence. In his mind's eye he could see Torres's nose broken and bleeding, jaw swollen and teeth missing.

Torres made no apology. Instead, he scowled and stood there waiting, his own hands curled into fists. Younger and probably faster, the rookie looked formidable. Keenan faked a punch, grabbed his wrist when he tried to block, then head-butted the prick with enough force to make his head ring.

The rookie reeled away from him, staggered, and went down on one knee. Keenan watched Torres's gun. He didn't know the guy, had no idea how far he'd go. Keenan leaned in toward him, still flexing his hands, wanting to do more damage.

'You don't know a damn thing about that night.'

Ready for a fight, knowing the disciplinary action he would face and not caring, Keenan braced himself. But when Torres looked up at him, Keenan saw the one thing for which he wasn't prepared. The last thing he would have expected.

Tears.

'You might be surprised,' Torres said through gritted teeth.

Keenan took a step back. Before he could figure out how to react, he heard a vehicle approaching and looked up to see a patrol car rolling down the street toward them.

Torres stood, quickly wiping at his eyes, and it was as if the tears had never been there at all.

'What do you mean by that?' Keenan asked, as

the cruiser pulled to a stop.

Torres opened the passenger door, turning back to face Keenan.

'Sorry, Detective,' the rookie said. 'My ride's here.'

He slumped into the seat and slammed the door. Keenan stood and watched the car pull away, his skull still ringing, trying to figure out what the hell had just happened. Everyone in Coventry started acting hinky when a big storm was on the way and the one due Wednesday was a monster. How else could he explain the way Torres had talked to him and the violence of his own reprisal? He'd never been a brawler, even when somebody pushed his buttons the way Torres had.

Maybe Torres had lost someone he loved in what they called the Big One. *The killer storm*, he thought. The upside was that now he knew there was at least one person as convinced as he was that Zachary Stroud could be found.

If the kid was out there, even if someone had snatched him up, Detective Keenan would find him.

Before the *next* storm rolled in.

★ ★ ★

Ella pulled into the driveway and killed the engine quickly, dousing the headlights, surprised to find her heart racing. She smiled to herself in the darkness inside her car, a strange excitement building. It seemed a pitiful thing that this many years into her marriage she ought to feel the sort of uncertainty that gripped her, the exhilaration that came with a moment of daring, a breathtaking venture out on a narrow limb.

Maybe that's what's wrong with us, she thought. *Not enough time spent out on a limb.* She and TJ had become expert at hiding their emotions instead of laying them bare, and Ella knew that was wrong. Love meant risking your heart, and she had spent too much time over the past few years swathing hers in layers of dissatisfaction and indifference that had more to do with herself than with her husband.

Ella stepped out of the car and closed the door softly, pressing the button on her key fob to lock it. A wave of reluctance swept over her — what if she made a fool of herself? Her face burned at the mere thought of it. After all the arguments and the nights they'd spent with their backs to each other in their marriage bed — the space between them taking on a weight of its own and growing heavier by the week — the wrong word or the wrong glance could end it. The past day or so, she had felt the ice beginning to thaw between them, but she knew it was a tenuous thing. One more ugly moment might kill the life they'd made together.

She took a deep breath, then went and unlocked the door. Slipping quietly inside, she paused in the foyer and breathed in the scent of something delicious in the oven. With a curious frown she went through the sitting room and stood in the open kitchen doorway, watching her husband stirring something in a small pot on the stove. Scruffy as ever, he wore a thick green cotton sweater, threadbare blue jeans, and socks with no shoes. In that moment it felt as if ten years had been erased from the calendar and they existed in a simpler time. Nostalgia stabbed her in the heart.

'Hey,' she said, her voice cracking.

TJ spun around, startled, and put a hand to his chest. 'Jeez!' he said. 'What are you trying to do, give me a heart attack?'

She smiled. 'What are you cooking?'

'That phyllo-wrapped chicken thing with the scallions and the red-pepper sauce. It won't be ready for a while, though. I didn't . . . '

'Didn't expect me for at least a couple of hours,' she said. 'Were you making this just for yourself?'

His brow knitted. 'Of course not. You haven't been eating at the restaurant lately and I figured when you came home, you might . . . ' He shook his head. 'You know what? Never mind.'

Ella sighed. 'I didn't mean it like that, sweetie. I swear to God. I just thought maybe somebody had called and tipped you off that I was coming home early.'

He looked like he might want to continue being angry, to fuel the argument, but instead he turned his back to her and stirred his sauce.

'What brings you home so early anyway?'

Heart pounding, she realized her palms were a little damp and chuckled softly at herself. Fortunately, TJ didn't hear — the last thing they needed was for him to think she'd been laughing at him.

She crossed the kitchen and stepped up

236

behind him, hands resting tentatively on his hips before she slid them around to his belly, embracing him and laying her cheek against his back.

'Us,' she said.

TJ stiffened but she did not back away, just held on to him and held her breath. After a moment he began to turn and she had to release him so that he could face her.

'What's going on, Ella?' he asked, studying her carefully.

'I left early. Gary's closing for me. I just . . . ' She dropped her gaze. 'I wanted to come home.'

She hated how fragile she sounded, hated the way she had just exposed herself to him. She knew how easy it was to be injured in a vulnerable moment; she had done it to him often enough.

TJ said nothing. Long seconds passed until at last she lifted her eyes and found him staring at her with a sadness so profound that it seemed to open a chasm in the floor beneath her.

'Should I not have come?' she asked, thinking about love and risk again, but not favorably this time. She spun away. 'Jesus, should I go back?'

Tears came to her eyes and she angrily swiped at them. They weren't born of sadness or even embarrassment, but surrender.

TJ touched her on the arm. 'Honey, listen — '

She pulled away. 'No, it's okay. I know problems don't vanish just because we pretend they're gone. I just thought — '

'Ella.'

He spoke her name with a quiet fragility of his

own that froze her in place and made her forget whatever words she had intended to speak next.

'I'm glad you're home,' he said in that same voice. She did not turn to face him, afraid that the walls between them that had somehow fallen might reappear. 'I'm always happy to see you, but I'm much happier when *you* want to see me. I want to have dinner together, have a glass of wine, talk about how bad business was today. I want desperately to pretend our problems are gone and hope they'll vanish if we wish hard enough.'

Ella felt so tired. Tired of fighting. Tired of things not going their way. She slumped back against him, letting him take the weight of her bones and her worries. His arms encircled her and he kissed her head and then her temple and then she slid around to face him and TJ kissed her mouth with what felt like a kind of surrender all its own.

'Is it so impossible?' she whispered into the space between them. 'I mean, if we try to stop thinking of them as problems, can't they go away?'

TJ exhaled, holding her hands tightly, and she felt one of the walls going back up between them.

'It's not that simple,' he said.

'I know I can be a bitch. I know it's unfair.'

TJ frowned. 'It's not that. We're both at fault. But no matter how happy I am that you came home and how much I've wished we could talk to each other without all the tension and bullshit . . . '

He glanced past her at the open kitchen doorway, looking wary and troubled. Ella turned to see if they were being watched, if Grace had come in, but they were still alone.

'But?' she asked.

'I think there's a problem we can't wish away.'

TJ looked over at the doorway again and suddenly she understood.

'Grace?' she said quietly. 'What are you talking about?'

He stepped away from her, ran a hand over his face, glancing around as if the words he sought might appear in the air. Whatever they were, he seemed to find them.

'It was weird this morning, right?' he whispered.

Ella nodded. 'A little. But she's — '

He halted her with a raised hand. 'Just listen. She came up to talk to me during my set today and it was even worse. She's talking like . . . '

'Like what?'

TJ cocked his head, staring at her with that imploring look that she knew so well, the one that said, *You know. You know, Ella, don't make me say it.*

'She talks like she's an adult,' he whispered.

'They all do that.'

'No,' he said, raising a finger. 'Not like this. It's like she's this wise, cynical old lady now instead of an eleven-year-old girl. And it's too weird, too . . . intimate. Like she knows us better than we know ourselves.'

Ella felt herself stiffen. She narrowed her eyes. 'I think you're overstating it a little, don't you?

239

Kids are always trying to redefine themselves, figure out what makes the difference between them and adults. When I was nine I told my parents that I had rights and they had no business bossing me around.'

TJ shook his head much more fiercely. 'This *isn't* that. I don't know what it is, but it isn't. Trust me. Better yet, go and take a look at her.'

Ella hesitated, then shrugged. 'Okay. Living room?'

'Yes,' TJ said. 'You go take a look out there and you tell me that she's not acting weird . . . that she's still the same kid.'

'What are you — '

'Go look,' he said with a quiet urgency that got her feet moving.

Ella went back out through the sitting room and foyer to the other side of the house. She could hear the sitcom laugh track even before she entered the living room and she allowed herself to wonder about the thing that had been sneaking around the shadowy corners of her mind for the past couple of minutes. *Is it really Grace who's acting strange, or is it him?*

Then she stepped into the living room.

Grace sat way back on the sofa, tucked primly against the cushions. She wore a yellow cardigan that Ella recognized as having come from her own closet; the eleven-year-old practically vanished inside it. Grace had buttoned the sweater all the way to the top. Across her legs the little girl had thrown an old blue blanket that TJ's late mother had knitted by hand. On the coffee table was a small tray, a porcelain teapot, and a little teacup to match.

Another ripple of laughter came from the television, drawing Ella's gaze to the screen, where a half-century-old episode of *The Dick Van Dyke Show* unspooled in crystal-clear black-and-white. Ella frowned, trying to force her mind to make sense of the scene before her. *It's a game,* she thought. *Some kind of make-believe, like a tea party, only she didn't have anyone to pretend with.*

More canned laughter on the television — Mary Tyler Moore giving her husband the cold shoulder — and it occurred to Ella that most of those laughs, recorded so very long ago, belonged to dead people. *It's like the ghost of laughter,* she thought, and a chill went through her unlike any she'd ever felt before.

Grace leaned forward to pick up her teacup and the motion startled a tiny noise out of Ella. The little girl froze for a moment, aware of her presence, and then continued as if nothing at all had happened, taking a sip of her tea.

Slowly, Grace turned to look at her, teacup in hand, the blue light from the television making strange shadows on her face, and Ella's little girl smiled at her.

'Come and watch with me, Mother,' she said, oh so properly. 'You'll adore this episode. It's one of my favorites.'

Dread traced cold fingers along Ella's spine. Heart pounding, body trembling ever so slightly, she backed up two steps and then fled the room.

13

On Monday morning, Allie stood on the sidewalk in front of Trumbull Middle School, monitoring the cars that were pulling up to the curb so that parents could drop their children off. The school put two teachers out front every morning, ostensibly to greet the students who did not take a bus, but Allie knew that a part of morning drop-off duty was chiding the parents who didn't follow the rules. The instructions were given at the beginning of the year and they were clear. Parents were not to allow students to exit their vehicles until they were at the curb in front of the school, and then only on the passenger side of the car, so they could step right out onto the sidewalk. Still, some of them bypassed the line and let their kids out in the middle of the street, never mind the traffic around them and the possibility that their children might be struck by another vehicle.

Allie hated those people and envied them all at the same time. She hated them for putting their children in danger and envied them for the innocence that allowed them to be so cavalier about the safety of their kids.

They're not safe, she wanted to tell them. *None of them are safe. Sometimes they die.*

It was twelve years since she'd lost Isaac and these thoughts still filled her head every time she

242

had to do morning drop-off duty. Twice a week for twelve years, watching parents take their children's lives for granted.

From time to time she knew that she took it too far, going into the street and sternly admonishing the parents, sometimes allowing a shrill edge to creep into her voice. In those first years after Isaac's death, most of the parents knew that she had lost her son and had the decency to look stricken when she reminded them of the rules. But as the years passed, those children had gone on to high school and their parents had gone with them and fewer and fewer people were aware that she had once had two sons instead of only one.

What an odd thing it was to have endured such a loss and to have daily contact with so many people who had no idea. Allie knew that everyone had tragedies, large and small, that were not visible to those who encountered them each day, and once that anonymity had returned to her school days she found that she appreciated it. She liked being just another teacher — just another mother — and hated those moments in conversation when people learned of Isaac's death for the first time. But morning drop-off was different. When she saw parents being so careless she wanted them to know what those few minutes they might save by skipping the line could cost them.

'Mr. Roche?' Allie said, stepping off the curb.

A couple of students stopped to watch but she smiled and waved them on. 'Get inside, guys. Please.'

The boys walked off, muttering to each other. Allie lifted a hand to signal the driver of a Subaru and moved between the cars waiting in line. Out in the street, Kitty Roche's father had stopped his red Volkswagen parallel to the line and the seventh-grade girl climbed out and then reached inside to retrieve her backpack.

'Mr. Roche?' Allie called, quickening her step.

Kitty — a skinny blond girl with a red bow in her hair — gave her an apologetic look and then slipped her backpack over one shoulder.

Inside the car, Mr. Roche kept one hand on the wheel as he leaned over the passenger seat to peer out at her.

'Sorry, Ms. Schapiro. Just couldn't be helped today. I'm late for a meeting.'

There were so many things she wanted to say to him, so many different ways she could express her fears. More than anything, she wished that she could let him feel for just a few minutes the pain that she carried with her every day . . . if only so that he would never have to feel it again.

'Mr. Roche,' she said, 'better to be late for a meeting than on time for Kitty's funeral.'

He gaped at her.

'Jesus,' Kitty whispered, shooting her a look of wide-eyed horror as she hurried off between the waiting cars and then onto the sidewalk and across the lawn toward the school.

'That's a little much, don't you think?' Mr. Roche said, his expression both angry and bewildered.

Allie felt her cheeks flushing with embarrassment. She hadn't intended the words to come out. She had already reminded half-a-dozen parents about the rules this morning.

'I'm sorry,' she said, as the line of cars continued to move behind her and an SUV coming up the street behind Mr. Roche's VW had to drive around him. 'There are a lot better ways for me to have gotten my point across.'

Mr. Roche looked as if he might still be angry but then his features softened.

'It's all right,' he said. 'I get how frustrating it must be out here, having to police all us rule breakers. But maybe cut down on the caffeine?'

Allie smiled. 'I'll do that if you'll use the line from now on.'

'I'll do my best,' he said. 'But right now I've gotta go.'

Kitty had left the door open because they were talking. Allie was holding him up. Confused and frustrated, wondering how the moment had reversed itself so that she was the one apologizing, she wished him a good day and swung the car door shut. She stepped back as Mr. Roche drove away, leaving her standing on the wrong side of the drop-off line, out in the street.

It's the storm, she thought.

Though it was cold enough for her to be wearing gloves and a scarf and hat, the sun shone, a beautiful blue-sky day, so rare for February. But if the forecast turned out to be accurate, in two days they would be in the middle of a major winter storm, the worst blizzard in years. With such a storm on the way, was it any wonder that her grief seemed heightened, that Isaac's death felt like it had happened twelve days ago instead of twelve years?

What was twelve years after all? She knew that once upon a time, when she was a little girl, she would have thought twelve years an eternity. But as she grew older she had begun to realize that a year was nothing. Twelve years was nothing. She still remembered details from her childhood with clarity, remembered things from a decade ago that seemed like fresh experiences to her. She wondered if she would reach old age and still look back and think the years had passed like nothing. A lifetime . . . was nothing. But it was more than Isaac had gotten.

'Morning, Ms. Schapiro!' a student called.

She turned to see Claire Nguyen waving to her as the girl hurried across the lawn from her mother's car. Allie smiled and waved back.

At least the kids will have a snow day or two, she thought, trying to make light of the dread that had coiled itself like a snake around her heart.

She glanced at the line of cars, made sure Claire's mother saw her, and then slipped between them. She had just reached the sidewalk when she heard the crunch of metal and a squeal of skidding tires. Students making their way across the snowy lawn spun around with wide eyes. Allie ran to Mrs. Nguyen's car and stood on her toes to get a glimpse of a dark blue Cadillac drifting away from the parked pickup truck it had just sideswiped on the other side of the street.

246

The Cadillac coasted toward the back of the morning drop-off line, its driver's-side mirror dangling from some wires.

Students were yelling, some hurrying toward the sidewalk to get a better look.

'Get back!' Allie said. 'All of you get — '

The Cadillac's engine raced, speeding up instead of slowing. It struck the last car in line with a whump of crumpling metal and fiberglass. The chain reaction slammed three or four vehicles into the cars ahead of them, and then it was over with the hissing of a cracked radiator and the enraged swearing of several parents who were already popping open doors and leaping out to survey the damage.

Allie whispered a prayer and rushed to the nearest car, looking in the passenger window at an eighth-grade boy named Ryan Morretti. The kid opened the door and stumbled out.

'Ryan, are you all right?' she asked. 'Are you okay?'

'I'm good,' he said, shaking his head. 'What just happened?'

Allie left him standing there and hurried along the line of cars as the students got out, none of them apparently injured, grabbing their backpacks and walking toward the group of parents who were gathered around the Cadillac. Its hood had buckled, the front end punched in, but the rear end of the little gold Ford Focus ahead of it had been demolished. Both airbags had deployed and now she saw that Lauren Cappuccio and her mother were still in the car. A parent Allie didn't recognize had opened the driver's door and was

247

helping Mrs. Cappuccio extricate herself, so Allie tried to do the same, but Lauren's door had been jammed shut by the collision.

The window had shattered, so Allie crouched and peered in at Lauren. 'Are you okay?'

Ordinarily full of confidence and sarcasm, the girl had gone pale, but she nodded.

'Feel like I got kicked in the chest, but I think I'm okay.'

'You can breathe all right?' Allie asked.

Lauren smiled wanly. 'If I say no, does that mean I don't have to go to school?'

'You probably should have a doctor look you over anyway,' Allie said.

'I can breathe fine, but my ears are ringing,' the girl replied.

'Sit tight. I'll make sure you're taken care of,' Allie said, turning back to the Cadillac.

A shouting match had begun. Mrs. Cappuccio seemed to be trying to calm everyone's nerves but the driver of the Cadillac had the misfortune to have included the queen bitch of the PTO, Helen Smith, in his collision.

'Is everyone okay?' Allie asked, looking for injuries.

Heads turned.

'Does it look like we're okay?' Mrs. Smith barked.

'Actually it does,' Allie said. 'But Mrs. Cappuccio's daughter might have a concussion.'

And how lucky you all are, Allie thought. *Banged up but alive. Your children alive.*

'Oh my god, Lauren,' Mrs. Cappuccio said, rushing around the back of the Cadillac so that

248

she could get to her daughter, passing right by Allie.

Only then did Allie realize that she recognized the driver of the Cadillac. Tall and broad and carrying thirty extra pounds, Eric Gustafson had won election to the city council the year before. His son, Kurt, was one of Allie's students, though Mr. Gustafson had not come in for parents' night or parent-teacher conferences — his wife had come alone. Allie recognized him only from his pictures in the local paper. With his Nordic features, chubby face, and buzz-cut red hair, it would have been hard not to remember him. She wanted to be furious with him but his expression was so pathetic and he was surrounded by so much anger that she could only pity him.

'Are you drunk?' Mrs. Smith demanded, poking Mr. Gustafson in the chest. 'Is that it? Don't think you're going to get away with this just because you're on the city council!'

The other parents — three of them, not including Mrs. Cappuccio — had seemed angry before, but with Mrs. Smith's tirade ringing in the air they all seemed to be feeling more awkward than angry now. All the students had slunk away to a safe distance on the snowy lawn where they could watch and mock with their friends. Even Kurt Gustafson stood twenty yards away, looking alternately enraged and humiliated by his father.

'I'm sorry! It was an accident!' Gustafson protested, his face reddening. He looked on the verge of tears.

'Drunk driving isn't an accident, it's a crime!' Mrs. Smith snapped.

'I'm not drunk!' Mr. Gustafson cried. He looked around as if searching for someone to back him up, and when his eyes lit on Allie, he pushed past the other parents to approach her. 'Ms. Schapiro, please. You can smell my breath. I swear I haven't been drinking.'

Allie stared at him. Maybe he hadn't been drinking but his behavior was certainly odd. Mr. Gustafson seemed on the verge of panic, like a child in trouble for something and trying to get out of it instead of a grown man — a city councilman, no less — facing people who were angry about the damage he'd caused.

'Mr. Gustafson, I have no interest in smelling your breath. You need to calm down.' She looked at the other parents, focusing on Mrs. Smith. 'You *all* need to calm down. It's a fender bender. They happen every day. I'm sure you've all been in one at some point or another.'

'I am going to be late for work!' Mrs. Smith declared, crossing her arms defiantly. The sun glinted off her glasses and picked out the cat hairs that clung to her jacket.

A siren blared in the distance; someone had called the police. Allie turned around and saw the principal, Mr. D'Amato, and the gym coach hustling the students toward the school. Relief flooded her. She would be happy to leave this mess to Mr. D'Amato.

'All of you please go back to your cars,' Allie said, glancing over at Mrs. Cappuccio, who had knelt down on the sidewalk to encourage her daughter. Lauren had begun to release herself from her seat belt and the airbag, making her way to the driver's door.

'Not until I get an answer,' Mrs. Smith said, striding over to where Allie stood with Mr. Gustafson, who had taken up position behind her as if she could shield him from Mrs. Smith's wrath.

'Look, I'm sorry,' Mr. Gustafson said, but he wouldn't meet Mrs. Smith's gaze. He kept shifting his weight from foot to foot, glancing around with an air of awkward frustration. 'But I'm not drunk.'

'If you haven't been drinking, then what the hell were you thinking?' Mrs. Smith demanded. 'You hit that pickup truck back there. I saw you coming in my rearview mirror. You were all over the road and then you hit your damn accelerator instead of the brake, like one of those ninety-year-old ladies who crashes through a convenience-store wall. We all had our children in the car! If you're not drunk, you must be high — '

'I'm not high!' Mr. Gustafson roared.

'Then what happened?' Mrs. Smith roared right back. 'And don't tell me your pedal stuck, because I will slap you right in the — '

'I don't know how to drive a car!' Gustafson shouted.

That silenced them all for a moment.

'I mean . . . ' he fumbled, 'I mean I don't remember how. Something happened to me. I . . . I had to get my son to school and he wanted me to drive him. His mother went in to work

251

early this morning and I was his only ride, but I don't know . . . I can't remember how to drive!'

They all stared. Allie knew there was something he wasn't saying but she could also tell that much of this was the truth because it hurt him so much to reveal it.

A police car turned the corner seconds ahead of an ambulance that came from the other direction. Principal D'Amato had been striding toward the gathered parents but now he redirected himself to meet the police car. Allie glanced around and saw that all the students had gone inside and only the cars involved in the accident remained at the curb. The school bell clamored inside, the sound rolling across the lawn.

Mrs. Smith abandoned them abruptly and marched toward the policeman, probably to insist that Mr. Gustafson be tested for drugs and alcohol. And that was the right thing to do, Allie knew. It might have been an accident, but Gustafson could have killed someone. She didn't like Helen Smith at all — nobody did, really, not even Mr. Smith — but Allie wondered if the bitch might be the only one who really understood what she could have lost this morning.

Penitent and yet somehow also a little petulant, Mr. Gustafson wiped his eyes and waited for the policeman and the principal. Allie stood close to him, though all the others had turned their attention elsewhere.

'Did you hit your head recently?' she found herself asking.

Gustafson looked at her. 'What?'

'Did you hit your head or fall down or something? I mean, people don't usually just forget how to drive.'

He turned away, unwilling to meet her gaze. As she studied him, something occurred to her that made her knit her brow.

'How did you know my name?' she asked.

His expression changed, turning from irritated to anxious. He cast a quick glance her way, as if he was guilty of something, but he didn't answer. A chill ran up her spine.

Then the policeman was there with a pad and pen out, ready to take a statement, and Mr. D'Amato swept Allie away for a private chat so that she could fill him in. As she spoke to the principal she kept glancing back at Mr. Gustafson, but he seemed determined not to look her way.

Leaving her to wonder.

★ ★ ★

Miri lay in bed, looking at the clock on her nightstand, telling herself she ought to get up. The darkness outside her window had begun to lighten with a hint of morning. Soon the sun would rise — as much sun as Seattle was likely to get in February. Sleep had eluded her, save for several brief respites when she had drifted off for fifteen or twenty minutes only to wake again, her late father's voice fresh in her mind, as if he had been speaking to her in her dreams.

The trouble was that he *had* spoken to her,

253

but not in a dream.

She studied the clock as it ticked over toward six A.M., but her true fascination lay not with the time but with the cell phone on the night-stand, just beyond the clock. She'd plugged it into the wall before going to bed to make sure it would be charged today, but she had also turned off the power. The phone lay dormant and harmless and yet she had found herself convinced that it would ring in the middle of the night. The prospect had alternately terrified and thrilled her.

Daddy, she thought, as if she could summon him.

Miri had been half convinced that she would have a different perspective in the morning. People said that sort of thing all the time and she had found it to be true, but not today. The passing of night and slow arrival of morning did not chase away the previous day's events, did not make her suddenly realize that it had all been a dream or that there was some legitimate explanation.

The voice on the phone had belonged to her father. Her father was dead. She had therefore spoken to a ghost.

She sat up and rubbed her eyes. Her hand strayed unconsciously toward the cell phone before changing trajectory. Picking up the TV remote, she clicked it on and climbed out of bed, peeling off her fading Decemberists concert T-shirt and heading for the shower. She splashed some cold water on her face at the bathroom sink and then found her mind drifting as she stared at her reflection in the mirror, studying the small rose tattooed on her hip. Her father had sometimes called her his beautiful flower.

Shaking off her fugue, she turned on the shower and let the water run until steam began to cloud the room. Only when she had stepped into the hot spray did the stiffness in her shoulders and neck begin to ease. As the water cascaded over her and she washed the previous day's grime from her body, she at last allowed her thoughts to drift.

Miri thought of home.

On an April morning during her senior year in high school, her mother had told her that she could no longer afford their house and that she had stopped paying the mortgage months before. The house was being foreclosed upon, and Angela would be moving into an apartment. Miri could stay with her until she went to college and during vacations, but Angela had made it clear that her one-bedroom apartment was not intended to be Miri's home. The fight that had erupted over this decision had been short, bitter, and one-sided. Although Angela had always had an ugly temper, she let Miri do all the yelling. The lack of emotion had been the thing that cut Miri the deepest. Her mother had made a decision and she was resolute; Miri's feelings didn't factor into that at all.

Angela might not have abdicated her responsibilities as a parent, but she had cast Miri adrift. As a little girl, Miri remembered her mother's constant refrain about giving a child roots and wings. Roots and wings. Now her mother wanted

255

to set the nest on fire.

Miri had never forgiven her for that.

The idea that her childhood home would be gone had distressed her, yet in some odd way it had freed her as well. She had spent that fall at UMass Amherst, and when her mother had asked what she wanted for Christmas, Miri had told her 'a backpack and hiking boots.' The day after Christmas she had abandoned everything she owned except what she could fit into the backpack, laced up her new boots, and hit the road, silently vowing never to sleep on the sofa in her mother's little apartment again.

Miri had hitchhiked all the way across the country, sleeping in parks and campgrounds. Despite the horror stories she had heard throughout her life, no one had attacked her, robbed her, or raped her. Out on the road she had found only free spirits and lost souls. Along the way, she had spent her time making bracelets and earrings with beads that she had brought along. She had been making jewelry as a hobby for years, and when she reached California she set up a blanket on the beach and began to sell the things she had made on her travels.

For three years she had wandered the roads of America, visiting forty-seven of the contiguous states but not returning to Massachusetts. Never going home. After those three years she had found herself in Seattle, where at last she decided that her odyssey had ended and a new journey ought to begin. She got a job and an apartment and went to college and tried to put Coventry, Massachusetts behind her for good, all except for Jake, her best friend from high school, with whom she had shared the worst night of both their lives.

Thoughts of Jake brought her mind back around to the phone call the day before, and suddenly even the hot water could not drive away the chill that raced through her. Rinsing out her hair, Miri shut off the tap and dried off, wrapping her towel around her hair and stepping out into the steam-filled bathroom. The mirror had frosted over with condensation, so she could not see her reflection, as if she weren't really there at all. As if she existed in the same world where that *other* phone call had originated.

After she'd dressed and dried her hair, she sat for a time on the edge of her bed in the company of muffled television voices and stared at her cell phone. Gray morning had arrived and muted daylight streamed through the window.

Miri picked up her phone, disconnected it from the charger, and powered it on. She hesitated for only a second before going to Recent Calls, where she saw JAKE at the top of the list. Her throat constricted and she felt her pulse quicken; she had thought that in the light of day, without a second call or some other evidence, she would be able to tell herself that it hadn't happened — that she had not spoken to her dead father on this very phone.

'Shit,' she whispered.

Leaving the cell phone on the nightstand, she went to her closet and dragged out a travel bag. There were preparations she would have to make, work to reschedule, people to whom she would have to apologize, so today was out of the question.

Tomorrow, though. Tomorrow she would go back to the only place she had ever really thought of as home.

★ ★ ★

Harley Talbot pulled his cruiser into Jake Schapiro's driveway shortly after three P.M. on Monday. The shadows of the towering pines and old oak and birch trees on the property had already grown long. It had been a beautiful day, the ground covered with pure white snow and the sky blue and bright, but the winter days were always ephemeral. Harley had no quarrel with the night — he had gone through several nocturnal periods — but on those abbreviated winter afternoons when the color began to seep from the land so early, he always felt cheated.

Who are you kidding? he thought as he put the cruiser in Park and killed the engine. *It's not the shortness of the day getting under your skin.*

Night falling meant the chief would halt the search for Zachary Stroud until morning — more than twelve hours, during which anything might happen to the boy, if he was still alive, out there somewhere. Harley had been with the search team all day, and now he had to pull a regular shift as well. Someone had to be out patrolling Coventry, especially at night.

As he climbed out of the car, relieved to be able to stretch his long legs, he glanced at the house and arched an eyebrow. In the fading light

258

and the long shadows, Jake's house looked abandoned. The shades had been drawn on every window.

'What the hell?' Harley muttered, dropping his hand to his side-arm and undoing the holster snap.

A quick survey of the property revealed nothing out of place. Jake's car sat in the driveway, nose up close to the door of the garage, which was too cluttered to serve its intended purpose. There were no tire tracks in the snow that still framed the vehicle's spot on the driveway — Jake hadn't driven anywhere since the storm had ended. Harley glanced into the car and then went up the front walk. With the placement of the house and the trees, the walkway didn't get much sun during the day and still bore a crust of ice that cracked underfoot.

Up close, Harley saw a ridge of light around the shades on the living room windows to his left. The sidelights around the front door had gauzy curtains over them but he tried to get a glimpse inside, to no avail.

He rang the doorbell, then rapped loudly on the door, the sound echoing off the snow and trees. Seconds ticked past. Normally he would have assumed that Jake had gone for a walk with his camera to take some pictures but the oddity of the drawn shades disturbed him, along with the fact that he had texted Jake half-a-dozen times today and left him two voice mails without getting any reply. He had dropped by to say hello, hoping to see if Jake was up for a late-night movie and Atomic Wings, a tiny worry in the back of his mind thanks to Jake's radio silence.

Now his worry had grown.

'Jake!' he called, knocking harder. 'You home? Open the door, man.'

You're overreacting, Harley.

Maybe he was, but he had only seen all the shades drawn on a house like this once before — drawn all the way down, so that nobody could get a look inside — and that had been at the LaValle murder house. The previous summer, a twenty-year-old college kid named Martin LaValle had come home from a night of partying with friends, taken his father's shotgun, and murdered his little sister in her bed. When his parents had come running, woken by the gunshot, he had blown them all over the faded floral wallpaper in the hall.

Harley didn't like those drawn shades.

'Jake, answer the door, goddammit!' he snapped, slapping his palm against the wood, shaking the door in its frame.

Fuck it.

He tried the knob but found the door locked. After staring at it for a moment, as if his scrutiny alone might open it, he rang the bell one last time and then pressed his ear to the wood, listening to it echo inside and hoping to hear movement. It seemed to Harley that he did hear something, a kind of rustle or whisper.

He flinched away from the thunk of the dead bolt being drawn back.

'Jake?'

The door opened ten or twelve inches and Jake Schapiro's face appeared in the gap, unshaven and smiling uneasily. He looked unkempt, hair mussed, wearing a T-shirt and old, baggy jeans. The way he stood reminded Harley of the times he'd come back to his dorm room in college only to have his roommate shoo him away because he had a girl in his bed.

'Hey,' Jake said. 'Sorry I haven't gotten back. I'm in the middle of a project. You know how I get.'

Harley stared at him. 'What kind of project?'

'Finishing the back bedroom upstairs. Gonna make it a library, I think.'

'Cool,' Harley replied.

He tilted his head to get a look inside the house but Jake shifted his body and narrowed the gap a little and there could be no question that he did not want Harley to see within.

'Look, I — '

'I have some time tomorrow,' Harley interrupted. 'I could give you a hand.'

'No, no, that's okay. It's been weighing on me, y'know? All the stuff I planned to do to fix the place up that I've just never gotten around to. I'm determined now, and I'd kind of like to accomplish that myself. No offense.'

Harley nodded, taking a step back. 'None taken.'

As Jake's friend, he wanted to force the issue, to give the door a shove. As a police officer, there were rules about entering a private residence uninvited and without a warrant.

Warrant? What are you thinking, that he's got somebody tied up in there?

Harley exhaled, smiling at himself. Yes, Jake

261

had gone all twitchy for some reason. Maybe he did have a girl inside and just wanted Harley to get the hell away from there so he could close the deal. Or maybe the story about the home improvements was the truth; Jake had an artist's ability to immerse himself in something and forget that the rest of the world existed. Harley had seen that part of him before.

'Tell me the truth,' he said. 'You got a girl in there?'

Jake rolled his eyes, his grin clearly forced. 'I wish. Look, I'll call you tomorrow, okay? We need a night out.'

'Atomic Wings,' Harley said.

Jake brightened. 'Exactly!'

'Tomorrow, then.'

Harley began to turn to go. As he did, he saw Jake edge back from the door. In the moment before it closed, Harley spotted something in his right hand — a fan of what appeared to be playing cards, although the yellow edges of the cards niggled at his memory, as if he ought to have recognized the design. Had they had illustrations on them? Harley thought they had.

Whomever Jake had been playing cards with, he clearly didn't want Harley to know about it. *Strip poker?* Always a possibility. Maybe the girl had been half naked already, sitting in the living room and waiting for him to depart. Harley figured it had to be someone he knew or Jake would've admitted he had someone inside.

You dog, Harley thought, smiling as it all began to make sense to him.

He climbed into his cruiser and started it up,

trying to figure out whom Jake might be hooking up with. Someone from the ME's office, maybe, or a crime-scene tech. Though given the effort Jake had made to keep him out, Harley wondered if maybe it was actually one of the women on the Coventry PD. There were several Harley wouldn't have minded seeing out of their uniforms.

Tomorrow he would pin Jake down.

Curiosity killing him, Harley backed out of the driveway and headed toward Carpenter Road, turning on his headlights as the twilight deepened around him.

14

The surface of Kenoza Lake had iced over by the turn of the year and wouldn't melt for another month at least. The weekend's snowstorm had left inches of fresh snow on top of the ice, and as the sun slid down behind the tops of the trees, the snowmobile tracks left behind that day looked like deep scars, carved in shadow.

'Where the hell are we going?' Baxter asked, glancing back at the small public lot in the lakeside park.

There were four cars there, one of them an old Chevy Monte Carlo that Doug had been restoring and one an Audi that he figured Franco had borrowed without permission from an unsuspecting customer at Harpwell's Garage. Doug had arrived first and waited in his car, chewing gum to fight the urge to smoke — a habit he'd given up two years before. He had been early on purpose and instantly regretted it, but he sat and watched the sun drift lower in the sky, people returning to their cars, couples and dog owners who'd been walking in the woods around the lake.

Franco had shown up ten minutes late with Baxter in the passenger seat. But now they were all here, and it felt like the beginning of something. Doug could feel the tension in the air and wasn't sure if it was the pressure pushing ahead of the huge storm on the way or just the animosity burning off Baxter.

Doug kept walking, leading the way along a path that vanished into the thick woods around the lake. When they plunged into the trees, the last of the daylight abandoned them, as if night had abruptly conquered the sun.

'I asked you where we're going,' Baxter said, an edge of danger and just a trace of nerves in his voice.

'Take a breath, man,' Doug said. He pulled a flashlight from his coat and clicked it on, throwing a strong, bright splash of illumination onto the path ahead.

Franco gave Doug a hard shove and he stumbled a bit, caught his toe on a rock jutting from the path, and nearly fell. Doug spun around and shone the flashlight in Franco's face, Baxter like an angry ghost hovering just outside their pool of light.

'What?' Franco demanded, grinning, eyes lit up with the violence that his kind of man always used to bludgeon the unknown.

Doug knew that his growing assertiveness was making Franco nervous and didn't give a damn.

'You've got a decision to make,' Doug said, shining his light first on Franco and then on Baxter. 'Are you going to shoot me? I'm not armed, boys. You want to put a bullet in me and leave me for the dogs back here, then do it.'

Franco looked like he might.

Doug glanced at Baxter, whose eyes were calmer. Baxter had his left hand stuffed in his jacket pocket but the right hand hung free, open but poised, ready to grab the gun that Doug had seen him jam into his rear waistband when he got out of the borrowed Audi back in the lot.

'Ease up, D,' Baxter said. He gave a little sniff of amusement as if to suggest he was above it all. 'If you're gonna be this wound up, man, there's no point in doing this job. Being with you is gonna be like walking through a mine field. We're gonna be trying not to get arrested; we can't be worrying about whether or not we put a foot wrong and you go off.'

Doug nodded slowly, lowering the flashlight. All their faces were in shadow, now. The slivers of sky visible through the branches overhead had turned to indigo, except to the west, where striations of pink and orange were visible but fading fast.

'Understood. But I can't be worried about you two, either,' he said, glancing pointedly at Franco. 'This is huge for me. For all of us. Huge risks along with huge rewards if we don't fuck it up. I have a plan. I'm going to explain that plan to you. If you're with me — '

'With you?' Franco sneered.

Baxter shot him a hard look. 'Shut it.'

'If you're with me,' Doug went on, focusing on Baxter, who had been transformed by the deepening darkness into a creature of shadows, 'then we do this thing together on Wednesday night. I've spent hours thinking about the angles of this thing, all the ways it could go wrong, and if we have the balls and a little luck, we'll all be happy as pigs in shit come Thursday morning. On the other hand, if you don't like my plan then you're welcome to go your own way.'

Baxter stepped nearer to him, close enough that the glow from the flashlight, which Doug still held pointed at the ground, gave strange contours to his face.

'You're saying we don't like your plan then you're out?'

'That's the way it's gotta be.'

'You think you know this shit better than me?' Baxter said, eyes narrowing. 'You're an amateur. You know how many houses I've robbed?'

Doug did not flinch. Instead, he thought of Cherie and of Angie, and of the new life he wanted for himself. The life he deserved.

'You know how many times I've been in prison?' he asked, chin high, close enough to smell the garlic on Baxter's breath. 'None.'

Franco snorted. 'Motherfucker can't be serious.'

Baxter tilted his head. Doug felt the violence radiating from him like body heat. The last color in the sky drained away as they stared at each other and now Franco might as well not have been there at all. In the reflected glow of the flashlight, it was just the two of them.

'I have a plan,' Doug repeated. 'Do you want to hear it?'

Baxter gave a slow nod. 'All right. Enlighten us.'

Doug turned away, shining the flashlight on the path ahead. 'Follow me.'

He thought Franco might bitch a little more but it turned out that Baxter had the leash on his attack dog a little tighter than Doug had realized, because Franco didn't say a word as Doug led them along the snowy path. The warmth of the

267

day had softened the snow but as they trudged through deeper woods, following a path that branched off to the right — away from the lake — the icy crust crunched underfoot.

After a minute or two without a word among them, Doug used the flashlight to pick out an even narrower path, again on the right. They had to duck beneath some low branches to follow it.

'This better be good,' Franco said.

Doug kept walking. When the path began to lighten ahead he turned off the flashlight and a moment later they emerged from the woods at the bottom of a snowy hill. An old house sprawled above them, its roofline painted darker by the light of the early-evening moon. The house was dark except for a single, small window that might have been the kitchen.

He turned to face his companions. His fellow thieves.

'I don't think you knew her, Bax, but back in high school there was this girl in my class named Tallie Hawes. Short for Natalie. Cute girl who never met a douche bag she didn't like. Married Andy Porter, who I hated back then and who lived up to all of my expectations for him. Rich, arrogant, executive for some bank or finance company or whatever.'

Baxter smiled. 'So this is, what, payback? You want to rob him because he shit on you in high school? I mean, not that there's anything wrong with that.'

Doug returned the smile, feeling good. Feeling fine. Thinking of Angie waiting in his bed.

'Nah. I don't want to rob Tallie. Shitty taste in

268

guys, but she was always kinda sweet.'

'They're not customers at the garage,' Franco said.

'No. They're not. I actually grew up in this city, man. I know a lot of people who don't bring their cars to Timmy Harpwell.' Doug pointed off to the left, beyond the big, rambling house. 'If you look, you can see the peak of another building back there. That's the stable. The Porters don't have horses, but the previous owners did.'

He expected Franco to make a crack about him wanting to be Butch Cassidy or something, rob trains from horseback, but to his surprise the bastard seemed to be paying attention at last.

Doug took a step nearer to them, boots crunching snow. 'There are four snowmobiles in there and plenty of gas.' He pointed up the hill, where a tall snowbank marked the bottom of Pinewood Circle. 'You go up the street, right across the road up there, and in a couple of minutes you're in some more woods, only the paths up there bring you right up to the backyards on Winchester Street. Three of the houses on our list are on the near side of the road. If this storm knocks out the power — and from the look of it, that's a pretty good bet — then we come in through the trees, go in through the back, and we may end up with a haul so big we don't bother with the other two houses. But if the night's going well and we feel safe enough, those other two are a few hundred yards down Winchester and then up Emerald Road.'

He turned and gestured back the way they'd come. 'We need a truck, something with power. Chains on the tires and plow blade on the front. We park in the lot by the lake and if anyone goes by, they'll think it's some driver on the city dollar taking a nap. We do the job, use the snowmobiles to get everything back to the truck, plow ourselves out if we have to, and we're home free.'

Baxter had a different sort of smile now, a distant expression that spoke of the future. He was already there, thinking about the haul.

'What about your friends, the Porters?' Franco said. 'They're just gonna let us take their snowmobiles?'

Doug glanced again at the dark house. 'They'll never know. They're in Florida for the whole month.'

'You know this?' Baxter asked. 'You're sure?'

'Completely.'

Franco narrowed his eyes. 'How do you know?'

'Same way I know those snowmobiles are in the stable,' Doug said, cocky now, not able to help it. 'Facebook makes people very stupid.'

Baxter actually laughed and after a second Franco did, too.

'You know we need to confirm,' Baxter said. 'Get into the stable, make sure the damn things run and that there's enough gas.'

'That's why we're here,' Doug replied. He cocked his head. 'Does that mean you're in?'

'In?' Baxter said, glancing at Franco. 'Fuck, yes, we're in.'

'We're in,' Franco confirmed. 'If that storm

hits as hard as they're saying, the power'll be out for days. Most of those rich pricks will do what they always do — head up to Vermont, stay in a fucking ski chalet or something until things are back to normal.'

Baxter held out his hand. Doug didn't like him and definitely didn't trust him, but he couldn't fight the sense of triumph that made his chest swell. He shook, but Baxter used the grip to yank him closer. The ex-con's eyes blazed with flint and fire.

'It's a good plan, Doug,' he said. 'Just don't get ahead of yourself. We go when I say go. This is my show.'

A tremor of fear went through Doug, but he fought it off. He had too much riding on this to be intimidated. If the night went the way he planned it, he could finally put his past to rest. His hometown had treated him like he was nobody. In his darkest hours, no one had so much as extended a hand. Coventry owed him, and as soon as he collected, he would put the whole city in his rearview.

Except Angie, he thought. *Could be she wants a fresh start somewhere, too.*

'I don't have any interest in being the boss,' Doug said. 'This is it for me. We do this and I'm gone. So, yeah, it's your show, man. As long as you're good with the plan, I'll follow your lead.'

Baxter squeezed his hand too tightly, shook, and then let go.

'All right then,' he said, turning to glance at Franco and then looking up at the clear, moonlit sky. 'Now all we need is the storm.'

★ ★ ★

Within Coventry's city limits there were four
bridges that spanned the Merrimack River. The
least traveled of these was Farmer's Bridge,
named for its original use as the primary route
for local farmers to bring their goods to the
downtown market in an era when a farmer's
market hadn't been something middle-class
suburbanites attended on leisure Sunday afternoons.

Trees leaned out over the water on both sides
of the river and covered much of the bridge with
shade. Joe Keenan liked to think of it as the
Forgotten Bridge, because so many people
ignored it. Many people who had settled in
Coventry over the past decade or so were barely
aware that it existed. The two primary river
crossings had been rebuilt in those years and
were wide and modern and had black,
wrought-iron streetlamps along their lengths.
The Farmer's Bridge seemed like a relic of the
past, connecting old farm roads on either side of
the river, neighborhoods whose houses dated
back seventy years or more. One either had to
know how to find it or stumble upon it by
accident, and even then crossing the bridge
seemed more quaint than practical, as it was only
barely wide enough for two full-size vehicles to
pass each other by.

The Farmer's Bridge — the Forgotten Bridge
— had been Keenan's thinking spot for his entire
life. As a child he had walked here with his
mother and played Pooh Sticks, the simplest

272

game ever invented, which they had taken from the pages of *Winnie-the-Pooh*. They would take small sticks and drop them into the river, then rush across the street and watch to see whose stick floated out from underneath first. Keenan cherished those memories of his mother, who'd been the most patient woman in the world. She had made the game seem both exciting and important, and they had both received a kind of sweet grace from the playing of it. A calm in their hearts.

His mother had been dead for thirteen years. He stood on the Forgotten Bridge and looked down at the icy river and could not bring himself to throw anything into the swath of open water, not even the broken stick he held in one hand. Just the thought of doing so made him picture pale arms struggling and a small head bobbing along with chunks of ice, cheeks turning blue, fingers reaching as he went down, carried under the bridge and emerging seconds later, floating, spinning lazily on the current, dead eyes staring up eternally at the night sky.

Headlights washed across the bridge and Keenan turned, shielding his eyes, and spotted a police cruiser rolling toward him. He'd parked his unmarked at the other end of the bridge and walked out here, needing time to himself. Time away from his phone and his radio and memories of past storms and fears of those yet to come. As he saw the cruiser, a flutter of trepidation hit him. The idea that a cop would be driving across this forgotten bridge while he was there seemed even less likely than that someone had come looking for him with news of Zachary Stroud. Could the boy have been found?

When the car rolled to a halt and he bent to peer in at Harley Talbot, he knew from the officer's expression that he'd been wrong to hope.

'What the hell are you doing out here?' he asked.

Harley arched an eyebrow. 'I could ask you the same.'

'You could. How did you know to look for me here?'

'Finch told me you used to come out here all the time back in the day.'

Keenan knew what he meant. Back in the months — hell, the first couple of years — after the storm that had killed Gavin Wexler and Charlie Newell and so many others, he had visited Farmer's Bridge often, tossing sticks into the water and not bothering to run across to see them float out the other side. The rushing water had brought him peace as he pondered the knowledge that all things were a river, every moment carried away from us, forever beyond reach. It had helped.

'Finch,' Keenan said. 'I wouldn't have figured him for the observant type.'

Only the older cops, like Finch and Lieutenant Duquette, would have remembered Keenan's visits to the bridge. But none of them had troubled himself to come out looking for him. Harley Talbot wasn't just a good cop. He was a good man.

'I guess you know they've basically called off

274

the search,' Harley said, pain in his eyes.

'I heard.'

'I tried calling you.'

Keenan gestured toward the end of the bridge. 'I left my phone. Radio, too.'

'Needed some downtime,' Harley said, smiling sheepishly. 'And here I am screwing that up for you.'

'No, it's okay.'

A line appeared on Harley's forehead. In the light from his dashboard, the massive cop looked grimly unhappy.

'Storm's coming in day after tomorrow,' Harley said. 'They'll have a skeleton crew out searching tomorrow and then they're done. Tomorrow the word will go out that we believe he may have drowned in the river, let the public know we've chalked it up as a drowning.'

'Of course,' Keenan said bitterly.

'Look, Detective, I figured you'd have heard already but I wanted to tell you face-to-face that I'm with you on this.'

'What do you mean, 'with' me?'

Harley smiled. 'I know you don't think this kid went into the water, so, officially or not, you're gonna keep looking.'

Keenan glanced out at the water for a moment, watched slabs of ice floating along the river in the moonlight.

'Yeah, I'm gonna keep looking,' he said. 'Maybe that's because I've seen too many dead kids and I just can't take another one. I get the impression that's what Marco Torres thinks.'

'Torres is a punk.'

Keenan smiled. 'Doesn't make him wrong. This whole thing could just be wishful thinking on my part. The kid's probably in the river.'

'Probably,' Harley agreed.

Keenan shot him a hard look, eyes narrowed. 'Is that what you think?'

Engine idling, dashboard lights turning his skin indigo blue, Harley frowned.

'I think every hour that passes it's more likely that the Stroud boy is dead. But I saw the accident scene and I have a hard time thinking the kid just stumbled into the water. My gut says no.'

Keenan nodded. 'Exactly. If this kid's still alive, then someone saw him. Someone knows where he is.'

'Like I said, I'm with you.'

'Thanks for that,' Keenan said. 'Really.'

'But you're not going to find him tonight,' Harley added. 'Get in. I'll run you to your car.'

Keenan hesitated, the broken stick in his hand taking on a strange new weight. He turned back to the railing, glanced at the icy water, and tossed the stick down into the churning current. He pulled open the cruiser's passenger door and climbed in. As Harley drove him the rest of the length of the bridge, he felt a pang of regret that he had not raced across the bridge to see whether it came out the other side.

Maybe it's better not to know, he thought, gazing out the car window at the gauzy halo around the moon. *At least then there's still hope.*

15

Miri's flight left Seattle at quarter to seven on Tuesday morning. She was used to rising early, but the buzz of her alarm at four A.M. had left her with bleary eyes and a persistent grumble until halfway through the flight, when she managed to drift off for a couple of hours of additional sleep. There had been seats available on later flights, but they had been more expensive and, with the monster blizzard all the weather reports showed moving toward New England, she wanted to get safely on the ground as soon as possible.

By the time she had landed and waited in line to pick up her rental car, it was a few minutes after five P.M. — the time change obliterating any hope of seeing daylight today. She had arrived at the airport in Seattle in the dark that morning, and night had already returned by the time she drove away from Logan Airport, in Boston, that afternoon. A glimpse out the window at the sky assured her that she wouldn't have seen much sun even if she'd arrived hours earlier. The thick of the storm might not be scheduled to arrive until after midnight, but the roiling clouds hung pregnant above and occasional flurries blew around the rented Ford, as if the storm was waiting just above the clouds, so full that the small flakes kept slipping through prematurely.

She drove north, discovering each mile as if

she had never traveled these roads before. There were new buildings visible from the highway and a new overpass on Route 93, but as she wended her way toward her childhood home she found herself igniting old memories that had lain dormant for years. Miri did not feel any desire to come back to live in New England, but still she realized that she had missed it, that she had a bittersweet love for the place that she had denied for a very long time. The feeling had a surreal quality that she had never before experienced.

She reached the exit for downtown Coventry just before six o'clock. In a parking lot that had once held a Toyota dealership, three snow-plows and a sander idled in the darkness, drivers sitting in shadows in the cabs, smoking cigarettes and talking through their open windows. Miri imagined them as early settlers, circling the wagons to prepare for an attack. The real snow wouldn't start for five or six hours, but the forecast had apparently forced the city to get its act together for once. They were ready.

Hipster music played on the car radio — she'd tuned it to her old favorite, The River, which was headquartered right here in Coventry. Gusts of wind buffeted the little Ford as she drove along Washington Street, looking at the warm lights burning in the windows of The Tap and Keon's and the other restaurants and storefronts that were part of the fabric of her memories of home.

Home, she thought. *Where are you going, Miri?*

The answer was *not* home. She knew she had to see her mother at some point, and she found that she wanted to see Jake. Needed to, urged on by a fondness in her heart. It had been so long since she had allowed herself to miss him, and now that she had let those feelings in, the strength of them surprised her.

Yet she found herself driving not to her mother's apartment or to Jake's house but pulling into a curbside parking space across the street from The Vault. Killing the engine — the sudden silence making her aware of the music she had barely been listening to on the radio — she sat for several seconds and just looked at the windows. Her mother had taken her to dinner at The Vault at least twice a month during high school, usually dragging Jake or another of her friends along. With strangers now living in her childhood home and the corridors of Coventry High no longer her territory, this felt like the closest she could find to a real homecoming.

Miri locked up the car, crossed the street, and pulled open the door of The Vault. From the bone-deep chill of winter, she stepped into the warmth of the restaurant's foyer and inhaled the delicious aromas that wafted from the kitchen. A blaze roared in the large fireplace and she felt the heat reach her core instantly. A twinge of regret touched her heart, not that she wanted to live here again but that the past was past, never to be lived again. She'd been so happy to put Coventry behind her forever, but now that she'd returned she realized that there had been much to love about this place.

'Can I help you?' a pretty brunette hostess

asked. She was young, with skin like caramel, and Miri wondered if she went to Coventry High or had recently graduated. For a moment she was tempted to ask about the teachers she remembered fondly, but resisted the urge.

'Table for one,' Miri said. Once she would have been embarrassed to eat in a restaurant by herself. As an adult, she had come to enjoy her own company.

Ensconced in a small, intimate booth by the front windows, she took off her knit cap and shook out her curly hair. She glanced around in search of Ella, the always friendly and energetic owner, or her husband, TJ, whose rich, sexy singing voice was half the reason The Vault had maintained such a cherished place in Miri's memory. Neither of them seemed to be around, but she found it didn't disappoint her very much. She was not sure how long she would be back in Coventry, but certainly long enough to pay The Vault another visit.

A frown creased her forehead as she wondered again how long she would be here.

Never mind how long, she thought. *The big question is: why? What the hell am I doing here?*

The phone call from her father seemed so unreal to her now. So much like a dream. Miri knew it had not been either dream or imagination. Her presence here — her plane flight and rental car and the lack of any tangible plan as to what she would do upon her arrival — was evidence enough of that. But what was she supposed to do now that she was here?

For the moment she had no answer, other

than to see her mother and Jake.

There were other people she knew in Coventry, other old friends, and there were a small handful that she would not mind seeing during her visit. Tonya Michelli. Adam Chang. But such wistful thoughts — unusual for her — vanished in the shadow of the haunting call that had brought her home.

The waiter came, a short Latino guy with incredible eyes and obvious muscles, a year or two older than she was, at a guess.

'Can I get you something to drink while you're looking at the menu?' he asked.

'I haven't been here in forever, but do you still do that little pot-pie dish?'

He smiled. 'We do. It's my favorite.'

Miri liked his smile very much. 'Then I don't need to open the menu,' she said. 'I'll have that, with a glass of water now and a coffee after.'

'A woman who knows what she wants,' the waiter observed.

'For better or worse,' Miri agreed.

The waiter gave her a curious look before he took her menu and went off to the kitchen. Though it was still relatively early in the dinner hour, there were a good number of people in the restaurant already, many of them at the bar, and she overheard talk of the impending storm along with other chatter and the clinking of glasses. Customers had apparently come in for a hot meal before the storm crashed in. She overheard several people at a nearby table talking about the chaos at the supermarket earlier in the day as people stocked up on groceries and batteries for flashlights and even candles.

A ripple of nausea went through her. Somehow Miri had managed to keep her feelings about the impending blizzard at a distance, but now with these hushed conversations all around her and the strange, breathless tension she felt among the diners in The Vault, dark memories returned, along with a terrible fear that she had tamped down inside her for a dozen years.

For the first time she worried about where she would spend the night. She had intended to get a room at the old Sheraton on the north end of town, not far from the New Hampshire border. But now the idea of being alone troubled her.

A sudden urgency filled her and she wanted the waiter to hurry. Perhaps it had been a bad idea for her to stop for a sit-down meal. She wondered if Jake would let her sleep the night on his sofa.

Of course he will, you moron, she thought. *He might hate you for leaving, but that doesn't mean he doesn't still love you.*

Some friendships were forever, and she and Jake Schapiro were connected by more than just love or friendship. They had shared the most terrifying and most painful night of their lives together. That linked them like nothing else could.

Miri glanced out the window at a passing car, its headlights and the streetlamps illuminating the flurries that danced in the air all along Washington Street.

A man stood on the opposite sidewalk, almost lost in the yellow glow of a streetlamp above him, snow flurries swirling around him. Miri couldn't breathe. Her heart seized in her chest. The snowflakes moved around him . . . and *through* him, as if he weren't there at all.

Icy fingers spider-walked along her spine.

'Daddy?' she whispered.

The figure stepped off the curb and began to cross the street toward the front of the restaurant and her heart leaped with fear and hope in equal measure. The snowflakes swirled through him, and though he was substantial and three-dimensional and as real as the cold glass against which she now placed her fingertips, she could see through him, his body translucent and turning to shadow as he stepped out of the dome of light cast by the streetlamp above.

The ghost gazed at her, a sad smile touching his darkened features as he reached the middle of the street.

As if coming awake from a dream, Miri bolted into action. She slid from the little booth, dragging the tablecloth and dumping her knife and fork and napkin to the floor as she ran for the front door, slammed it open, and stepped out into the night. A blast of wind gusted so hard that she staggered a bit.

Miri looked up and saw that the flurry had ended. The sky still hung heavy with snow, but for the moment it had ceased to fall. Wind eddied a few flakes along the pavement, but the real storm had yet to begin.

Of her father's ghost, there was no sign.

★   ★   ★

283

Doug watched Angela glide across the ice on rented skates and couldn't help smiling. She wore a white knit hat pulled down far enough to cover her ears and a thick blue cotton scarf that hid her smile, but somehow he found her more beautiful than ever. He still remembered the irritable, dissatisfied, volatile woman she'd been when they had first dated, but over the past couple of days those memories had been quickly fading. As she did an ice pirouette, her hazel eyes lit up with joy, and he knew that he would do whatever he had to do in order to see that joy again and again. Tomorrow's burglaries would go a long way toward making that happen. He wasn't stupid enough to give her any of the jewelry they planned to steal, but something bought with the proceeds . . . that would make her eyes sparkle.

The ice skating at the rink in Veterans Memorial Park — the stretch of green between City Hall and the town library — had been a Coventry winter tradition for more than fifty years. Doug knew how to skate well enough, but growing up he had never understood the point of doing it without a hockey stick in his hands and a goal to shoot pucks at. Then he'd met Cherie, and that had changed. The outdoor rink, little more than a wooden frame full of frozen water, had been her favorite place in the world. Her mother had brought her there as a little girl and she had always said that it brought her back to those days, that the Christmas lights strung in the bare branches of the trees all over the park and her hair flying as she skated made her feel ten years old again.

Angela turned to him, skating backward and beckoning him to follow, which he did in the long, powerful strides that his body still remembered from high school hockey. He had his own nostalgia for the rink, for the cold air and the couples skating hand in hand, some of them old enough to have skated there the first year it opened. But his nostalgia was bittersweet.

Making the turn at the far end of the rink, Angela swept into another pirouette, this one less graceful. She spun around once and then hit a rough patch of ice and went down on her behind, sliding several feet before she burst out laughing, her scarf sliding down to reveal the rest of her face.

Doug skated to a hard stop, spraying ice at her.

'Hey!' Angela cried, pouting. 'That's not very nice.'

'I said I could skate,' Doug said, reaching out to give her a hand up. 'I never said I was graceful.'

She took his hand and he hauled her up onto her skates, then pulled her against him for a kiss. Angela smiled against his lips, then responded more fully, grabbing the back of his head to deepen the kiss. His body reacted instantly and he pressed himself against her, nearly unbalancing them both, so that they had to retreat to arm's length to keep from falling.

Grinning, Doug skated a few feet away from her. A pair of high-schoolers went by, shaky on their skates, arms out as if bracing for a tumble.

'You never told me *you* could skate so well,' he said.

Angela glided after him. 'You mean fall on my ass? Yeah, that was lovely.'

'You know what I mean. Were you into figure skating as a kid? I didn't know you and Cherie had that in common.'

They'd been close friends. Doug figured they must have bonded over a shared love of skating, but he didn't remember either Cherie or Angela ever bringing it up.

'I've always loved to skate,' Angela said, turning around to skate backward and yet still catching up to him and smiling as she passed him by.

'Did you two ever go together?'

'All the time,' Angela said quickly, but she glanced abruptly away and he had the strangest sense that she was lying to him.

'That's weird.'

She cocked an eyebrow. 'What is?'

'I took her skating all the time during the winters we were together. How come you never came along?'

With a sad smile, she reached out and took his hand as they continued to skate face-to-face.

'I did, baby. Trust me. I was with you every time.'

'What is that supposed to mean?' he asked.

But he had barely made it halfway through the question before she pulled away and turned from him, skating off into the crowd and wiping her eyes. Just before she'd spun away, Doug thought she had begun to cry.

What are you hiding? he thought.

Through a gap in the crowd circling the rink, he saw her skating alone in the center of the ice. She had taken off her hat and her hair flew behind her as she glided along, enjoying the sensation, as if only here on the ice could she find peace.

Doug waited for a gap in the line of skaters passing him by and then went to her. When Angela turned to him, her tears were gone but her eyes held a haunted sorrow that he had never seen in them before.

'What is it?' he asked.

She took his hand. 'Just skate with me, baby. I want to remember this, no matter what happens.'

Doug touched her face, tucked her hair behind her ear. Was she worried about what might happen to him tomorrow night? About the burglaries?

'What's going to happen?' he asked.

'Silly man,' Angela said, tugging him along beside her, the air full of chatter and laughter and distant music. 'It's going to snow.'

★ ★ ★

Detective Keenan walked into The Tap, relishing the heat blasting from the vent above the restaurant's foyer. He shivered a little, but from the warmth instead of the cold, and some of the stress eased from him. A glance at the clock above the bar — an antique Elvis Presley whose hips swung from side to side to tick the seconds away — showed that eight P.M. had come and gone, which meant that he was officially off duty.

The Tap was a combination restaurant and brewhouse, complete with vats of beer in the cellar. The bar and dining room were separated by a wall whose lower half was wood and whose upper half was frosted glass. As he walked to the bar he peeked through the opening between the two rooms and saw that only a few tables were occupied, which explained the bored look on the face of the tall, soccer-mom-looking woman by the hostess stand. She started to reach for a menu as he approached, but he waved her away and pointed to the bar and she went back to her desultory slouch.

Several people recognized and greeted him as he moved through the bar, all cops. The Tap had been unofficially adopted by the Coventry PD in the years since their old haunt, the Lasting Room, had closed. Keenan gave halfhearted hellos and clapped more than one officer on the shoulder as he made his way to an empty stool, but he did not linger or stop to chat. He had come here because it was familiar and comfortable and because he liked the Coventry Winter Ale they brewed, not to look into the eyes of his fellow police and see the regret and apology they felt over failing to find Zachary Stroud.

As he slid onto a stool, the aging blond bartender noticed him and came down the bar.

'Evening, Joe,' she said, her voice a cigarette rasp.

'Morgan,' Detective Keenan said. 'Glad to find an empty seat.'

288

'Aw, we're just a little light tonight. Hell, it's a Tuesday,' Brenda said, the makeup crinkling on her face, worn by nicotine and years of tanning. 'It's the restaurant that's dead.'

'I'm just teasing,' Keenan said. 'I'm actually surprised you've got a crowd at all. It's gone very quiet out there tonight.'

Brenda wiped down the counter like some bartender in an old Western.

'You know what it's like before a snowstorm. Coventry always holds its breath,' she said, then met his gaze. 'What can I get you? Winter Ale?'

Keenan smiled, his tension relaxing further. 'How do you do that? I hardly ever come in here anymore.'

'Yeah, yeah, ever since you made detective,' Brenda teased, grabbing a glass and going to the tap to draw his beer. 'But you've been drinking the same thing every winter for, like, ten friggin' years.'

She poured a perfect glass — just a skim of foam on top — put out a coaster, and set his beer on top of it.

'If my wife ever throws me out, I'm going to propose to you,' Keenan said. 'Any woman with that kind of memory should be cherished.'

'Yeah, right. Tell that to my asshole ex-husband.'

Keenan took a swig of his beer and was about to reply when someone tapped his shoulder. He turned to see Marco Torres standing behind him, looking pissed off. After the week he'd been having, Keenan had run out of patience.

'What the hell's your problem?'

289

Torres shuddered as if he might cry and stepped in close.

'Personal space, asshole,' Keenan said, but when he reached up to push Torres away, the younger man grabbed his wrist and twisted his arm aside.

'He's still out there, you son of a bitch,' Torres whispered. 'You're here having a beer and another kid is going to die on your watch.'

'Fuck off!' Keenan shouted, shaking loose and shoving Torres backward, so that he crashed into the wall, his head cracking a panel of frosted glass.

Other patrons at the bar shuffled away from them, but the cops who'd been drinking there moved nearer, all of them ready to step in if things got out of hand. One of them was Ted Finch, who gave Keenan a conspiratorial grin.

'Didn't think you had it in you, Joe,' Finch said.

Keenan felt all the fight go out of him. If Finch approved, he knew he had crossed a line. He stared at Torres, who stood in a kind of defensive crouch, eyes wide with what looked more like sadness than fear. A chill went through the detective, a crawling, icy thing that spread through him with a shiver. Something about the way Torres looked at him made his stomach knot with unease.

'Why me?' Keenan demanded. 'Yeah, I want to find the kid. It's killing me. But why the hell do you put this just on me when there's a whole department — a whole goddamn city — that should still be out searching?'

Torres straightened, his eyes narrowing angrily.

290

His lips were a thin white line until he took a single step nearer and spoke so quietly that even Keenan could not be completely certain what he said.

Then Torres bolted, running for the exit and slamming out the door.

A lot of chatter filled the wake of his departure, patrons reacting to the scene and cops muttering about rookies coming unraveled because of the job. Finch came up beside Keenan and offered to buy him a beer as soon as he'd drained his glass.

'Another night, Ted,' Keenan said, drinking half of his beer in a couple of gulps and then dropping a ten on the bar. He glanced up and saw Brenda watching him. 'Tell the owner he can reach me at the department about the glass. I'll cover it.'

His voice sounded as if it were coming from somewhere other than his own lips.

Keenan ignored Finch's exhortations to finish his beer, to stick around and join the other cops in the bar for another round, and headed for the door. He stepped outside into the frigid February night, the wind cutting through his jacket, the air heavy with the threat of the coming storm. He shoved his hands into his pockets and glanced around for any sign of Torres, but the rookie had gone.

The last thing Torres had said had been spoken so quietly that even Keenan, who had been the closest to him, wasn't sure he had heard correctly. But he knew what those words had sounded like.

'Because I'm betting you still remember what my boy's skin smelled like when it burned.'

* * *

Miri sat in her rental car, bathed in the green glow of the dashboard lights. Hot air blasted from the vents and yet she could not get warm inside. There were only two possibilities. Either she had seen her father's ghost standing on the sidewalk across the street from The Vault in the middle of a snow flurry . . . or she had lost her mind. Such thoughts made it almost impossible for her to breathe.

She had loved her father deeply and still missed him so much that it hurt every day, so the idea of being able to see him and speak to him caused a flutter of anxious joy in her heart. But the existence of ghosts, the possibility that the dead lingered on and might be around her even at this very moment, made her shiver. What did they want, if they were there at all? Were they merely sorrowful, or jealous and spiteful of the living? The mere thought made her uneasy, and cold despite the car heater as it fought the winter chill. Miri sat behind the wheel as the car shuddered with every ominous gust of wind, and glanced anxiously out at the darkness, fearful of the silent yearning of the dead.

'Where are you, Daddy?' she whispered, her voice barely audible above the groan of the heater and the purr of the engine.

What the hell am I doing out here?

Miri glanced out the windshield at the house

292

diagonally across from the spot where she'd parked. She remembered it well, had seen it both in dreams and in nightmares. As far as she knew, Allie Schapiro still lived there, and judging by the warm lights inside and the car parked in the short, narrow driveway, the woman was at home. Though Miri had stayed friends with Jake all through middle school and high school, she had not set foot inside that house since the night of the blizzard that had claimed her father's life, the night that Isaac Schapiro had fallen to his death.

How hard is it? Just go up to the door and ring the bell.

Jake was the only person in the world with whom she felt she could talk about what had been happening to her. The only person who would not outright dismiss her. But at some point she would need to talk to Allie as well. The blizzard had changed the course of all their lives. If not for that storm, Miri had no doubt, Allie would have been her stepmother. They'd have been a family. If her father had a message for her, Miri was sure he would want her to share it with Allie as well, but this was premature. She wouldn't know where to begin.

Miri shivered, still unable to let the warm air penetrate the chill inside her. She turned on the headlights, put the car into Drive, and pulled away from the curb, following a route she could have navigated with her eyes closed. As long as she had been away from Coventry, its streets were ingrained in her subconscious like the lines she'd memorized for her eighth-grade play. Discovering just how deeply Coventry was rooted inside her made her wistful and yet depressed her as well. In some ways it would always be home, and yet she hoped that once she put it behind her for a second time, she would never have to come back. All her ghosts were here, real and imagined. And now she found herself driving toward them, instead of away.

Her mother had an apartment in Hamel Mill Lofts, less than a ten-minute drive from Allie Schapiro's house. Her childhood home had long been sold and her mother could be a total bitch, but that ninth-floor apartment at the Lofts was the closest thing she had to a home in Coventry these days.

'This should be fun,' she muttered to herself as she turned into the big lot behind the Lofts, a complex of old mill buildings that had been converted into some of the best apartments in the city.

The old smokestack, now nothing but a giant accent piece, loomed against the low, winter storm clouds. She craned her neck to glance at it, but pulled her attention away in time to notice a parking space halfway across the lot toward the center building. Miri had never visited her mother here, but she knew from talking to Angela that this was the right spot, and had the apartment number written down. Once she'd parked the car, she consulted the strip of paper she'd stashed in her tiny purse.

921.

Shouldering her duffel, she locked up the rental and crossed the lot to the door. A big, scruffy guy with glasses came out as she

294

approached, leading a tiny dog wearing a red snowflake-pattern sweater. He held the door for her and Miri smiled and thanked him, thinking that this was better, that seeing her mother face-to-face when she opened the apartment door would somehow be less awkward than talking to her over the intercom from the building's foyer.

She could not have imagined how wrong she'd be.

The elevator whirred up to the ninth floor and she found herself wishing for the distraction of Muzak. Alone on the elevator, it was too quiet, with too much room for ghosts.

The long, turning corridor surprised her, with its freshly scrubbed brick and exposed wooden beams left over from the original mill building. At the door to apartment 921, Miri paused and took a breath, wondering if she really wanted to do this. She could always go to the shitty little Best Western on the north side of the city. She exhaled, realizing the truth. No way would she tell her mother about seeing her father's ghost, not just yet. But if this was real, and not just some breathless, fevered wish come to frightening life, she would need to tell them all in time. Jake and Allie Schapiro, and her own mother. Although Angie and Niko were divorced, they had loved each other once. His death had scarred Angela deeply, especially coming on the same night as her best friend, Cherie Manning, had died.

The worst night, Miri thought. *Ever.*

Shifting her duffel to the other shoulder, she

rapped on the door, then waited through twenty seconds of silence before she knocked again, louder this time. She had just started to wonder if her mother might not be home when she heard low voices behind the door.

'Who is it?'

So strange hearing her mother's voice in person after years away.

'It's me,' she said. 'It's Miri.'

More talking inside, and Miri began to get a terrible, sinking feeling. Her stomach dropped and she swore softly, wincing with awkwardness as she heard the lock thrown back, and then her mother was opening the door.

Miri wasn't prepared for Angela's pleasant smile or the way her mother stared at her as if in discovery, looking her up and down as if it had been forever since they'd last seen each other. But she supposed that, in a way, it had.

'God, it's really you, isn't it?' Angela said, tucking her hair behind her ear.

Miri took in the unruly hair, the pink flush of her mother's cheeks, the hastily tied bathrobe, and any hope that her suspicion might not be warranted went up in smoke.

'Hi, Mom.'

Several awkward seconds passed before Angela seemed to notice the duffel, and then realization lighted her face. She gave a kind of sad smile and stepped back to let her daughter in, opening the door wider, which gave Miri a glimpse of Doug Manning farther inside the apartment, hastily buttoning his shirt. Though it had been years, Miri recognized him immediately. Doug had

296

been the husband of her mother's best friend, and he'd always been kind to young Miri, teasing her about boys and ruffling her hair. At the city's memorial for those killed in the blizzard, with Doug grieving for Cherie and Miri for her father, he had stood beside her while Charlie Newell's sister sang 'Amazing Grace' and put a protective arm around her, both of them quietly weeping.

'Hey, kid,' Doug said now, the way he always had, as if no time at all had passed.

As if it made all the sense in the world for her mother to be screwing the husband of her dead best friend. And probably it did — Miri was no expert — but in that moment it made her want to throw up.

'Come in, sweetie,' her mother said, oh so tenderly — so carefully. 'It's so great to see you.'

Angela's smile seemed almost sincere, but the *sweetie* sickened her. In her whole life, her mother had never called her sweetie. Girl, sometimes, or babygirl, as if it were all one word. Mirjeta, her full name, if she was angry. Bitch, more than once. But never sweetie.

An image of Doug and her mother having sex swam into her mind and it was too much for her to take.

'This was a mistake,' she said, shaking her head and taking a step away from the door. 'I'm sorry. I should have called. I should have . . . '

The thought left unfinished, she turned to walk away. Her mother stepped out into the corridor and called after her, voice cracking with a plaintive sadness, a vulnerability that Miri never would have associated with Angela Ristani, and it very nearly stopped her in her tracks. But *sweetie* rang in her ears and the image of the pink, mid-sex flush in her mother's face made her rush down the hall to the elevator.

Only when it had arrived and she'd stepped in did she allow herself to look back down the hallway to confirm that her mother had not given chase. The combination of relief and disappointment confounded her.

The doors slid shut and the elevator hummed as it began its descent.

Shitty little Best Western it is.

*   *   *

Sometime after one A.M., Allie Schapiro woke from a dream in which Isaac rushed into her room and slid into bed with her, afraid of the rattling of the windows caused by the storm and the whistle of the icy wind. It was the sweetest of dreams, lying there under the covers, whispering assurances to her little boy in the dark, and when some noise or other roused her from sleep, she still felt him in her arms, felt the softness of his hair against her cheek. The dream dissipated like smoke, and she tried so hard to hold it inside her heart and her memory, but like all dreams, it had never been meant to keep.

Outside her window, it had begun to snow in earnest. This was no little flurry but the beginning of the blizzard that forecasters had been warning about for days. The wind gusted and the window rattled and the frigid air howled

298

in through the single inch that she had left it open.

Allie rose tiredly and went to shut it, closing out the wind and the chill and turning the lock to secure it.

Out on the corner, just at the edge of a pool of golden light from a streetlamp, she saw the ghost of Niko Ristani staring up at her.

With a small cry she backed away, her hand over her pounding heart. She shook her head, not understanding. Pinched her arm to make sure she was awake. Looked around the room to see if somehow she might still be dreaming.

When she returned to the window, the street below was empty.

It would have been so easy for her to tell herself that it had been a stray thread of her dreaming mind that had shown her something impossible, but Allie could not do that. She was awake, and she knew what she had seen. If she hadn't seen Niko's body herself, hollow and forlorn in the casket on the night of his wake, she would have thought that somehow he had faked his death. But she had loved him, and so she knew that her love had died.

Niko, she thought.

Ghost or not, it would have made her happy to know that somehow his soul still endured, but she had seen the tortured look in his eyes, the worry there. The fear in the eyes of a dead man.

And it terrified her.

16

On Wednesday morning, the banging of a loose shutter roused Jake from a deep sleep. He came awake with barely conscious irritation, his brain trying to make sense of the sound as he took a deep breath and forced himself to open his eyes. Gray light filtered through the bedroom windows and thick, wet snow pelted the glass. So much had already built up on the sill that a diagonal slash of white covered the bottom quarter of the window.

The banging drew his attention again and he frowned for a moment before putting it together. *Shutter. Right.* On this side of the house's exterior, the previous owner had left the original old-world shutters intact. In an era when the fear of Indian attacks was still fresh in the minds of settlers, such heavy wooden shutters were typical, useful as they were for stopping arrows. Later, they became a common architectural feature, even when the prospect of Indian attack was a distant memory. Though their hinges were rusty, and they had probably not been closed in decades, the old shutters on the east-facing side of the house remained. Something else he hoped to rectify someday.

The hinges squealed as the shutter banged against the house, the blizzard gusting as if its winds were the breath of some icy billows. As the sleep-fog retreated from his mind, it occurred to him that he would have to go outside and secure it, and he swore under his breath and turned over, burrowing his head into his pillow.

Then he went rigid as true wakefulness returned.

'Isaac,' he said, his voice muffled by the pillow.

Jake glanced at the clock on his bedside table to find that it was nearly eleven A.M. They had stayed up until almost three o'clock in the morning, talking and watching superhero movies. Isaac had always loved comics and Jake had remembered how they had fantasized about what it would be like if Hollywood ever managed to make a movie of The Avengers. Last night, Jake had helped make that fantasy come true for his little brother and had been content to let the movies fill the quiet that had fallen between them as the hour grew first later and then earlier. Just when he had begun to think that Isaac would never sleep, he had heard the soft snoring of the little boy and realized that — ghost or not — his physical body had passed its endurance threshold. He had slept, and Jake had done the same.

Still tired, eyes gritty with sleep, he sat up in bed. Small stacks of comics shifted on top of the bedspread as he moved beneath the covers.

'Isaac?' he called, glancing at the bedroom door, which had been tightly shut.

A tiny voice at the back of his mind suggested that he'd dreamed or hallucinated all the events of the previous two days, but that was ridiculous. Here were the comics, after all, and he knew that if he went into the living room he would find stacks of DVDs, open board games, and the little white boxes of Chinese food they'd eaten the night before and which he now realized he'd forgotten to put into the fridge. The food would have stunk up the living room and the kitchen, but he could not bring himself to care.

All that mattered was Isaac.

Jake threw back his covers and climbed out of bed, discovering that although he was barefoot he still wore the rest of his outfit from the night before. He'd fallen asleep in jeans and a thin cotton sweatshirt — not the most comfortable pajamas.

'Ike?' he called toward the bedroom door, which stood two-thirds of the way closed.

'Here,' a small, frightened voice replied from Jake's closet.

He spun toward it, heart thundering. The door hung halfway open, and he heard the sound of Isaac shifting on top of the shoes and sneakers arrayed on the floor of the closet. Jackets and shirts moved as Isaac poked his head out, a wary look in his eyes.

'I'm hiding,' the boy said, as if that needed to be explained.

'What are you hiding from?'

Isaac looked disappointed. Almost hurt. 'You *know* what.'

The gray storm light barely illuminated the shadowy recesses of the closet, so that Isaac's face seemed to float there, suspended amid the hanging clothes. Staring at his features, Jake felt the world shift underfoot. The eyes belonged to his brother, or at least he thought they did. He certainly saw Isaac there. But the other features had been unfamiliar to him only days ago. Jake had turned on the television each day after his shower, with Isaac in another room, and watched the local news just long enough to get an update on the search for Zachary Stroud. This face that floated out from the darkness of his closet belonged to that missing boy, but to Jake, it was fast becoming his brother's face. Somehow, Isaac's spirit had returned and had slipped inside this lost boy, this boy whose parents had died and made him an orphan. It might even have been that Zack Stroud had died and Isaac now inhabited his body in some peculiar resurrection. Jake's life had left him equipped to look upon death without flinching, but it had not prepared him for this.

The only thing he really knew — and over these few surreal days he had come to understand that it was the only thing that mattered to him at all — was that Isaac was back.

'Why don't you come out of there?' Jake asked.

'Huh. No,' Isaac replied. 'Why don't you come in?'

Jake crouched in front of the closet. 'Really, Ike. Look around. There's a storm, yeah. But it's just snow and wind. The banging you hear is a shutter. I'll go out and secure it in a bit, and we'll — '

'No!' Isaac shouted, then clapped a hand over his mouth, obviously regretting the loud noise. He let his hand drop and Jake saw that his lips were quivering and his eyes looked on the verge of tears. 'You can't go outside. Promise you'll stay in here with me until the storm has gone.'

Jake swallowed dryly, unnerved by the fear in those familiar unfamiliar eyes. 'Okay.'

'Promise.'

'I promise.'

'Now come into the closet,' Isaac said.

Jake sat on the floor, leaning against the doorframe. He put out his hand and Isaac slipped his thin, pale one — the hand of Zachary Stroud — out of the shadows to clasp it. The fear and sadness in his eyes gave way to a single, urgent plea.

'You're safe here, Ikey,' he said. 'I promise.'

Isaac's lips trembled again and tears began to well in his eyes. 'You didn't believe me that night. About the ice men.'

Jake had to look away, a nauseous twist in his gut. 'I know. You have no idea how sorry — '

'Will you believe me now?'

With a shuddering breath, Jake pushed away his guilt and forced himself to look again at his brother.

'I've asked you a dozen times to explain it all to me. How you can be here and what *they* are and . . . everything. You just change the subject, and I understand that. I do. You don't want to talk about it. But if we're in trouble now, if we're in danger — '

'They're coming,' Isaac insisted, tugging on his hand. 'Coming back for what's theirs. We have to hide until the storm passes. We *have* to.'

Jake tried to imagine spending the rest of the day and all night in his closet, and what that would entail. Flashlights. Snacks. Comic books.

Maybe a board game. Quiet time in which to tell his brother what had transpired in the twelve years since his death. They had mostly skirted the subject in the days since the boy had first appeared. Isaac resisted any discussion of his death and the fact that the world had gone on without him. But if he was going to stay, that would have to change.

Jake shuddered, closing his eyes and turning away. How could he stay? With everyone looking for the boy whose face Isaac now wore, a boy who might or might not even still exist somewhere beneath that face, how could Isaac stay here? How long could Jake keep him hidden?

An image swam up into his mind, a memory of icy fingers reaching through the screen of his childhood bedroom window and grabbing hold of Isaac. A current of fear swept through him, fear to the bone, fear to make him remember the terror of that night as if it had been last night. The idea that the ice men might come for Isaac made him feel like screaming. He had let his brother down once before, and he refused to do so again.

'Okay,' he said at last. 'I'll hide with you. We'll make a game of it. Though maybe the basement would be better — more room, more air to breathe. Or the attic — '

'Not the attic!' Isaac said sharply, shivering. 'Too many drafts. Open spaces.'

'Okay. The basement it is. But you have to tell me everything you know about them, Isaac. Everything.'

Isaac nodded. 'Whatever you want, Jakey. Just don't let them touch me again.'

Jake gripped his hand tightly. A stranger's hand. His brother's hand.

'That's not going to happen.'

For a few seconds, Isaac just held on. Then the boy let out a long breath and looked up at him.

'Y'know, maybe you should go out and fix that shutter after all,' Isaac said. 'But don't leave it open. Close it tight. Close 'em all tight.'

* * *

The snow fell so hard that the world outside the windows was nothing but a blur of white. Doug and Angela had been up late, and not woken until after nine. Now noontime had come and gone as he emerged from the shower and crossed Angela's bedroom to peer outside. White, yes, but really the world had turned gray. Pressing his face against the cold glass, he looked up in search of some sign of daylight. Tomorrow — morning or sometime in the afternoon — the sun would return, the sky would be blue, and then the massive snowfall would attain the whiteness that nature intended.

Today, though . . . today he saw nothing but gray. It occurred to him that this was the true state of the world, endless gray, trapped between light and dark. He laughed at himself for even thinking it.

Now you're a fuckin' philosopher, he thought, turning from the window and grabbing the overnight bag he'd brought in the night before.

Clean socks and underwear, a fresh T-shirt, some deodorant, a toothbrush. He pulled on his clothes, including the jeans from the night before, brushed his teeth, and then left the bedroom, lured through the apartment by the delicious aroma of frying bacon.

'Something smells good,' he said as he walked down the short hall that opened into the large space that included the living room on one side, a dining area in the middle, and the kitchen tucked away on the other side.

Angela stood at the stove, hip cocked as she used a fork to flip the bacon slices. She had slept in a flannel pajama top and nothing else, but while he'd been showering she had located the bottoms and slipped them on. Though he'd have preferred her without them, he couldn't deny that she looked adorable.

Jesus, there's a word you'd never have tagged her with in the old days.

But then again, the old days were just that, and he was interested in starting over.

'Good morning, sleepyhead,' she said, arching a playful eyebrow.

'Please. You slept just as late as I did. You just don't have anywhere to be.'

Angela pointed to the small television on the counter with her fork. The volume had been turned down low, and soft voices emanated from it. On the screen, a reporter stood in the driving snow in heavy winter gear, standing with her legs apart to keep from being blown over by the powerful wind.

'Nobody has anywhere to be,' Angela said.

307

'Schools are canceled everywhere. The governor has asked businesses to let people work from home to keep cars off the roads and let the plows and sanders do their jobs.'

She had cracked three or four eggs into a bowl and now began to beat them with a whisk.

Doug barely noticed, staring at the TV screen. 'Perfect.'

A map of central New England showing snowfall totals appeared onscreen. For a moment he thought this was a forecast for the entire storm, but then he caught the words despite the low volume and realized that while they'd been sleeping, sixteen inches of snow had already fallen. He glanced at the clock about the stove — nearly ten A.M. Nearly a foot and a half in nine hours or so, and no end in sight. He felt a twist in his gut and wasn't sure if it was fear or anticipation.

He retrieved a glass from the cabinet and turned back to Angela.

'If we're doing breakfast for lunch, I'm going to have some OJ. Can I pour you some, or are you sticking with coffee?'

She poured the egg mixture into a large nonstick pan, focused on the work as if he hadn't said a word. Doug frowned, watching as she added salt and pepper and then dumped a handful of shredded cheddar cheese into the eggs.

'Angie?'

'Get out some bread, would you?' she asked. 'I forgot . . . '

Her back to him, she began to shudder.

'Hey, hey,' Doug said, going to her and putting his hands gently on her shoulders. 'What's going on?'

Angela shook him off, using a plastic spatula to chop and scramble the eggs. The bacon had started to burn, so Doug turned off that burner and slid the pan onto one that she hadn't been using.

'Angela. Look at me.'

When she turned, her face was flushed pink and there were tears on her cheeks. She pursed her lips as if trying to hold back words she refused to speak.

'Oh, shit,' he said. 'What did I do?'

Rolling her eyes, she allowed herself a little laugh, but the sadness quickly returned.

'You didn't do anything,' she said. 'It's just this storm. And you're going out, and I don't know what's going to happen.'

The eggs had been on too long now, and Doug moved to her and kissed her forehead and whispered for her to let him take over. She stepped back, swiping at her tears and taking deep breaths to get herself under control. As he slid the eggs around in the pan, he lifted it off the stove and shut off the burner.

'Plates?' he asked.

Angela nodded, wiping her eyes one last time before standing on tiptoe to get a pair of plates from the cabinet. Doug used the spatula to scrape the eggs onto the plates in equal portions.

'That's too much for me,' she said.

'They're good for you,' he said, handing her the plate. 'Get your bacon and sit. I'll bring over

309

your coffee and get us some juice.'

She did as he'd asked and in another minute they were facing each other across the small table. Doug couldn't resist stuffing a slice of bacon into his mouth while she played with her eggs and took a sip of juice.

'We forgot the toast,' Angela said quietly, not looking at him.

'Screw the toast.'

She picked up a forkful of eggs and gave him a weary smile. 'Kinky.'

As beautiful as she was, for the first time he noticed just how dark were the circles beneath her eyes.

'Did you have trouble sleeping last night?' he asked.

'Maybe a little,' she said, and they both knew this was a lie. She'd had a lot more than a little.

'What's going on, Ange?' he asked, and then he let the question float there. He picked up his orange juice to give her time to gather herself, watching her over the rim of the glass as he took a sip. She hadn't wanted him just to hold her, to comfort her, so he needed her to talk.

She cupped her hands around her coffee mug, enjoying the heat coming through the ceramic. Cherie had always done the same thing when the weather turned cold and it reminded him just how close the two women had been.

Angela fixed him with a hard look, no trace of a smile. 'Take me with you.'

'Take you where? You think I'm leaving — '

'Today,' she said. 'Take me with you today.'

Doug blinked, mouth opening in a silent *O*.

He sat back in his chair and slowly shook his head.

'Babe, you know I can't do that.'

'You have to.'

He studied her face. Where the hell was this coming from? He liked the new Angela Ristani — might even be able to love her — but if her transition from bitch to sweetheart included this neediness, that was going to be a problem.

'You don't know what you're asking,' he said grimly, leaning forward to put emphasis on his words, studying her eyes. 'This isn't some kind of boys' outing. We're not going sledding or ice fishing or something. Baxter and Franco would not react well to you showing up. Hell, Baxter might just shoot us both.'

Angela scoffed, picking up a piece of bacon. 'Bullshit.'

Doug grabbed her wrist as she tried to put the bacon into her mouth. He squeezed, knowing it might hurt her a little but needing her to pay attention. Her eyes brightened with surprise and anger.

'Listen. Franco's an asshole, but I don't think he'd kill anyone. Baxter, though . . . I've known that guy most of my life. He did time in prison. I've heard rumors, some drug thing, once upon a time. Point is, I have no doubt that if it came down to him going back inside or pulling the trigger, we'd both be dead. So, I'm sorry, but you're staying right here. The guy's not going to commit a whole fucking boatload of felonies with someone he's just met.'

He saw that she wanted to argue, watched the

311

struggle in her eyes, and then she turned away, her breakfast forgotten. Doug got up from his seat and went around the table to kneel beside her, touching her hair, turning her face toward him.

'You know this. You're a smart woman. So what gives?'

When she spoke, it was barely above a whisper and with eyes downcast.

'I just think we should stay together,' she said. 'I'm afraid something's going to happen.'

'I'll be fine, I swear,' he said, trying to reassure her. 'I'll be careful.'

'It's not . . . ' she began, faltering and then finally lifting her gaze. 'I don't want to be taken away again. I just got back to you.'

Doug knitted his brows at the odd phrasing, but the message was clear enough. The first time they had dated, he'd had no idea how much she cared for him. He wasn't going to make the same mistake again.

'I told you I'm not going anywhere,' he said. 'Neither are you. I know it's early days for us, but I like this . . . like being with you . . . very much. It was a little weird the last time. I felt like we both loved Cherie so much that in some way she was still between us. But now it's just you and me, and I think she'd approve.'

Her smile was bittersweet, but did not erase the worry in her eyes.

'I think she would,' Angela said.

'And I want to see where it goes.'

'Me too,' she said, closing her eyes as if it hurt her heart to say it. 'You have no idea.'

Angela sighed and kissed him, first on the forehead and then on the mouth, lingering for a while, her tongue touching his.

'Just promise me you'll take care of yourself,' she said, searching his eyes as if trying to memorize them in case she never saw them again. 'And watch out. You never know what's going to be waiting for you in a storm like this.'

★ ★ ★

Harley strode through the storm, fighting the wind and the snow that pelted his face. It was midafternoon but it might as well have been midnight for all the daylight the storm let in. He would have cussed about it but his jaw was clenched in aggravation at the bitter cold that seemed to bite right through his clothes and cut him to the bone. The wind raged and swirled so much that it drove snowflakes down the back of his jacket and the collar of his shirt. Violent meth-heads and back-alley gangbangers he could handle — hell, he'd made short work of his fair share — but out here in the storm he felt like a little kid again. He just wanted a blanket and his old sofa and the TV remote. And cookies. Hell yeah, he wanted cookies, still hot from the oven.

The crew from National Grid had arrived and was already raising the bucket on their truck to reach the power lines. One of the lines had come down and the transformer had blown. The good news was that the downed line wasn't going to electrocute anybody; the bad news was that thousands of people in Coventry were without

313

power. On the way over here, Harley had driven through several neighborhoods that had gone dark. Tonight there would be candles and flashlights and lots of blankets. The ones who could manage it and were smart would visit relatives or get a hotel room somewhere with power and heat, but that would also mean traveling in the blizzard, and that might be more dangerous than a frigid night at home.

'You guys need anything?' he called, raising his voice to be heard over the roar of the blizzard.

Several of the crew looked up at him, then went back to their work. An older guy, winter hat pulled down tightly over his ears, waved to Harley.

'We're good. Long as you keep anyone from plowing into us, we'll get this bitch purring again.'

'You got it!' Harley said, waving as he turned back to his vehicle. Only once he had climbed back inside and moved the car to block oncoming traffic, flipping on the blue lights, did he continue grumbling to himself.

There had been plenty of shifts that he had spent sitting on speed traps and lots of overtime working traffic details for road construction. It bored the crap out of him. If it hadn't been for the weather, he would at least have stood outside and directed traffic, giving him a chance to talk to the crew or to passersby, but nobody would be passing by tonight. And no way in hell was he going to stand around in the middle of a blizzard when the blue lights were all the warning that drivers needed.

314

He left the engine running so that the heat would stay on, watching the blues strobing off the trees and the National Grid truck and every fat snowflake and listening to the static and garbled voices on his police radio. It had already been a long day and it was barely half past one. He didn't want to think about what the night would bring. The shift he'd been scheduled for wouldn't normally take him into the evening hours, but he was fairly low in seniority and he had a feeling some of the older guys would be playing that card, leaving the rookies and the young guys out in the cold.

Harley sighed and slouched in the seat, leaning his head back. Idly, he slipped his cell phone out and glanced at it to see if he'd had any calls or texts. In the past couple of days he'd left three messages for Jake Schapiro and hadn't heard back. Something was definitely going on with Jake and Harley worried that his friend was in some kind of trouble. Had he not gone out to the house and seen Jake with his own eyes, he might have been worried that he had somehow offended the guy. But whatever had gotten into Jake's head, he hadn't seemed pissed at Harley. Just preoccupied and a little paranoid. Harley thought of the way the shades had all been drawn and how strangely Jake had acted when he'd gone to the door. At first Harley had thought Jake had a woman inside, but when he'd ruminated on it later, he'd decided that didn't seem likely. If he'd been having some kind of torrid sex weekend, that would explain how tired he looked and maybe — just maybe — the shades being drawn. But Jake had been unshaven and appeared not to have taken a shower. He'd looked skittish and not a little ill. That wasn't the look of a man who'd fallen in love, or even a guy who'd gotten very lucky.

What the hell are you up to? Harley thought, checking to make sure he hadn't missed any texts.

'What are you hiding?' he said aloud, and then he frowned. The question had come unbidden, as if surfacing from his subconscious, but now that the idea had been voiced it stuck in his mind.

The way he'd stood in the doorway that day, blocking Harley's view into the house, holding those cards . . .

Harley stopped breathing. Closed his eyes and focused on his memory of those cards. He leaned forward and put his forehead against the steering wheel, slowly exhaling.

'Oh, fuck,' he whispered in the confines of the car.

He'd thought they might be playing cards, even tarot cards, but something about them had been familiar. He hadn't seen the backs of the cards or he would have recognized them right away. The way Jake had been holding them, he'd gotten only a glimpse of the front, and even then only the mostly yellow borders at the tops of the cards. They had seemed familiar and now he understood why. He'd played the game often enough as a little kid.

They were Pokémon cards.

A dreadful suspicion filled Harley. He stared

out the windshield at the National Grid crew but barely saw them, his mind turning inward. What the hell was Jake Schapiro doing playing Pokémon with all the shades drawn, and whom had he been playing it with?

He reached for the radio but his fingers froze a few inches from it. *This is Jake we're talking about*, he told himself. *The guy's your friend. You're gonna ruin his life on a damn hunch?*

No. He wasn't going to do that. He felt guilty enough just to be thinking the things he was thinking. Jake Schapiro had never been the kind of guy to share his most intimate emotions or his secrets, but the same could be said of Harley. They were friends, and he had never gotten any indication that there was anything deviant about the guy. He had to go about this carefully.

Please, he thought to himself *Please, don't be a monster.*

His cell phone had been acting hinky ever since the storm began, so it didn't surprise him that his call didn't go through the first time. By the fourth try, he'd grown frustrated enough that he was on the verge of leaving the National Grid crew on their own, but then the static on the line cleared and he heard it ringing.

On the fourth ring, there came a fresh burst of static and then a voice. 'This is Keenan.'

'Detective, it's Harley Talbot. We need to talk.'

★ ★ ★

As night came on, Ella popped a fresh pod into her coffeemaker and hit the button, listening to it

317

gurgle and hiss for a few seconds before the French roast began to flow into her mug. Just the smell of it was enough to please her. Once she'd added the cream — she wouldn't dare taint it with so much as a grain of sugar — she held the mug up and blew ripples across the liquid surface. The coffee would help warm her. Even with the heat on and the thick, black sweater she'd donned, the view out the kitchen window made her shiver. The storm raged out there and it didn't look like there would be any end in sight.

Part of her was relieved. Business at The Vault had been thinner than usual with all this inclement weather and somehow it had lifted the burden of worry from her shoulders when she had realized that she had no choice but to stay home and keep the restaurant closed.

Of course, home had its own worries.

Ella sipped her coffee and tried to ignore her fears.

'Hey.'

She flinched, spilling hot coffee onto her hand.

'Son of a bitch,' she said, putting the mug down and rinsing her hand in the sink.

TJ came over and ripped a paper towel off the roll, wiping up the mess with a penitent expression.

'Sorry. Didn't mean to startle you.'

'I'm just jumpy,' Ella said. One hell of an understatement. 'Been jumpy all day.'

Paper towel balled in his hand, TJ leaned against the counter and looked at her. Ella used a dish cloth to wipe the coffee off the exterior of the mug and then took another sip, grateful that she had spilled only an ounce or two.

'What are we going to do about the little old lady in the living room?'

Ella stared at her coffee, not looking up. This was the conversation she'd been dreading all day. With the three of them snowbound together, it ought to have been an opportunity to watch movies or play games, a chance for Ella and TJ to continue to repair the cracks in their relationship and to shower attention on their daughter. That was what snow days were meant for, not this tension, this breathless confusion.

'I don't know,' Ella said quietly, glancing at the kitchen door to make sure Grace had not come in after her father. 'I thought it must be just a game she was playing, but this morning she's even worse. Even more . . . strange.'

Strange wasn't the way she had intended to finish that sentence. Even more of a bitch, maybe. More like an old woman.

'We need to bring her to a therapist or a psychiatrist or something, get her evaluated,' TJ said.

'God, I hate that word. 'Evaluated,' as if human emotions are fucking mathematics.'

TJ put a hand on her arm and Ella felt her anger draining away, leaving only her sadness and confusion. She turned to face him.

'You want to take her out in this storm?' she asked.

'No. But I want to make an appointment for her. I'll make some calls, get some recommendations. I know the day's getting away from us, but the doctor's office will probably at least have the answering service covering the phones, even with the blizzard.'

'Hell,' Ella said, 'maybe we should get an exorcist.'

A soft, girlish laugh came from the kitchen door and they both spun to see Grace standing there on the threshold, framed in the entrance to the room. Only she didn't look like Grace; not really. Not now that Ella was looking at her dead-on and the girl had surrendered the effort she'd been making at normalcy.

'That's pretty funny,' Grace said, her voice the same but with a harder edge. Her little girl, but with a jaded weariness that only adults ever achieved. 'I always knew he'd marry a girl with a sense of humor.'

'Grace?' TJ said.

But Ella could tell that he no longer believed he was speaking to his daughter. She could see it in her husband's eyes and hear it in his voice and for a moment her heart swelled with terror as she wondered if she might not have been too far off . . . if it was possible, after all, for a demon to have inhabited her baby girl.

'She's here,' the girl said, 'but I think we all know you're not talking to her right now. Come on, Thomas. You were always very intuitive, for a boy.'

TJ raised a hand to cover his mouth, his eyes wide. Ella felt the wave of fear that came rolling out of him and it gripped her as well. Her eyes welled with tears. She had been half kidding before, but her whole world had just shifted.

320

'What the hell — ' Ella began in a whisper.

Then TJ spoke a single word that shut her up. 'Mom?'

Ella turned to stare at him, pieces falling into place in her mind. Impossible pieces. The house was silent except for the brutal rushing of the wind that made it creak and sway and battered it with heavy snow.

'TJ?' Ella said, her voice cracking.

Grace stepped toward them.

'No!' TJ shouted, one hand up, shaking his head and trembling with emotion that seemed caught between fear and anguish. 'You stay right there! Right fucking there!'

Grace watched them with ancient eyes. The little girl tilted her head and sighed impatiently, an aura of sadness around her.

'I'm sorry,' she said. 'Thomas. Ella. I swear to you that I didn't plan for any of this, and I certainly never wanted to hurt or frighten you. But it's too late for apologies now, and too late for tears. You're going to have to hide me, you see.'

'Hide you?' Ella echoed.

Grace turned to the window, chin high, looking stronger and wiser than any eleven-year-old girl ever ought to look.

'I can feel them out in the storm.'

Snow struck the screen outside the window, whiting out the world.

Grace turned back to them and looked at her mother with a stranger's eyes.

'They're coming.'

17

Miri had spent most of the day hiding away from the storm. She'd had to fight the temptation to pull the drapes, order room service, and find a marathon of nineties' sitcoms on TV, ride out the storm with *Friends* or *Seinfeld*, which seemed to be on one channel or another twenty-four hours a day. Instead she was out driving in the snow, hands white-knuckled on the wheel. The wind slammed her rental car hard enough to rock it from side to side and the blizzard punched at her windshield, snow falling so hard that her wipers couldn't keep up. She sat forward in the seat, heat blasting at her face and heart slamming in her chest, doing her damnedest to see more than five feet beyond the nose of the car.

A burst of static came from the radio and she jumped, startled, and glanced down, only to find the panel dark. The radio had been silent before and it was silent now because she had turned it off when she'd gotten behind the wheel, not trusting herself to avoid distraction. Frowning, she tapped it on and listened to the music fill the car, an old Dave Matthews song that she had entirely forgotten until it sparked to life in her brain right then, filling her with thoughts of middle-school dances and the arrogant boys who'd always been her fascination. That had been her undoing, really. She loved Jake, but with him there was always the painful undercurrent of their shared anguish. With those arrogant boys, she had always been able to forget, but she had regretted every kiss and fumbling backseat fondle.

Inhaling sharply, she hit the button to silence the radio again. To silence the past.

Tonight, arrogant boys would not do. She needed not to forget but to remember, and she needed to talk to the one person who would understand what she was feeling. If she told Jake about going to her mother's house the night before and finding her with Doug Manning, he would understand the pain in her heart implicitly. He knew her better than she knew herself.

Which is exactly why you moved three thousand miles away.

The thought stung her, but there was truth in it. She had left to escape her mother's indifference, but also to put the past behind her. Put the pain behind her. And as much as she loved him, she could never separate Jake from that past or that pain.

Still, ever since she had decided to return to Coventry she had intended to go to see him. She had seriously entertained the possibility that she was losing her mind, and that was one of the reasons she needed to see Jake. Being in his presence, wrapping her arms around him and getting the rib-crushing hugs that she had only now begun to realize she had desperately missed . . . that would give her perspective. This morning, with the storm in full swing, she had decided to call him and arrange a visit for

323

tomorrow. She'd tried several times and left messages, even sent texts, but received no reply. Miri knew that Jake owed her nothing after the way she had abandoned Coventry, and the way she had abandoned him, her best friend. But it still hurt.

Unable to reach him, she had decided to dare the storm, to roll the dice and hope that the tires on the rental car were up to the task. Only now that she was out driving in the middle of it did she realize that she had never really intended to make the drive out to Jake's farmhouse. That could wait until the storm passed, until the city plows finally got around to clearing the side streets that they had thus far mostly ignored.

Last night she had seen her father's ghost in the middle of a flurry of snow, and when the snow had stopped falling, the ghost had vanished. What now, then, with the blizzard raging around her? Every time her cell phone rang, she had hoped to hear his voice again, if only to erase whatever doubts she had about that first call. But she had not heard from him since.

You saw him, she thought. *That's better.*

Leaving the hotel, she had stood in the parking lot and let the snow and wind pummel her as she called out to him, her voice stolen away by the storm. She had glanced around the parking lot, hoping to see him, wishing for any sign that he had not left her behind again.

Now she drove carefully, trying to stick to roads that had been recently plowed and sanded, but in most places it was difficult to tell. The snow fell too fast for the city to keep up. Still, she managed to get across the new bridge and, sticking to main roads, found her way to Allie Schapiro's house — the last place she had seen her father alive.

Pulling to the curb, she killed the engine and shut off the headlights and sat in the darkness, watching the snow fall. Bent over the steering wheel, she looked up at the darkened windows of the room that Jake and Isaac had shared as boys. The window to the right drew her attention, though it could not have been any darker. Nothing moved there. The window had nothing at all remarkable about it except for the fact that once upon a time a little boy had fallen from it to his death.

The engine ticked as it cooled. Miri sat there watching the house, watching the snow swirl and eddy and gust with the storm, hoping. A light burned in an upstairs room — maybe Allie's room — and the living-room windows on the first floor held a dim golden glow. The car rocked and the wind whistled around it and after a time the engine ceased its ticking, too cold to make a sound.

Miri sat in the car long enough for her hands to start to hurt from the cold.

'This is stupid,' she whispered, her voice seeming somehow louder than it should.

Despite her frustration, she could not bring herself to leave yet. Instead, she popped open the door of the car, a little alarm dinging inside until she plucked the keys from the ignition. She wore leather gloves and a knit cap and a handwoven scarf, but these were slight protection against the ferocity of the storm. It tore at her, hammered the cold into her bones. Stuffing her gloved hands into the pockets of her coat, she stepped into the middle of the street and inhaled deeply of the frigid air. Somewhere far away, a plow scraped pavement. The bell in the library tower rang, the sound echoing strangely in the storm and rising and falling with gusts of wind.

'Dad?' Miri called, looking around, feeling foolish as the cold wind bit at her exposed skin.

She went to the spot where Isaac had died. Memory rushed into her, stealing away her breath. She squeezed her eyes shut but grief waited for her there, inside her head, and so she opened them again to escape the images that still remained — images of little Ike Schapiro broken and twisted and then carted away on a gurney, his face the last thing visible as they zipped him into a body bag.

Miri glanced up at the window from which Isaac had fallen — or been dragged, the way Jake told it.

A face looked back down.

Her mouth opened, a tiny sound of terror escaping her lips as she backed away from the house. Her hands were shaking and her heart thrummed so loudly that it took her a moment to realize that the face looking down upon her belonged to Allie Schapiro. Ms. Schapiro put a hand over her mouth in surprise, but now she slid the window open.

'Miri? Is that really you?'

'Yeah,' she called up. 'Sorry, Ms. Schapiro. I didn't mean to scare you.'

326

'What are you doing out in this weather?' she asked, but with an edge to her voice that very few people would have understood. What she meant was, *What are you doing out in this storm when you know what can happen?*

'It's hard to explain,' Miri said, glancing back at her car.

'You wait right there, then,' Allie said. 'You might as well tell me over coffee.'

'That sounds — ' Miri started to say, but Allie had already slid the window shut.

Miri smiled to herself. She had always liked Allie, even back when the woman had just been Ms. Schapiro, her teacher, instead of her father's girlfriend. During that brief time when she'd thought that they might all be a family, she had fantasized about what it might be like, and worried about what it might mean for her love for Jake.

Little-kid stuff, she thought. *Puppy love.*

She spared one more glance at the snow-packed road beneath her feet, remembering Isaac. Her father had gone for help, rushing off to chase the distant sound of a plow — quite like the scrape and roar she could still hear, even now.

Miri turned to look off in the direction her father had gone that night, when she'd watched him vanish into the storm.

And he was there. Translucent, unaffected by the snow and the wind, the storm passing through him as if he weren't there at all. But he was.

Her heart lit up. She had expected to be afraid

327

or disoriented. Instead she felt nothing but joy, so powerful that she began to weep tears that felt warm on her cheeks.

'Daddy,' she said, and she started toward him.

Her father's ghost smiled, his eyes even kinder than she remembered. He reached out a hand as if he might touch her, but when she went to take it her fingers passed right through him.

'*I'm sorry*,' the ghost said. '*I can't . . .* '

A scream cut him off, then stopped abruptly, echoing in the storm. Miri spun just in time to see Allie faint dead away, tumbling headfirst out her front door and into the snow.

Miri took a step toward her and then halted, remembering the way the ghost had vanished the night before. She spun around, her heart aching at the thought of him going away again, but this time the ghost remained.

'*It's all right*,' her late father said. '*Go to her. There are things you both should know.*'

★ ★ ★

The key was not to get greedy. Doug had reminded Franco and Baxter of that half-a-dozen times leading up to today and he knew they were sick of hearing it. Fortunately, it seemed they had been listening. Baxter had been a thief for most of his life and Franco had taken to it easily. Doug had taken more convincing and he had felt bad after each burglary, especially the night they had stolen a Bose stereo system. Yes, the sound was amazing and it was worth a mint, but at the end of the day it was just a stereo.

Their shopping list was supposed to be simpler than that — jewelry, cash, credit cards, and anything kept in a safe that looked valuable. He dreamed of finding a stack of old bearer bonds, the kind of thing that people stole in movies from the seventies.

In the past they had taken art and small antiques when those things were given a special display in the house, but two-thirds of that stuff had turned out not to be worth the hassle. Since none of them was an expert and because they had four houses they wanted to hit during a single storm and they could steal only what they could transport by snowmobile, they had decided to forgo anything about which they were uncertain.

Doug moved across the carpet in Ted and Paulette Harcourt's master bedroom. He held a backpack in one gloved hand and had already dumped the contents of Mrs. Harcourt's jewelry box inside. From the nightstands he had snatched a gold watch and several rings, and cuff links that seemed forgotten at the bottom of Ted Harcourt's sock drawer. Mrs. Harcourt would be wearing her wedding and engagement rings, but he had found an enormous diamond in an antique setting that he presumed had belonged to the woman's mother. Guilt had plagued him as he slipped it into the backpack and he had considered putting it back — just that one item; the other guys would never know — but the clock was ticking and it would take too long to fish it back out.

That was the only twinge of guilt he had felt

since they'd hit the first house, well over an hour earlier. The Harcourts — and the owners of those other houses — were rich as hell. Doug would have bet that none of them had ever had to wonder where his next meal would be coming from, never worried about being fired from a job or having to find a new one. People who came from this kind of money would never understand how good men could be driven to burglary. Other kinds of theft, certainly — white-collar thievery on a scale so huge that it was hard for Doug to wrap his mind around it — but small-time robbery? Never.

Fuck 'em, he thought.

It had become his mantra today.

The storm had hit so hard and so fast that a quarter of the city had lost power before noon, but still they had waited until sundown to get moving. The forecast showed the blizzard raging all night long, so they had plenty of time. Once he and the guys had reached the barn and borrowed the snowmobiles that were waiting for them there, they had ridden through the woods to take a closer look at their first target, the home of Sean Duhamel. The house had been pitch black, without so much as a candle flame inside. Without power or heat, the Duhamels had abandoned their home. Even if they had an alarm system hardwired to a security company, it wouldn't be working unless they had a generator. And if they'd had a generator, they wouldn't have bothered leaving home.

Sean Duhamel kept four thousand dollars in cash in an envelope in his sock drawer. Franco

330

had laughed as he counted it, almost giddy.

The Nathansons' house had been next. Mrs. Nathanson's weakness was for diamonds. They had a decent safe, but Baxter had made short work of it. Inside, they'd found a diamond necklace that Doug figured must be worth tens of thousands of dollars, two stacks of rainy-day money, a handful of other jewelry, and a baseball signed by Babe Ruth. They'd argued over the baseball. Franco wanted to snatch it, but Baxter sided with Doug: it would be impossible to fence something so easy to trace without getting caught. Furious at having to leave such a valuable item behind, Franco had grabbed a Sharpie from Alan Nathanson's office and blacked out Ruth's signature.

If Doug hadn't already been nursing a profound hatred for Franco, he would have hated him after that.

Now Doug entered the Harcourts' walk-in closet and started digging through the clothes and pushing aside hanging jackets, looking for a safe. A black dress hung there, beaded and slinky and probably worth thousands, and he was filled with anger at the thought that Angela would never be able to afford a dress like this, that he had never been able to take care of Cherie the way he had always wanted to, and she'd died before he'd ever had a chance to spoil her.

He found no safe or trick panel, so he reverted to the more reliable tactic of opening shoeboxes and hatboxes and upending them onto the floor, but he was only half paying attention to the task. All day his thoughts had been returning to the oddity of the conversation he'd had with Angela before he'd left her place that morning.

I just got back to you.

What the hell was that supposed to mean? Doug knew he shouldn't let semantics bother him, but those words had been niggling at the base of his brain. Of course he knew what she'd meant to say — *I just got you back* — but the phrasing had been quite awkward and she hadn't even seemed to recognize it. Even so, he doubted he would have noticed if not for the statement that had followed. Angela had said that she didn't want to be 'taken away' again.

The more he thought about it, the more he began to believe that she really had been taken away somewhere. Until she had shown up at his door over the weekend, he hadn't seen her for four or five months. Now he wondered if she had literally been taken away, either to rehab or into some kind of psychiatric facility. Either way, there were clearly some vital bits of information that Angela had not yet shared with him.

'Anything?'

Startled, Doug jumped a little as he turned to find Franco standing just outside the huge walk-in closet.

'Nah. No safe. No more jewelry. No secret stash.'

Franco scowled. 'What the fuck were you doing in there, trying on the bitch's shoes?'

Doug shot him a hard look. 'You fare any better?'

'Not much. Stack of credit cards in the guy's desk. Jeweled egg from a glass case — '

'An egg?'

'Like one of those Russian things,' Franco said. 'Baxter figures the stones are real, so it could be worth a mint. If you're done in here, let's go. We've got all we're gonna get.'

Doug nodded. Franco hesitated for a second, as if trying to decide if Doug had challenged him somehow. Baxter was the ex-con, but Doug had come around to the opinion that Franco was the more dangerous of the two. If something went wrong with this job, he was sure Franco would be the source of the trouble. He bore watching, so Doug slid his foot through the mess he'd left on the floor of the closet as if taking one last look for valuables, and waited for Franco to turn around and lead the way out.

Baxter met them in the corridor. He seemed to sense the tension in his partners and glanced from one to the other before gesturing toward the stairs.

'I checked the windows. Still no power in any of the houses I can see. There's someone home three houses up on the other side of the street — candles or flashlights or something — but other than that, the whole area's deserted. Not even a goddamn plow.'

Franco grinned. 'I love it.'

'Don't get cocky,' Doug said. He shouldered his backpack and brushed past them, heading down the stairs.

Franco swore at him, but he and Baxter followed a second later. They moved through the kitchen to the French doors that led out onto the snow-covered deck. Their footprints were clearly

333

visible out on the deck and in the yard, but the snow kept falling and soon there would be only slight indentations in the white sprawl to mark their passing.

Baxter held up a hand to caution them, took a second to scan the backyard, and then opened the door. In silence broken only by the crunch of snow underfoot, they hustled out into the blizzard. The wind shrieked around them. Doug had expected it to die down by now but it seemed only to have grown more powerful. Despite the biting cold, he smiled to himself. They were pulling it off. Hell, they *had* pulled it off. They could all go home now and come out way ahead. But they wouldn't do that. Doug had one more key, and there was no reason for them not to use it.

Franco and Baxter hurried across the yard. Doug followed, backpack heavier over his shoulder now, but he wanted it heavier still. They were out here freezing their balls off, getting tired from rushing through the ever-deepening snow. Only a fool would be out in the middle of this blizzard without a damn good reason, and they had the best reason of all.

The shrieking of the wind grew so loud that Doug slowed down, glancing around in search of some other source for the sound.

Ahead of him, Baxter stopped short and Franco ran into him from behind, nearly knocking them both over.

'What the fuck?' Franco grunted.

Baxter ignored him, his attention diverted toward the elaborate wooden swing set in the

334

middle of the broad backyard. The swings swayed back and forth with the ticktock creak of old metal hinges, but as Doug blinked melting snowflakes from his eyes, he realized that it wasn't the swings that drew Baxter's attention.

'You see this?' Baxter asked aloud.

In among the swings stood two figures, tall and thin and the same blue-white as the storm. They stood there, silently observing, and for a second Doug wanted to run. Then he understood that they were only an illusion, that someone had built snowmen or that the children who lived here had made some kind of scarecrows that the storm had crusted with ice and snow.

'Christ, they're spooky,' Franco said. He nudged Baxter. 'Come on. Let's go.'

They started for the woods again, headed for the snowmobiles, but Doug kept staring at the figures beneath the swings. His pulse quickened. Something about them drew his attention, made him give the swing set a wider berth. Whoever had built the snowmen had made icy scarecrows out of them. *Not kids*, he thought, a shudder running down his spine as he craned his neck to watch the things. Kids couldn't have made them so tall and thin. And how the hell had the gleam on those eyes been achieved?

Jesus, how did I not notice them before? Had the things been there forty minutes ago, when they had arrived? Of course they must have been. It wasn't as if someone had sculpted them in the short time he and the others had been inside the house.

Doug had just about convinced himself when the things began to dance.

They swayed languidly from side to side, arms out, beginning to twirl and to rise, moving with each gust of wind.

'Holy . . . ' Doug began, taking two steps backward, his throat going dry. A cold deeper than the chill of the air dug into his heart. 'I'm not . . . this can't . . . '

He couldn't finish a sentence.

One of them glanced slowly at him, ice-dark eyes upon him, and the frozen surface of its face cracked in a jagged smile of such malevolence that he felt a screaming terror awaken within him, a terror he hadn't known since he'd lain in the dark as a little boy, unable to breathe for fear of the dark whisper that he believed he'd heard beneath his bed.

The wind shrieked, snow stung his eyes, and as he blinked it away his terrified paralysis snapped. He turned to race after Baxter and Franco, and saw another one off to the left, in among the high, bare branches of the trees. It darted down through the branches toward Baxter and Doug felt fresh terror blossom in his chest. Impossible. It was all impossible.

But somewhere in the primal core of his brain he believed what he'd seen, because his hands were already moving. He tugged off one glove and reached for the gun tucked into the rear of his waistband, shouting for Baxter to look up.

Franco had stopped and turned, but he hadn't seen the thing in the trees. He was staring into the sky . . . into the storm.

Doug glanced up into the blizzard and saw others overhead, riding the wind, falling with the snow, moving out across Coventry like frozen angels.

Off to his right, the swing-set hinges creaked, and he spun to see the things sliding toward him through the falling snow.

Behind him, Franco began to scream.

★　★　★

Isaac had gotten his way after all. Jake had tried to take him into the basement, where he had a stack of old board games like Life and Monopoly and Pictionary, but it was cold down there and growing colder now that the power had gone out. With flashlights and extra batteries and thick blankets, plus a goose-down comforter that had once belonged to their mother, the Schapiro brothers had retreated to the closet and bundled themselves up. When the games had grown too boring for Isaac, Jake had decided to read to his little brother. Now they were a third of the way through *The Westing Game* and every few pages Jake would forget what they were doing there, forget what they were hiding from, forget that Isaac was dead and his ghost possessing the body of a little boy for whom the whole town had been searching.

Nobody was looking for him right now, of course. They had at least until the blizzard ended before they needed to worry about anyone continuing the search for Zachary Stroud. Tomorrow morning, when it had all passed and

337

the cleanup begun, they would worry about what to do next.

'You'll love this part,' Jake said, smiling in the glow of his flashlight off the page. 'Turtle is the best.'

Isaac didn't reply. Jake continued reading, but after a moment he heard a quiet sniffle and he looked up to see Isaac weeping in the yellow glow.

'Hey, Ikey, no,' Jake said, putting the book aside. He reached for his brother and pulled him close. 'It's okay, little bro. I've got you.'

Isaac shivered in his arms, as if the cold that had crept inside him could never be warmed. When he spoke, his voice was choked with tears.

'You don't understand,' Isaac said. 'I missed so much. You're so . . . you're old, now, and I'm still just me, and I missed so, so much.'

'Ssshh, it's okay,' Jake whispered, as his heart clenched and his own tears began to flow. 'It's okay.'

Isaac shoved him away and punched him in the chest, face red and twisted with anger.

'It's not okay!' he cried. 'You're not — '

Eyes widening, Isaac cut himself off, glancing in terror at the closet door, visibly holding his breath and waiting for some terrible repercussion to come from his raising his voice. Seconds passed and Jake only stared at him, until at last he reached out and gripped his brother's wrist and squeezed. Isaac met his gaze, eyes still wild with fear.

'I told you. It's okay. We'll have time together now.'

Isaac looked at him and for the first time Jake saw not only fear but real sorrow, aged and steeped in painful wisdom. They were the eyes of innocence lost.

'I'm not afraid just for me,' Isaac whispered, cradling his flashlight against his chest as if he wanted to curl into a ball and pretend he could not be seen. 'The ice men take all the heat from inside you. That's what happens when they kill you, Jakey. It's like they drink it all up, your heat. And then you belong to them, even after you don't have a body anymore, and they keep drinking from you, like forever.'

Isaac took Jake's hands in his own, crying softly.

'I don't want what happened to me to happen to you,' he said.

Jake could not muster a reply. Instead he shuddered and pulled Isaac to him again, the two of them under the blankets and comforter. They sat back against the wall with only each other for protection, both of them listening to the storm howling outside and staring at the closet door, hoping it would not come in.

★ ★ ★

Allie regained consciousness on the sofa in her living room, damp and cold and with a headache that started between her eyes and radiated in branches across her skull. She had a few seconds to wonder why her blouse was wet and then she heard a rustling noise and gentle footsteps and she shot upright, turning to see someone coming

339

toward her. Her heart jumped and then she exhaled as she recognized her visitor.

'Miri,' she said. 'It really *is* you.'

'It's me,' Miri replied. 'I made you a cup of tea, Ms. Schapiro — '

'Allie, please. And you didn't have to . . . '

Her words trailed off. Allie watched as Miri set the steaming mug of tea down on the coffee table and connections slammed together in her brain. She *had* seen Miri outside in the snow. That hadn't been her imagination. Allie touched the front of her blouse and felt the damp fabric and an image fluttered through her mind, the snow rushing up to greet her, the sensation of falling.

'I fainted,' she said, staring at the teacup.

'Yes.'

Slowly, she drew her gaze from the cup and studied Miri, the dark curls of her hair, her copper eyes like bright pennies, her tentative smile, hopeful, and full of worry.

'I saw . . . ' Allie began, and then she began to shake. Her hands trembled and she pressed them together, lacing her fingers as if afraid the pieces of her — broken for so long — might fall apart after all these years. She pressed her eyes shut and fought the tide of confusion and fear and hope long enough to speak the words.

'I saw Niko,' she whispered. 'I saw your father, out in the storm. I think I'm going crazy.'

She felt Miri settling onto the sofa beside her. The girl took her hand but she kept her eyes tightly shut.

'You did,' Miri said. 'And I'm so glad you did,

340

because it means that *I'm* not going crazy.'

Allie opened her eyes, turning to stare at Miri.

'That can't be. We both know — '

'And we both saw. He's here, Allie. Here with us, right now.'

Allie scooted back on the sofa until she could retreat no farther, glancing anxiously around the living room at the floral drapes and the unused hearth and the doorways that led to the foyer on one side and the kitchen on the other.

She let out a shuddering breath as a door slammed shut in her mind. The image she'd seen in the storm had to have been someone else.

But he was transparent. The snow passed through him. He was —

Her imagination.

Allie glared at Miri. 'Why are you doing this? What do you want? It's hard enough for me when it snows like this. You know that. After what we all went through, I can't believe you would — '

Something shifted in the shadows near the old fireplace.

'*She wouldn't,*' someone said in a low rustle of air. '*You know she wouldn't.*'

Allie covered her mouth, eyes wide, trembling with the urge to scream or flee or weep with joy, or perhaps even all three. The thing in the shadows could not have been called a man; it was barely more than a silhouette. A phantom.

'Oh my god,' she said behind her hand.

She wanted to faint and yet refused to allow herself to do so. She feared even closing her eyes, worried that the ghost would be gone when she opened them.

341

'Niko?' she said, her eyes filling with tears, her heart breaking all over again, pain as fresh as it had been that night twelve years past when she had lost her love and her baby at the same time.

A ghost, she understood, was a terrible thing. It gave her the pleasure of seeing his face and hearing his voice one more time, but he had only the specter of life in his eyes. Seeing the ghost of the man she'd loved felt like an assault, a mocking reminder of all that she had lost when he and Isaac had died, not just love and joy but her faith in the world and her hope for a future she would never have.

'Why?' she whispered.

The ghost hung his head, but not before she saw the pain in his eyes and knew that he understood that his presence was not welcome, that he had hurt her.

'*You have lost so much,*' Niko's ghost said, his voice a gentle touch. '*I would never wish you more pain. But there will be much more if nothing is done. Others will die, maybe others you love.*'

'Daddy, what are you talking about?' Miri asked, gripping Allie's hand.

'*Jake told you the truth,*' the ghost said, sliding nearer, emerging from the shadows. '*The ice men are real. And they're here.*'

18

Miri found it difficult to focus on her father's words. If she did not look directly at him, didn't peer too deeply into the shadows, it was possible for her to listen to the rumble of his voice and pretend — for several moments at a time — that he was still alive. In the presence of his ghost she had found that she could barely breathe. Niko Ristani had died when she was only eleven years old, young enough that when she wanted to remember his voice she had to put on old family videos and just listen. Now he was right here with her. Right here in this very room.

She felt damp streaks on her face and was surprised to find that she was crying. Tears reached her lips and she brushed them away, tasting salt. Her chest ached as if her heart had swollen within her, near to bursting.

The ghost hesitated.

'*Miri?*'

She closed her eyes, not wanting to look at him. Miri had seen him strike out into the blizzard that night in search of help, already traumatized by Isaac's death, and the next time she had seen him he was lying dead in his casket, the funeral home not quite able to cover up the blue sheen left behind from lying dead in the snow for days before discovery. And now he was here.

Niko had been a great father. The best. When he and Miri's mother had gotten divorced she had been too young to truly understand that there was enough blame to go around for both of them and she had believed Angela to be completely at fault. Those years when she'd had her father to herself had been the best years of her life. He had always told Miri that he could never hate her mother, because Angela had given him the greatest gift anyone could ever have. Even at the age of nine or ten she would roll her eyes, but in her heart she cherished those words. Busy as he was, he would always find time to hug her, and when he had days off he would take her to the beach or just huddle with her in his living room to read a book together, taking turns reading to each other. When he died they had been halfway through the second Harry Potter book. Miri had never picked up the book again, couldn't bring herself to read the rest of the series.

For her eleventh birthday, he had taken her to the Grand Canyon and they'd ridden mules all the way down and camped at the bottom. That night, they had lain on some rocks and looked up at the stars framed between the upper edges of the canyon walls, and Miri had cried because it was all so beautiful, and because she wished things could have been different and her mother could have been there with them and her parents still in love. That had been the night that Niko had told Miri that he was falling in love with Allie Schapiro. Though it had been so strange to think of her father with her former teacher — and she had reached an age where she could not trust the prospect of happiness — she had let herself think that perhaps there would be a new family and begin wondering how she would manage it, being around Jake so much without letting on how much she liked him.

The memories overwhelmed her. Niko hadn't been the perfect father — he could be short-tempered and often became too wrapped up in his work, and sometimes he said things about Angela that a child should never have to hear about a parent — but he had loved Miri and tried his best to show her that love.

'*Hey,*' the ghost said, startling her.

Then Allie's voice. A human voice. Alive. 'Miri, honey, please.'

'*Miri,*' the ghost echoed. She felt a chill and wondered if it had come from some draft in the house or off of him. '*Honey, I'm really here.*'

Opening her eyes, she spun on him, hands shaking as she gestured at the air as if she might wave him away.

'No, you're not. You're *not* here, Daddy. You're dead.'

She stared at him, forced herself to look at him and through him, to see the bricks of the fireplace that were visible through the gauzy nothing that her father had become.

Allie put a comforting hand on the back of Miri's neck, but she felt no comfort.

The sorrow in the eyes of her father's ghost broke her heart into even smaller pieces.

'*Yes,*' the ghost whispered, and his voice seemed to be everywhere and nowhere at once. '*I'm sorry that I left you that night. I would never have done it if I'd known that I wouldn't*

345

be coming back. But Isaac was dead and I couldn't stand to see you and Jake standing there by his body, to see Allie so broken. I went for help.'

'It never came!' Miri shouted at him, shaking off Allie's hand.

The ghost rushed at her so abruptly that she let out a scream. Allie scrambled back on the sofa but Miri did not move as Niko came up to her, almost nose-to-nose.

'Listen to me. Awful things happened in Coventry that night and help never came for anyone. Well, now those things are going to happen again, but tonight can be different. You and Allie and I . . . we can help, and not just the living.'

Miri stared at him, growing numb, as if so many conflicting emotions had simply overloaded her.

It was Allie who spoke up. 'What do you mean? Are you saying . . . ' Her voice lowered to a whisper. 'Is Isaac here, too? Like you?'

'Not like me, but yes, I think he's here in Coventry. And if we can't warn him and the others . . . '

The ghost shifted away, retreating to the shadows as if he found solace in them. And perhaps he did.

'Dad?' Miri said. 'I'm listening, now. Tell us what we need to do.'

The ghost remained in the shadows. They gave him more substance, somehow, and Miri studied him at last, hoping to etch the details of her father's face more deeply into her memory. The

346

slight curl to his short hair and high cheekbones and dark, serious eyes that could turn bright with laughter . . . only not now. Perhaps never again. Death had taken that from him.

'*Jake called them the ice men*,' the ghost began. '*I remember that. He got the phrase from Isaac and it's as good a term as any. The truth is that I don't know what they really are, though I have my suspicions. They live in the storm, but it's not just any storm. They exist in a kind of endless blizzard that is somehow its own place, a kind of frozen limbo. When it snows anywhere, this other, unnatural storm overlaps with our world.*

'*They killed me, of course. That night I was running toward the sound of the plow on the next street and two of them just plucked me up off the ground like birds of prey. I've never been so cold, not before and not even now . . . and then they dropped me. The fall did me in.*'

Miri shuddered and took Allie's hand.

'*They strip the ghost right out of you — that's the only way I can express it — and then you belong to them, dragged along in their wake from storm to storm. They survive on something they take from us at the moment of death, and then after, too, like leeches. Heat or life or soul, I don't know what. When you're in the storm you can sense the living world, feel its warmth just out of reach. That's the worst part, knowing how close you are to love and light.*'

'I'm so sorry,' Allie said.

Niko smiled softly and nodded to her. Miri wiped her eyes.

'I thought of you — both of you — during my time in the storm. I grieved for myself and at the thought of never seeing either of you again. Somehow I kept a little ember burning inside me, a purpose I held on to, and the last time it snowed here in Coventry, I could feel it. I willed myself toward it. That final ember gave me the strength to pull myself from their gravity and I found myself here, fully aware for the first time. When the snow falls, my thoughts are clearer.

'The others noticed. Isaac and the Newell boy and Cherie Manning and the rest from Coventry. I had left a trail for them and they slipped out after me, but none of them seemed to be able to focus the way I can. They decided that the only way to survive, to hide from the ice men, was to have a living body as an anchor.'

'What do you mean, 'anchor'?' Miri asked.

Niko's ghost looked at her. 'They've taken over the bodies of living people.'

'That's awful,' Allie said, crow's-feet turning to wrinkles as she frowned.

'Is it?' the ghost replied. 'They're afraid, Allie. They're hiding. I think some of them just want a chance at a proper good-bye, but I wouldn't be surprised if others intend to run off and start new lives in those bodies. The one thing I know for certain is that they were all hoping that escaping meant they were free, but it isn't that simple. The ice men noticed. They had to wait for a real storm, something powerful enough for them to come through.'

'And now it's here,' Miri said quietly.

'And now they're here,' her father said.

Allie tucked a stray lock of hair behind her ear. 'You said you had suspicions about what they are.'

The sight of her father's ghost shrugging with uncertainty was the strangest thing that Miri had ever seen. The strangest thing she ever hoped to see.

'They could be the gods of winter, the tattered remnants of long-forgotten deities, left over from an age when people worshipped the elements.'

Miri studied him. 'But you don't think so.'

'No, I don't. I think they're like me. I don't know how it started or who the first of the ice men might have been, but I think these things only look demonic. I think they're just hungry ghosts, searching for warmth. I think they're what will eventually become of us if we let them take us back into their storm.'

'Oh my god,' Allie whispered. 'Isaac.'

Niko's ghost nodded. *'Exactly. Isaac, and the rest of us. But they have limits. They can only exist here for as long as the storm rages. Once it begins to die down, they'll have to retreat along with it.'*

'So, if you can keep from being taken again until the blizzard ends . . . then what?' Miri asked, knowing that the answer would not be what she desired. Seeing her father like this would be the closest to a miracle she would ever get.

'I don't know,' he said, glancing away from her, the fireplace visible through the side of his face. *'I'd like to think that we can go on, then . . . to whatever waits for us all when we die.*

Wherever we're supposed to go. All I know is that I won't be dragged back to that frozen hell, and I have to do whatever I can to help the others. There may be places they can hide, places the storm can't reach them, but only if they know it's possible. I have to find them all, give them hope —'

'But you can't go out into the snow,' Allie said quickly. 'What if they find you?'

'*I broke away from them once already, Allie, and I have to believe I can do it again. We have to find the others —*'

'You don't know whose bodies they've . . . possessed?' Miri asked, barely able to get the word out. It felt so strange to say such a thing and have it be real.

'*I saw a few faces but I don't know the names.*'

'We have to call Jake. He'll help,' Miri said.

'*Will he believe you?*' the ghost asked.

'He saw them, remember?' Miri said. 'The ice men. If anyone will believe us, it'll be him. In fact, given the call he made to me the other day, it may be that he knows this already. But he hasn't been answering his phone all day.'

'Isaac,' Allie said, with a hopeful glint in her eyes. 'If his spirit really is here, and he hasn't come to me, he'll have gone to his brother if he can. He has no one else.'

'Then we go to Jake's,' Miri said, getting up from the sofa. 'I just hope the plows have done their job.'

Allie rose as well. She took a deep, shuddery breath and for the first time she approached

Niko's ghost, reaching out as though to caress his cheek. Her hand passed through him and when she turned away, Miri averted her gaze, hating to see the regret in Allie's eyes.

'We go,' Allie said. 'But we have a stop to make on the way.'

'*A stop?*' the ghost asked, his smoky form wavering a little, as if he might vanish.

Allie turned to look at him again, then glanced at Miri.

'I think I know where at least one of them is,' Allie said.

'Who is it?' Miri asked.

Allie frowned. 'I'm not sure, but it's one of the children and I think he's very confused and very frightened.'

'*It's good that he's afraid,*' the ghost said, stepping from the shadows and becoming even less substantial. '*Fear may be the one thing that keeps him safe.*'

★ ★ ★

At first, TJ had found it difficult to look at his daughter. His uncle Jim had once told him that Grace had 'her grandmother's eyes,' and the memory of that moment made him want to scream. He'd loved his mother — still loved her — but his conception of reality didn't allow for something like this. The idea that they both existed now, his mother and daughter both in one body, made him want to crawl out of his skin. It was simply wrong, truly abominable. All he wanted was to hold Grace in his arms but he

351

couldn't bring himself to do that now.

'Is she still in there?' he asked, forcing himself to look at the little girl with her grandmother's eyes.

'Of course,' Grace said.

But she's not Grace, TJ thought. *She's Martha.*

'Get out!' Ella screamed, making TJ jump. She strode the few paces that separated her from Grace and grabbed the girl by the shoulders, shaking her. 'God damn you, get out of her! How dare you do this?'

'You don't understand,' Grace said.

'Then make us understand,' TJ said, putting a hand on Ella's shoulder and drawing her back. 'Explain this . . . this insanity.'

And Martha did. Through her granddaughter's voice, she told the story of the night she died, of walking out into the blizzard and the things that came for her there, of the years living in a constant snow, a storm so cold that she knew she would never be warm, and a sudden opportunity for freedom.

'Mom,' TJ said when she was done, his heart like an aching pit in his chest, all the guilt of a dozen years burning inside him. 'I'm sorry. I wasn't here. I told you I'd stay with you and I . . . I'm so sorry.'

'No,' Martha said, and for a moment Grace's young features — just eleven years old — did look uncannily like her grandmother's. 'Don't do that to yourself, TJ. If you'd been here they'd have had you as well, and that would be another kind of hell for me altogether.'

'And now what?' Ella asked, anger and confusion darkening her eyes. 'What about Grace?'

'She's lovely,' Martha said. 'And as soon as this storm is over, I'll leave her. I think as long as I'm here, inside her, they won't notice me. If they're searching for the dead, they'll never realize — '

The wind gusted so hard that it shook the entire house, rattling the windows in their frames. They all flinched, startled, and stared at the window above the kitchen sink. A few seconds passed and TJ exhaled, turning back toward Grace, when the wind kicked up again, shrieking and battering the house, and this time it did not let up.

'What the — ' Ella began.

Something scraped along the outside of the house and TJ's mouth went dry. They heard scratching at the window and turned again, this time to see the fleeting image of a face outside in the snow, a hideous, jagged rictus of ice and glaring eyes. And then it was gone.

Ella screamed, even as Grace — Martha — grabbed both her parents by the hand and tried to drag them from the kitchen.

'We've got to hide!' she cried.

'You said you were already hidden!' Ella shouted. 'That they wouldn't find you!'

With terror in her eyes, Grace almost looked like their little girl again. TJ put himself between his family and the window, then glanced back at his daughter.

'What's going on, Mom?' he demanded. 'Why

353

aren't they just breaking the windows?'

'They move like the storm,' the late Martha Farrelly said in her granddaughter's voice. 'Solid as they can be, they can't come in unless the wind can find an entrance — an open door or window or a draft space.'

TJ glanced at Ella. 'Is the bedroom window still open?'

'I don't think so,' Ella said, flinching and twisting around at every scrape and scuffle on the roof and walls, her eyes frantic.

TJ had a moment to think about losing her — not just her leaving him, but losing her forever, and losing Grace as well — and a grim calm touched him.

'They'll find a way in,' he said. 'We need to — '

Ella did not have his calm. She spun on Grace . . . on Martha . . . and rushed to the little girl, grabbing her by the arms again.

'Let her go!' Ella shouted, her face etched with rage, hair falling wild across her face. 'These things are here for you, not Grace! You're willing to risk your granddaughter's life for your own! I don't care what kind of hell you were in — '

'I do,' TJ whispered.

Ella twisted to glare at him. 'What?'

'These things are *here*, Ella!' he said, stalking around the kitchen, turning at every sound, ready to fight if it came to that. 'We're all in danger, no matter what my mother does now.'

'What kind of person does this?' Ella demanded, eyes wide with disbelief.

Grace . . . Martha . . . pulled free of her grip,

staring at Ella. 'You haven't been where I've been. You don't know. I only need to stay safe until the storm dies down — '

'Will it ever?' TJ asked. 'Will they let it?'

'They don't bring the storm,' Grace said in that wise old little-girl voice. 'They only ride it.'

TJ racked his brain, trying to figure out where they could hide where the wind could never reach them.

Overhead, he heard the attic roof beams groan with the weight of the snowfall, threatening to cave in.

And what then?

★　★　★

Detective Keenan sat on his sofa, wrapped in a blanket and reading *Lonesome Dove* by candlelight. Without heat or electricity, the only sounds in the house came from the rattle and creak of glass and wood as it stood firm against the storm outside. His wife, Donna, had taken the boys and gone to her parents' house in Hingham the night before. They had lost power during the last three major storms to hit the Merrimack Valley and Donna had just not wanted to deal with keeping the boys warm and worrying about keeping them calm when they both were so afraid of the dark.

He missed them, but a night or two of quiet would be welcome. Or it would have been, were it not for the lack of heat and the way the cold seemed to take root in everything, its icy grip tightening as the temperature dropped. Had he

355

been able to go with them down to the South Shore, where they would be getting half as much snow and the storm couldn't even be called a blizzard, he would eagerly have done so. But Lieutenant Duquette had made it clear that, on duty or not, the entire department was to stay on call in case of emergencies, particularly once the storm had ended.

So here he was, alone on his sofa with his book and a couple of candles and a plate with the crust from his peanut butter and banana sandwich on the coffee table.

Headlights washed across the living room, casting his surroundings in an unearthly glow. Keenan glanced up from his book, listening for the scrape of a plow, but this engine was too quiet for one of those lumbering metal beasts.

Folding the page of his book, he set it on the coffee table and rose, going to the window. The snow fell so heavily that he could barely make out the snow-covered vehicle parked at an angle in front of the snowbank at the bottom of his driveway. Then the blue lights turned on, strobing the blacked-out houses up and down the street, and he saw the driver step out. The officer was a giant, and as he made his way through the sixteen inches or more of snow already on the ground, Keenan knew who he was long before he reached the front steps.

The detective didn't wait for the cop to knock. He pulled open the door.

'Evening, Harley,' Keenan said. 'Not much warmer in here than it is out there, but come on in.'

Officer Talbot stepped inside and stomped the snow off of his boots and Keenan swung the door shut behind him.

'Better get your coat, Joe,' Harley said. 'I kept trying your numbers but the landlines are tied up and your cell is all static. The storm is messing with everything.'

'Shit,' Keenan muttered.

All through this storm he had been unable to avoid thinking of the blizzard twelve years past and all those lives lost. Sitting alone in his cold, dark house, he had been grateful that he would not be the one to respond first if something awful happened. Yet here was Harley, dragging him out into the snow, and he wondered if the night would be any less terrible simply because he hadn't been first on the scene.

'What's goin' on?' Keenan asked. 'Don't tell me we got a homicide in the middle of this.'

Harley narrowed his eyes. 'No. It's nothin' official, actually. Nothing I wanted to call in.'

Keenan had grabbed his boots from the spot by the door where he'd left them to dry, but now he paused to shoot Harley a curious look.

'What's that mean?' he asked.

'Remember how I said Jake had been acting weird?'

'Jake Schapiro?' Keenan said, pulling on his boots.

Harley frowned. 'Yeah. Who else? I went — '

'Up to his door, right? You thought he had a girl inside.'

Harley looked queasy, like whatever thoughts were in his head had made him sick.

357

'He had someone inside,' Harley said. 'But it wasn't a girl.'

Keenan had knelt to tie one boot, but he snapped his head around to look up at Harley. A little tug of suspicion pulled at his gut, but he didn't want to believe it.

'Whatever you're trying to say, I wish you'd spit it out.'

'He had cards in his hand when he came to the door,' Harley said, his nose wrinkling in disgust or perhaps dismay, the words coming reluctantly to his lips. 'I thought they were playing cards, man. But a little earlier, I realized they were something else. I recognized them, Joe. The guy was holding a bunch of Pokémon cards.'

Keenan's gut gave a sickening twist. 'You're saying he's hiding a kid out there?'

Harley only stared at him, jaw grimly set.

'You think it's Zachary Stroud,' Keenan said.

'I think it could be,' Harley admitted. 'But if we report that and we're wrong, Jake'll never live it down. Never mind forgive us. He's my friend, Detective.'

'And if he snatched a lost kid whose parents were just killed?' Keenan asked.

'Then that isn't my friend out there in that farmhouse. It's a damn monster.'

Keenan finished tying his second boot, then grabbed his jacket and gloves and hat from the chair by the door.

'Let's go find out.'

★   ★   ★

358

Allie sat in silence in the passenger seat of Miri's rental car, wondering where Niko had gone. Swaddled in her white down coat, she huddled into herself, constantly checking her peripheral vision for ghosts. *Stop*, she told herself, but she couldn't deny the chill that danced along her spine. No man had ever been as kind to her as Niko Ristani. She had loved Jake and Isaac's father but they had married because she had gotten pregnant with Jake and just assumed that true intimacy would come in time. That had never happened; the army had kept him away from her more than he was with her, and then he had been killed in action. Allie had never really understood what it meant to be in love before Niko, never felt as if her heart had set sail from her body. Allie had lost him and grieved for that loss ever since, had wished for just one more day, one chance to tell him what he truly meant to her.

But not like this.

She felt as if she ought to be thankful, but instead she was terrified, pins and needles all over her skin, unable to catch her breath as she looked for some sign that the ghost might be in the car with them. It — he — had vanished into the storm the moment they had left Allie's house, but had said he would be with them. Allie felt something in the car, an unsettling frisson in the air that might have been the presence of the dead or simply a prickling fear that would be with her for the rest of her life.

'You okay?' Miri asked.

Allie jerked in her seat, turning to stare a

359

moment at Niko's beautiful, grown-up girl. She uttered an anxious laugh.

'Are you kidding?'

Miri frowned, hands tight on the wheel, driving so carefully in the storm as the wind buffeted the car.

'You're afraid of him? He'd never do anything to hurt you.'

Allie shuddered and covered her face with her hands. 'I know. I do know that.'

Miri said nothing. After a moment, Allie dropped her hands and looked over to see a tear sliding down her otherwise expressionless face.

'I'm afraid, too,' Miri said. 'I don't want to be, but I can't . . . '

Allie lowered her voice to a whisper. 'He's dead, Miri. He's not supposed to be here. People . . . we're just not meant to know the dead.'

If Niko's ghost was in the car with them, it gave no sign of having heard. Still, Allie felt his presence, felt a chill that the car's heater could never drive away. As Miri turned onto Bridle Path Road, trying to keep her tires in the tracks of other cars that had passed through the inches of snow that had fallen since the last plow had passed that way, the two women fell into a wary, fearful silence.

I'm sorry, Allie thought, knowing she should speak the words aloud. Her fear felt like a betrayal.

'Check it out,' Miri said. 'Gustafson's got company.'

Allie had told her the story of Eric Gustafson crashing his car into others in the drop-off line in front of the school on Monday and the way Gustafson had behaved, the way he'd cried while confessing that he had no idea how to drive a car. When Niko had been talking about the return of those killed that awful night, her thoughts had gone immediately to the city councilman and the frightened, childlike look in his eyes that morning.

Now they pulled up in front of his house to find that they were not his first visitors. A police car sat in Gustafson's driveway, only a fresh dusting of snow on the windshield — it hadn't been there very long.

Miri put on the car's hazard lights and they climbed out, instantly assaulted by the freezing white savagery of the storm. Bent against the wind, they trudged up the driveway, calf-deep in snow. Allie kept glancing around to see if Niko's ghost would appear but saw nothing out of the ordinary.

'Weird,' Miri said. 'The cop just plowed in here. No way he's getting out.'

Allie looked at the police car and understood immediately. The driver had plunged his vehicle into the unplowed driveway and must already have been lodged there in the entire blizzard's depth of snow.

'Let's be careful,' she said.

'And ready to run,' Miri replied.

They went up the steps and rang the bell. Councilman Gustafson's neighborhood was one of the few they'd passed through where the power was still on, but though there were plenty of lights burning within, the bell brought no reply. Allie rapped hard several times, and then again. They didn't have time to be polite. Niko's ghost had said they needed to warn all the spirits of the dead who had escaped the hell the ice men had made for them, and she was willing, but not until after she had seen that Jake was safe and learned whether Isaac's spirit had found its way to his brother's house.

And what then? she thought. *Will you be afraid of him, too? Of your baby boy?*

Allie knocked again, even harder. She had agreed to this first stop because she had seen Gustafson with her own eyes and because the house was practically on the way to Jake's.

'Forget it,' Miri said. 'Let's just — '

The door opened, but it wasn't Mr. Gustafson who greeted them. The policeman who'd so deeply committed his car to the snowed-in driveway stood staring at them. His name tag read TORRES.

'Can I help you?' Officer Torres asked.

'Is everything all right, Officer?' Allie asked. 'Is Mr. Gustafson — '

'Who the hell are you people?' the cop said, his eyes narrowing.

'We need to talk to Mr. Gustafson,' Miri said. 'And I'm wondering if maybe we need to have a talk with you as well.'

Allie saw the suspicion with which Miri and Officer Torres regarded each other and suddenly understood what Miri was suggesting. It all seemed so unreal to her that if she had not seen Niko's ghost for herself she would have thought that Miri had lost her mind, and if she was

362

wrong about this cop they might both end up in handcuffs.

'My name is Allie Schapiro,' she said. 'Mr. Gustafson's daughter is a student at the school where I teach. I need to speak to him.'

'In the middle of a blizzard?' Officer Torres demanded.

'Dad,' said a voice inside the house. 'It's okay. Let them in.'

Allie took a step back. *Dad?*

Officer Torres opened the door wider and they saw Gustafson inside, that same scared-little-boy look in his eyes, and Allie knew, then. She understood it all. Only one father-and-son pair had died during the blizzard twelve years past.

'Did you know they never found your body?' Allie said, barely aware that the words had come out of her mouth. 'Everyone assumed you had died that night, but we could never be sure.'

The cop's eyes went wide for a moment, and then he dropped his gaze, embraced by a sorrow it pained Allie to see. Gustafson came up beside him, one comforting hand on his back.

'Gavin?' Miri said, looking stricken.

'Hello, Miri,' Gustafson replied.

Allie could find no words, not even the warning she had intended to offer. Carl Wexler and his son were reunited, but in the bodies of a policeman and a city councilman, both of whom must also have people who loved them. They had no right to intrude upon these lives. When the storm had passed, perhaps their spirits would go on to a final rest, but what if they tried to hold on? The thought revolted her. The dead were

363

dead. They did not belong to the world any longer.

'Does your mother know?' Miri asked.

Gustafson shook his head.

'And she's not going to,' Officer Torres said. 'She has a new life, a new husband and a little girl. This is temporary. Telling her would only hurt her.'

'On that we agree,' Allie said, her skin crawling. 'We came to warn you — '

'They're here,' Gustafson said.

'Yes,' Miri said. 'But if you can make it through the storm . . . '

She faltered. Allie didn't know what had silenced Miri until she saw Gustafson's gaze and the fear in his eyes. She spun and saw something darting through the storm, a figure moving in the snow, saw it stop and turn and look at them, hanging there as the blizzard howled through it. Its eyes were like holes bored through into a frozen world of endless winter. Ice seemed to grip her heart and race through her veins, all warmth driven from her, and a terrible sorrow enveloped her. It felt as if the bottomless pits of its wintry eyes were leeching out her soul.

'They're *here*,' Gustafson said again. And this time there was no misunderstanding.

'*Get out of here, Allie*,' the wind whispered in her ear, snapping her alert as if she'd woken from a trance. The snow whirled beside her and became Niko's ghost, his face etched with panic. '*Miri, go! It's not you they want, but they'll kill you if you stay!*'

Allie tore her gaze from the thing in the storm

364

and felt her fear become hatred as she remembered Jake talking about the ice men. Another of them slid through the blizzard and circled the first and they seemed almost to be dancing. She had thought Jake had imagined it all, had constructed some fantasy to accompany the trauma of his brother's death. She had turned her own heart to ice that night and her relationship with her surviving son had never been the same.

'Bastards,' she whispered.

Then Miri grabbed her wrist and Allie was in motion, lurching and stumbling down the snowy steps and across the deep snow of the yard toward Miri's car.

'The wine cellar,' she heard Gustafson shout behind her. 'Dad, come on!'

Allie heard Miri screaming her name and looked up just in time to see the thing flying at her through the snow, its face chiseled from ice, its mouth open in a shriek of frigid wind that showed jagged white teeth. It reached for her with spindly icicle fingers and grabbed fistfuls of her coat and Allie screamed as her feet left the ground. The wind seemed to aid the force that carried her aloft. She felt its cold insinuate itself into her flesh and bone and heart, felt unclean in her own spirit as its malignance washed over her. The storm spun her around in the air and she kept screaming, thinking of the frozen limbo that Niko had told her about and that perhaps it wouldn't seem quite so much like hell if they were together.

Please, no, she prayed. *I don't want to die.*

For years she had been grieving, a shadow of herself, and now she mourned all the time that she had lost.

Allie saw Miri thirty feet below, arms reaching skyward, crying out for her.

And then she saw Niko. His ghost appeared beside Miri, reached out to touch her hair with insubstantial hands, and then lofted himself into the air with a gesture. He did not so much fly as appear and reappear in different snowy gusts, a violent winter zoetrope that lasted only heartbeats. Allie twisted in the demon's grasp to get another glimpse of the ghost, and even as she did Niko appeared in front of Allie's captor and swung his spectral fist. The ice man felt the blow and bared its needle teeth, whipped around, and dived after Niko's ghost. It lost its grip on Allie and she screamed, flailing at the air, snow whipping at her as she fell, landing on her back with an impact that knocked the breath from her lungs.

Miri appeared beside her. 'Anything broken?'

'I don't — ' Allie began, and that was all she managed before Miri grabbed her hand and hauled her up out of the nearly foot and a half of snow that had broken her fall.

Disoriented, it was all Allie could do to keep her feet beneath her as they raced toward Miri's rental car. She heard shouting behind her and turned to look back at the house, at the dead father and son who were haunting the bodies of the cop and the politician.

'Go, go!' Officer Torres shouted, but inside, Gustafson was calling to him — Gavin Wexler

366

pleading with his father, Carl.

Torres slammed the door and turned to face the snow as it built itself into a pair of ice men, spindly ice fingers curled into claws as they rushed at him. Allie head Gavin screaming inside the house, the ghost of a little boy with the voice of a man.

'Get to the wine cellar!' Torres shouted, but he didn't turn his back on the demons that flew at him. And then, loud and anguished, as if the words had been torn from his chest, he screamed out his love to his son.

Miri shouted at Allie, who turned in time to find herself careening into the side of the car. She bumped against it and then flung open the passenger door as Miri raced around to the driver's side. They tumbled in and Miri jammed the key into the ignition and started it up. As the engine roared, Allie glanced out and saw Niko's ghost reappear once, just ahead of them, beckoning them down the road. Her heart soared, knowing that he had escaped being dragged back into that hell. Not alive, but not one of *them*.

As Miri hit the gas and the tires spun in the snow, Allie glanced to the right and saw the ice men bent over Torres, digging into him and ripping out strands of a vapor she could barely see through the storm, ribbons of the thing she could only think of as Carl Wexler's soul.

'Faster!' Allie said as they pulled away. 'Get us to Jake's!'

'What about the rest of the ghosts?' Miri asked.

Allie thought of Carl and Gavin Wexler and how they had not wanted even the people who loved them and were still living to know they had returned. She realized that they had no way to predict the wishes of the dead.

'My concern is for Isaac and for your father, and for the living. The rest of them will have to fend for themselves.'

19

Timmy Harpwell drove his battered red F-150 through the storm, massive plow blade adding all the weight he needed for traction in the snow. He had three other drivers out working for him tonight, plowing a handful of private developments and business parking lots. A storm this size, they couldn't just wait until morning and deal with it then. Timmy understood that, but he sure as hell hadn't planned to be one of the grunts freezing his ass off tonight. He'd made the mistake of hiring his wife's nephew and the little puke had called in sick. Timmy had tried calling Franco, who hadn't been answering his phone all damn day.

'Assholes,' he muttered. He'd been in a perpetually pissed-off state for the past fourteen hours or so.

Lukewarm air blasted from the truck's vents. The truck's heater had chosen today to shit the bed, and he couldn't get properly warm. His fingers were cold on the steering wheel, even with gloves on, and his toes were cold, too.

I'm too young to feel this damn old, he thought.

The engine groaned under the weight of the plow blade as he hit the brakes, slowing down to turn into the parking lot of Dudley Plaza, a rinky-dink little strip mall whose anchors were Domino's Pizza and White Hen Pantry. Working the lever, he put down the plow blade and gunned it, clearing a swath of pavement. Six inches of snow had fallen since the last time he'd been by and the snow just kept falling.

'Fuckin' snow,' he whispered.

Timmy missed the shithole video store that had once been next to White Hen; they'd had the most interesting porn section in town. There wasn't anything you couldn't find online these days, no matter how perverse, but there had been something about perusing those video racks that he liked. For some reason, his wife would watch porn with him back when he could bring a videotape or a DVD home, but she thought there was something more unsavory about watching it on the computer.

Tonight his balls were so cold he didn't think he'd ever be able to get turned on watching porn — or doing anything else — again. When he got home, he'd wake Amy up and see if she wanted to try to warm them up. The thought brought the first smile to his face in hours.

He put it in Reverse, raised the plow, and took a swig of coffee as he backed up for another run. When he looked up, someone was standing in his path, headlights barely able to illuminate more than a silhouette.

Timmy leaned forward to peer through the windshield.

'What the hell?' he muttered. 'Out of the way, moron.'

Shifting into Drive again, he revved the engine, having no interest in rolling down the window and letting the storm in. Whoever the idiot in the middle of the parking lot in front of Domino's was, he didn't get the message.

'Oh, for Christ's — '

Timmy never finished the sentence. His mouth hung open and he stared, cocking his head to one side. The figure ahead had moved nearer as if sliding or gliding along the just-cleared pavement, crossing a dozen feet in an eyeblink, and now that it had come closer he could see it more clearly.

No way, he thought. *It's got to be some kind of* —

It flew at the truck, dagger fingers reaching, jaws wide, teeth bared, and shrieking in harmony with the storm. It struck the truck's grille just above the plow blade and vanished in an explosion of ice crystals that scattered across the windshield. Only then did Timmy realize that the shrieking had been his own and that the horrible, inhuman, keening wail was still coming.

Heart thundering, his whole body numb, he clapped a hand over his mouth to silence his screams. Taking long, hitching breaths, as cold as he'd ever been in his life, frozen to the bone, he looked at himself in the rearview mirror and saw the terror in his eyes and knew that he was not the man he had always believed himself to be. He felt his heart racing, felt himself on the verge of tears he refused to shed, and knew something had broken inside him. A strange sort of anger overcame him.

Franco, you motherfucker, he thought.

Whatever the hell had just happened — *a hallucination,* he told himself, *had to be —* he

371

never would have been out here if not for Franco. As Timmy exhaled slowly, his heart still banging, trying to get himself under control, he promised himself that he would make Franco's life hell for a while.

He frowned, realizing that the cold he felt was not just fear. His heater had finally died completely; nothing but frigid air was blowing in through the vents.

'Goddammit!' he shouted, liking the anger in his voice. It made him feel better.

He reached for the temperature-control knob . . . and something reached back. Ice crystals poured through the vents and sculpted themselves into sharp icicle fingers and grabbed on to his wrist.

Timmy shrieked as its face began to slide in through the vents, jaws wide.

He looked into its blue-ice eyes and saw a terrible nothing that seemed to fall into some soulless forever, and he pissed himself, the last of his dignity leaving him.

And then he died.

* * *

Doug stood in the storm, fighting the wind and the snow that whipped at him, and watched things carved out of ice drag Franco into the air. They were like wraiths, jagged, frozen bogey-men, and they whirled about on crushing gusts of wind for a second or two before they rushed head-on toward the sprawl of a tree's bare branches. Franco shouted for help, his voice

372

rising near a scream as he tried to fight them, and then there came through the storm the most sickening sound, a wet crunch as the wraiths impaled him on a pair of jutting, skeletal branches.

'Jesus,' Doug whispered, and he turned to bolt for the snowmobiles, furious with himself for the seconds he'd wasted by watching Franco's murder. Shock had paralyzed him and now terror freed him again.

A gunshot cracked the night, echoes swirling in the blizzard. Doug spun around to see Baxter pointing a gun at him.

'Is this you, Dougie?' Baxter asked, eyes wide with fear. 'Did you do this?'

'Fucksake, Bax . . . we gotta go!' Doug shouted over the screaming of the snowstorm. His heart banged against the inside of his chest. His face had lost all feeling; he had never felt such cold.

Baxter marched at Doug with the gun aimed at his face, as if the wraiths were not still there in the woods, watching, and whipping back and forth in the blizzard overhead. Had he really lost it so completely?

'Baxter — '

'What the hell *is* this?' Baxter shouted. Doug saw the frost that had started to form on his face and stuck his eyelashes together.

A crunch of boots on snow made them both turn and Doug had to shield his eyes from the snow to confirm what he thought he'd seen. Angela stood there, long ringlets of dark hair whipping in the wind, eyes wide with a sadness that broke his heart. Her thick winter coat and gloves and scarf might have made her look adorably comical any other night, anyplace other than this.

'It's exactly what I feared!' she said.

Baxter marched toward her, aiming at her chest. 'Who the hell are you?'

'No!' Doug yelled, darting between them, hands raised. 'She's with me, man.'

'So you had fucking backup? You had some double cross in mind?' Baxter screamed.

Doug knew then that he'd snapped. The things were watching, gliding lower, sliding from the woods and coming across the backyard toward them, the swing set left behind, and Baxter acted as if they were no threat at all, even though Franco's body hung impaled on a tree, blood already freezing in red icicles beneath him.

'It's not like that,' Doug said, his feet crunching in the deep snow as he backed up to where Angela stood.

'No? Then what's it like?' Baxter screamed, panic breaking him. 'What the hell is this shit?'

'They're coming,' Angela said quietly, and yet somehow — through some trick of the blizzard — her voice carried to both of them.

Baxter must have seen that she wasn't looking at him anymore. He turned to see what had drawn her attention and it was as if he awoke to the truth in that moment.

'Franco!' he screamed.

Instead of fleeing, Baxter raised his gun and ran toward the wraiths, firing again and again. Doug saw one bullet strike home, shattering the

374

heart of one of those ice demons without slowing it down. And then they were on Baxter, fingers stabbing and tearing.

Angela had Doug by the arm and they turned to each other, shouting at each other in unison that they had to run. They went headlong, practically falling forward through the deep snow, the effort pulling hard at the muscles in Doug's legs so that by the time he reached his snowmobile he crashed into it before throwing one leg over. Angela jumped on behind him, straddling the seat and screaming at him to go.

He started it up and the engine roared as he twisted the throttle. The snowmobile gunned forward, its single headlight picking out a path ahead as he raced for the street. No way would he try to backtrack through the woods, not now. He'd dropped his backpack but the saddlebags on the snowmobile were full of what he'd taken from the other houses. He forced his fear down, packed away his childhood terrors deep in his heart where they had always lain in wait. Where he believed they lay in wait for all of us when we are fragile, or alone in the dark.

Enough of fear, he told himself. This could still be a fruitful night, but only if they lived.

'Dougie,' Angela said, speaking close to his ear.

He glanced back and saw two of them rising and diving in the storm, and then starting in pursuit.

'Hold on!' he shouted as they went up over a snowbank and down into the street. He swung the snowmobile to the left and gunned it again.

Snow kicked up behind them as they shot off down the street with the headlight leading the way, knifing through the darkness, as if trying to outrace the killing grip of winter itself.

'Dougie, listen,' she said, so close and warm at his ear, though their speed blew the snow so hard that it stung as it hit them. 'It's me, babe. I missed you so much. I know you blamed yourself for not being there that night, but I forgive you, Dougie. All I wanted was to feel your skin against mine again. If they get me . . . if they take me back, at least I'll — '

'Cherie?' he said, so quietly that in the raging storm she could not possibly have heard.

'God, I love you,' she said, squeezing him tightly.

They reached a corner and he swung right, headed for Greenleaf Street, praying the power would be working there or on Route 125 just beyond it. *As if streetlights will save you*, he thought, and his heart broke.

'How?' he asked.

She screamed, then, and he twisted around to see her being lifted off the back of the snowmobile by her hair, kicking her legs and trying to reach for the spindly ice demon that dragged her into the air. It caught her wrist and climbed higher until she was only another shadow in the storm. Doug turned, screaming her name — not Angela, but Cherie — so much that had not made sense about the previous days suddenly making heartbreaking, breathless sense at last.

His gaze was still searching the whited-out sky when he hit a snowbank he hadn't seen coming,

376

jostling him hard enough that he lost his grip on the handlebars. The sled went out from under him, its engine racing as it took air, and it crashed a dozen feet farther along even as he hit the snow, rolling violently. He felt his left forearm give way with a loud crack and cried out his pain.

Lying on his back, staring up at the whipping snow, he saw Cherie fall, end over end, before she struck the ground. Again he roared her name. Cradling his broken arm, he stood and staggered thirty feet, over the snowbank and back into the street, where he found her bleeding and shattered.

'No, baby, no,' he said as he crumpled to the snow-covered pavement at her side.

Doug felt hollow inside, utterly bereft, unable even to summon the tears that his soul wanted to cry. He glanced skyward, expecting to see them descending upon him with their icicle fingers and bottomless eyes, but they were gone.

Then he felt her move. Her eyes fluttered and his breath caught in his throat when he saw her focus on him. Her brows knitted in confusion.

'Doug?' she said weakly.

His heart seized on the tiniest shred of hope that she might live, that he would not lose her a second time.

'I'm here, honey,' he said. 'I'm right here.'

Her confusion flared to anger. 'But how did *I* get here? What happened to me?'

The bitter, cutting edge in her voice gave her away.

'Angela?' he said, his last hope extinguished.

Her eyes rolled up and she passed out from shock, her injuries too great. But he had heard that bitter edge, had seen her eyes, and he knew that whatever part of Cherie had been inside her, the demons had torn it out again.

'Why didn't you tell me?' he whispered to the broken woman before him, the snow already beginning to accumulate on top of her, turning red and melting where it touched her blood. Things could have been so different if only he'd known.

Still, he could not cry. Doug laid his head back and gazed up into the storm, and amid the whipping snow and punishing wind he saw a single pair of eyes glaring at him, dark pits like holes in the world.

He screamed as the demon hurtled down at him through the blinding snow, long icy talons outstretched. Heart seizing, breath frozen in his throat, he rolled away from Angela and threw himself sprawling across the road. He felt those talons at his back, slashing, tugging, ready to eviscerate him. He reached the snowbank and launched himself over the top, twisting around to see how close he was to death.

The snow swirled around Angela's broken, motionless body, but of the ice demon there was no sign. Wherever it had gone, Doug prayed it would never return.

★   ★   ★

TJ grabbed his wife by the hand and looked into her eyes, all the tension between them forgotten.

378

The scraping continued on the walls and roof and TJ kept his eyes averted from the window over the sink, afraid that he would see another of the winter ghosts staring back at him with those empty, frozen eyes. Hate-filled eyes, as if the things despised him for the warmth of his flesh and wanted to strip it from him.

'The upstairs bathroom has no windows,' he said, turning from Ella to Grace, still unnerved by the aged wisdom in her eyes. 'We can stuff a towel under the door — '

'It may not keep them out for long,' Grace said, her voice sounding even more like her grandmother's.

TJ put a hand on her back, hustling her along in front of himself and Ella. 'I don't see another option. They'll find a draft eventually, get into the house. If we're waiting out the storm, we've got to buy time.'

He felt as if his pulse throbbed throughout his body, banging in his temples and the tips of his fingers and beating a rapid rhythm in his chest, but he had to stifle his fear. Grace — Martha — rushed for the stairs and started up, with TJ and Ella ascending behind her. At the top of the stairs, TJ started to turn toward the hall bathroom, but Grace had stopped short in the corridor, staring through the open door of her bedroom.

Ella grabbed her daughter by the arm. 'Hurry!'

Grace pulled her arm free, turning to glare at Ella with Martha's eyes. 'Look outside!'

TJ and Ella crowded behind her and saw that she had stopped to peer into her darkened room.

The purple, frilly curtains that Grace loved had been drawn back and beyond the window the snow fell at a less drastic angle and the flakes seemed diminished. The storm had not ended, but it seemed to have weakened slightly.

'Listen,' Ella said. 'The wind has died down.' She turned and searched TJ's face with hopeful eyes. 'Do you think — '

A terrible noise erupted in the attic overhead, a squeal like nails dragged out of wood followed by a little pop that TJ recognized as a lightbulb bursting.

'Oh my god,' Ella whispered, grabbing his arm so hard that her fingernails dug through his shirt and into his flesh.

'It's so cold,' TJ said, and he saw his breath fog in front of him.

'They found a way in,' Grace said. 'A vent or someth — '

The attic had a hinged door with a drop-down ladder and as the three of them stared it began to shudder and bang with pressure from above. TJ stared in mute horror as the pull-string hanging below the trapdoor began to ice over.

The shrieking began again, but this time it wasn't the gale outside but the howl of frigid wind whipping through the house's eaves. TJ looked at Ella and Grace, saw the sorrow and surrender in their eyes, and knew he could not live if he lost them. He thought of all the times he had held Grace in his arms when she was a baby and even later, as she grew — thought of all the nights Ella had fallen asleep curled against him in bed with her head resting in the crook of his arm — and he moved.

Grabbing Ella, he shoved her to the bathroom. She careened through the open door and fell, sliding on the Italian tiles, scrambling to get back to her feet.

'No, TJ, don't — '

He picked Grace up and went through the door, shouting for Ella to shut it even as he pushed Grace into the bathtub, thinking how absurd it all seemed, how wrong. How grimly mundane.

'It's not going to work,' Ella said quietly, her breath fogging in front of her.

Ice crystals had formed on the vanity mirror. TJ refused to look at it or to think. He grabbed towels from the linen closet and jammed them under the door, pushing with his fingers, filling the gap there, ignoring the fact that there were thinner gaps all around the doorframe.

'Thomas,' his mother said, in the voice of his little girl, and TJ felt his heart seizing in his chest as he ignored her, pressing himself against the door, hoping to narrow the spaces around it.

Supposed to protect them, he thought. *Mom. Ella. Gracie. You're supposed to take care of them.* But he'd broken his word to his mother and she'd died as a result, and now the things that had killed her had returned to murder the rest of his family, to drag him into a hell constructed of his inability to love them enough. To be the man he'd always aspired to be.

He slumped against the bathroom wall and stared at the doorknob, watching as ice began to form around it.

381

Ella fell to her knees on the fuzzy blue throw rug, shaking her head as she stared at Grace, trembling with grief.

'Mrs. Farrelly,' Ella said, staring into the little girl's old-woman eyes. 'Martha. Please, you can't let this happen.'

Grace stiffened, chin raised. 'The storm is dying.'

'Not fast enough,' Ella said. 'I don't care what happens to me, but Grace — '

'We'll be all right,' the girl replied, and for the first time TJ saw the selfishness in her, saw that in her fear she would say anything.

Ella slapped Grace so hard that it spun her back against the wall of the tub.

'Stop it!' TJ snapped.

The bathroom door began to tremble, and they heard long, icy claws drag along the wood.

Tears ran down Ella's face as she turned to stare at her husband. 'Don't let this happen.'

TJ squeezed his eyes shut against the scratching noises and the anguish in his wife's eyes. But even with his eyes closed, he felt the grip of the cold, the temperature still falling. His chest hurt as he inhaled the frigid air and opened his eyes, turning toward his wife and daughter — his 'girls,' he called them.

He went and knelt beside Ella, nudging her aside as he reached into the bathtub for Grace, who stared back at him with the fearful, hurt, suspicious eyes of his dead mother.

'Mom,' he said, and Grace allowed herself to be pulled in her father's embrace . . . Martha into her son's.

TJ held her there, wincing at the rattle of the door in its frame, at the scrape of those icy claws on the wood. The gap was small but it had to be enough. Why weren't they coming through? Were the creatures toying with them? TJ thought they must be and hated them for it.

He breathed in the scent of his daughter's shampoo and felt her little heart beating against him. A thousand images of his mother crashed together in his head, memories that he cherished but that he had stored away like a much-loved photo album, there to be drawn out when he missed her most.

'Losing you was so hard,' he whispered to his mother. 'Blaming myself made it even worse. But the living are the living and the dead are the dead.'

The scraping on the door grew louder and a gust of frigid air blew into the bathroom through the gap between door and frame, and he knew the evil that had come for them had decided to end it.

'TJ,' Ella said, and he heard her crying behind him, needing him.

He tightened his embrace on his daughter, shuddering with a sadness the likes of which he'd never known.

'I'll always love you, Mom, but I can't lose my Grace. She's only eleven. She deserves to have a life. She deserves a *chance*. The Martha Farrelly I know, the woman who wanted grandkids so badly, she'd never put Grace at risk. I know you're scared — '

He felt Grace relax in his arms, felt her breath

383

on his cheek as she exhaled, nearly hanging from his neck.

'Daddy?' she whispered.

TJ couldn't breathe. He jerked back, holding her at arm's length, staring at his little girl. When he glanced over his shoulder he saw a gossamer shadow moving out through the door, passing through it as if it weren't there, and he nearly called for her to come back.

'Gracie?' Ella said beside him. 'Is it you?'

'Mom,' the girl said, almost impatiently, 'I'm cold.'

Ella grabbed hold of her husband and daughter both and dragged them into a family embrace, Grace practically falling out of the tub on top of them.

'Oh, God, thank you,' Ella said.

TJ said a silent prayer of thanks as well, but his was not to God. He thought of all the things that he wished he'd thought to say to his mother and now never would. But he thought perhaps that was for the best.

'Hey,' Ella said, reaching up to caress his cheek, searching his eyes. 'It's gone quiet.'

And so it had.

The only sounds in the bathroom were the hum of the overhead fan and the quiet dripping of water as the ice on the doorknob began to melt.

20

'*Jake. Wake up.*'

Inhaling sharply, Jake sat up and found his head amid the clothes hanging in the closet. He gave an amused grunt and shook himself. Isaac shone a flashlight in his eyes and he squinted and turned away.

'I'm awake.'

'Listen,' Isaac said, nudging him. 'Do you hear that?'

The boy might not have Isaac's face, but his voice sounded so genuine, so right, that it made Jake shiver. He wondered if it was just his imagination — twelve years had passed, after all; how could he really remember what Isaac's voice had sounded like back then? Maybe all ten-year-old boys sounded the same.

'I don't hear anything,' he said.

But he frowned even as he spoke the words, because maybe he actually did hear something, a thumping noise that was not the sound of the shutter banging against the house. His heart skipped a beat, then began to race. He hadn't been completely asleep but he had definitely been drifting off, despite that it was hours earlier than he usually went to bed. Now he couldn't have been more awake. It felt like every cell in his body was on alert.

The sound stopped. He shifted, knocking over some shoes that he'd piled up to get them out of the way and tipping all the contents out of the open Monopoly box at his feet. His head hit the clothes again and some bare hangers jangled.

'Is that . . . ?' Jake asked.

Isaac shook his head. 'I don't think so.'

The muffled sound of voices reached them, impossible to understand but clearly human. The thumping came again and Jake exhaled, realizing how stupid he'd been. He started to get up and Isaac grabbed his arm.

'No!' the boy said.

'Someone's here. They're banging at the door.'

'Don't answer,' Isaac pleaded.

Jake hesitated, but he heard the muffled shouting again and thought whoever was out there didn't seem likely to give up. A terrible thought occurred to him.

'What if something's happened to Mom?'

Isaac glanced around the dark closet, forlorn, and then he nodded. 'Okay, go. But don't go outside. And if you see anything weird, shut the door fast.'

Jake smiled. 'Promise.'

He took the second flashlight and climbed out of the closet, groaning as he stretched his legs and back. He was only twenty-four but already his body didn't adapt well to being cramped in a closet for a few hours. Once upon a time he and Ikey could have camped in there for days, eating junk food and telling ghost stories. Now the idea of ghost stories made him nauseous. Fear had lost its entertainment value.

'Stay there,' he told his dead brother, and he shut the closet door.

Clicking on the flashlight, he hurried through the house, realizing just how loud the banging and shouting was. As he hurried to the front door, he recognized one of the voices as Harley's, and then his other visitor identified himself.

'Jake, this is Joe Keenan, and this is your last chance. If you're in there, open the door. Otherwise we'll have to assume you're in some kind of trouble and we're coming in! I'll give you a count of ten!'

A heavy fist hammered on the door. *Harley*, he thought.

'Open the damn door, Jake!' his friend shouted.

Outside, Detective Keenan began to count loudly down from ten. As Jake reached for the dead bolt his hand wavered. If something had happened to his mother, he wanted to know, but what if they were there for another reason? Detective Keenan had been instrumental in the search for Zachary Stroud.

'Shit,' Jake whispered to himself.

Harley shouted his name and banged again.

'Seven!' Keenan yelled. 'Six! Five!'

Shit, shit, shit, Jake thought, and then he slid back the dead bolt and turned the knob, hauling the door open. They were coming in one way or another; better that they did so without destroying his front door. He stood in his foyer and shone his flashlight in their eyes.

'You sound like you're about to blast off,' he said, scratching his head and pretending to yawn.

Harley and Keenan looked surprised that he'd opened the door and he saw them straighten up. They'd actually been prepared to break in.

'Where the hell have you been?' Harley demanded.

Jake scowled at him. 'Sleeping. In my house. The house of an idiot who did not buy a generator after the last two times he lost power. Not a lot else to do in the middle of a blizzard . . . except, I guess, for going around hammering on people's doors when you should be home. What is *with* you guys? It's kinda late, don't you think?'

Detective Keenan visibly shifted gears, going from friend to cop in half a second. 'Can we come in?'

Jake shrugged and stepped out of the way to admit them. 'Of course. Sorry, still half asleep.'

As they entered, he glanced out the door, searching the snow-streaked darkness for inhuman things.

'What are you looking for?' Detective Keenan asked. 'We're alone.'

Jake's heart skipped. He hadn't thought about it, but that was a good sign. They'd come without the cavalry.

'Just wondering how you got here. Did you park out on the street?'

'Not like we could get into your driveway,' Harley said. 'Even getting up your street wasn't easy. If the plow doesn't come by soon — '

'If the plow comes by soon, your car is probably going to get demolished,' Jake said. He gestured toward the living room and they followed his lead. 'Wish I could offer you guys some coffee. I might have some beers, but — '

'We're good,' Detective Keenan said wearily.

Jake could barely breathe as he picked up a matchbook from the coffee table and lit two candles he'd left there earlier, in preparation for the storm. There were also two empty mugs on the table, left from when he'd made hot chocolate earlier for himself and Isaac, and he saw Keenan eyeing the mugs. You didn't have to be a detective to count to two.

From the moment Jake had let them in, Harley had been watching him with open curiosity, not quite accusatory but definitely suspicious. He hated to have his friends look at him that way, but the idea of trying to explain the truth to them seemed absurd.

'So, I assume you guys didn't pay me a visit just because you were bored.'

The sarcasm didn't earn even a smile, and that was when he knew he was in real trouble. These guys weren't going to content themselves with asking him; they were going to want to search. Of course they were. He'd been stupid not to realize it right away. If they didn't have strong suspicions, they would never have come all the way out to his house in the middle of a blizzard.

'We didn't,' Detective Keenan said, sitting forward on the sofa and studying him, trying to look casual but ready for whatever Jake might do.

This is really happening, Jake thought.

'Last time I was out here, you wouldn't let me

389

in,' Harley said. 'The shades were all down. Most of 'em are still down. I had the idea you had a woman here, maybe a new girlfriend or something.'

Detective Keenan looked pointedly at the two mugs on the coffee table. Jake faked a smile and he knew they saw its falseness. Both cops stiffened a little, sensing his panic. He knew it, but he could not get the thin, fake smile off his face.

He struggled to think of some way to get rid of them. If they wanted to arrest him, to take Isaac away, they could do that, but only if they waited until the storm had passed. The idea of Isaac out there in the blizzard with the ice men hunting for him . . . Jake couldn't let that happen.

'I know I must've looked like a wild man that day,' Jake said. 'But I've been having trouble sleeping. That's why I had the shades down. I didn't fall asleep till dawn. I hadn't even been up long when you — '

'Bullshit,' Harley interrupted.

Jake almost expected Detective Keenan to protest. He was the detective; he was the one who should have been asking the questions. But Keenan just watched.

'It's not bullshit,' Jake said, allowing himself to look irritated. 'Seriously, what the hell's going on with you guys? Why are you here?'

'Pokémon,' Detective Keenan said.

Jake flinched. 'What?'

'You had Pokémon cards in your hand,' Harley said. 'Spread out, the way you would if you were playing, so don't tell me you were getting ready to sell them on eBay or some shit. You've got about five seconds to explain yourself, Jake. Convince me you're not some kind of . . . '

Harley glanced away, shaking his head, not wanting to speak the words.

Jake hated it. At twenty-four, he was old enough to know that the older people got, the harder it was to make close friends, and he and Harley had been close.

'Harl,' he said, ignoring Keenan. 'I swear to God, it's not what you think.'

Detective Keenan stood up, staring at him, a little spark of hatred in each eye. 'Tell me right now, kid. Is Zachary Stroud in this house?'

Jake stared back, thinking of trying for Keenan's gun and knowing how ridiculous an idea it was.

'It's not what you think, Joe.'

'Jesus Christ!' Keenan said, sneering as he spun around, glancing around the living room. 'The whole city's been looking for the boy and he's right here? Everyone's given him up for dead!'

Keenan paused, then stormed over to Jake, one hand on his gun. 'Is he alive, Jake? Tell me the boy's alive?'

'He's alive,' Jake said. 'But he's not Zachary Stroud.'

Detective Keenan jerked his head, gesturing to Harley.

'Officer Talbot, search the house. Find the boy.'

Harley looked like he wanted to spit in Jake's face. He opened his mouth to speak and then thought better of it, turning to leave the living room.

'Listen to me, Harley. You can't take him out of here! It's not safe, you understand? *The ice men are going to take him back.* If you take him out into the storm they'll come for him, and they'll probably kill you while they're at it!'

As if he hadn't spoken, Harley stormed from the room. Moments later Jake heard doors slamming open and closed, then heavy footfalls on the stairs. The wind still gusted hard, rocking the house and making the beams creak, and snow whipped at the windows, but Harley Talbot's footsteps were the loudest sound that Jake had ever heard.

His heart breaking, he looked at Detective Keenan.

'Please, Joe, you've gotta listen.'

Keenan's upper lip curled in disgust. 'Don't even talk to me.'

Upstairs, Isaac began to scream. They heard Harley's voice, too, trying to reassure the boy, but the sounds of struggle continued and got closer.

'What the hell?' Detective Keenan muttered.

When Harley reappeared, he had Isaac over one shoulder.

'Jesus, Harley, put the kid down!' Keenan shouted.

Harley complied, but the second that Isaac's feet were on the ground he started punching the massive cop, screaming at him.

'Dammit!' Harley snapped.

He knelt and tried to put his arms around

Isaac to restrain him. The boy grabbed his right arm with both hands and bit him hard. Harley swore and gave him a little shove and Isaac fell on his butt on the hardwood planking, then scrambled to his feet and rushed through the living room.

'Zack, listen,' Detective Keenan said, crouching to try to intercept the boy. 'We're here to help you. I know you're in . . . '

The boy dodged around him and threw his arms around Jake.

'Don't let them take me, Jake. Please don't let them. I can't go out in the snow.'

'I know, I know,' Jake said, kneeling down to take the boy in his arms. Cupping the back of Isaac's head in one hand, he clutched the boy to him and looked over his shoulder at Harley and Detective Keenan.

'I tried to tell you. This isn't what you think.'

'Then what the hell is it?' Harley demanded.

'The kid's in shock,' Detective Keenan said. 'After the accident, he'd have to be. I don't know if you did anything to him or if you've just got some bizarre idea that you're helping him, but — '

'You're not listening!' Jake snapped.

Isaac had calmed enough to turn to face the officers. Jake stayed on his knees beside him, the Schapiro brothers united.

'Okay,' Detective Keenan said, frowning as he tried to make sense of their closeness. 'What is it, then?'

'Twelve years ago, Joe . . . there were demons in that storm.'

'Demons,' Harley echoed, a terrible sadness in his voice. Pity in his eyes.

'I saw them with my own eyes. They came right through the screen of my bedroom window and dragged my little brother, Isaac, out into the snow. The screen didn't give way . . . they pulled him out.'

'I remember hearing about this back then,' Keenan said. 'But you're a grown man now. You can't possibly — '

'It's true,' Isaac said quietly, his voice full of such pain that the others in the room could not help but stare at him. He lowered his gaze, scuffing his foot, fearful but not surrendering. 'They took us all, everybody who died that night, and they've kept us ever since . . . till a few days ago. We got away, but they know we're here and they're out there now, in the blizzard, hunting for us. I'm sorry for the boy whose body I'm in. He hit his head and when he got out of the car his parents were drowning and he tried to save them. He went into the river and dove under the water and tried to smash the window but he was too little and then he was choking and swallowing the water and he was going to drown when I went inside of him.'

Keenan and Harley stared at him openmouthed, neither of them knowing what to say next.

'I'm sorry,' Isaac said. 'But I think he did something to his brain, going that long without breathing right. I can't even feel him thinking in here with me.'

'Holy shit,' Harley whispered.

394

'Harley. Joe,' Jake said. 'Meet my little brother, Isaac.'

Detective Keenan backed up. 'No. No way, man. Do you have any idea how crazy you both sound? You've had three days up here by yourself to mess with this kid's head. His parents may be gone but he's still got family.'

Something in Keenan's expression suggested that he doubted his own words, like he struggled with a memory he wished he could forget.

'Joe,' Harley said quietly.

Keenan shot him a hard look. 'Don't even think about it. Get your cuffs out.'

'No!' Isaac shouted.

Harley took out his handcuffs but he looked unsure.

Jake put an arm around Isaac. 'I can't let you do this, Joe.'

Detective Keenan pulled his gun. He didn't take aim, but suddenly the weapon was in play, and Jake slid Isaac behind him, blocking his brother with his own body. Harley started toward him with the handcuffs.

'Don't make this ugly, Jake,' Harley said, obviously troubled. 'Whatever this is, we'll work it out.'

'Are you kidding me?' Jake snapped. 'Keenan's got his gun on us! What are you going to do, Joe, shoot a kid? If you guys don't believe him, nobody will, and if you bring him out in that storm I'm going to lose my brother all over again!'

'Jake,' Detective Keenan said. 'You lost Isaac a long time ago. There is no 'again.' Nobody wishes there were more than I do, but there are no second chances.'

Isaac stepped out from behind Jake.

'There might be,' the boy told him. 'Charlie Newell says you cried over him and Gavin. They weren't much older than I was and they've been suffering all this time. We all have. Maybe it's not really a second chance, but we don't want to suffer anymore. We just want to rest. Don't you think Charlie deserves to rest?'

The gun shook in Detective Keenan's hands. His eyes were wide and damp and he trembled with something that did not seem much like rage until he turned and looked up at Jake and sneered.

'You son of a bitch,' he said, 'putting this shit in the head of a ten-year-old. What is *wrong* with you?'

'Joe — ' Jake began.

'You have to listen!' Isaac cried.

Detective Keenan stared at the boy as if trying to see inside him. In that moment's hesitation they all heard the storm blowing outside.

'Officer Talbot,' Keenan said, 'I swear to God if you don't cuff him right now I am going to shoot *you* instead.'

Harley swore under his breath but he moved toward Jake. When Isaac tried to interfere, Harley shoved him onto the couch and grabbed Jake by the arm, slapping a cuff on one wrist. Jake shouted and shot an elbow into his gut, got away for a second before Harley grabbed the back of his neck with one huge hand and slammed him to the floor, one knee on his back, forcing his other arm around. Jake fought against it until he thought his arm would break, and at last there was nothing he could do about it. The cuffs were on.

'Stop!' he screamed. 'You don't know what you're doing!'

Jake twisted around, trying to get Harley off him, and saw Isaac beating on the huge cop's back and arms and head until Keenan grabbed Isaac from behind, holstering his gun.

Such was the brutal tableau on display when they heard the front door open, all of them turning toward the sound of a woman's voice.

'Jake?'

Two figures stepped into the foyer, dusted with snow, and then stood at the living room entrance, staring inside with wide eyes. One of them was Jake and Isaac's mother, but it was the other whose presence astonished him. Even then, in the middle of the chaos, he couldn't help thinking how beautiful she looked.

'Miri?' he said.

Something shimmered in the air behind them and Jake wondered if they had brought someone else along.

'Let him go!' his mother said, rushing into the room. 'Harley, for God's sake, what are you doing? You've had dinner at my house. What do you think you're — '

Isaac rushed at her, throwing his arms around her waist. He buried his face in her chest and began to sob, trying over and over again to speak to her but unable to get out the words. At last, breath hitching, everyone in the room staring, he spoke a single word.

'Momma.'

Allie Schapiro stared down at him, her eyes welling. She searched that unfamiliar face — the face of a stranger — and pushed the hair away from his eyes to get a better look.

'Isaac? Is it really . . . '

She sank to her knees and embraced him.

'This is a goddamn madhouse,' Keenan said.

Outside, the wind began to scream and they all stiffened. Jake spun around, staring at the windows. Had he seen something flit by out there? The fear that had been enveloping him wrapped itself around him like a shroud. Once upon a time, twelve years earlier, Isaac had watched the ice men dancing in the snow and made the mistake of thinking them harmless. Playful. They couldn't make that mistake again.

The house shook and a barrage of noise filled the air, beams creaking and glass rattling, and then they could hear a terrible sound, like a hundred iron hooks being dragged along the roof and outer walls of the farmhouse.

'They're here, Momma,' Isaac cried, spinning around in terror, eyes wide. 'Don't let them take me again.'

Jake looked at Harley. 'Get these goddamn handcuffs off.'

'This is impossible,' Detective Keenan said.

Miri snapped her fingers in front of his face twice. 'Wake up, Detective. The impossible can kill you.'

21

Keenan spun around, trying to figure out where the sounds were coming from, and then he realized they were coming from everywhere. His thoughts were a maelstrom of doubt — whom did he believe, here? Whom could he trust? Despite the icy air and the plummeting temperature in the room, he felt beads of sweat dripping down his back and wondered if he might be having a nervous breakdown.

Breakdown? It's not that simple. I'm losing my damn mind.

Losing his mind, because with every word out of the mouths of these people, he kept seeing the face of that rookie, Torres, in his head, and trying to tell himself that the young, seemingly unbalanced cop had not said the words Keenan thought he'd heard in The Tap the night before: *'I'm betting you still remember what my boy's skin smelled like when it burned.'* He'd thought Torres was having some kind of psychotic episode, convincing himself that he was Carl Wexler. Hell, given his age, he might have gone to school with Wexler's son. Or so Keenan had told himself.

Now, he didn't know *what* to think.

The fingers of his right hand twitched and descended toward the gun he'd just holstered. He had to force himself not to draw the weapon, worried that he might pull the trigger. Instead, he stared at Zachary Stroud. The kid might be orphaned, but somehow he'd survived . . . if he was still even Zachary Stroud. The way he held on to Allie Schapiro — kids didn't clutch at strangers that way. He knew her, saw her as his mother, but if Keenan allowed himself to follow that train of thought it would lead him to things he simply refused to believe.

Harley had moved behind Jake and was taking off the handcuffs.

'What do you think you're doing?' Keenan demanded. He felt like he was floating, like the people in the room around him were retreating into shadows and he was starting to lift off the ground. 'He's in custody, dammit!'

Harley froze and stared at him, eyes narrowing. Could the younger cop see how untethered from reality he had become? Keenan thought perhaps he could, and it was almost a relief when Harley hurried to him, moving between Allie Schapiro and Miri Ristani.

'Joe, snap out of it,' Harley said, grabbing his arm.

The whole house shook with a massive gust of wind, boards groaning, and the Stroud boy cried out again, this time pointing at the window. Keenan glanced over and thought, for just a second, that he had seen a face at the glass, an obscene mask of ice with jagged teeth and eyes that were hideously, cruelly intelligent. He turned away, shook his head to clear it, and looked again to see that it had been only a pattern of snow stuck to the window screen.

Harley grabbed the front of his jacket and

hauled him up onto the tips of his toes, so they were practically nose-to-nose.

'Detective Keenan!' he shouted. 'Wake the hell up!'

Keenan flinched, inhaling sharply, as if Harley had struck him. He shook himself loose and for a moment he just stood there listening to the pounding of his heart. When he turned to look at Allie and the boy again, Miri and Jake were with them . . . and beyond them, in the shadows at the corner of the room, stood what could only be a ghost.

'There!' Keenan shouted, pulling his gun, knowing bullets would do nothing. 'All of you get back!'

'No!' the Stroud boy said, looking at him with wide, desperate eyes. 'He's here to help! That's Miri's dad!'

Gripping his gun so hard that his knuckles ached, Keenan watched the ghost drift to the boy and kneel in front of him.

'*Hello, Isaac,*' it said.

Keenan's jaw dropped at the sound of its voice and a ripple of emotion went through him, some combination of wonder and horror that he had never felt before.

'You got away, Niko,' Isaac said. 'We all thought we could get out, too.'

'*I know, pal. I know.*'

Of all things, it was the sorrow in the eyes of a ghost, the regret in the voice of a dead man, that brought it all home to Keenan. He glanced around the room at the people gathered there and realized that they were a family. Allie had been in a relationship with Niko at the time of the blizzard that had killed Niko and Isaac, and here they were. Niko and his daughter. Allie and her boys. Keenan stared at Zachary Stroud and the boy's story came back to him, the firsthand account of a ghost who had watched a boy try to save his drowning parents and ended up nearly drowning himself, brain damaged by oxygen deprivation.

This wasn't Zachary Stroud at all.

Sound rushed in. It had been there all along, the scraping at the farmhouse's walls and roof and the rattling of the windows, but he had been lost inside his head for a minute or two. Now he felt as if he had woken from sleep to discover that the ordinary world had been a dream and this land of impossible things was reality.

'There are others,' he said, looking at Jake. 'How many are we talking about?'

'All of them, I think,' Jake said, but he could barely take his eyes off the ghost in the room. 'Either like Isaac or . . . I don't know, maybe like that.'

'No,' the ghost said. '*There are no others like me.*'

'We found Gavin Wexler and his father,' Allie said quickly, glancing around at the walls as if they were closing in. 'They've possessed Eric Gustafson and a policeman named Torres — '

'Torres,' Keenan said. 'God, it all makes sense now.'

'Nat Kresky was acting weird,' Harley said. 'Like he couldn't — '

Miri threw up her hands. 'Solve the mystery

402

later, guys. We need to get somewhere they can't reach us and right now. Allie and I have seen these things up close — '

'The cellar,' Jake said, picking up Isaac — *And now I'm thinking of him as Isaac*, Keenan thought — and rushing out of the room.

'Move it!' Keenan snapped at Harley, but the other cop was already moving.

Miri and Allie raced after Jake and Isaac, each but the boy holding a flashlight, and Keenan and Harley brought up the rear. When Keenan glanced into the corner where he'd seen the ghost, Niko Ristani had gone. A flush of warmth went through him, relief that the dead man had abandoned them, but when he hustled into the corridor and saw the others rushing for the cellar door, which Jake held open, the ghost appeared again, standing just behind Jake and urging them on.

He forced himself to breathe, to just keep moving. To believe. These people were depending on him.

His teeth chattered. It had become so cold in the house, and so quickly, that the chill cut through his jacket and made the gun feel like ice in his hand. Miri went downstairs first, followed by Allie and Isaac, the little dead boy who held his mother's hand to keep from falling. *Just move*, Keenan told himself, trying not to be thrown by his thoughts.

'You think this door will hold?' he asked, looking past Jake at the ghost of Niko Ristani.

'*If anything will*,' the ghost replied, his voice seeming to come from everywhere and nowhere.

403

'It's sturdy and secure and the weather stripping will lessen the chance of a draft. The storm is weakening; we just have to hope it spins itself out before they can get to you.'

The whole house seemed to sway. It sure didn't feel to Keenan like the storm was weakening.

'Go,' Jake said, nodding to him and Harley as he dug into his pocket and pulled out a jangling set of keys. 'I can lock it from inside.'

Harley patted him on the arm — all forgiven, apparently — took out his flashlight, and hurried into the cellar after the others. With the ghost looking on, Keenan paused.

'Jake . . . '

'Now's not the time.'

Keenan nodded. 'Lock it up tight.'

He had his foot on the top step when they all heard a massive crack and a splintering of wood, followed by a crash.

'One of the vents. The attic or the bathroom,' said the ghost. 'They're inside.'

Keenan felt like his heart shriveled up in his chest, felt the prickle of heat on the back of his neck even as the air filled with ice crystals, fogging their breath and frosting their hair, and he had the lunatic idea that it might snow inside the house. Jake came at him and Keenan turned, hurtling down the steps as Jake locked the door behind them. The darkened stairwell gave way to the eerie yellow glow of the cellar, flashlight beams crossing in the swirl of dust, picking out the gleam of cobwebs. The furnace had fallen silent, a metal monolith in the corner, and stacks

404

of old boxes and two huge old televisions took up most of the wall space. A small, doorless entryway led into a smaller room, and Keenan saw the edge of a clothes dryer in the dim light.

'How do we fight these things?' Harley asked, drawing his gun as he turned to Miri and Allie. 'Is this gonna do me any good?'

'I have no idea,' Miri said. 'But quiet down, will you? Maybe they won't hear us.'

'They don't have to hear us,' Isaac said, reaching out for his older brother's hand. 'I feel them up there. I feel how hungry they are. And if I can feel them, I'm pretty sure they know I'm here.'

The little boy turned to his mother. 'You should go. You could get away if you left me here.'

'I can't,' Allie said, her voice quavering. 'I lost you once. I'll die before I let you go again.'

Isaac's voice got very small. 'I don't want you to die. I don't want any of you to die.'

Keenan tuned them out, focusing on the door lost in shadows at the top of the stairwell. It shuddered with the wind and he knew that whatever these ice men were, they were definitely inside, now. Cabinets and doors banged shut with the breeze of their passing and things fell over, crashing to the floor. He wondered where the ghost of Niko Ristani had gone, but he imagined the spirit had hidden itself away. If these things wanted him back, he'd be a fool not to hide.

But he wouldn't have gone far. Not with his daughter here. Keenan turned to look at Miri.

Of all of them, she seemed to be the steadiest, as if none of this surprised her. It made him wonder how long her father's ghost had been visiting her. Whatever happened, she would fight. They all would, because they all had something to fight for.

He watched Jake and Miri exchange a loaded glance. Jake checked to be sure Isaac was safe with their mother and then went to her, the two of them sharing a brief, powerful embrace.

'Sorry I didn't answer when you called,' she said. 'Long story.'

'I didn't leave a message,' Jake replied, studying her. 'And yet here you are.'

'A story for another day,' Miri said. She pushed the ringlets of hair away from her face, reached out and caressed his cheek. 'I'd say it's good to see you — '

'Let's save it for tomorrow,' Jake said.

Keenan heard the hope and the courage in Jake's voice and read many of the unspoken words in the air. He looked back at the door at the top of the stairs and knew that none of them stood a chance. The only person with any possibility of getting out of this was already a ghost, and he had vanished.

Pushing away from the bottom of the stairs, he went to the pile of old boxes and then started checking the shelves behind them. He holstered his gun and started digging through boxes.

'Harley,' he said. 'Look around for things to burn.'

'Burn?' Miri said. 'You'll kill us all. There's nowhere to run down here.'

Keenan shot her a grim look. 'Fire's about the only thing I can think of to combat these things. If we can make it too hot in here for them, maybe we can outlast them.'

'I don't think that will work,' Isaac said. 'They carry the winter with them. A fire . . . '

The boy trailed off, but Keenan was barely listening. He couldn't just sit and wait for death without fighting back. As Harley and Jake and Allie started to go through the boxes, he slipped his flashlight into his right hand and went into the laundry room. A workbench in the corner included a table saw and there were tools hanging over it. Any of them would have made an effective weapon against something made of flesh and blood.

'Oh boy,' Miri said from behind him.

She had come into the laundry room, and when he turned, he saw what had shaken her. Above the washer and dryer was a small, rectangular window he hadn't noticed before. The concrete wall had a crack that led away from the corner of the window frame.

'Shit,' Keenan whispered.

He held a hand up in front of the window and felt the cold air that blew in from outside. Climbing on top of the dryer, he looked outside. The snow still fell, but the flakes had gotten smaller and it drifted gently from the sky. The wind kicked up a bit, but nothing like the gale that had been battering the house.

'It's barely a blizzard anymore,' he said, turning to face her. 'The worst of it that's been hitting the house must be coming from them. It can't be long, now.'

Another crash came from overhead and Miri flinched. Her eyes shone with fear.

'We don't *have* long.'

Keenan knew she was right. He looked at the small window, thinking that Isaac would fit through, and probably Miri and Allie, but that he and Harley and Jake would never manage it. Jumping down from the dryer, he shone his flashlight around the laundry room and froze as its yellow beam picked out a heavy metal door at the back. Hanging his head, he chuckled softly.

'Is that a bulkhead door?' Miri asked.

Keenan grinned, then hurried past her to poke his head back into the main area of the cellar. Harley, Jake, Allie, and Isaac all looked up at him, dropping whatever conversation he'd interrupted.

'We're done hiding,' he said. 'We stay here, we're dead.'

'We can't fight them,' Harley said.

'Who said anything about fighting?' Keenan replied. 'We stand a better chance of outlasting the storm if we're on the move, and the cars are just down the end of the driveway. Put your butts in gear. We're getting the hell out of here.'

'You're crazy,' Allie told him.

As if summoned by her words — and perhaps he had been — Niko's ghost resolved itself into being beside her in the gloom.

'No,' the ghost said. '*I've been watching them. They're playing with you. They'll be down here any minute, but most of them are inside the house now, or above it. If you run, you may not*

408

make it, but if you stay you are all going to die.'

Jake swore under his breath. 'I guess we're running, then. I just wish I'd brought a coat.'

★ ★ ★

Miri followed Detective Keenan up the steps, the frigid wind stinging her cheeks. The moment she emerged at the rear of the farmhouse, she realized that the blizzard had diminished. The snow still fell and the wind still blew, but the whiteout had ended. She could see all the way across the yard and into the trees. Turning, she saw the massive drift that marked the roadway and heard the scrape of a plow at work. It was this last, mundane detail that made her think that all would be well, that somehow they would make it out of this alive.

Keenan beckoned the others out of the cellar. 'Move it. Before they realize . . . '

He didn't have to finish the sentence.

Jake came up after Miri. When he emerged, he reached for her and she took his hand as if it were the most natural thing in the world. Perhaps it was and always had been precisely that. Amid her fear and desperation, she felt a wave of bittersweet emotion, so reassured by his presence and yet cursing herself for all the time she had spent running away from the life they could have had.

'Quickly,' she said to him. *Run,* she thought, *before they can ruin us again.*

'Come on,' Keenan whispered, clomping across the deep snow. He turned to look up at

409

the roof of the farmhouse, his expression urgent with fear and expectation, but the ice men were nowhere to be seen.

Miri and Jake hesitated until his mother and Isaac had cleared the bulkhead, and then the gigantic cop, Harley, emerged behind them. His badge gleamed silver in the night.

'Go. We're right behind you,' Allie said.

Jake nodded, gripped Miri's hand more tightly, and the two of them started hurrying across the yard as best they could in the deep snow. It had not hardened to ice but still the noise of their passing was considerable, the crunch and shush of each step and the rustle of their clothing spreading out to fill the white silence. Miri had never been in better shape in her life but already her legs felt heavy from the effort, and she heard Jake curse under his breath. Running in snow like this was impossible. The best they could do was slog their way to the road, cutting a diagonal path across the yard.

Halfway across the property, barely discernible in the falling snow, her father's ghost watched her progress. Transparent, fading in strength along with the storm, he waved her onward and she bent into the hard trudging. Snow went down inside her boots and she had to bring her knees practically to shoulder height with each step, but she forged a path.

She and Jake had come up almost parallel with Keenan when they all heard Allie utter a little cry behind them. Miri turned to see that Isaac had fallen. The boy struggled to right himself in the snow, one arm plunged deeply as Allie held his other, trying to help him up.

'Dammit,' Jake said. 'I'm an idiot. It's too deep for him.'

He started back toward his brother, but he hadn't gone two steps before Harley lifted Isaac into his arms.

'Hang on, kid,' the massive cop said. 'Whoever you really are.'

Miri smiled, squeezed Jake's hand, and had started trudging again when she felt the wind pick up. The chill sliced through her and the gust made a roar in the bare branches of the nearby trees, nearly a howl. She pulled her coat tighter around her throat and glanced at Jake as they struggled through the deep snowfall, thinking how cold he must be without a jacket.

Her teeth chattered and her eyes felt like weighted iron orbs in her skull. Her face had gone numb, as if she wore a mask that covered the muscle and bone beneath.

She heard her dead father's voice in her ear.

'They're coming.'

A fresh gust of fear erupted inside her, heart drumming as she spun. Off to her left, Detective Keenan had already realized that time had run out. Out of the corner of her eye she saw him pull his gun, but her focus was on the silhouettes that had just appeared above the farmhouse, a pair of wraiths who flitted back and forth on gusts of wind, watching their progress through the drifts.

Jake tugged on her hand, forcing her to look him in the eye.

'Keep going,' he said. 'As fast as you can.'

Then he went back for his mother. Miri saw Allie reaching for his hand and Harley lumbering after them with Isaac in his arms. She felt the burning in her calves and thighs from clambering through the snow and she knew they were never going to make it . . . knew they were all going to die.

A tiny breath escaped her lips — perhaps it was the last of her hope leaving her — and she turned to look for her father's ghost. He had vanished once more, still trying to keep out of reach of the ice men so that he would never have to endure the torment of their frozen hell again.

'What are you doing?' Keenan snapped at her. 'Move your ass!'

The detective managed to shuffle sideways through the snow so that he could watch the figures gliding through the storm above the house and still have his gun at the ready. It slowed him down, that move, but he seemed ready to fight for Miri and the others. The only thing that kept her moving was the idea that lagging behind would put the man in further danger, and he deserved more than that.

She glanced back at Jake and Allie as she broke a fresh trail across the snow. They'd covered half the distance to the road, but the cars still seemed a thousand miles away in this storm. Fear kept her warm, and a dread that clutched at her insides and made her want to weep for all the days she had not yet lived.

Miri glanced over her shoulder and regretted it, for the ice men had multiplied. There were four of them now, and two had begun to slink

412

through the air currents and the dwindling snow, descending toward them.

No, Miri thought. *Nononono.*

She ran right through her father's ghost, a shudder going through her at the contact. It startled her so much that she lost her footing and tumbled into the snow, kicking at the white stuff as it slid into her collar and down her back. Her father's ghost was intangible and yet she had felt a warm frisson of contact as her flesh had passed through him, and when she inhaled sharply she realized that she could smell his cologne. The ghost of a scent she had long forgotten.

It was that — having forgotten that precious, sensory piece of him — that broke her heart afresh.

'Daddy!' she shouted, realizing what he meant to do.

The ghost of Niko Ristani stood between his daughter and the ice men that scythed down through the eddying snow. Detective Keenan fired twice, shots that punched through the ice men, blowing holes in their bodies and driving them back half-a-dozen feet. They'd been staggered.

Miri rose to her knees in the snow. Jake and Allie were on either side of her now, helping her up as she watched the snow rush in to fill the demons' wounds, restoring them.

'Keep firing!' she called.

Her father's ghost turned to them all. '*You can't kill them.*'

'I can slow them down!' Keenan said, firing again.

Harley lumbered past them all, never slowing,

his grim face set on the singular task of getting Isaac to safety. The boy remained silent in his arms, perhaps knowing how little hope they really had.

A loud metallic bang sounded across the yard, echoing off the house and the snow. Side by side with Jake and Allie, knees pumping and heart thrumming, Miri looked back again to see that one of the bulkhead doors had clanged shut behind one of the ice men, and even now another emerged from the side of the bulkhead that remained open.

She looked ahead. They had perhaps twenty yards to cover before they reached the street, where they would at last be able to really run and where the cars were waiting. They were the longest twenty yards she had ever seen, the most impossible twenty yards imaginable.

The ice men from the bulkhead hurtled toward them across the snow, following the trail they'd broken like bloodhounds. No longer were they teasing or dancing or playing; the time for killing had arrived.

'The storm is . . . dying,' Allie said, trying to catch her breath. 'They're in a . . . hurry, now.'

Keenan fired at the things that chased them over the snow, staggering them, blowing off the left side of the face of the one in the lead. It seemed for a moment ready to drift apart, the lower half of its body turning to swirling snow, and hope sparked in Miri's heart. Then it shook itself, solidifying, and turned its single remaining eye on Keenan with such frigid malevolence that Miri screamed.

Jake shouted her name and she turned to see the two who'd come off the roof knifing toward her from the sky. Her father's ghost shot through the air and latched on to one of them, pulling it aside, drawing its attention as he slid off into the trees and the demon followed. The other kept coming, long fingers reaching for her, knives made of ice that she could practically feel cutting her flesh. Something tugged deep within her, as if it had already begun to feed on her spirit before even touching her.

And then Jake plowed into her, knocking her into the snow again, covering her with his body. She saw his eyes go wide and vacant and a bit of frost form instantly on his skin as the demon dug those dagger fingers into his back. Hot blood spilled onto her and Jake grunted, his eyes full more of sorrow than of pain.

Isaac screamed, fighting Harley's grasp. Tearing loose, he dropped to the snow and started back toward Miri and Jake.

'Kid, don't do it!' Harley managed, before he swore loudly and pulled out his gun.

With his long stride, Harley covered the distance in no time. Miri watched as the ice man stopped its attack on Jake and turned hungrily to Isaac. Rage flashed in its white-blue eyes, a black spark that went impossibly deep, as if its eyes were bottomless wells falling away into the winter limbo from which the demons hailed.

The demon flew at Isaac, arms outstretched.

Harley knocked the boy aside, set his feet firmly apart, and fired his gun twice at close range, obliterating the ice man's head. The rest of it blew apart in a spray of ice crystals and wet snow.

Feet crunched in the snow and Miri looked up to see Allie standing above her and Jake.

'My boy,' Allie said, falling to her knees.

Jake groaned and slid off Miri, landing on his back, blood melting the snow around them. Isaac threw himself on top of his brother, whispering things to him that the others were not meant to hear.

Harley shot at another, and Miri saw that there were more of them now, gliding through the air overhead, circling on frigid currents like winter's carrion birds. Keenan had made his way over and now they made a small cluster, so close to the road but impossibly far.

'Don't let them . . . ' he managed, turning to Miri, his eyes alight with purpose. 'Protect Isaac.'

Miri nodded, turning to Allie. 'Stay with them.'

Something moved to her right, at the corner of her eye, and she turned with the hope that her father had come back, only to see an icy wraith darting at them, much withered by the lessening of the storm, eyes hard and soulless as it slashed at Harley's chest and arms. The huge cop roared in pain and dropped his gun, staggering away.

Miri lunged for the gun, her motion taking her out of the path of an attack that might have torn her head clean off. The wraith that had set its sights upon her slid past her and she felt ice form on her exposed skin and the breath dragged right from her lungs as she landed in the trodden snow and scrambled for the gun.

Her father's ghost stood beside her, barely there, the sketch of an image in the dark, but his eyes were fierce.

'*Keep fighting*,' he said. '*The storm is fading.*'

Another dived at her and Niko Ristani's ghost lunged at it, diverting it upward, the two fragile creatures attacking each other. The demon ripped at the insubstantial nothing of her father's spirit and Niko — though dead — let out a shout of anguish, pounding at the ice man's face. He could not touch his daughter, could not kiss her forehead the way he always had when she was a girl, but he could strike these unnatural things. As Miri watched, the ice man began to tear her father's ghost to ribbons, and she leaned forward, and seemed almost to inhale the essence of him . . . and then the wind gusted, and the ghost was gone, leaving the demon to flail at thin air.

As she turned, gun in hand, she heard Allie crying out and saw the ice man that had tried to kill her — latch on to Isaac, its dagger fingers digging into his skin as it began to drag him into the air.

'No!' she cried, taking aim but afraid to fire for fearing of hitting Isaac.

★ ★ ★

With a cry of pain, Jake reached up and grabbed hold of Isaac's ankles. Fresh rivulets of blood trickled down his back and pain radiated from his wounds, but the pain was good — it kept him awake. Gritting his teeth, he held on to his

417

brother and felt himself rising to his feet. Jake stared up into Isaac's terrified eyes, knowing that he couldn't let go and knowing that if he didn't, he might break his little brother's bones. Above Isaac, the ice man sneered down at them, baring rows of long, sharp, icicle teeth and staring with those bottomless, nightmare eyes.

Jake shouted for help and his mother was there beside him, grabbing Isaac by the belt and then by the hand, giving Jake time to get a better grip, wrapping one arm around Isaac's leg and battering at the demon's grip with the other. One of its arms cracked and Jake let out a roar of triumph.

'Don't let go!' Isaac yelled, meeting his brother's gaze. 'Don't let them take me again!'

'We won't!' their mother shouted.

Jake mustered strength from deep inside himself, pushing away the pain and the smell of his own blood and the sight of the desperate tears sliding down his mother's face. This was a time of second chances. He felt that so keenly. A night when time might be turned back, when they might all wake from nightmares that had haunted them for a dozen years, if not the same then at least with a chance at something new and good. Pain seared his back — something had torn in the muscle tissue there — but he would not let go as long as he still lived . . . not of Isaac and not of Miri, now that she'd come home.

It was a night when so many mistakes might be undone.

'Leave him!' he screamed, glaring at the demon that held his brother, looking into eyes

418

that seemed full of centuries of malice. 'Leave us alone!'

Jake heard his mother scream and turned to see another ice man clutching at her hair and wrapping one arm around her belly, pulling her into the sky. The demon had thinned to almost nothing but still had the strength to carry her along on the wind. As Jake watched, it paused, glanced at the sky with a frozen grimace that looked almost like fear, and then plunged itself *into* her. Its arms seemed to merge with his mother's flesh, passing through her the same way Niko's ghost moved through solid objects. Ice showered down from the place where his mother and the demon met, as if the thing were crumbling with the contact, and in a moment of recognition that made Jake roar in panicked fury, he realized that the demon was entering her, trying to possess her the same way Isaac had possessed the dying body of Zachary Stroud.

'No!' he screamed, but he could do nothing for her from the ground, and that knowledge made him scream all the louder.

A gunshot cracked the sky and the bullet shattered the ice man's head, just as it had begun to dip toward his mother's chest — to submerge itself within her, seeking an anchor to keep it in this world. The wraith shattered into ice shards that turned into a spray of crystals before they hit the ground and Allie fell perhaps a dozen feet to land with a whispered thump in the snow. Instantly she was up and moving, scrambling to be sure none of them tried to grab her again.

Jake spun to see Joe Keenan staring at the

place where she'd hung in the air above, wide-eyed with breathless horror at the hideous violation he had just prevented. In the sky, an opening had appeared in the clouds and a white veil of mist was all that separated the earth from the stars in that one place. The storm was passing. The ice men looked ever thinner, growing almost as insubstantial as Niko's ghost . . . and they were furious.

They attacked as one, riding the wind with spindly fingers outstretched. Another took hold of Isaac and Jake shouted, knowing he could not win this battle. Keenan kept firing, destroying two more, but Jake felt his feet leave the ground and wrapped both hands around his brother's waist. A demon slashed at his arms and then another grabbed him by the back of his shirt and now they were both being dragged upward.

Gunshots came from the other direction, only one bullet striking home, blowing the arm off an ice man a dozen feet above them. Jake twisted to see that it was Miri who'd been firing, but now she tossed the gun aside and ran to him, jumping to wrap her arms around his legs. The storm had thinned dramatically and Jake heard ice cracking and felt something snap above him. For just a moment he feared that it had been Isaac's neck, but then they were falling, he and Isaac and Miri, and they hit the snow in a tumble of limbs.

Miri held Isaac, looking for injuries. Jake gritted his teeth against the pain in his wounded back, enjoying the freezing snow beneath him. He let his head loll to the left and saw Harley shuffling toward them, bloody and cradling one arm.

Jake heard his mother cry out and dragged himself up again, the pain in his back like fresh daggers as he saw the ice men concentrating on her, half a dozen of them — all that remained — dragging at her clothes and hair with their pitifully thin fingers. They were barely more than ghosts themselves but they swept her from her feet.

Detective Keenan took aim, but his gun clicked on an empty chamber. Whatever ammunition he'd had was gone. Jake staggered to his feet but knew he would never reach her.

'Joe, please!' he shouted.

Keenan did not hesitate. He hurled himself into their midst, using his bare hands to snap icy limbs, curling himself around Allie and driving her to the snow, covering her with his body to protect her, screaming as the ice men slashed at his back.

And then they had him.

As the snow became nothing but a flurry, the last of the ice men came together to drag Keenan into the sky. Jake could no longer stand and fell to his knees as his mother and Miri, Isaac and Harley gathered around him and the five of them watched the ice men carry Joe Keenan into the storm clouds, so high that they lost sight of him.

They heard him screaming as he fell, thirty yards away, crashing through tree branches before hitting the ground with a puff of white and a crack of bone that echoed across the snow.

'Oh my god,' Miri whispered.

Side by side, Jake and Harley staggered through the snow, bleeding and exhausted, until they reached him. Detective Keenan's eyes were open and his chest rose and fell with wet, guttural breaths, but one leg had folded beneath him and a tree branch jutted from his abdomen, pinning him to the snow.

'Joe,' Harley said. '*Jesus*, no.'

Keenan gazed up at them. 'I found him, didn't I? The lost boy?'

Jake frowned for a moment and glanced at Harley, who slowly nodded.

'You found him,' Harley said quietly, as the last snowflakes floated to the ground around them.

'He's home, now,' Jake said, glancing back at Isaac and Allie and Miri. 'He's with his family. With his mother. You saved her, Joe.'

But Keenan didn't respond. The rattle of his breathing had ceased, and when Jake moved nearer, he saw that the light had gone from the detective's eyes. They were dead, now, and bottomless, as if the void left by his spirit's passing went down and down and down, forever.

Jake grieved for him, and yet he knew that, in a way, even Joe Keenan had gotten his second chance tonight, and made good.

22

Coventry had never been more beautiful than in the days that followed the storm. Blanketed in snow two feet deep and with drifts three times that height that gave the illusion of a frozen white ocean, the city was enveloped in a gentle calm. The skies were blue, the days warming up just enough that by Friday, the ice and snow that had caked trees and power lines had melted away. The streets had been plowed. To the delight of children, the sidewalks had not been completely cleared in time for school on Friday morning, allowing them the pleasure of a third snow day in a row.

On Friday morning, just after nine o'clock, Allie Schapiro drove her five-year-old Nissan through the gates of Oak Grove Cemetery and followed the familiar, narrow, curving roads until she came to the place where Niko Ristani had been buried, twelve years past. Another car had already parked beside the high snowbank near Niko's grave, and though she was expecting them, it took her a moment to recognize the car as Miri's rental. Miri waited by her father's grave, a red knit cap on her head and a matching scarf setting off the somberness of her long black coat.

As Allie drove up, the doors of the rental car opened and Jake and Isaac stepped out. She parked behind Miri's car and put on the parking brake, her heart fluttering at the sight of her two sons. It jarred her, looking at Isaac — knowing he was Isaac — and seeing the face of Zachary Stroud. The other dead who'd returned had all inhabited the bodies of people whose spirits were still intact, but to hear Isaac tell it, Zachary Stroud's spirit had left his body when the little body had begun to drown, and Isaac had stepped in before the body could surrender its life in full. She had to believe him; surely Isaac would not lie to her. And yet she shuddered a little whenever she thought of it, wondering if some shred of the Stroud boy's consciousness remained there, a prisoner of his own flesh and blood. She prayed that his soul was gone, told herself that it had to be.

It had to be, if only so that she could sleep at night.

'Hi, Mom!' Isaac said, rushing to throw his arms around her. She hesitated for only a fraction of an instant before returning that love, and hoped he would not notice.

'Hello, Ikey,' she said, kissing the top of his head. 'I like the outfit your brother bought you.'

Isaac stood back and glanced down at his clothes as if he'd forgotten what he had put on that morning, a blue-and-red-striped sweater with a gray winter coat, black boots, and jeans. Allie smiled; that was just like him. He'd never paid any attention to what he wore. No matter whose face he had, this was her little boy. She hoped that she would be able to get used to that.

'Hey, Mom,' Jake said. 'You look good.'

Allie thanked him, frowning as she noticed the

stiffness in his posture and the tightness of his expression. Beneath his clothes — his outfit similar to Isaac's — Jake had tape and bandages covering much of his back, protecting the stitches that had been required to close the worst of the puncture wounds there.

'You, on the other hand, *don't* look so good.'

He arched an eyebrow. 'Gee, thanks.'

Allie went to him and kissed his cheek, ruffled Isaac's hair, and turned to watch Miri, who had both hands on top of her father's marble headstone, leaning on it as if it were the only thing keeping her upright. Her mother had been badly injured during the storm, sustaining broken bones and severe internal injuries in a fall that the authorities could not explain. Angela remained in intensive care and had still not regained consciousness more than twenty-four hours after the storm had ended. Allie could only imagine what Miri must be thinking, here at her father's grave with her mother in such dire straits, but the girl was strong. No doubt about that.

After a moment or two, Miri shifted, seemed to take a deep breath, and turned to smile wanly at Allie.

'Together again,' she said.

Only two words, but they echoed back across the years, hinting at the familial promise that Allie and Niko's relationship had held before the evil came to Coventry. Whether or not the ice men were truly evil did not matter to her. Their malice and hunger had destroyed her happiness and taken the lives of people she loved. She hoped that wherever they were now, they were starving.

'Come on, boys,' Allie said, taking their hands.

With Jake shuffling painfully on one side and Isaac on the other, and her own cuts and bruises still aching, she clambered over the snowbank until the four of them stood together around Niko's grave.

'It's like we're burying him again,' Miri said.

Allie wanted to argue with her, but she felt the same way. Jake put a comforting arm around Miri, and Allie wondered where their lives would take them, now. Miri had run pretty much as far away from Coventry as it was possible to go without leaving the country. Could she stop running, now?

'Mom?' Isaac said. 'Am I buried here?'

A dreadful ice slid through Allie's veins, colder than the touch of the demons they'd faced in the storm. She looked into her son's eyes — into the face of a stranger — and she could not reply. Instead, she hugged him tightly.

'Hey, Ike,' Jake said, grabbing his little brother playfully by the ear. 'You're not buried anywhere, man. You're right here with us.'

Isaac stared at him for a moment, then looked at Miri. He had died at the age of ten and had spent a dozen years aware and alert — thinking — trapped in a kind of hell Allie could only imagine. He still had a boy's face and manner, but he understood far more than he let on.

'Okay, Jake,' Isaac said. 'Okay.'

An agreement. A contract, Allie thought. They wouldn't speak of it again.

'Thank you guys for coming,' Miri said. Her curls framed her face and Allie thought she looked adorable, not at all like a girl who'd been in mourning for more than a decade.

'Of course,' Jake said.

Miri glanced away, her smile fading, and then turned to focus entirely on Isaac.

'Hey, Ike,' she said, 'can I ask you something?'

The little boy looked up at her with a terrible wisdom in his eyes.

'You want to know if they got him,' Isaac said.

Allie's heart quickened. 'No,' she said. 'Miri, you saw him escape. He vanished, you told me.'

'I thought so,' Miri replied, 'but he hasn't come back. I guess I just thought that he'd . . . ' She turned to look at the headstone again, at the letters of her father's name so deeply engraved in the marble. 'I thought he'd stay.'

Isaac hugged her. 'I don't think they took him. I think he's gone wherever we were supposed to go back then, the night we died. He'll be all right, now.'

Allie and Jake exchanged a look. After a second, Jake shoved his hands into his pockets and peered down at his brother.

'What about you? Are you staying?'

Isaac would not face him. 'Not if I have to be Zachary Stroud. So I guess we'll see.'

The boy stared down at where his boots were plunged into the snow until they all heard the approach of an engine, and car tires crunching over the grit left behind by the sander. Allie turned to see a silver Mustang rolling toward them. The car drew to a halt but she could not see through the tinted windows. The door opened but it took several seconds for Harley Talbot to extricate himself from the driver's seat. His height forced him to fold himself into the car, and the sling on his right arm had to have made it difficult to drive.

'You must love that car a lot to be willing to jam yourself in there,' she said.

Harley grinned and slammed the Mustang's door. 'A man's got to have style.'

She smiled. 'Thank you for coming.'

'We needed to have this conversation,' he said as he strode toward them, stopping on the other side of the snowbank, as if he felt he'd have been intruding if he came any nearer. 'I can't think of anywhere more private to have it. First thing you should all know is that the department's likely to release Joe Keenan's body on Monday, which means the funeral will probably be Wednesday or Thursday.'

'He saved my life,' Allie said quietly. 'We wouldn't miss it.'

Jake put a hand on Isaac's shoulder. There were circles under his eyes that had never been there before. 'Seriously, Harley. Thanks for being here.'

'Don't thank me yet,' he said.

Miri stepped up beside Allie and took her hand, and for a moment — there by Niko's grave — they really were the family that she believed they had always been meant to be.

'What are you saying?' Miri asked. 'Don't keep us in suspense, Harley. Please.'

Harley nodded, reaching up with his good

hand to rub the stubble on his chin. He was on medical leave, and while his right arm healed he had apparently given up shaving.

'Nobody believes it was a bear,' he said, his voice a low rumble. 'If it had just been our injuries they might have gone for it, but with Keenan and Torres and that Harpwell guy dead, and what happened to Miri's mother, they're going to have to take a closer look.'

'Shit,' Jake muttered.

'What do you think will happen?' Allie asked, a strange calm enveloping her.

Harley shrugged. 'No idea. When Lieutenant Duquette pressed me on it, I asked him if they'd ever closed the investigation into the weirder deaths from twelve years back. He said those cases were still open. I figure that's where this will go. As long as we keep telling our story and stick together, the investigation will go on forever.'

Miri exhaled. 'Do you think they realize they're never going to find answers that satisfy them?'

'I think they do.' Harley glanced away, across the trees and graves and the gate, toward the rooftops of downtown that were visible from the hilltop cemetery. 'I think it's over.'

Allie put an arm around Isaac's shoulders. 'Not for us.'

'I'm going to do everything I can,' Harley said, but this time his focus was on Isaac. 'I swear to you, kid, I'll do my best. It's not going to be easy.' He glanced at Miri and Jake before turning to Allie again. 'My statement's with Child

429

Services now, just the way we talked it out. You were driving over to Jake's when the storm really hit hard. You found the kid wandering on the side of the road and took him to Jake's. Miri and I were already there, having dinner with him, and we all rode out the storm together. You took care of the boy, formed a bond with him.'

'But he has family,' Miri said quietly. 'Zachary Stroud.'

'Mrs. Stroud has a sister in California who doesn't seem to give a damn,' Harley said. 'But there are cousins in Portsmouth who seem to want custody. Maybe when the reality of what that means — the responsibility — settles in, they won't be so eager.'

Allie took a deep breath. 'He's my son, Harley.'

'I know,' Harley said. 'I know.'

★ ★ ★

On Sunday morning, the sky turned gray again and the clouds moved in. TJ lay inside the massive snow fort he and Grace had built into the enormous snowbank at the end of the driveway with his back to the wall, breathing hard and grinning like a fool. He had a snowball in one hand and another half dozen ready to go.

'Ready to surrender yet, Daddy?' Grace called from the driveway.

'Not on your life, kid!' TJ declared.

A pair of snowballs came over the wall of the fort in rapid succession, one of them hitting his shoulder and sending a spray of snow down the collar of his jacket. He laughed out loud at his daughter's audacity. She'd used his voice to aim by. *Smart kid*, he thought.

'Graahhh!' he shouted, scaling the inside of the wall and kneeling on top of the snowbank, prepared to nail her with the snowball in his hand . . .

Grace had vanished.

He blinked, a flutter of fear in his heart, and then he heard the scuffling behind him and realized he'd been duped. TJ turned just in time to see her emerging from the tunnel that led from the driveway into the fort.

'Oh, you sneak!' he shouted, sliding back down the snow wall.

But Grace was too fast for him. Laughing that little-girl laugh that had always broken his heart, she lunged for his pile of premade snowballs, grabbed two, and began to barrage him with his own arsenal. One hit him on the thigh and he turned instinctively and let the other hit him in the head so it didn't get him in the face.

'That's it!' he cried, laughing, and tackled her in the snow.

Grace giggled uncontrollably, trying to catch her breath as he rolled around with her in the snow, pretending the two of them were in a life-or-death wrestling match. He maneuvered her so that he ended up on his back on the floor of the snow fort with Grace astride his chest, victorious.

'No!' he yelled. 'Don't hurt me! I surrender!'

'You are defeated! Now you must do my bidding!' Grace declared, echoing things she'd heard him say in similar play-battles over the years.

'Yes, master,' TJ said, marveling at the happiness in his daughter's eyes.

She remembered nothing of what had happened in the days leading up to the blizzard, and for that he would be forever thankful.

They heard a car horn honk as it pulled into the driveway.

Grace jumped off him. 'Mom's home!'

She dived for the tunnel and TJ's pulse quickened. He scrambled after her, grabbed her by one boot and the back of her jacket, and hauled her to him. Grace kicked at him, playful but obviously irritated.

'Let go!' she yelled, giving him a look that made him dread her teenage years.

'Hang on.' He climbed up to look over the top of the snowbank, watching Ella park in the driveway and turn off the engine. 'Okay, now you won't get run over. Go ahead.'

In one smooth movement, Grace turned and grabbed a snowball from his stash, hurled it at him, and then rabbited through the tunnel. TJ could only laugh as he clambered over the top of the snowbank and slid inelegantly down to the driveway.

'No fair!' Grace said when she saw him.

She might have protested more, but Ella popped open her car door and emerged with a cardboard tray of Dunkin' Donuts cups. TJ caught her eye and she rewarded him with a smile. What they had been through together — the fear they'd felt for themselves, for each other, and most powerfully for their little girl — had changed things between them. It was as if they had seen each other clearly for the first time in a very long time.

'I thought you guys might want something to warm you up out here,' Ella said.

'Hot chocolate!' Grace announced, throwing her arms around her mother and hugging her before stepping back with hands outstretched to receive her drink.

'And coffee for Daddy,' Ella said as she handed Grace her hot chocolate. 'Cream, no sugar, and a double shot of espresso.'

'A double shot?' TJ said. 'Daddy's going to be wide awake tonight.'

Ella gave him a sly grin. 'There's something to be said for a wide-awake Daddy.'

Grace blew on her hot chocolate but it was too hot for her to drink yet. Instead, she began to regale her mother with tales of the glorious snowball fight that she and her father had been engaged in, complete with a blow-by-blow account of her cunning deceit and the claiming of his personal stash of snowballs. Ella listened closely, nodding her encouragement in all the right places.

Watching mother and daughter together, TJ felt a fresh lance of sorrow pierce him. He missed his mother and he feared for her soul, now that he knew with utter certainty that such things truly did exist. He had prayed every night since that somehow she would find peace . . . find rest. In his prayers, he always thanked her, hoping that somehow she would hear him or know how grateful he was to have his daughter back.

He and Ella had been on the verge of tearing apart their beautiful family. His mother had sacrificed herself to give them a shot at making things right, and he had no intention of letting that go to waste.

'Here you go,' Ella said, handing him his coffee as Grace took a careful sip of hot chocolate. 'Sounds like Daddy got his butt kicked.'

'It won't be the last time she outsmarts me.'

Ella nodded proudly. 'It's what daughters do.'

TJ smiled. 'I wouldn't have it any other way.'

★ ★ ★

At lunchtime on Saturday, Jake and Miri walked together along the sidewalk on Washington Street, careful not to let their hands stray into the narrow gap between them. Jake wanted to take her hand, but he had wanted to hold Miri's hand for more than twelve years. They had come downtown to have lunch at The Vault, and he knew it would be foolish of him to make more of it than it was, no matter what had passed between them on Wednesday night. That had been amid terror and desperation and they had clung to each other for assurance based on the deep fondness they'd always had for each other.

He told himself that and tried to believe it, for her sake if not his own.

'It took them forever to get the sidewalks clear,' Miri said.

'I think they were more focused on getting the power back on,' Jake replied. 'I hear there are a ton of neighborhoods in Atkinson and Methuen and Jameson that are still blacked out.'

When she didn't reply, he realized that she had paused to stare at the low-slung gray sky with wide, haunted, hopeful eyes.

'It's snowing,' Miri said.

She glanced around and Jake followed suit, understanding instantly that she was looking for her father. For several long seconds they stood there waiting, but if Niko Ristani's ghost still lingered in their world, he did not show himself then.

'Just a flurry,' she said.

Jake went to her. 'Maybe that's best. We don't know what another major blizzard will bring.'

Miri took a deep breath and then exhaled, nodding as she started walking again. A few lonely snowflakes floated down around them, a winter afterthought. She had been at the hospital with her mother all the afternoon and evening before, and then had gone to sit with her again that morning. Angela was out of intensive care but still had not regained consciousness, and her doctors were troubled. Miri had made it clear that she did not want to dwell on it. Their lunch was meant to be a break for her, a chance to breathe the air and think about the rest of her life, not just her mother's fate.

'Come on,' she said. 'I'm starving, and it wouldn't hurt my feelings if I could get a cup of coffee.'

'I think we can manage that.'

'Of course, you can't get a decent cup of coffee anywhere here. I used to think Dunkin' Donuts was the alpha and omega of great coffee, but now I've been spoiled, living in Seattle.'

Miri glanced sidelong at him as they passed in front of a little antiquarian bookshop.

'When I go back, maybe you should give it a try,' she said.

Jake tried to meet her eyes but she looked away. He felt the space that separated them more keenly, now, their hands parallel pendulums never meant to touch and yet drawn together as if magnetic.

'Me in Seattle?' he asked.

Cars went by. Across the bridge, Mass had ended and the church bells began to ring.

'Why not? You like coffee, don't you?'

Jake let that sink in, let it slide around in his brain for a while. They passed the red awnings of the pizza place that had retained all the decorations from the Mexican restaurant that had occupied the space before it. Coventry kept changing, always evolving, but it was still home.

'I'm in the middle of half-a-dozen different projects at the house,' he said. 'Nothing's finished. And with Isaac here . . . I can't leave now. Not when we don't know what's going to happen with custody and everything.'

Miri nodded again. 'I know. Of course you can't.'

She turned her face to the sky, trying to catch one of the few, errant snowflakes on her tongue. With her hair a wild tangle of curls falling around her face, she looked perfect and innocent, the same pretty girl he had fallen in

436

love with in the sixth grade.

'I know you're not going anywhere until you know how things will work out with your mother, but maybe you could think about something a little more long-term,' Jake said.

Miri cast a thoughtful glance at the sidewalk beneath her feet. They had gone another half-dozen paces before he felt her hand brush his, fingers seeking his grasp. Jake smiled as they continued on, hand in hand.

'Maybe,' she said. 'It's something to think about.'

And the snow continued to fall.

★ ★ ★

In his heart, Doug knew what he had experienced, knew that Cherie had somehow taken up residence in Angie's soul, that for a short time he and his wife had been reunited. She had loved him, and she certainly hadn't blamed him for her death. That ought to have lifted a weight off him and to an extent it had: much of his guilt had been exorcised. But he missed her now more than ever. Her death had haunted him before, and now he was plagued by the ghost of the second chance he had lost.

The snowmobiles were all back in the Porters' barn. He'd had to backtrack and take the one Franco had been using and drive it over to the next street, banging on doors until he found someone with a working phone. Once the EMTs had carted Angela away, he had worked fast, dumping all the stolen goods onto the back deck of the first house they'd robbed. He'd put all three snowmobiles back in the Porters' barn, wondering how long it would be before the Porters noticed the bent strut on the one he'd crashed and if they would figure the whole thing out.

The Coventry police had a whole host of mysteries to unravel, according to word on the street and the local paper. Bodies all over town, including two dead cops. A bunch of stuff stolen during the blizzard and then just left behind, not far from where the corpses of two known felons had been found. Thanks to Angela's injuries, the trail might lead back to Doug eventually — the police seemed far from convinced that she could have sustained such serious internal injuries in the snowmobile crash he'd concocted — but as far as he knew, the only person who could actually connect him to Baxter and Franco was Keenan, and the detective was dead.

It didn't seem fair, even to him. A white hat like Keenan dead and Doug Manning, whose hat had always been gray at best — still alive. If the cops never put it all together, if he had really made it through all this untouched, maybe that was the universe making its apologies for taking Cherie from him. He'd gotten to see her again, talk to her again, make love with her again, even if it had been through Angela. He had been furious to have her taken from him a second time, until he realized what a gift it had been.

He had been given a reminder of what it felt like to see himself through her eyes. It had him thinking that maybe fate gave second chances for a reason, that maybe the trouble in his life had never been that he wasn't successful enough, but that he'd never tried hard enough to appreciate what he had. He missed Cherie desperately and Angela was definitely *not* the answer, but he was alive, and that was a start.

While she had been in the ICU, the hospital wouldn't let him visit because he wasn't family. Her condition was still considered critical, but she had her own room now and visitation rules were different. Miri had put him on a list of approved visitors, and he was grateful for that. Angela might not be Cherie, but they had known each other a long time and he was partly responsible for the events that had gotten her busted up in the first place. Whatever came now, he would look out for her as best he could. It was what Cherie would have wanted.

Now he sat in a hard plastic chair beside Angela's hospital bed, watching sitcom reruns whose laugh tracks seemed like cruel taunts to the unconscious woman whose situation seemed so dire. From time to time he glanced over to see if she had woken or at least moved, but there was no indication of life save for the steady rise and fall of her chest. The machines monitoring her vital signs blinked in silence.

And then she stirred.

'Hey,' Angela said weakly.

Doug turned to her, smiling. 'Hey, yourself. You're alive, in case you're wondering.'

She turned to him, eyes fluttering open as she reached out to take his hand.

Her eyes were a bottomless, wintry blue.

And her touch was like ice.

439